Praise for *Writing Winning Proposals: PR Cases*

"Thanks to his book, Tom Hagley is helping to raise the bar in the public relations profession. When I started to review the first edition of this book, I couldn't put it down. *Writing Winning Proposals* addresses one of the greatest weaknesses in public relations. I was so pleased to see someone take a bold step not only to define the components of a PR plan, but to establish rules for writing them. Tom's clear delineation of how to put a plan together is engaging and the best blueprint I've seen. Students who master the principles in Tom's text will certainly have taken a big step toward being ready to enter the profession."

Christopher K. Veronda, APR
Manager, Corporate Communications, Eastman Kodak Company
Former Chairman, Honors & Awards Committee and National Board Member
Public Relations Society of America

"Tom Hagley provides a tremendous foundation for future public relations practitioners by focusing campaign planning on the goals of the client organization. He does a superb job of linking public relations practice to the interests of CEOs and others trained in management and marketing."

Jim Van Leuven, Ph.D., APR
Professor Emeritus Colorado State University

"Thanks to this book, Tom Hagley has become a permanent part of my classroom and contributor to PR instruction on many other campuses. His book is a great piece of work. I say that with respect to its contents, but even more so with respect to the author. *Writing Winning Proposals* comes from a person I always believed was destined to take the "real world" to the classroom. It is no surprise that in this book he insists on writing by the rules to develop winning proposals. He comes to academe knowing precisely what executive managers want from public relations practitioners."

Glen T. Cameron, Ph.D.,
Maxine Wilson Gregory Chair in Journalism Research
University of Missouri School of Journalism

"Through his masterful teaching, Tom Hagley has been bringing his years of 'real world' public relations experience into the classroom for students fortunate to have him as their professor. With the publication of his *Writing Winning Proposals*, Hagley's expertise will benefit thousands of students beyond his classrooms as well as professionals wanting to sharpen their skills."

Lynne M. Sallot, Ph.D., APR, Fellow PRSA
Josiah Meigs Distinguished Teaching Professor
Advertising and Public Relations Department
The Grady College, University of Georgia

WRITING WINNING PROPOSALS
PR CASES

BY TOM HAGLEY

Second Edition

Forewords by

Glen T. Cameron, Ph.D. and Christopher K. Veronda, APR

cognella™
San Diego, CA

First published in the United States of America in 2010 by Cognella, a division of University Readers, Inc.

Trademark Notice: Product or corporate names may be trademarks or registered trademarks, and are used only for identification and explanation without intent to infringe.

14 13 12 11 10   1 2 3 4 5

Printed in the United States of America

ISBN: 978-1-934269-96-1

www.cognella.com 800.200.3908

Dedicated to my students
who enabled me to learn how to teach them
what they must know to succeed in public relations, and

to my loving wife Peggy,
whose support through the years
contributed so much to the success of my
professional career, which is the foundation for this book,

and to our precious little friend
Truffles
1996–2009

Contents

Foreword

By Glen T. Cameron, Ph.D.

Thanks to this book, Tom Hagley has become a permanent part of my classroom and contributor to PR instruction on many other campuses. I first became acquainted with Tom when I was teaching at the University of Georgia where I schemed whenever possible to get him into my classroom. He was director of public and investor relations for Alumax, a Fortune 200 company located in Atlanta when he became a favored guest lecturer and internship mentor in the Grady College of Journalism and Mass Communication. In addition to bringing his considerable experience to the classroom, Tom provided the students with structure, guidance, and an opportunity to grow–the same ingredients that make his text a must for our classrooms.

When Tom retired from his distinguished career as an executive in corporate and agency public relations–with a stint running his own public relations firm thrown in for good measure–I was teaching at the Missouri School of Journalism. I tried to recruit Tom, knowing that he had spent three decades striving to make the profession better in every way. Tom is committed to embracing innovation as a basis for tempering the metal and sharpening the edge of the profession. Although we competed unsuccessfully with the lures of the Northwest, I feel that we have finally captured Tom by way of his wonderful textbook. It's not the same thing as having an experienced, compassionate, creative professional in our classroom, but it is the next best thing.

His book is a great piece of work. I say that with respect to its contents, but even more so with respect to the author. Writing Winning Proposals comes from a person I always believed was destined to take the "real world" to the classroom. I saw that when Tom spoke to my classes at the University of Georgia and here at the Missouri School of Journalism. He has a passion for teaching, coaching, and counseling. He listens, recognizes, shares, encourages, tolerates, and even admits his own mistakes to those he mentors. His internship assignments made students stretch far beyond what they ever thought they could do with so little experience.

It is no surprise that in this book he insists on writing by the rules to develop winning proposals. He comes to academe knowing precisely what executive managers want from public relations practitioners.

Glen T. Cameron, Ph.D.
Maxine Wilson Gregory Chair in Journalism Research
Missouri School of Journalism

Foreword

By Christopher K. Veronda, APR

___

Thanks to his book, Tom Hagley is helping to raise the bar in the public relations profession. When I started to review the first edition of this book, I couldn't put it down. Writing Winning Proposals addresses one of the greatest weaknesses in public relations. I was so pleased to see someone take a bold step not only to define the components of a PR plan, but to establish rules for writing them. Tom's clear delineation of how to put a plan together is engaging and the best blueprint I've seen. Students who master the principles in Tom's text will certainly have taken a big step toward being ready to enter the profession.

The second edition of *Writing Winning Proposals* is a great reference and review tool even for veteran practitioners. In judging hundreds of Silver Anvil Award entries over the years, I noticed that many lacked quality plans. It was common to find goals confused with objectives and strategies combined with objectives. Plans that suffer such deficiencies don't win, or don't even get implemented.

To student readers of Tom's book I would say: You have an opportunity to distinguish yourselves in the profession by learning to write winning plans and proposals. You stand out from the crowd of professionals, especially by understanding how you build research and evaluation into any plan. I can't emphasize that enough.

There are no secrets to creating winning plans or winning Silver Anvils. If you develop a good plan, you shouldn't be in a position of having to look around afterwards, trying to identify success indicators that might or might not be attributable to PR activities, and claim them to be measurements of success. It seemed to me that too many "plans" were written from a shower of communication activities that happened to rain some indicators that could be claimed as results. Your plan or proposal should be like a business contract that puts research, clear objectives and means of measurement up front. I am excited for people just starting a career who have a big opportunity to write plans worthy of respect and high recognition.

Christopher K. Veronda, APR
Manager, Corporate Communications, Eastman Kodak Company
Former Chairman, Honors & Awards Committee and National Board Member
Public Relations Society of America

About the Author

An accomplished instructor of public relations, Tom Hagley teaches public relations principles, advanced writing, plans and campaigns courses in the School of Journalism and Communication at the University of Oregon. He has been welcomed also as a guest instructor at The University of Georgia, Georgia State University, Missouri School of Journalism, Central Washington University, Linfield College and The University of Portland. He was inspired to teach by experiences over five years with 21 interns from the Henry W. Grady College of Journalism and Mass Communication at U.G.A., in his program regarded as one of the best the school offered.

Hagley is a consummate professional with 30 years of progressive experience as a corporate public and investor relations executive, private consultant, worldwide public relations agency executive and metropolitan daily newspaper reporter. He managed staffs and annual program budgets of $6.5 million, including the title sponsorship of an IndyCar racing team, and corporate philanthropic contributions of $10 million. He directed corporate communication in publicizing a company's rapidly rising value from its spin-off as a public entity in November 1993, through a corporate takeover attempt, to the acquisition of Alumax Inc. by ALCOA in 1998 that formed the world's largest aluminum producer with a combined company of 100,000 employees in 250 locations in 30 countries with estimated 1998 revenues of $17 billion.

A published writer, Hagley is recognized nationally by public relations practitioners and educators as a contributor of knowledge with many articles published in business and professional journals, including seven featured in The Strategist magazine published by the Public Relations Society of America. He is a master of all forms of public relations writing, including plans, Congressional testimony, executive speeches, a white paper that the U.S. Trade Representative used as a base document in solving an international trade crisis, and persuasive documents, such as a grant requested and received from the federal government totaling $1.25 million for before and after school programs for a public school district. He is now author of the second edition of *Writing Winning Proposals*.

Introduction

Writing by the rules creates winning proposals. Some of you are reading this book because you want to learn how to write winning proposals. Some of you are experienced in writing public relations plans and are curious about what this author has to say about rules for writing winning plans. And some of you would like to see how the techniques presented here apply to writing proposals for related areas of communication designed to influence the behavior of people. This book is designed to be of benefit to plan developers in all areas of the communication profession.

Students of public relations, as well as seasoned practitioners anywhere in the world, will be challenged by this book to achieve a level of clarity and credibility seldom seen even in award-winning public relations plans. The challenge lies in understanding how planning relates to public relations, knowing what is involved in the planning process, and being able to apply specific rules in writing the components of a public relations plan.

What distinguishes this book is that its instruction is presented from the perspective of those who review public relations plans and communication proposals and authorize the resources necessary for their implementation. In short, it tells specifically what plan reviewers want to see in a plan and how they want the information to be presented.

With this book you can study the basics of developing a plan and apply your skills as an individual or in a team in solving problems, seizing opportunities or meeting challenges in many diverse, real world case situations, all having compelling needs for public relations action. The cases have been classroom tested over a dozen quarters in university-level instruction and have proven to be effective lessons for a classroom or professional workshop environment.

Something in your interest brought you to this book, now it's my job to make your effort worthwhile by showing you how to develop plans with a potential for success.

Understanding Why Planning Is Important, and How It Relates to Public Relations

Why is planning important and how does it relate to public relations? One reason planning is important is that a plan is the instrument used to propose and obtain approval for executing public relations activities. Executive managers who have responsibility for allocating an organization's resources require various methods, such as a traditional request for authorization, that provide a basis for evaluating expenditures. A public relations plan serves as a proposal to spend a certain amount of an organization's time and money on public relations activities. The 10 components of a plan provide the information necessary for managers to evaluate proposed public relations activities and approve their execution.

Another reason planning is important is that a plan provides a mechanism for measuring results of public relations activities. A good plan provides objectives with measurable outcomes. This provides plan reviewers with evidence that a plan is making progress toward achieving the plan's goal. It also provides a sound basis for evaluating results.

Another reason planning is important is that a plan is a product, the quality of which can distinguish its developer as a star among practitioners of all levels of experience. This is because the quality of public relations plans throughout the industry leaves so much room for improvement that well conceived plans easily take on a brilliance that wins approvals and adds credibility to the profession.

Communication professionals who serve as judges for the industry's most prestigious Silver Anvil award competition sponsored each year by Public Relations Society of America review hundreds of public relations plan entries. Judges are outspoken in saying that many industry professionals need to go back and learn the basics of developing successful public relations plans. The criticism is leveled at all but the few plans selected for recognition.

So planning is important because a plan is the instrument used to propose and obtain approvals, a mechanism for monitoring and evaluating and a product that distinguishes true public relations professionals.

To fully appreciate how planning relates to public relations, it is necessary to know precisely what public relations is and what can be expected of its practice.

What exactly is public relations?

I like to challenge people to define public relations in two words. Other professions define themselves in two words—doctors practice medicine, lawyers practice law, accountants keep records. People in these disciplines define their work in two words, issue invoices and get paid accordingly for their expertise.

Not everyone in public relations can receive compensation so readily for their work because many people—yes, many people—in public relations cannot define what they do.

And if you can't define what you do, you can't measure what you do. If you can't measure what you do, you can't evaluate what you do. If you can't evaluate what you do, you can't very well expect to be paid for what you do.

To arrive at a two-word definition of public relations, I looked back over the years, made a list of untold numbers of projects and programs I had completed and summarized them.

I convinced people to support, to vote, to consider, to learn, to champion, to follow, to testify, to read, to buy, to trust, to invest, to listen, to become informed, to join, to leave alone, to contribute, to believe, to participate, to think, to work, to authorize, to accept, to welcome, to compromise, to accommodate, to cooperate, to wait, to attend, to decide and the list went on and on and on.

The common denominator, the two-word definition, became perfectly clear. That is, in public relations, we influence behavior.

Whose behavior do we influence?

The answer for a public corporation, private company and for a not-for-profit organization is the same. We influence the behavior of anyone who has or could have an effect—positive or negative—on the organization's ultimate performance.

That would include, as examples, employees, suppliers, customers, shareholders, industry and financial analysts, labor unions, voters, government regulators, special interest groups and many more.

Is that ethical?

Of course it's ethical. The ethical principles applied to public relations are no different than those applied to any other profession. Is it ethical to convince someone to replace a heart, a tooth, a roof or a brake cylinder? Certainly it's ethical if there are valid reasons to replace one.

How do we influence behavior?

We influence behavior through strategic planning and communication. And therein lies the "magic of the profession" that few public relations practitioners possess and for which fewer still get proper recognition.

True expertise in strategic planning and communication is the work of masters. That's why I call it the "magic of the profession." Strategic communication requires knowledge, skills and problem-solving experience in the dynamics of persuasion, human interaction and communication design.

In public relations, we influence behavior through strategic planning and communication.

I define strategic communication as having seven characteristics:

1. skillfully planned and managed;
2. public—open to discussion, debate, mutual discovery and compromise;
3. engaging—intended to connect directly with individuals and/or reach others through constructive interactions with traditional, as well as new media:
4. holistic—able to see in a broad context the need to alter one's own behavior in order to influence the behavior of others;
5. authoritative, accurate, accountable, transparent;
6. two way—receptive to exchanges of differing views and collaboration toward the greater good;
7. authentic—promoted on the merits for achieving a desired behavior.

How do we evaluate the effectiveness of our strategic planning and communication?

The answer, simply: Did we influence behavior or not?

Public relations, then, is the practice of influencing behavior through strategic planning and communication. Planning is the central function in this process.

Before we move on, I would like to emphasize, and illustrate with a case, that the art of influencing behavior, ethically, centers on a deep, respectful and sensitive appreciation and understanding of human nature and not what I have witnessed too often as a random application of communication tools by others to address a situation, for example, "We can fix this with a news release and a fact sheet."

Case One
Community
Relations

The St. Lawrence River below The Plains of Abraham in Quebec City looking upstream toward the village of Deschambault and Montreal

MYSTERIOUS SOUND IN DESCHAMBAULT

I would like to take you with me to revisit what was the destination of many memorable business trips. They were made memorable by relationships developed with a welcoming community of residents of the French-Canadian village of Deschambault in the province of Quebec. I'm going to describe a particular experience, then ask you to think about it, not in any structured, strategic way, but rather in ways that you feel about it, intuitively. Your intuitive judgment as an individual, as a human being, is an important factor in determining your success as a professional public relations practitioner. So go with your intuition on this case and recommend what you think is the right thing to do.

As you study this case, think about why it would be important to have a planned approach . What would you propose and why? What research would you initiate? How would the actions you propose be implemented and, most importantly, evaluated?

This is a case of responding to the concern of an elderly woman who says, now that a major production plant nearby has been completed and is in full operation, she hears a continuous low-level sound inside her house. She sent a letter to the plant manager stating that the sound is audible enough to be annoying and asking if he "would be so kind as to investigate and do something to eliminate it."

The woman, 82 years of age, is a highly respected elder of the community. She has written books about the region, has kept local traditions alive, and has supported efforts to improve the local economy.

She lives in one of the historic cottages made of local limestone in the village of Deschambault situated on the north bank of the St. Lawrence River between Montreal and Quebec City. It is on Chemin du Roy, built in 1734, the first road to link the two cities.

The nearby production plant is a billion-dollar operation built as a global model in the use of best technology available for the handling and processing of mate-

Historic limestone cottage

rial resources exceeding all standards of environmental control.

Noise, however, is of concern to some residents. For many years, villagers have enjoyed the country charm and serenity of the lower Saint Lawrence. People who regard the peacefulness of the area as a special value would consider any new noise a disturbing intrusion. But the region is in a state of transition. The Societe d'expansion de Portneuf provided a full range of services inviting projects ranging from cottage industries to mega plants. No matter how hard businesses and industries try to integrate their operations with the environment, things will never be the way they were in this agrarian region.

A world class aluminum production plant, now owned by ALCOA with the St. Lawrence River in the background.

Village of Deschambault.

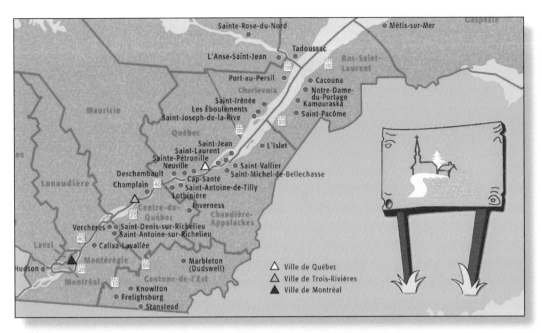

Deschambault is located between Montreal and Quebec City.

So, these were the circumstances under which the plant manager received a letter from the woman asking for relief from the low-level sound that fills her home.

1. What do you think the plant manager should do?
   - Write a letter defending the plant
   - Deny the problem
   - Argue the cost/benefits of industrial development
   - Minimize responsibility with excuses
   - Blame the community for inviting industry
   - Pay a personal visit and apologize
   - Do something to accommodate the resident's request.
2. What should the company do if the plant manager investigates

A bed and breakfast inn

the sound and cannot detect with scientific equipment any low-level sound inside the house?

3. Should the company retrofit the house with insulation and storm windows, whether or not a sound is detected?

4. How would you counsel the plant manager in discussing this problem with the elderly woman?

- Is it best to separate facts from emotions?
- If so, what should be discussed first, facts or emotions?
- What is your reasoning?
5. What about the factor of control?
   - What type of control does the resident have?
   - The plant manager?
   - Why is it important to think about that?
   - Should control be shared?
   - How could control be shared?
6. How does accommodation relate to public relations in this case?
   - Does accommodation have a useful purpose in this case? Explain.
   - What are the upsides and downsides of using accommodation in this case?

Village of Deschambault on the north bank of the St. Lawrence River.

2 Meeting the Challenges of the Planning Environment

Public relations plans are developed in many different environments—publicly owned and privately owned companies, government and non-government organizations, not-for-profit and various other entities. These environments have characteristics that can have a bearing on how plans are developed, whether or not plans are approved, modified or rejected, and even whether plans succeed or fail. So planning cannot be done in a vacuum. Planners must take into account the characteristics of their respective organizations, which will enable them to understand how to meet the challenges of the planning environment.

Let's take a look at some major challenges of the planning environment in three areas: organization, leadership and resources.

Organization

A publicly-owned corporation, for example, can be mission driven or financially driven. Organizations, of course, can and do fall somewhere between these aims, but for our purposes we will look at these as points on opposite ends of the spectrum.

In a mission-driven organization, employees are considered the key to success. When employees are motivated by meaningful work they invest more than their time in an organization. They work with a purpose that captures their interest and taps their creativity as they reach out to customers with innovative solutions and extraordinary service. By building relationships with customers, an organization grows in sales, profit, market share and, ultimately, in overall value to its shareholders.

In a financially-driven organization, management tends to take employees for granted and simply goes through the motions of showing respect for other stakeholders. The serious interest is in impressing securities analysts and shareholders with short-term performance improvements—quarterly profits. The focus on profits can be so intense that management will do whatever it takes—acquire this, sell that, lay people off, cut back, borrow more—to obtain an attractive stock price.

Developing a public relations plan in a financially-driven organization can be a challenge because management in many cases will be inclined to resist plans that

- don't yield an immediate, virtually guaranteed return;
- propose costly benchmarking or other investigative or evaluative research measures;

- require an investment in the long term for building relationships with any of the organization's stakeholders;
- have strategies requiring consistent values, such as telling the whole truth internally and externally and not spooning it out according to the differing tastes of stakeholder groups;
- offer effective solutions but require added costs of using outside services, such as photographers, graphic designers, multi-media studios and public relations firms.

Developing plans in a mission-driven organization presents a different challenge. The plan developer is in competition for resources with other areas, such as operations, marketing, sales, customer service and research and development. However, the allocation of resources is evaluated in terms of the organization's mission, rather than short-term financial goals. Management reviews plans for their potential to benefit all stakeholders. The focus is on investing for the longer term.

In a mission-driven organization, management is interested in investing in public relations plans that

- motivate and empower employees to provide innovative, superior service to customers;
- win the loyalty of suppliers;
- build long-term working relationships with all stakeholders;
- strengthen the bottom line in terms of economic performance, social investment, community involvement, ethical and values based performance and environment values.

Leadership

Let's look next at the challenges of the planning environment in the area of leadership. Approval of public relations plans is, in large part, under the control of executives who have no academic education in public relations. This paradox deserves a deeper look.

Next to the ability to manage people and budgets, public relations skill is the most sought-after attribute in top executives by today's corporations, according to private research by a worldwide human resources organization. Yet few executives have any formal education in public relations and slow progress is being made to equip future business leaders with these critical skills.

Business schools develop leaders for businesses and governments throughout the world. What these leaders are taught has an influence on the daily lives of millions of people–an enormous responsibility that business schools try to address with the traditional focus on finance, accounting and marketing.

But examine the dramatic transformation taking place in the role of chief executive officer and one can easily surmise that market demand for formal public relations training is heading toward academe like a high-speed train. Executive leadership today is about building and maintaining trusting relationships with employees, customers, suppliers, investors, analysts, board members and all major stakeholder groups. It's about influencing the behavior of people through persuasive communication. It's about showing empathy for others. In sum, it's about public relations.

In recessionary times especially, building relationships with compassion and open, candid communication is imperative for today's business leaders. These core values are critical to corporate America's struggle through traumatic upheavals marked by acquisitions, mergers, downsizings and restructurings that are leaving employees with feelings of instability, insecurity and uncertainty about their work and personal lives. Business schools are going to have to expand functional areas with formal public relations training.

It has been said that CEOs are hired for their skills and fired for their personalities. CEOs who entered the business world years ago with no formal training in human relations skills are beginning to yield to executives who are learning to lead as compassionate communicators. But it's a slow and, in some cases, painful transition. For example, I returned from a small-ship exploration of Alaska. We traveled through the pristine areas of Prince William Sound that are still struggling to survive Exxon's corporate arrogance and spilled oil. It was more than a decade ago that the chairman of Exxon, Lawrence Rawl, at the time head of the nation's third largest corporation in sales, said, "We would have liked to recall the oil off Prince William Sound. We called, but it didn't hear us." I picked up a local newspaper and shook my head in disbelief as I read that Exxon was planning to bring its ill-fated Valdez oil tanker back to operate in Alaska where its presence is sure to rekindle memories of great loss and destruction. Exxon still has much to learn about compassion—about being empathetic to public interests.

Public relations textbooks are revised frequently to include updated cases of corporate leaders failing to live up to public expectations of good citizenship. Why is living up to public expectations of corporate behavior a continuing challenge to corporation after corporation?

The problem is the absence of formal public relations training among executive managers. Let's consider what can happen, practically speaking, when a chief executive officer has to manage a crisis situation. Without formal training in public relations, a CEO has no basis on which to make self-confident decisions and instead must rely heavily on the advice of others.

In a crisis situation, a CEO often turns to corporate counsel for legal advice. However, some attorneys can be so intimidating about liability issues that they paralyze a CEO into a state of inaction. With solid PR training to balance legal counsel, a CEO might, as one did, say in a crisis situation: "I've been advised by our law department that the company is not responsible, but we are going to act as though we are."

Or a CEO could hire a PR firm with a track record in successful crisis management, but the CEO without PR training could be putting the fate of an entire enterprise into the hands of experts he or she has little or no skills to evaluate or direct.

Or a CEO could turn to what Warren Buffett calls the "institutional imperative," or the tendency of executives, he says, "…to mindlessly imitate the behavior of their peers, no matter how foolish it may be to do so."

We will continue to see major corporations failing to live up to public expectations of corporate citizenship until the top jobs are filled with executives who have the formal training necessary to feel self-confident in directing the public relations function, building trusting relationships through good communication and leading with compassion.

Developers of public relations plans will continue to be challenged to educate senior executives in the practice of public relations. We know that the profession operates on a body of knowledge in the social sciences that has been developed over many years. We practitioners know how to put that experience to work in all areas of public relations. Many executives have yet to learn even the fundamentals of influencing behavior.

Some plan developers are fortunate to have chief executives who are better educated in public relations. These enlightened executives enjoy working with plan developers. A plan developer can show a CEO, for example, that by understanding and participating in the creative process the chief executive can lead with visions that trigger in all stakeholder groups convictions to act in support of an organization's mission.

In a business Week article from early 2003, Jeffrey E. Garten, dean of the Yale School of management, wrote this timeless advice: "Industry can't climb out of its funk just by cutting costs and meeting quarterly goals. CEOs must bet on their vision. Betting on a vision is a risk that many CEOs are hesitant to take." Some prefer to play it safe, managing costs and fine-tuning strategies. Some prefer to mark time, waiting for economic circumstances to improve. Some have promising visions, but lack confidence in their ability to carry them out.

Launching a vision is like launching a ship. If you don't know how to score the bottle, you shouldn't swing the champagne. The result could be an embarrassing clunk, instead of a spectacular splash.

Let's consider what it is like to launch a vision with a leader who understands the principles of influencing behavior. First the leader holds someone accountable for developing the vision. The person held responsible is usually a professional communicator, such as the plan developer. Some executives believe that planting a seed with an individual is the same as assigning an individual to the seed's development. It's a safe position for the executive who doesn't want to take the risk of sharing an idea and possibly being challenged, debated or criticized about its potential or validity. But there's a big difference between sowing a seed and holding someone accountable for the seed's growth and development. Without a process for development and accountability for driving it, a vision will be no more than a pipe dream.

There is no inherent certainty for a leader that what he or she has in mind as a vision, especially in its embryonic state, is clearly right for the organization. Executives must have the courage to engage in constructive debate. Open, on-going dialogue with others serves to clarify and perfect a vision. A plan developer shows a leader how to share a vision with others, perhaps in a small brainstorming group or among confidants. The developer knows visionary ideas are fragile. They're not complete. They're not perfect.

A plan developer knows how to shepherd delicate ideas through the creative process, and how to pursue all of the pathways of human engineering necessary to energize the interest and action of individuals who have a potential stake in the organization's success. A plan developer is quick to point out that a vision is not a directive. It's not a figment of someone's imagination. It must be an achievable condition, an irresistible state of being with the power to turn belief in an idea into a conviction to act on its behalf.

An enlightened leader will work closely with a plan developer, knowing that conveying an idea is difficult and requires a variety of professional communication skills. A leader can turn to a plan developer for the draft of a vision the same way the executive turns to a writer to request a draft of a speech.

The leader and plan developer know the aim of a vision shouldn't be to shoot for the moon. Its aim should be to orchestrate readily available resources to achieve results that move an organization to a higher level of innovation, competitive strength, market position and profitability. An experienced public relations plan developer has the position and skills to move freely throughout an organization to expose an idea to a broad spectrum of expertise in sales, marketing, law, finance, and R&D and to meld ideas into a vision with universal appeal.

The leader and plan developer know that a vision must contain appeals to all stakeholders—employees, existing and potential investors, industry analysts, bankers, journalists. Enlightened executives know that to have the power to trigger convictions to act, a vision must have ownership by all of its stakeholders. It is not a one-sided opportunity. It must be a multifaceted, irresistible opportunity for stakeholders within and outside the organization. No one in an organization has a better grasp of the diverse views of stakeholder groups than an organization's experienced public relations professional. Research is a cornerstone of the profession and public relations professionals who perform the function in developing annual reports, establishing Web sites, preparing news announcements, drafting speeches, position papers and other forms of corporate communication are well equipped with the skills to research and develop the basis for a vision.

An astute leader knows that once crafted, a vision must be delivered, but not by a "town crier." It's not an edict. It's a vision. It's the seed of an idea. It needs time to unleash its power in the imaginations of people it captivates. It needs time to be considered, studied and evaluated.

As a vision is pursued by the chief executive and plan developer and evidence of its potential develops and is shared with its stakeholders a vision gains validity. It is assimilated and communicated with personal conviction by its stakeholders. Results of the vision continue to validate its potential and trigger in the minds of its stakeholders convictions to act in support of the vision. As the process unfolds it energizes employees to produce, customers to buy, investors to invest, bankers to lend, analysts to recommend, journalists to write, suppliers to support.

For public relations plan developers who are fortunate to have chief executives who are enlightened and willing to explore what can be accomplished by leveraging the credibility of public relations in a vision, the challenge to planning can be an exciting experience.

Resources

Finally, let's look at the challenges of the planning environment in the area of resources. The plan developer might have a choice of using resources within the organization or outsourcing work to various service firms. Or the plan developer might have to rely entirely on the organization's resources.

The advantages of using the organization's resources are:

- people involved have a vested interest in the organization's mission and are likely to have a personal commitment to contributing to its success;
- control of the plan is internal among the people involved with its implementation;
- expenses are minimized by enlisting the involvement of existing personnel and obtaining support from existing budgets.

The planning challenge increases when the plan developer must outsource work. A plan developer might not have a choice but to outsource work to a firm already retained by the organization. Whether the developer must use a designated source or select a source, careful management of the source's performance is essential. To illustrate, let's consider what is involved in managing the outsourcing of work to a public relations firm.

Generally speaking, public relations firms are service driven. However, some PR firms are cost driven. Unless one is prepared to lose one's shirt, it's best to select a service-driven firm.

By selecting a service driven firm, a plan developer is far more likely to develop and execute a winning plan.

So what distinguishes a service-driven from a cost-driven PR firm?

Use of time is a major distinguishing factor. A service-driven firm uses time to provide service. A cost-driven firm uses time to cover costs at the expense of client service. Firms become cost driven when the cost of operating—office rent, auto and electronic equipment leases, salaries, and other overhead—is so high that meeting those expenses drives the business.

A service-driven firm provides a plan developer with an experienced account representative. A cost-driven firm provides an experienced account representative, initially, then might switch to a less experienced representative, but at the same high billable rate.

A service-driven firm:

- provides a plan developer with the full depth of the firm's expertise. A cost-driven firm limits client service to the experience of the account representative to allow others in the firm to concentrate on more lucrative business.
- provides a plan developer with high-quality resources for graphic design, photography, video production and whatever is needed. A cost-driven firm attempts to use its own, often mediocre resources to keep profits in house.
- drives the plan developer's assignment to completion. A cost-driven firm is less responsive, causing the client to do the account representative's work of staying on schedule and on budget enabling the account representative, instead, to handle more accounts.
- is willing to tailor its services to a plan developer's own performance criteria. A cost-driven firm insists on its own way of providing service and resists client attempts to manage and evaluate the firm's performance.
- knows how to serve as an extension of a plan developer's staff. A cost-driven firm keeps its independence and functions to its own advantage.
- keeps working until the work meets the plan developer's expectations. A cost-driven firm is in a hurry to collect its fee. It offers excuses for substandard work and sometimes tries to get the client to accept and pay for the PR firm's mistakes, inability to follow directions, poor writing, careless editing and other unprofessional practices.

To manage a plan that will involve the services of an outside firm, a plan developer must understand the challenges involved in outsourcing and directing various forms of services.

A plan cannot be developed or implemented in a vacuum. The environment in which a plan is developed can present substantial challenges in the areas of organization, leadership and resources.

The Plan Developer

There is one more factor to consider before studying the public relations plan and its component parts and that is you—the plan developer. Acceptance of plans that you propose will depend, in large part, on plan reviewers' confidence in your ability to deliver what you propose. Such confidence comes from how reviewers see you as a public relations practitioner. So let's consider the matter of professional image.

The traditional characterization of practitioners suggests that public relations professionals fall somewhere on a continuum ranging from lower-paid tacticians to higher-paid strategists and that the ultimate career position is having the stature necessary to gain acceptance by the leadership of an organization. This characterization suggests that practitioners have a choice to make between being a tactician or strategist, that if an individual chooses to be a tactician, the individual will not have the esteem of a consultant in the eyes of senior executives.

I would like to offer a different view. Having worked with colleagues in all aspects of public relations for more than 30 years , I would characterize effective practitioners as having unique combinations of tactical and strategic communication talents and skills. I believe practitioners, through their academic training and education and professional experience, develop a professional capability as tacticians and strategists.

Practitioners have the ability to confer on situations, from simple to complex, and recommend ways to influence people—even millions of people—to behave one way or another in response to meaningful communication activities.

A skilled practitioner has, for example, the consulting skills to recommend communication strategies and, in addition, has all of the technical skills to develop a news announcement, guide it through the review process, reconcile reviewers' differences, disseminate the announcement worldwide, and handle resulting inquiries from reporters providing more information and/or effectively correcting erroneous reporting errors. A skilled practitioner has the consulting skills to recommend strategic use of online media, and has the technical know-how to create projects in the cyber world.

The combination of tactical and strategic skills is a great strength. However, I do caution young men and women to be conscious of the image they project–someone who scurries around with a pencil behind one ear, clutching a clipboard and dangling a camera from a neck strap is going to have a difficult time being regarded as a strategist, rather than a tactician. If you enjoy working as a tactician, that is fine and there are many rewarding positions for you to pursue. The point is to cast an impression that is in keeping with your career goals.

Young men and women entering the profession should take delight in acquiring a combination of tactical and strategic communication skills and to enjoy developing that unique professional capability to the fullest extent possible.

In this chapter, we explored major challenges of the planning environment in the areas of organization, leadership, resources and you as plan developer. Before we move ahead, I would like you to experience the challenges of an extraordinary planning environment in the case of battling a wildfire in Central Oregon.

Case Two
Public
Information

BLACK CRATER WILDFIRE

As a class, take turns reading the updates in the wildfire time line. Begin each one with the day, date, time and headline imitating the voice of a newscaster. Stop at each Discussion Break to write answers or discuss answers to the questions. When you have completed the time line, study the Points of Importance to see how the lessons learned might add to your earlier discussions.

On Monday, July 24, 2006, my wife Peggy and I and our 11-pound dog, Truffles, a Coton deTulear, rode into the town of Sisters to enjoy some leisure, outdoor activities in Central Oregon. Instead, we became victims of a wildfire that caused the evacuation of three residential developments and threatened evacuation of Sisters.

In a matter of a few days, the fire became a number one national priority and command was quickly passed from local to regional to federal control.

Observing the management of public information throughout the emergency period provided a special opportunity to document the incident as a case study. I want to acknowledge contributions to the points of importance that follow the time line from C.J. Norvell, information officer for the federal Southeast Interagency Incident Command.

ROLE PLAY

Take turns reading the entries in this time line in the voice of a news broadcaster. Include the day, date and heading of each entry. Pause at the discussion breaks to discuss appropriate actions.

BLACK CRATER FIRE TIME LINE
Tuesday, July 25, 2006 10 AM
Fire burns on Black Crater

A wildfire estimated at between 50 and 70 acres continued to burn uncontrolled, this morning, on the south side of Black Crater within the Three Sisters Wilderness.

The fire, which was discovered Monday morning after a Sunday evening lightning storm swept across the area, is located about 10 miles southwest of Sisters.

Tuesday, July 25, 4:44 PM
Black Crater Fire is spreading

After 12 hours of relative calm, the Black Crater Fire was again spreading to the north and northeast this afternoon. Firefighters struggled to control the fire blazing in dense, beetle-killed timber and dead and down trees on the south and east slopes of Black Crater. Estimates of the fire's size range up from 120 acres.

Wednesday, July 26, 1:57 PM
Black Crater Fire triples in size

The Black Crater Fire burning west of Sisters tripled in size yesterday and now is burning on 300 acres, according to fire information officer David Seesholtz. Increasing winds combined with heavy dead and down trees caused the fire to

spread. Some 197 firefighters are now on the fire including seven 20-person crews. In addition, there are 13 engines and two dozers on the fire.

DISCUSSION BREAK I

Assume that you have been designated spokesperson for the command now in charge of coordinating emergency services. You think to yourself, the town has a weekly newspaper and inactive Web site, no local commercial radio or TV, phone messaging hasn't been in use. The town has a population of about 1400 people. Businesses on town streets can easily be covered by walking. The big question you keep asking is what can we use as a 24/7 channel for frequent updates on the fire?

What would you suggest using as a way of conveying public information to the town? Make a list of all possible ways to disseminate timely information to residents and business owners.

Wednesday, July 26, 10:48 PM
Black Crater Fire holds at 400 acres

Ash from Black Crater fire fell in town and surrounding subdivisions today. The fire is burning approximately 7 miles southwest of town.

Thursday, July 27, 10:42 AM
Black Crater fire increases to 820 acres

The Black Crater fire revealed itself last night. Infrared aerial surveying of the fire showed the fire area to be 820 acres, up from the 400-acre estimate earlier in the day. Not all of the 820-acre area is burning. The infrared survey showed areas of high intensity burning at the southern edge of the fire and another area burning "hot" at the eastern end of the fire. The rest of the fire area is checker-boarded with patches of fire and patches that have escaped the flames.

Thursday, July 27, 11:23 AM
Residents advised of evacuation plans

Evacuation plans for the subdivisions of Crossroads and Tollgate, as well as other residential properties scattered in the area southwest of Sisters, have been developed in case the Black Crater Fire blows up and threatens these communities.

Thursday, July 27, 1:45 PM
Black Crater air attack is underway

An air tanker and helicopter made retardant and water drops on the Black Crater Fire this afternoon as firefighters tried to keep the 820-acre blaze from spreading toward the Crossroads subdivision. As of 1:30 p.m., the fire remained 3.5 to four miles away from the subdivision and two

miles away from the line the Deschutes County Sheriff's Office is using as a trigger point to initiate an evacuation. No evacuation procedures have been launched.

Thursday, July 27, 4:15 PM
Crossroads is being evacuated

Fire officials and Deschutes County Sheriff's deputies are evacuating the Crossroads subdivision and the Edgington Road area. Sisters High School is the designated evacuation center. The Red Cross asks that evacuees check in at the center even if they plan to stay elsewhere. The Tollgate subdivison has been placed on notification.

Thursday, July 27, 6:53 PM
Black Crater Fire advances

A public meeting on the Black Crater Fire situation has been scheduled for 7:30 p.m. tonight at Sisters High School. The fire has advanced to within three-quarters of a mile of the demarcation line that would trigger an evacuation of Tollgate. It is within one and three-quarters miles of a second demarcation line that would trigger an evacuation of the City of Sisters.

DISCUSSION BREAK 2

Evacuation plans have been developed for the subdivisions of Crossroads and Tollgate areas. The evacuation order will be given by loud speakers on sheriff's vehicles. Once the order is issued and the areas evacuated, no one will be permitted back until the areas are declared safe.

Residents will want answers to questions, such as, what about my pets if I go to work in Redmond or Bend? What about my livestock? As spokesperson, you will have to have answers to residents' questions. Make a list of all the questions you believe residents could be expected to ask at the public meeting scheduled for 7:30 p.m. at Sisters High School.

Thursday, July 27, 9:45 PM
Governor declares state of emergency

The Black Crater Fire has grown to between 1500 and 1700 acres and forced the evacuation of approximately 600 residents of the Crossroads subdivision and another 70 or so from the Edgington Road area. The fire is currently about two-and-a half miles from Crossroads. The Tollgate subdivision is on notice for possible evacuation, with the fire about one-half mile from the point at which authorities will initiate an evacuation there.

Friday, July 28, 11:31 AM
Black Crater Fire grows to 2,684 acres

The Black Crater Fire grew to 2,684 acres yesterday, according to an aerial infrared survey conducted last night. Some 425 Crossroads residents (the number was revised down from 600) remain evacuated, along with the residents of the Edgington Road area. The fire is approximately two-and-one-half miles from Crossroads. The fire is still about 1 mile from a demarcation line that would trigger an evacuation of some 1,500 Tollgate residents.

Friday, July 28, 11:48 AM
Forest closure announced

Fire officials have closed all National Forest lands west of Forest Service Road 16 (Three Creeks Road). Forest service personnel are notifying campers and recreationists to leave the area.

Friday, July 28, 1:00 PM
Winds quiet in the morning

The winds that fire officials fear could push the Black Crater Fire toward residences in the Edgington road area and the Crossroads subdivision did not materialize as early as expected today, according to a meteorologist with the Northwest Oregon Incident Management Team. She told firefighters at a briefing at noon that winds are now expected to start rising at 1 p.m. and by 3 p.m. "It should be blowing pretty good."

Friday, July 28, 1:40 PM
High 'possibility' of Tollgate evacuation

Fire officials are saying that there is a 'high possibility' that Tollgate will be evacuated by tonight; and a 'reasonable possibility' that the City of Sisters will be evacuated by tonight.

Friday, July 28, 5:30 PM
Black Crater Fire burning toward the north

The column of black smoke that loomed over the Black Crater Fire late this afternoon was from fire activity along the north rim of the fire. The fire, which is the number one priority fire in the nation, is now approximately 3,000 acres in size.

Friday, July 28, 8:30 PM
Firefighters have made progress

Firefighters held the eastern edge of the Black Crater Fire where it had pushed toward residential areas on yesterday and forced the evacuation of the Crossroads subdivision and the Edgington Road area.

Saturday, July 29, 11:17 AM

"There is a good chance the Tollgate subdivision will need to be evacuated today or Sunday," Sisters/Camp Sherman Fire Chief Tay Robertson told a large crowd of homeowners at a public meeting this morning at Sisters High School. The fire has grown to the east and the north to about 4,700 acres. It is currently 5 percent contained, and lies about two-and- one-half miles to the west of Tollgate, and three-and-one-half miles south of Black Butte Ranch.

Saturday, July 29, 5:00 PM
Tollgate Is Evacuated

The call went out at about 3:52 p.m. today to evacuate the Tollgate subdivision near Sisters. The wind picked up and blew the Black Crater Fire over the trigger line, according to Tim Edwards, captain with the Deschutes County Sheriff's Office.

Saturday, July 29, 9:30 PM
Using fire to fight fire

There is a 50–50 chance that the City of Sisters may be evacuated by late tomorrow morning, according to Black Crater Fire Incident Commander Carl West.

Sunday, July 30, 8:15 AM
Night crew makes strong headway on blaze

A fire-fighting crew worked all night to secure an eight-mile section of the eastern and northeastern perimeter of the Black Crater Fire where it has been pushing hard toward residential areas. A burnout operation to rob the fire of fuel and to help firefighters secure a line around the head of the fire was successful and the incident

DISCUSSION BREAK 3

Assume you are now public information officer for the federal Southern Area Blue Team incident command that is about to assume control of the fire from the regional command. Your unit has been put on alert about the Black Crater Wildfire. You have a short time to quickly research the situation before your unit hits the ground and takes over command from the Northwest Oregon Interagency Incident Management Team. Make a list of all information you would like to have before arriving in Sisters. You will have under your supervision on site, three staff members, an expert Webmaster, a person who was a former newscaster, and a person with experience in telecommunications. You have been told that the principal of the local high school has suggested the possible use of Outlaw Radio, FM 106.5, a new station to be operated by students when school begins this fall.

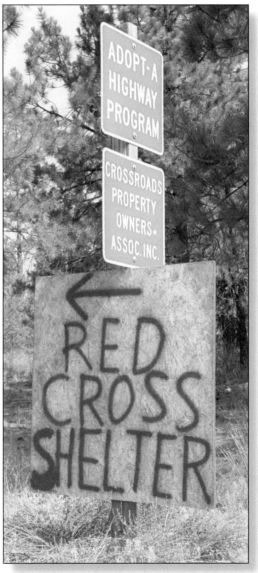

management team's morning briefing was upbeat and optimistic as a result.

Sunday, July 30, 11:30 AM
Winds will test the 'black line'

Winds gusting in the 25 to 35 miles-per-hour range on Sunday will test the "black line" created in an all-night burnout operation on the Black Crater Fire, according to Incident Commander Carl West.

Sunday, July 30, 3:00 PM
Firefighters pound blaze from ground and air

Fire crews are taking advantage of cooler temperatures and cloud cover to capitalize on ground gained during Saturday night's burnout operation. Crews are using both air and ground resources to cool down remaining hot spots and mop up along the fire line perimeter.

Sunday, July 30, 8:30 PM
A 'good day'

Firefighters built on the successful burnout operation conducted by the Saturday night shift to consolidate their grip on the

Black Crater Fire on today. "It was a good day," said Dale Gardner of the Northwest Interagency Incident Management Team at an evening tactical briefing. The Northwest team is handing command of the fire to the federal Southern Area Blue Team, a Type 1 (large fire) management team from Georgia.

DISCUSSION BREAK 4

Assume that you must introduce yourself and members of the federal Blue Team incident command at your first meeting with town residents. More than 800 people, half the town, is expected to attend. How will you introduce yourself and members of the team, beginning with incident commander, Mike Quesinberry. What can your team say to instill in the hearts and minds of residents trust that their personal safety and security of their property are in good hands? What will you have the federal team say as it assumes command from the regional Northwest team?

Monday, July 31, 8:15 AM
Firefighters are on the offensive

Firefighters are on the offensive against the Black Crater Fire, mopping up and strengthening lines on the east side of the fire where it had pushed toward residential areas and forced evacuations of Crossroads, Edgington Road and Tollgate. The fire covers about 9,000 acres and is 20 percent contained. As the Southern Area Blue Team took over management of the fire from the Northwest Oregon Interagency Incident Management Team, new Incident Commander Mike Quesinberry said,

"You've done a lot of firefighting; we've got a lot of firefighting left to do."

Monday, July 31, 12:45 PM
No word yet on evacuee return

Despite significant progress on containing the Black Crater Fire, fire officials have not yet determined when evacuees can return to their homes in Crossroads, Edgington Road and Tollgate.

Monday, July 31, 5:06 PM
Tollgate residents to return home at 6 p.m. Monday

Captain Tim Edwards of the Deschutes County Sheriff's Office has announced that residents of Tollgate may return home at 6 p.m. tonight. Crossroads and Edgington Road remain under evacuation until further notice.

Tuesday, August 1, 11:30 AM
More evacuees could return home today

Residents of Crossroads and the Edgington Road area may be returning home on Tuesday afternoon. Black Crater Fire Incident Commander Mike Quesinberry told a smaller-than-usual crowd at Sisters High School that he planned to tour the fire at lunch time, but that "all indications are that you folks will be back in your homes this afternoon."

Tuesday, August 1, 5:00 PM
Evacuation order lifted

As of 5 p.m. today, Crossroads and Edgington Road residents will be allowed to return to their homes, fire officials announced.

Tuesday, August 1, 5:29 PM
Sisters community rallies in face of fire

The Black Crater Fire rallied the community spirit of Sisters–and the rest of Central Oregon. As the flames and smoke rolled closer and closer to Sisters, more and more people began to prepare for the eventual evacuation of their homes. At the same time, residents safe from the advancing fire and those who felt they could help were also gearing up. The first

to open its doors was the Sisters School District. Without delay, school officials put out the welcome mats at the middle and high schools and cooperated with the agencies that needed a place to set up headquarters. The Northwest Interagency Incident Management Team set up fire camp at Sisters Middle School, while the Red Cross established an evacuation center at Sisters High School.

Tuesday, August 1, 5:44 PM
Weather aids Black Crater fire fight

A lack of firefighting resources dogged the effort to fight the Black Crater Fire, but that effort was aided by the weather. Though some nasty winds played a large roll in the blow-up that forced evacuations of Crossroads and Edgington Road on Thursday, the weather overall was more cooperative than might have been expected at the end of July. Temperatures in Sisters dropped into the 70s (and the 30s overnight) on Sunday and Monday and humidity rose, allowing firefighters two days in which to consolidate gains made in an all-night burnout operation on Saturday.

Tuesday, August 1, 6:28 PM
Firefighters gain upper hand on Black Crater Fire

Firefighters seemed to have gained a strong hold on the 9,200-acre Black Crater Fire west of Sisters by this morning. Tollgate residents, evacuated Saturday, as the fire spotted over notification lines, were allowed to return home at 6 p.m. yesterday. Residents of Crossroads and Edgington Road, who had been out of their homes since Thursday, anxiously awaited news that they, too, could go home.

Thursday, August 3, 1:20 PM
Black Crater blaze is 50 percent contained

Firefighters continued to mop up hot spots on the Black Crater Fire as they worked to complete the last eight miles of containment line around the 9,200-acre blaze. The fire is 50 percent contained.

Friday, August 4, 8:30 AM
Fire containment expected Sunday

The 9,400 acre Black Crater fire is 70 percent contained, according to fire officials.

Full containment is expected Sunday at 6 p.m. Sixty-five firefighters were mobilized to a spike camp in the wilderness area on Wednesday. With the camp established, firefighters have four additional hours a day to construct a line.

Monday, August 7, 9:29 AM
Black Crater Fire is 95 percent contained

The Black Crater Fire was 95 percent contained as of yesterday. Expected containment has been pushed back to August 11.

DISCUSSION BREAK 5

Now that you have read the time line, review the lessons learned from the Black Crater Wildfire experience. Discuss the following Points of Interest. Make notes about points that have a bearing on earlier discussions and discuss revisions.

Also discuss the characteristics of the planning environment for this case. How would you describe this situation in terms of organization, leadership, resources and your role as spokesperson? What are the challenges in each area?

POINTS OF IMPORTANCE

Black Crater Fire will be remembered as a model of cooperation between citizens and firefighting personnel at all levels of government. The incident provides a slate of lessons in public relations that I have titled Points of Importance.

1. Treat victims with respect. For example, the rapport between town residents and firefighters was exceptional and resulting citizen cooperation was extraordinary.

2. Give immediate access to information. For example, information was made available through print, broadcast, telecommunication and Internet channels.

3. Give information the priority of operational strategies. For example: "Firefighting comes first …" is an attitude, not a viable principle. Public information must have the same priority in order to have public support and cooperation.

4. Begin public briefings with detailed information. For example, public meetings are most effective when opened with details people want most.

5. Make incident command the authoritative public information source. For example: www.NWOregonIMT.com was established and later moved to www.fs.fed.us/r6/centralOregon with a link to "Black Crater Fire."

6. Give tough-to-take instruction without hesitation. For example, residents were told "Once the evacuation order is given you will not be permitted back into the area."

7. Answer all questions. For example, in public meetings, especially, all questions must be answered. One question was asked three different ways by three different people and each query was treated with respect as though it were asked for the first time.

8. Completely address areas of intense public interest. They will not go away. For example, questions about the location of power lines and the use of air support, were answered completely in follow-up meetings.

9. Fully explain processes and procedures. For example, evacuation notification and procedures must be explained in detail. How will residents be notified? Will there be a pre-alert? How much time will there be between the pre-alert and the evacuation order? Will the town be notified all at once or in phases and, if so, in what sequence? If we go to work in Redmond or Bend and an order is issued can we get back into Sisters? In other words, should we go to work tomorrow? What about our pets? Should we leave our doors unlocked? Will "Reverse 911" phone notification include cell phones?

10. Avoid jargon and technical terms. For example, people appreciate it when experts take time to explain or avoid using technical or jargon terms such as containment, tractor line, hand line, cat line, black line, water bar, mop-up, hose and wet plumbing, trigger, back burn, backfire, moppin' in, moppin' up, hose ways, retardant line, structural crews, root out, transitional pattern, hot shots and hot shot crews, rehab work and emergency restoration work.

11. Instill confidence in leaders. When there is a change in incident command, the commander's first remarks can instill public confidence in a new leader.

12. Consider the children. Emergency situations provide teachable moments for children.

13. Expect public information challenges. For example, the local fire chief said, "You can expect public information challenges in three areas: the situation itself; staffing and technology.

14. Use opportunities to garner goodwill. For example, the Sisters fire chief said, "You can rest assured that we are taking good care of your property. We're even watering your plants while you are away."

15. Provide continuous information. For example, public briefings on a regular schedule (10 a.m. and 7:30 p.m. daily) are invaluable in an emergency situation.

16. Be particular in selecting a public meeting place and facility. For example, Sisters High School became the evacuation center–conveniently located, able to accommodate nearly the entire town for meetings, fully equipped with a sound system, computer projection equipment, laser pointer, large screen, chairs, rest rooms, and a radio station, Outlaw Radio 106.5 FM with a feedback e-mail address: KZSO@outlawnet.com.

17. Focus the public meeting agenda on specifics. For example, brief people with military-type precision and detail–What exactly was accomplished today? How was it done? What resources were used? What's the plan for tonight and tomorrow morning? What additional resources are needed? Are we going to have them? If not, why?

18. Let experts speak. For example, people want information directly from the sheriff's office, incident commander, meteorologist, fire behavior analyst, state fire marshal's office, Oregon Department of Forestry, Red Cross, local fire chief, U.S. Forest Service.

19. Make public information a two-way exchange. For example, give people what they want to know, then have them listen to what they need to know.

20. Take advantage of existing communication resources. For example, Sisters High School radio station was used to broadcast public meetings live and

replay them during the day along with interviews of experts on the fire team, statements were given to The Nugget, Sisters' weekly newspaper, for posting on www.nuggetsnews.com, and to the Bend Bulletin for posting on www.bendbulletin.com. Regional TV was included.

21. Be respectful of every question and concern. For example, during one public meeting a woman from an RV parked in the evacuation/information center parking lot said, "We don't have an FM radio; how will we know when it's OK to go back to our house?" The commander of the federal Southeastern Area Interagency Incident Management Team kindly replied: "I will come over and tell you."

22. Use visuals. For example, project Web addresses and emergency help and information phone numbers on a screen and give people plenty of time to copy them.

23. Use handouts. For example, explain the evacuation notification process that will use media releases, the incident team phone line 549-3211, Oregon Department of Transportation number 511-8, phone calls to evacuees who register with the Red Cross, Outlaw radio 106.5 PM; police car sirens, house-to-house door-belling,

24. Spike rumors. For example, an evacuee who was eager to get back into his home spread the word that houses were being looted. Authorities immediately challenged the rumor with accurate information.

25. Accept volunteered resources. For example, Clearchannel.com provided free wireless Internet connections at the Red Cross evacuation center, along with 20 drops throughout town, and it offered free long distance phone service.

26. Walk in the victim's shoes. For example, sit with 800 people voicing their questions, concerns and anxieties to fully appreciate the importance of providing information fast, accurately and in great detail.

27. Be forthright and honest. For example, the lead public information officer for the federal Southeastern Area Interagency Incident Management Team said: "Whether news is good or bad you can count on us to tell you the truth."

28. Drop boundaries. Promote cooperation among local, state and federal officials and the people they serve and the rewards will be bountiful. For example, when the Type II Northwest Interagency Incident Management Team turned command of the emergency over to the federal Type I Southeastern Area Interagency Incident Management Team, the Northwest team received a standing ovation from hundreds of residents and the federal team quickly came to regard Sisters as "the most giving and patient community."

29. Support each other. Meeting the challenge of a life and property-threatening situation is a significant accomplishment to be recognized. For example, parents helped children make cookies and fudge and take it to fire fighters. Residents and merchants posted thank you signs around town. When one resident during a public meeting asked what more the town could do to show its appreciation to the fire teams, the incident commander said, "Just give 'em a smile and a wave."

30. Use multiple channels. For example, the Incident Management Team staffed a bulletin board briefing at the town park and ran a daily information trap line to key businesses and local government offices.

31. Keep the media informed. For example, the IMC conducted frequent and scheduled briefings and took reporters and photographers on trips to the fire line. The Incident Management Team treated the media as a partner to ensure that accurate information would be conveyed to the public.

32. Consider related impacts. For example, the Incident Management Team, thinking of the economic impact the emergency could have on a small town, made a special effort to communicate with visitors and included them in the information trap line with a staffed in-town sidewalk briefing.

33. Use a phone bank. For example, the Incident Management Team provided information through a phone bank and also used this channel to spike rumors with accurate facts. Out-of-towners used the phone bank to ask about the smoke and whether or not they should come to Sisters.

34. Use public meetings. For example, regularly scheduled public meetings at Sisters High School—the official evacuation center—gave residents, visitors, business owners, evacuees the opportunity to get to know eyeball to eyeball leaders of the fire suppression organization, particularly "the outsiders" of the Southeastern Area Incident Management Command. When first introduced, the incident commander said in a typical Southern drawl, "I may talk slow, but I fight fires real fast." Instantly, he had a close rapport with the hundreds of people attending the meeting.

35. Win trust. For example, truth established trust for the Incident Management Command. It was made clear from its first public appearance that the IMC would "always tell the truth, whether the news was good or bad."

36. Accept help and resources. For example, the Incident Management Command could have ignored the Sisters High School principal when he offered the use of the school's radio station that was due to come on line at the fall start of school. Instead the IMC partnered with the school and Outlaw Radio 106.5 FM became a major information source that

taped and aired the public meetings repeatedly along with interviews of fire officials from the interagency team. The station, thanks to the high school principal, just happened to be available–something that doesn't happen for most fire fighting emergencies. When the public meetings were discontinued, the IMC continued to provide briefings on Outlaw Radio 106.5.

37. Messaging must be consistent. For example, the information function was seamless, mainly because messages to the public were consistent from all sources within the interagency group. In contrast to the commonly seen, sharp bickering over turf among government agencies, collaboration between local, state and federal authorities, the media and citizens in fighting the Black Crater Fire was commendable beyond everyone's belief.

38. Announce and celebrate success. For example, as one incident command official said, "I am not sure you could have a more comprehensive program. In return the community served pie and ice cream!!"

3 Writing and Leading with Integrity

One of my students at the University of Oregon was asked in a job interview to identify weaknesses in the PR profession. Unable to think of any, she turned to the interviewer who admitted that she couldn't think of any either. Understandably, we don't dwell on our weaknesses.

However, public relations, as a relatively young and developing profession, does have vulnerabilities. As practitioners and particularly as plan developers, we have a responsibility to be aware of them and to help ensure that public relations continues to grow in practice and in character.

What can we do as plan developers to strengthen the profession?

One thing we can do is market and deliver what we do best. We are strategic communicators. A review of Silver Anvil winners in the category of PR tactics showcases the tremendous talent we have in communication.

Public relations is not clearly defined–it has hundreds of definitions, so expectations of results can be wide ranging. It is better to market our core competencies in communication than to promise more than we can deliver. The temptation exists to pursue hot markets, like social media networking, high-tech, health care and corporate governance, with loosely formed but firmly hyped "expertise." This tendency oftentimes sets up great expectations, only to be dashed by disappointing results and invoices that make boards of directors resistant to return to the profession for services.

Another thing we can do is bring public relations planning into sharper focus as we strive to do in the classroom and in this book. Because there is limited textbook instruction in developing public relations plans, practitioners have almost as many different definitions of goals, objectives, strategies and activities as we have for defining the profession itself.

A public relations plan that puts its audience into a state of confusion and rejection over terms and form brings great injury to the profession's reputation.

Public relations is not an exact science, so we cannot guarantee the outcomes of plans. However, we can show how we draw on bodies of knowledge in the social sciences and methodically and strategically formulate plans to increase our effectiveness in achieving objectives.

We can strengthen the profession by ensuring that our practice of public relations is always service-driven. Examples exist of public relations firms whose overhead costs for expensive office space, leased cars, furniture and office equipment–instead of quality service–drive the practice, demanding more and more billable hours any way a firm can get them. There are examples of individual practitioners whose work is driven by personal ambitions at any cost rather than by a genuine desire to provide quality service. The profession's reputation cannot afford these excursions any more than today's corporations can afford the liberties many have taken with accounting practices.

Being rock solid in upholding the principles of the profession, as enumerated in the Public Relations Society of America's Code of Ethics, is especially important at a time when public relations is heavily engaged in counseling others about reputation management. Public relations has yet to be fully accepted as a true profession. There are no standardized educational requirements. There is no mandatory licensing or certification. There is no effective self-regulation.

When we market our core competencies in strategic communication, when we bring public relations planning into sharper focus, when we ensure that our practice of public relations is service-driven, we are leading with integrity. We are demonstrating a passion for principles that commands respect and develops mutual trust. By leading and writing with integrity we enable the profession to grow in practice and in stature.

While we are on the subject of integrity, read the following case titled, "What could go wrong." This is a case of an industrial operation that presents a clear and present danger to the lives of people in the surrounding community. Think of yourself as the public relations consultant in this case.

Case Three
Risk
Communication

WHAT COULD GO WRONG?

The case on the following page is written as a role play to give participants in a class or workshop a sense of how it must feel to work in a poorly managed high-risk environment. In this situation, a public relations consultant has been called on to assist management in announcing to employees and community residents that a new piece of equipment is being added to the plant operation which will require the use of two, in addition to the current use of 17 toxic chemicals.

The consultant interviews employees in dangerous areas of plant operations, then conducts a focus group of community leaders.

The case situation is actual and while it represents an extreme situation, it makes people even in well managed industrial operations think twice about potential risks in their own businesses.

How would you advise the plant manager? What are the regulatory, moral and social implications in this situation for the company, the consultant and government?

In the mid-1980s, the federal government made it the public's right to know about hazardous materials used in the work place. Companies using dangerous chemicals were mandated by law, under SARA Title III (EPCRA), to disclose their use of these substances by completing and making available Material Safety Data Sheets. Information reported tells where hazardous chemicals exist and in what quantities. Residents of many communities throughout the country, initially, were shocked to discover the risks posed to their personal health and safety by their industrial neighbors. Today, the risks continue to exist; the public is less interested and informed and has abrogated the safeguarding of its health and safety to local, state and federal agencies.

A fire chief gave this perspective: "Material Safety Data Sheets are of interest to local emergency planning committees, state emergency response commissions and first responders; the general public is relatively uniformed, and largely uninterested. There seems to be a willingness to rely on government to protect people from bad things in their community. In my opinion, interest in chemical risks by the public peaked within the first decade of SARA Title III (EPCRA), and has since waned. Fortunately, my experience has been that industry still cares and is sensitive to public expectations."

While people have gained a right to know about the use of hazardous materials in the work place, they would be misguided to think that the risks in using toxics have been eliminated. They must rely on employer and government oversight to ensure their health and safety. Most of all, they should seek information and know for themselves what hazards exist and how they are being managed.

> "I work five different areas. Each has a computer. Ya can't know each one very well. So when something's going wrong I just wait 'til it's bad enough for the computer to tell me what to do."
>
> —Plant Worker

To give you a sense of what it is like to work in a high-risk environment, the role play on the following pages will take you into an industrial operation and let you feel, vicariously, through interviews of workers and community members what it must be like to end each day grateful that a crisis did not occur.

Conduct the role play as a class or as a professional workshop. Think about how you would advise the plant manager? What are the regulatory, moral and social implications in this situation for the company, the consultant and government?

This role play serves as an introduction to the subject of risk communication. Communicating matters of risk effectively requires: a.) information needs to be met to the receivers' satisfaction; b.) information from a known and trusted source; c.) a sense of control provided by an independent party, such as an emergency response service; d.) safety claims based on a track record of performance and evidence that lend them credence. Is this company in a position to talk convincingly about risks to health and safety?

ROLE PLAY
Cast

Narrator
Public Relations Consultant Vince Brockwell
Plant Manager Harry Holderman
Employee Mike
Employee Arvin
Employee Rich
Employee Bill
Employee Bob
County Commissioner Iffert
Chamber of Commerce Executive Dorothy
Fire Chief Sonders
Police Chief Jefferies
Mayor Hunt
State Senator Winchester
State Representative Gritmeyer

Plant Manager's Office

PR Consultant Vince Brockwell meets with plant manager

Plant Manager Harry Holderman

Vince, I asked you to see me because we are going to make an addition to the plant.

PR Consultant Vince Brockwell

And you want an announcement.

Plant Manager Harry Holderman

I wish we could do it without any fanfare.

PR Consultant Vince Brockwell

What are you going to add?

Plant Manager Harry Holderman

Just another piece of equipment.

PR Consultant Vince Brockwell

So why the serious look?

Plant Manager Harry Holderman

You know we already use 17 hazardous chemicals. Well, this will add two more and the community, by law, has a right to know. We made the big disclosure about our chemical use back in the mid-'80s. Now that the information is accessible, people don't seem to have as much interest. But this is going to wake the sleeping dog.

PR Consultant Vince Brockwell

This has always been considered a dangerous place to work, Harry. And I don't know that the perception has changed.

Plant Manager Harry Holderman

I'm afraid that's true. The head shed just wants to make money–at anyone's expense.

PR Consultant Vince Brockwell

Why don't I have some informal conversations with people inside and outside the plant. I'd like to interview some employees. I'm sure I could arrange a focus group of community leaders like the mayor, chamber director, police chief. That will give us an idea of how people feel about accepting more risk.

Plant Manager Harry Holderman

You might wake the sleeping dog.

PR Consultant Vince Brockwell

Let's do this, Harry.

Interviews at the Plant with Employees

Brockwell, having made arrangements to interview employees in the most dangerous areas of the plant, begins with Mike.

PR Consultant Vince Brockwell

Mike, tell me about your job.

Mike

First thing to know when we go to work is which way the wind's blowing. If you smell a foul order, you know to run away from the wind. That's how we watch for chemical leaks.

PR Consultant Vince Brockwell

So what are you supposed to do in an emergency?

Mike

There's been spills. That should be a sign that we need some written procedures, but there aren't any.

Brockwell completes the interview and moves to another dangerous area of the plant and talks to another employee.

PR Consultant Vince Brockwell

Arvin, where do you work?

Arvin

Can I say, without getting in trouble?

PR Consultant Vince Brockwell

Sure.

Arvin

They say I work in the "powder house." My area is a danger zone.

PR Consultant Vince Brockwell

Is it like a bomb?

Arvin

Kind of …

PR Consultant Vince Brockwell

Are you worried about that?

Arvin

I was told that I would be safe. It's designed to explode up into the air and not out to the sides.

PR Consultant Vince Brockwell

What would you do in an emergency?

Arvin

I'd try to find the foreman.

PR Consultant moves to another dangerous area of the plant.

PR Consultant Vince Brockwell

Rich, I see that you work with computer controls. This room looks like a military command center.

Rich

I'm working five different jobs now; each one has computers to work. Ya know, it's hard to get to know computers on five different jobs, especially when you don't really know the programs.

PR Consultant Vince Brockwell

So what do you do in an emergency?

Rich

There's no written procedures.

PR Consultant Vince Brockwell

So you just …

Rich

You just wait until the situation gets bad enough to set off an alarm and see what the computer tells you to do.

PR Consultant Vince Brockwell

You're pretty much on your own.

Rich

Pretty much.

PR Consultant talks to another employee.

PR Consultant Vince Brockwell

Bill, tell me about your job. What do you do?

Bill

I monitor equipment. I get a little nervous sometimes when the supervisor is gone for two or three weeks. Even when he's around, he's always tied up some place in meetings.

PR Consultant Vince Brockwell

What are you afraid might happen?

Bill

I worry about seeing a bad chemical reaction and not having anyone around to explain it.

PR Consultant Vince Brockwell

Like what?

Bill

Tanker trucks come and go. No one checks them in. They pull up to a tank, fill it and leave. I've seen more than one driver put something into the wrong tank.

Consultant walks over to a railroad siding.

PR Consultant Vince Brockwell

Bob, you work in a hazardous area of the plant. Tell me what it's like.

Bob

I do chlorine hook-ups.

PR Consultant Vince Brockwell

You unload chlorine from railroad tank cars.

Bob

Yea.

PR Consultant Vince Brockwell

Is there a training program for that?

Bob

No. You know how it goes. One guy learns from another.

PR Consultant Vince Brockwell

So how did you learn?

Bob

From Hank.

PR Consultant Vince Brockwell

Who taught Hank?

Bob

Someone else. I know that's not good. If the first guy's not trained no one does it right.

PR Consultant Vince Brockwell

Tell me. How would you feel standing around one of these tank cars while someone else does the hook-up.

Bob

Not on your life, man.

PR Consultant Vince Brockwell

What would you do in an emergency?

Bob

You mean like in a chlorine attack? I can always count on three or four other guys for help.

Vince Brockwell slowly bows his head, closes his notebook and heads for the office.

Focus Group at Chamber of Commerce with Community Members

PR Consultant Vince Brockwell conducts a focus group session with a county commissioner, the chamber of commerce executive, fire chief, mayor, police chief, a state representative and state senator. Brockwell begins by focusing on the group's knowledge of plant safety hazards.

PR Consultant Vince Brockwell

As you know, I am working on behalf of the local plant management to assess the plant's relationship with the community and, in particular, communication regarding health or safety issues. Let's start with the subject of safety.

Commissioner Iffert

I don't think anybody knows whether it's safe or not.

Chamber Executive Dorothy

We know there are hazards down there.

Fire Chief Sonders

There could be problems with safety. There are potential hazards with the transportation of chlorine.

PR Consultant Vince Brockwell

What's your view, chief. Does your department have any concerns about safety?

Police Chief Jefferies

We're not aware of any particular hazards.

Mayor Hunt

We've seen people evacuated from that area twice. The chemical leaks tend to be irritating. I don't think anybody outside the plant has had to be treated.

State Senator Winchester

The most obvious concern is the chlorine. It comes by rail right to the plant. Tank cars sit there on a side rail. I'm not aware of others. But they have some pretty heavy duty stuff.

State Representative Gritmeyer

The plant is a very hazardous place to work. But they have worked at it, so it's much better than many small businesses.

PR Consultant Vince Brockwell

What do you think about the odors from the plant?

State Senator Winchester

Son, that's the smell of Greenbacks!

State Representative Gritmeyer

That question is very difficult to answer.

Commissioner Iffert

In my opinion, the odors are from harmful stuff. But the plant represents a lot of money. So it's a trade-off. In all honesty, I don't think anybody knows what's coming out of the plant.

Chamber Executive Dorothy

I was caught on Labelle St. when they released something. I was scared! I thought I'd been gassed!

Fire Chief Sonders

Fortunately, practically nothing solid is coming out of the stacks. It's more like steam.

Police Chief Jefferies

I don't believe the odors are harmful. It's just part of the manufacturing process. There are environmental controls, and I'd assume they're operating in limits.

Mayor Hunt

It can't be too bad for ya. They spent millions to take particulate and harmful crap out of the air.

Subject of the focus group changes to see where members get information about the plant.

PR Consultant Vince Brockwell

I would like to know how you keep informed about the plant and management decisions that might affect the community.

Commissioner Iffert

I read the newspaper.

Chamber Executive Dorothy

I talk to the plant manager.

Fire Chief Sonders

I go straight to the head of the company.

Police Chief Jefferies

I usually talk to employees.

Mayor Hunt

We've had real problems getting information. A lot of times we don't know what's going on until something is published.

State Senator Winchester

I go to the highest person I can find.

State Representative Gritmeyer

I've been wanting to talk to someone for a long time.

Focus of the group changes again, this time to determine if the plant manager is a well-known, trusted spokesperson for the plant.

PR Consultant Vince Brockwell

Let's talk for a minute about the plant manager. At the chamber, do you know the plant manager?

Commissioner Iffert

Sure, I know him.

PR Consultant Vince Brockwell

How would you describe the plant's involvement in the community?

Chamber Executive Dorothy

It took a long, long time to persuade them to put someone on the chamber board.

PR Consultant Vince Brockwell

What about you, Commissioner. Do you know the plant manager?

Commissioner Iffert

If I've met him, I don't recall.

PR Consultant Vince Brockwell

Chief, have you met the manager?

Fire Chief Sonders

I can't remember.

PR Consultant Vince Brockwell

What about the plant's involvement with the community in your area?

Fire Chief Sonders

I'd say their involvement is four or five on a scale of one to 10. The plant doesn't want to appear to run the town, so it keeps its involvement down.

PR Consultant Vince Brockwell

Have you met the plant manager, Representative Gritmeyer?

State Representative Gritmeyer

No. I haven't met him.

PR Consultant Vince Brockwell

How would you describe the plant's involvement in state legislative affairs?

State Representative Gritmeyer

Why, I'd call it laid back.

PR Consultant Vince Brockwell

Would you agree with that Senator?

State Senator Winchester

Their community activity is sporadic. There's no corporate obligation. It's purely a business involvement with the community.

PR Consultant Vince Brockwell

Have you met the plant manager?

State Senator Winchester

No. Don't think he's involved much in the community.

PR Consultant Vince Brockwell

Has the manager had any contact with you, Mayor Hunt?

Mayor Hunt

Yeah. He's a busy guy. Their involvement with the community is limited. Either they don't see their value to the community, or they have made a decision to keep to themselves.

PR Consultant Vince Brockwell

Is there any plant contact with the police department?

Police Chief Jefferies

Not really. I don't know the manager.

Subject of the focus session shifts to the matter of control to see if the plant shares with the community, through local emergency services or some government agency, any sense of control over health and safety hazards.

PR Consultant Vince Brockwell

Chief, when the plant has to make a decision that affects the community, is there an opportunity for the community to participate?

Fire Chief Sonders

They just decide what they want to do and do it. We would like to have some input.

Police Chief Jefferies

We don't have a say in anything.

Chamber Executive Dorothy

I don't find things out until I read them in the paper. If I didn't get the paper I'd be completely in the dark.

PR Consultant Vince Brockwell

Mayor, have you been consulted by the plant?

Mayor Hunt

Well, not directly, I guess.

State Representative Gritmeyer

Don't ask me. I'm never called.

State Senator Winchester

I'm not sure what to say. Within the company there's some unpredictable behavior. Let's move on.

The PR Consultant now looks for evidence, such as a jointly developed emergency plan or track record of cooperation, that the plant could use to back up any claims or statements it makes about safety.

PR Consultant Vince Brockwell

Is there a plan for a major emergency?

State Senator Winchester

I think we're extremely well prepared.

State Representative Gritmeyer

I don't think we are. There's no plan.

Commissioner Iffert

There's no plan. No alarms. No evacuation plan or anything.

Chamber Executive Dorothy

Maybe that's an area we need to work on. There's always concern about what we would do in a major emergency.

Fire Chief Sonders

There's no major response plans in place, but there should be.

Police Chief Jefferies

No plan. No drills. No alarm.

PR Consultant Vince Brockwell

So what would you do if there was a gas leak?

Police chief takes PR Consultant outside to his patrol car. Opens the trunk.

PR Consultant Vince Brockwell

What are all these, chief?

Police Chief Jefferies

These are different gas masks or respirators. Five.

PR Consultant Vince Brockwell

How would you know which one to use?

Police Chief Jefferies

Oh, someone from the plant would call and tell me.

Public relations consultant Vince Brockwell, now in deep thought about what he has learned and about his responsibilities as a consultant, slowly closes his notebook, returns to his office to prepare his report for Harry Holderman.

Plant Manager's Office
PR Consultant Vince Brockwell

Harry, I finished my interviews.

Plant Manager Harry Holderman

So, is this going to let the cat out of the bag?

PR Consultant Vince Brockwell

Look, Harry, this isn't about announcing new equipment. Good grief, man! You are sitting on a powder keg! The employees I talked to in the most dangerous areas of the operations are not safety trained. They're not computer trained. They're barely supervised. They devised their own ways to stay safe. They're sitting at their workstations with a big fat false sense of security. What I … no …

Plant Manager Harry Holderman

What Vince?

PR Consultant Vince Brockwell

No, I shouldn't be …

Plant Manager Harry Holderman

What? So constrained? Go ahead. Pound my desk with your other shoe.

PR Consultant Vince Brockwell

I can't believe the feds haven't shut this place down. Actually, I do know why they haven't. The whole town is protecting you. Without this plant there wouldn't be a town.

Plant Manager Harry Holderman

So what did people in town have to say?

PR Consultant Vince Brockwell

For one thing, they don't know if the plant is safe or not. There's lots of doubt that it is and little interest in finding out–even among the emergency services–would you believe? What they know is what they read in the paper, or what they hear over the fence from a friend in the plant.

Plant Manager Harry Holderman

It's a small town. Everybody knows everybody.

PR Consultant Vince Brockwell

Not you, Harry. Not everybody knows you! If you had to talk to people in this town, they'd want to see your ID. The fire chief can't remember if he ever met you.

Plant Manager Harry Holderman

Well, we have a lot to handle.

PR Consultant Vince Brockwell

I hope you have your own fire truck.

Plant Manager Harry Holderman

It's a good thing we're good friends, or I'd of thrown your butt out of here by now.

PR Consultant Vince Brockwell

Harry. Seriously. This is not good. Employees and the town's people are taking a big risk. They could die in their beds at night if those tank cars ... Are you prepared to handle an emergency? The town isn't. No alarm. No drills. No evacuation plan. You need to be prepared to manage and communicate in an emergency. You need to have some agreements up front, among yourselves, and with others, about how you're going to function in a crisis situation.

Plant Manager Harry Holderman

It's not that simple, Vince. We have never gotten the resources we need. To the headquarters we're nothing but a cash cow and all that counts is the milk.

PR Consultant Vince Brockwell

What about the company's responsibility to the town? ... to all the people who are virtually risking their lives to keep the cow productive? Surely, there must be some sense of social responsibility up there.

Plant Manager Harry Holderman

Not much I can say about that.

PR Consultant Vince Brockwell

Then what about the human values right here? How are you and your staff getting along with each other and the rest of the workforce. You must have some shared values.

Plant Manager Harry Holderman

We do, Vince. And that's really why I called you.

4 Beginning the Planning Process with Accountability

I t is easy to get caught up in the excitement of developing a public relations plan, especially if its creative elements are likely to delight or impress reviewers. However, focusing mainly on creative strategies could be a serious miscalculation on the part of a plan developer. That's because a plan, regardless of its degree of creativity, must be backed by accountability for cost, completeness, effectiveness and measurability.

A plan reviewer could be expected to ask, How do you justify this plan in terms of cost, benefits and need? In other words, will the benefits you expect to derive from the plan be worth the time, money and energy that have to be put into the plan to accomplish its goal? A question of equal importance that a reviewer must contemplate is, How does the need for this action rank among all of the other pressing needs of the organization?

A public relations plan could require from $5,000 to well over $500,000 to develop and implement. A request for such an expenditure, assuming that it is an expense over the existing budget, must compete on its merits with all other special requests for an authorization of funds. So the plan's costs, benefits, and necessity must be made absolutely clear to a reviewer.

With regard to cost, a plan also must be affordable to the organization receiving the proposal. That's not to suggest cutting corners or lowering standards to suit an organization. If a public relations action can't be done right it shouldn't be attempted. Fortunately, in public relations, there are many different ways to accomplish communication objectives cost-effectively.

So, a plan must establish a clear need for public relations action and must propose a cost-effective orchestration of communication activities that is within the sponsoring organization's budget.

A plan reviewer also could be expected to ask, What's the basis for your justification of this plan? With this question, the reviewer is holding the plan developer accountable for completeness. The reviewer wants to see that you have all of the information necessary for the reviewer to make a thorough assessment of the plan in order to decide whether or not to approve it. That means the plan developer must be diligent in writing each of the 10 components of the public relations plan. As you will see in the next chapter, a reviewer has specific interests in every component of the public relations plan: 1) problem, challenge or opportunity statement, 2) situation analysis, 3) target publics, 4) goal, 5) objectives, 6) strategies, 7) activities, 8) time line, 9) evaluation, and 10) budget. So as you develop a plan, ask yourself if you are presenting all the

Plan reviewer

information a reviewer would require in each area of the plan to enable the reviewer to make an assessment and reach for a pen to approve your plan.

A reviewer also could be expected to ask, How do you know this plan will be effective? With this question, the reviewer, many of whom have no formal education in public relations, is looking for assurances that what is proposed in the plan is what will be necessary to obtain some reasonable measure of success in achieving the plan's goal. It is incumbent on the plan developer to educate the reviewer in knowing that public relations plans are based on proven principles of communication and persuasion, and practice calling on the body of knowledge in the social sciences that has been acquired by the profession over several decades.

Another important way to assure effectiveness is with research. The use of research, despite its immense value, has yet to become fully established in the profession. The term research, by its own definition, connoting formal, costly, time-consuming study, documented investigation, examination of a condition in one past moment or period of time–retards its use. Heads of organizations who have ultimate control of public relations spending historically have resisted spending money on research. However, research is becoming much more affordable with new Internet technologies.

Measuring effectiveness doesn't always require formal research. The fact is there are many forms of research that are not costly and time-consuming. In the broadest terms, everyone conducts research. We all gather information to find solutions to problems. It is an important function in our daily lives and not as a formal process. Research is vitally important in the development of plans and should not be summarily dismissed.

A plan reviewer could be expected to ask, What indications will you have to show that your public relations plan is, in fact, proceeding effectively toward accomplishing its goal? With this question, the reviewer is holding the plan developer accountable for measurement. Assuming the plan is being implemented, how can its effectiveness be measured? The answer should be that the plan's objectives–all of them–are measurable. Every one of a plan's objectives should be written, as will be explained later, to include a desired behavioral outcome and the resulting behavior can be measured in qualitative or quantitative terms.

Case Four
Event
Planning

GETTING NOTHING FOR SOMETHING

The case on the following page is about being accountable. Read or conduct the role play about an open house for a new health care job training center. Explain why the case is titled, "Getting Nothing for Something." Explain what it means to be accountable in this case. Also answer the questions posed in the introduction to the case.

This is a case of getting nothing for something. An open house is held to introduce community residents to a new health care job training center. It costs thousands of dollars and leaves guests with no more than a "nice impression."

Read the role play on the following page to get a sense of what two executive managers think about the event and how it was managed. Then return to this point to answer the following questions about how you would hold yourself accountable for conducting a successful open house.

1. How would you determine a need for the open house?
2. How would you assess alternative ways to fill the need?
3. How would you discuss the costs and benefits of the event with the executive manager?
4. How would you answer the question, What if invitations are sent and no one attends?
5. How would you answer the question, How can you be sure the guests will get our message?
6. How would you answer the question, How can you be sure that you will get everyone's full support of the event?
7. How would you answer the question, What if the media has no interest in the event?
8. How would you answer the question, How will you measure the event's effectiveness?

ROLE PLAY
Cast

Dave, retired executive
Frank, retired executive

Restaurant

Two retired executives, Frank and Dave, are talking over breakfast.

Dave

Did you go to the open house yesterday?

Frank

Yes. I went over after lunch.

Dave

Did you meet the director?

Frank

He was the CEO of that chain of methadone clinics. Wouldn't have been my pick for the new center.

Dave

Ironic that in management it's easier for an inadequate CEO to keep his job than it is for an inadequate subordinate. That's what Warren Buffett says.

Frank

Sad, but true. Look at that guy. Not much of a performer and they make him head of a new health care job training center. He'll keep that position forever. Chances are good that he has no specified performance standards from the board. Most CEOs don't.

Facsimile of a new health care job training center where an open house could have been held to introduce the facility, its services and staff to community residents.

Dave

Or they're easily explained away. Buffett says too many bosses shoot the performance arrow, then run over to paint a bull's eye around the spot where it lands.

Frank

You like Buffett.

Dave

Yea. I especially agree with him about boards of directors. He says relations between a board and a CEO are expected to be congenial. Any criticism of a CEO's performance is seen as socially unacceptable as belching. Nothing like that stops an office manager from coming down hard on employees.

Frank

Someone should come down hard on the new director for that open house.

Dave

Why so?

Frank

Well, for one thing, they obviously spent big bucks on food, entertainment and giveaways and what did they get for it?

Dave

Yea, that was apparent to me too. I left with the impression that it's a nice place with nice people and that's about all. What's the point of spending the money?

Retired executives, Frank (left) and Dave (right) having a casual conversation over breakfast.

Frank

The invitation was an expensive piece. Except, I would have sent some information with it for people who couldn't attend. At least they would be a little more knowledgeable about the center and the mailing wouldn't be a complete waste of money.

Dave

If I were a board member I'd hold the new director accountable for spending money on an event like that and getting virtually nothing for it.

Frank

I remember an open house we had. Talk about impressions! Our PR woman … Boy was she tenacious!

Dave

Pretty aggressive.

Frank

Aggressive about getting results! Why are we doing this? What's the message you want to give to everyone who attends and to those who don't attend? What's the impression you want to make on the whole community? She kept firing questions then came back with a detailed plan and budget.

Dave

I remember that grand opening. So does the whole community, I'll bet. You probably needed therapy after shaking so many hands.

Frank

Yea. We had greeters, well-rehearsed tour guides, information stations with important points on sign boards, good, but not lavish refreshments, and mementoes that were useful to keep as reminders. Our PR woman wouldn't have launched the event without a clear, measurable objective.

Dave

Well, I think yesterday's open house showed a clear lack of capital-allocation skills on the part of the new director.

Frank

There's plenty of unintelligent capital allocation going on in corporate America.

Dave

Hey listen, Frank. It's my turn to pay for the eggs. Let's do it again next Friday.

Frank

Sounds good to me. We can talk about the Dingle deal. You know what they say about investment bankers, "Never ask a barber if you need a haircut."

INTERNSHIP PROGRAM
Assist With White House Social Events

The White House Internship Program provides a unique opportunity to gain valuable professional experience and build leadership skills. This hands-on program is designed to mentor and cultivate today's young leaders, strengthen their understanding of the Executive Office and prepare them for future public service opportunities.

In addition to typical office duties, interns will supplement their learning experience by attending a weekly lecture series hosted by senior White House staff, assist at White House social events, and volunteer in community service projects.

"This program will mentor and cultivate young leaders of today and tomorrow and I'm proud that they will have this opportunity to serve," said President Obama. "I look forward to working with those that are selected

Accountability
A special way to learn about event planning and accountability is through The White House Internship Program.

to participate and I want to commend all who apply for their desire to help through public service to forge a brighter future for our country."

White House Internships are full-time unpaid positions and participants are responsible for arranging their own transportation and housing for the duration of the program.

Applicants are encouraged to contact educational and other non-profit organizations to apply for funding or housing assistance. Applicants can contact local colleges and universities for housing opportunities.

Applicants must be:

US Citizens; eighteen years of age on or before the first day of the internship; enrolled in an undergraduate or graduate program at a college, community college, or university (2–4 year institution) or must have graduated in the past two years from undergraduate or graduate school; or be a veteran of the United States Armed forces who possesses a high school diploma or its equivalent and has served on active duty at any time over the past two years.

5 Measuring the Effectiveness of Public Relations Programs and Activities

In this chapter, we will use the case of Quality Out of Control to illustrate the invaluable use of research and emphasize the absolute necessity of evaluation in the practice of public relations. Following the case is a Gold Standard Paper developed by the Commission on Public Relations Measurement & Evaluation titled, "Guidelines for Measuring the Effectiveness of PR Programs and Activities by Dr. Walter K. Lindenmann and published by the Institute for Public Relations. Pay special attention to this chapter and know that if you can't measure what you do, you can't evaluate what you do. If you can't evaluate what you do, you can't very well expect to be recognized for what you do.

I would like to provide a broad context for the case of Quality Out of Control. First is an excerpt from an article from the June-July 1994 issue of *Public Relations Journal* titled, "CEO serves as chief communicator of TQM (total quality management) program:

> Total quality management (TQM) has been tried, with varying degrees of success, by many organizations since it became a management buzzword in the late 1980s. Many U.S.-based firms, as well as concerns around the globe, have adopted TQM strategies and tactics, such as cycle analysis, process efficiency and customer-driven systems. Employee empowerment and total organizational commitment are two, sometimes conflicting, elements of any successful TQM "deployment," according to the experts. Communication strategies play a crucial role in achieving these goals.

Second is the opening paragraph of an article titled, "The Five Messages Leaders Must Manage," by John Hamm in the May 2006 issue of *Harvard Business Review*:

> If you want to know why so many organizations sink into chaos, look no further than their leaders' mouths. Leadership, at any level, certainly isn't easy—but unclear, vague, roller coaster pronouncements make many top managers' jobs infinitely more difficult than they need to be. Leaders frequently espouse dozens of cliché-infused declarations such as "Let's focus on the key priorities this quarter," "Customers come first," or "We need a full-court press in engineering this month." Over and over again, they present grand, over arching—yet fuzzy—notions of where they think the company is

going. Too often, they assume everyone shares the same definitions of broad terms like vision, loyalty, accountability, customer relationships, teamwork, focus, priority, culture, frugality, decision-making, results ... [and in this case, quality, standards, priorities and needs].

Case Five
Employee Communication

QUALITY OUT OF CONTROL

The case on the following page illustrates the use of personal interviews to research an internal communication problem. Each interview was 60 minutes in length and to expedite analysis of the findings, each person interviewed, including the plant manager, was asked to summarize his or her responses to each of six questions in one or two words. Your assignment is to characterize the overall response to each question, the overall response to the plant manager's answers, and explain conclusions you could draw from your characterizations or analyses. When you complete your work on question six, characterize responses to all six questions by each staff member and determine what conclusions could be drawn from their responses relative to their particular job functions. An extension of this exercise is to read the Guidelines for Measuring the Effectiveness of PR Programs and Activities and explain how this research could be used in measuring the effectiveness of an employee communication plan that would assist the plant manager in achieving total quality control.

All businesses, service as well as manufacturing, have one objective in common and that is to deliver quality in whatever they have to market. Quality is the cornerstone in building a business and so over the years many different Q programs, such as TQM or Total Quality Management, have been put to work to ensure quality in products and services. TQM means, essentially, that there are quality requirements in every phase of providing a product, such as taking orders, purchasing materials, manufacturing, shipping, billing, etc. This case points out what many companies have learned—without effective communication, you will not achieve a high standard of quality even if you have checks and balances in every phase of the business.

Better Bags manufactures various forms of paper packaging. The manager of one of the company's plants that manufactures paper shopping bags for grocery stores asks you to meet with him to discuss a problem. At the meeting he says, "I have been talking quality around here for months and it's like talking to a brick wall! Quality seems to be lacking in everything we do and I don't know what more I can do. We're beginning to lose customers. We get reports about handles falling off bags and bottoms falling open. One lady is suing us for letting a jar of Bobos Bread & Butter Chips fall through a bag and break her toe. We have had everything tested and we know the problem is not with paper or glue. It's a problem with how we work together to run the equipment that makes the product. It's a very serious situation, and just when I'm getting ready to retire. I don't want to reinvent this place at this point in my career. I'm just asking you, as our PR department experts, to see if your expertise in communication can help get my quality message across to everybody."

You and your staff begin work by interviewing members of the plant management staff. Results of six interview questions are shown on the following pages. Each interview was 60 minutes in length and to expedite analysis of the findings the interviewer asked each person interviewed, including the plant manager, to summarize his or her responses to each of six questions in one or two words. Your assignment is to characterize the overall response to each question, the overall staff member response to the plant manger's response, and explain conclusions you could draw from characterizations or analyses. When you complete your work on question six, characterize responses to all six questions by each staff member and determine what conclusions could be drawn from their responses relative to their particular job functions. On the next page you will find a fact sheet about Better Bags.

Better Bags, Inc.
Paperville, U.S.A.

Employees: 276
Product: Paper grocery bags with paper
               handles
Customers: Grocery stores—chains and independents
Established: In business since 1972
Manager: Tom Jones, 64; 30 years of service; degree in mechanical
               engineering from the University of Engineering

Bag operation: The bag operation is automated. Movement of material is along an assembly line of machines that cut, fold, glue and attach paper handles. The equipment adjusts to changes in temperature. Paper jams are infrequent, but require setup and adjustment time. While the equipment is automated, it must be closely monitored which requires diligence on the part of equipment operators, accurate reading of gauges and recording of data by workers and coordination between shift supervisors. Sometimes the equipment runs 24/7. To reach an optimum operating level that results in efficiencies that produce a margin of profit, managers, supervisors and workers must operate as a team, focusing on quality standards that are demanding of the equipment and the entire workforce. Similar bag operations in other company locations have shown that to achieve optimum production levels, quality standards must be clearly defined and effectively communicated. It has also been learned by industry that many factors are to blame for poor quality, including company politics, shortsighted thinking and poor management. However, at Better Bags, Inc., product quality at six of the company's plants was improved substantially and measurably just through improved communication.

Communication: The plant operates three shifts: 1) 7 a.m. to 3 p.m.; 2) 3 p.m. to 11 p.m.; and 3) 11 p.m. to 7 a.m. On each shift employees are given a 20-minute lunch break. Supervisors conduct safety meetings every day at the beginning of each shift. Supervisors also conduct communication meetings once each month. The plant manager talks to employees quarterly by shift. The most effective ways to communicate with employees are 1) through supervisors; 2) by weekly newsletter; 3) by monthly video tape; and 4) by closed circuit TV. Employees function in work groups and, for special efforts, in teams. Team members can select a team leader. The team effort is coached by the shift supervisor.

Plant Manager

Is quality one of the plant's main priorities?

Plant Manager: "Yes"

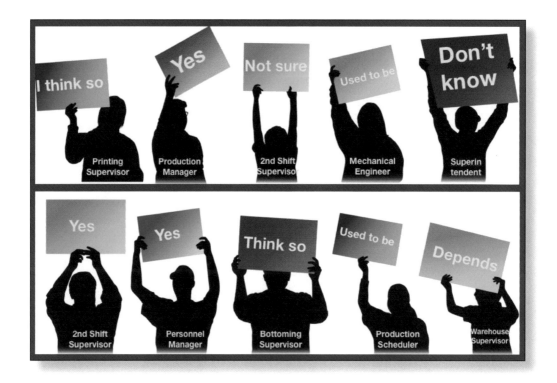

How would you characterize the overall response to personal interview question #1 and to the overall staff member responses to the plant manager's response? What conclusions could you draw from your analyses?

Plant Manager

What seems to be management's main focus?

Plant Manager: "People"

How would you characterize the overall response to personal interview question #2 and to the overall staff member responses to the plant manager's response? What conclusions could you draw from your analyses?

Plant Manager

Describe the plant's quality standards.

Plant Manager: "Customers specify."

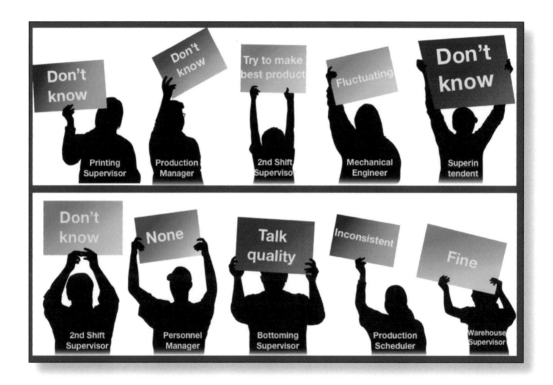

How would you characterize the overall response to personal interview question #3 and to the overall staff member responses to the plant manager's response? What conclusions could you draw from your analyses?

PERSONAL INTERVIEW QUESTION #4

Plant Manager

Who sets the quality standards?

Plant Manager: "All"

How would you characterize the overall response to personal interview question #4 and to the overall staff member responses to the plant manager's response? What conclusions could you draw from your analyses?

Plant Manager

How well are the

quality standards met?

Plant Manager: "Good."

How would you characterize the overall response to personal interview question #5 and to the overall staff member responses to the plant manager's response? What conclusions could you draw from your analyses?

Plant Manager

What's the greatest need for improvement in this plant?

Plant Manager: "Money."

How would you characterize the overall response to personal interview question #6 and to the overall staff member responses to the plant manager's response? What conclusions could you draw from your analyses? What conclusions could you draw from looking at the responses of individuals and their areas of responsibility?

ARTICLE: DOES YOUR COMPANY HAVE THE 'WRITE' STUFF?

Now why would an executive manager want to give an organization a writing test?

To increase profitability. That's a good reason. Just when you're beginning to think that "re-engineering" was the last great hope to increase profitability, someone comes along with the simple suggestion that improved writing skills can improve an organization's bottom line.

So, how can something as basic as good writing impact financial performance? I'll illustrate the point six ways. Once you begin to think about it, you will discover more ways that are specific to your business.

1) **Customer Service.**   Why are your customer service costs as high as they are? Don't ask your customer service department; its goal is not to reduce or eliminate itself. Make your own assessment. Is the volume of customer calls high because product instruction sheets are unclear; because product manuals fail to adequately explain product features; because special offers, discounts, or ordering procedures are confusing? The goal should not be to improve customer service, but rather to reduce the need for it with more clearly written materials.

2) **Web Presence.**   Why hasn't your Web site reduced expenses as you originally expected? You set up a station somewhere in cyberspace thinking that it was going to save you money. Instead you find that customers are like shooting stars. They can appear at your cyberspace station as quickly as they can disappear from it. Why? If they can't find what they're looking for quickly, they can go instantly to competing sites to find what they want. The aim should be to have your Web site messages written so well that customers can easily find and navigate to exactly what they want.

3) **Competitive Information.**   Why aren't your employees sharing information that could benefit the company? Information that employees acquire in doing their jobs can be extremely valuable to your business. In fact, most of the competitive information you might like to have is probably right under your own roof. The goal should be to show employees writing practices and forms that encourage interpersonal communication and greater sharing of information throughout the organization.

4) **Stock Value.**   Why aren't investors recognizing the full value of your company? Your company's most valuable assets are its core competencies. If you ask industry analysts, investors and potential investors to name your company's

core competencies, could they do it? The aim should be to ensure that written materials communicate strategically with financial audiences.

5) **Competitive Bids.** Why haven't you been winning a greater number of business bids? When no one asks a single question after your company's sales presentations, is it because the presentations are so thorough as to answer every conceivable question? Or is it because they didn't stimulate any interest? The aim should be to have presentations and proposals written that are highly persuasive and compelling enough to win new business.

6) **Quality Control.** Why are your error rates higher than they should be? If you asked each of your employees to describe what is meant by "quality" in your particular operation, would you hear one concise definition, consistently, throughout the organization? Or would each person have a different idea of what is meant by quality in your organization? The aim should be to have standards clearly written and understood by the entire organization.

I have raised questions about profitability in six areas of business. You won't find answers to my questions in financial statistics, such as return on investment, net earnings and total debt to invested capital. You don't need to hire an MBA from Harvard to find the answers. You just need to give your company a "writing test." Make a simple assessment in each area covered above, asking yourself or your customers, securities analysts, investors and other important audiences, "How well is it written?"

Assess your company's writing skills and how effectively they are applied, then take steps to raise the bar to its highest level of proficiency. You are likely to find more than one significant opportunity to improve profitability through good writing.

GOLD STANDARD PAPER
Commission on Public Relations Measurement & Evaluation

GUIDELINES FOR MEASURING THE EFFECTIVENESS
OF PR PROGRAMS AND ACTIVITIES

by Dr. Walter K. Lindenmann
Published by the Institute for Public Relations
Copyright © 1997, 2003 Institute for Public Relations
www.instituteforpr.org

Contents

FOREWORD

For years we have been told that we can never expect to get proper credit for what we do in public relations until we can find an effective way to measure our effectiveness.

Most other professions have recognized measuring tools—engineering devices, chemical reactions, case law, charts and figures. But public relations efforts have always been gauged in a variety of ways—each using a different kind of measuring stick.

In an attempt to begin to find a uniform "ruler" we can all use for measurement, a Public Relations Evaluation Summit was called in October, 1996 in New York City. This gathering of top leaders interested in public relations research was sponsored by the Institute for Public Relations, INSIDE PR, and the Ketchum Public Relations Research and Measurement Department.

As a result of that Summit, a booklet was published and distributed in 1997 under the title, "Guidelines and Standards for Measuring and Evaluating PR Effectiveness" as a first attempt to establish guidelines for how we might begin to agree on uniform ways to measure public relations by using the same measuring sticks. In the light of new developments relating to PR measurement overall, this booklet was revised in 2002 and given a new title, "Guidelines for Measuring the Effectiveness of PR Programs and Activities," to more accurately reflect its contents. We view the revised version of this book as a companion to "Guidelines for Measuring Relationships in Public Relations," and "Guidelines for Setting Measurable Objectives," both of which were published in 1999.

We believe you can use the ideas and suggestions in this booklet as a working document of ways we can continue a dialogue on measuring the effectiveness of public relations.

Jack Felton President & CEO

OVERVIEW

What is public relations measurement and evaluation?

Basically, it is any and all research designed to determine the relative effectiveness or value of what is done in public relations. In the short-term, PR measurement and evaluation involves assessing the success or failure of specific PR programs, strategies, activities or tactics by measuring the outputs, outtakes and/or outcomes of those programs against a predetermined set of objectives. In the long-term, PR measurement and evaluation involves assessing the success or failure of much broader PR efforts that have as their aim seeking to improve and enhance the relationships that organizations maintain with key constituents

More specifically, PR measurement is a way of giving a result a precise dimension, generally by comparison to some standard or baseline and usually is done in a quantifiable or numerical manner. That is, when we measure outputs, outtakes and outcomes, we usually come up with a precise measure—a number; for example, 1,000 brochures distributed … 60,000 hits on a web site … 50% message recall … an 80% increase in awareness levels, etc.

PR evaluation determines the value or importance of a PR program or effort, usually through appraisal or comparison with a predetermined set of organization goals and objectives. PR evaluation is somewhat more subjective in nature, or softer, than PR measurement, involving a greater amount of interpretation and judgment calls.

Interest in public relations measurement and evaluation has surged in recent years, as the public relations field has grown in size and sophistication, and as those who practice in the field have found themselves more often than ever being asked to be accountable for what they do.

Those who supervise or manage an organization's total communications activities are increasingly asking themselves, their staff members, their agencies and consulting firms, and their research suppliers questions such as these:

- Will those public relations and/or advertising efforts that we initiate actually have an effect—that is, "move the needle" in the right direction—and, if so, how can we support and document that from a research perspective?
- Will the communications activities we implement actually change what people know, what they think and feel, and how they actually act?
- What impact—if any—will various public relations, marketing communications, and advertising activities have in changing consumer and opinion-leader awareness, understanding, retention, attitude and behavior levels?

As questions such as these have increased in number in recent years, many public relations practitioners—as they seek to justify what they, themselves, do—have sensed a need to establish guidelines or criteria that the industry can follow, when it comes specifically to public relations measurement and evaluation.

This guidebook, which has been revised and edited under the auspices of the Institute for Public Relations Commission on PR Measurement and Evaluation, seeks to set minimum standards when it comes to measuring and evaluating the effectiveness of specific short-term PR programs, strategies, activities and tactics against pre-determined outputs, outtakes and outcomes. Those interested in measuring and evaluating the effectiveness of PR efforts aimed at enhancing the long-term relationships that exist between an organization and its key constituents should consult the companion guidebook, "Guidelines for Measuring Relationships in Public Relations." (www.instituteforpr.com)

SOME GUIDING PRINCIPLES

In focusing on PR measurement and evaluation, here are some guiding principles or key factors to consider at the outset. These guiding principles are discussed in more detail in the main sections of this booklet.

Establish clear program, activity, strategic and tactical objectives and desired outputs, outtakes and outcomes before you begin, to provide a basis for measurement of results. PR goals should tie directly to the overall goals of the organization.

Differentiate between measuring PR outputs, which are usually short-term and surface (e.g. the amount of press coverage received or exposure of a particular message), PR outtakes, which are usually more far-reaching and can have more impact (e.g. determining if those to whom the activity was directed received, paid attention to, comprehended and retained particular messages) and PR outcomes, (e.g. did the program or activity change opinion and attitude levels, and possibly behavior patterns?).

Measuring media content, while of great value, needs to be viewed as only a first step in the PR measurement and evaluation process. It can measure possible exposure to PR messages and actual press coverage; however, it cannot, by itself, measure whether target audiences actually saw the messages and responded to them in any way.

There is no one, simple, all-encompassing research tool, technique or methodology that can be relied on to measure and evaluate PR effectiveness. Usually, a combination of different measurement techniques is needed. Consideration should be given to any one or several of the following: media content analysis … cyberspace analysis … trade show and event measurement … polls and surveys … focus groups … experimental and quasi-experimental designs … and/or ethnographic studies that rely on observation, participation and/or role playing techniques.

Be wary of attempts to precisely compare PR effectiveness to advertising effectiveness. The two forms of communication are quite different from each other and the fact that placement of advertising messages can be controlled, whereas placement of PR messages usually cannot be controlled, needs to be taken into consideration.

PR effectiveness can best be measured if an organization's principal messages, key target audience groups, and desired channels of communication are clearly identified and understood in advance.

The PR measurement and evaluation process should never be carried out in isolation, by focusing only on the PR components. Wherever and whenever possible, it is always important to link what is planned, and accomplished, through PR, to the overall goals, objectives, strategies and tactics of the organization as a whole.

MAJOR PR MEASUREMENT AND EVALUATION COMPONENTS

For any PR evaluation research to be credible, five major components of the process need to be taken into consideration. They are:

1. Setting Specific Measurable PR Goals and Objectives

This has to come first. No one can really measure the effectiveness of anything, unless they first figure out exactly what it is they are measuring that something against. So, to begin, the public relations practitioner, counselor and/or research supplier ought to ask: What are or were the goals or objectives of the specific public relations program, activity, strategy or tactic? What exactly did the program or the activities hope to accomplish—through its public relations component?

This is not always easy to do, since it is often difficult to separate public relations programs and activities (such as publicity efforts, distribution of informational materials, the holding of special events or shows, etc.) from marketing communications (point-of-purchase promotional activities, coupon redemption programs, special contests and give-away activities, etc.) and from advertising (paid print and broadcast messages, cyberspace commercials, etc.)

In setting PR goals and objectives, it is usually important to recognize that measuring PR effectiveness per se—that is, the management of an organization's overall communications activities with its target audience groups or publics—can be quite difficult to do unless the individual elements or components of the program are clearly defined. We suggest that instead of trying to measure PR as a total entity, steps be taken to measure the effectiveness of individual or particular PR activities, such as measuring the effectiveness of specific publicity efforts, or a particular community relations program, or a special event or trade show activity, or a government affairs or lobbying effort, or a speaker's program, or an investor relations activity, and so on.

Additional ideas and suggestions pertaining to the setting of measurable PR goals and objectives can be obtained in the IPR Commission on PR Measurement and Evaluation guidebook, "Guidelines for Setting Measurable Public Relations Objectives." (www.instituteforpr.com)

2. Measuring PR Outputs

Outputs are usually the immediate results of a particular PR program or activity. More often than not, outputs represent what is readily apparent to the eye. Outputs measure how well an organization presents itself to others, the amount of exposure that the organization receives.

In media or press relations efforts, outputs can be the total number of stories, articles, or "placements" that appear in the media ... the total number of "impressions"—that is, the number of those who might have had the opportunity to be exposed to the story ... as well as an assessment of the overall content of what has appeared. Media Content Analysis (see page 83) is one of the principal methodologies used to measure media outputs.

For other facets of public relations, outputs can be white papers, speaking engagements, the number of times a spokesperson is quoted, specific messages communicated, or specific positioning on an important issue or any number of quantifiable items that are generated as a result of the effort.

Outputs also might be assessment of a specific event, a direct mail campaign, the number of people who participated in a given activity, how a CEO handles himself or herself at a press conference, or the appearance and contents of a given brochure or booklet.

In any event, both the quantity and quality of outputs can be measured and evaluated. Media can be evaluated for their content; an event, as to whether the right people were there; a booklet or brochure for its visual appeal and substance; and so on.

3. Measuring PR Outtakes

Although it is obviously important to measure how well an organization presents itself to others and the amount of exposure obtained, it is even more important to measure PR outtakes—that is, determining if key target audience groups actually received the messages directed at them, paid attention to them, understood and/or comprehended the messages, and whether they retained the messages and can recall them in any shape or form.

When a PR program is launched or when given PR activities or events are initiated—such as the distribution of a brochure or a booklet, the placement of announcements on web sites, or the delivering of a speech—it is important to assess what, if anything, did the intended recipients "take-away" from this effort.

The first unit of outtake measurement could very well be that of favorability. Was the PR program or effort favorably received? Were the creative design elements or "packaging" received favorably? Was the "language" received favorably? Was the "ease of use" of the PR effort favorably received?

The second unit of outtake measurement relates to understanding and comprehension. Did the messages that were being disseminated make sense to the intended recipients? Were those to whom the messages were targeted able to decipher them and put them into appropriate context?

The third unit of measurement at the outtake level is message recall and retention. It measures whether the messages we craft for inclusion in our brochures, booklets and related PR programs and activities make enough of an impression on the intended recipients, that they become memorable. Can the intended recipients recall the embedded messages and can they retain them for any length of time?

The final unit of measurement at the outtake level is that of attention and possible immediate response. Did the receiver respond positively to the receipt of the messages? Did he or she do something with the information now in hand, for example, by passing on materials or messages to friends or colleagues? Did the recipient request more information, for example, by going to a web site?

It is possible to compare the outtake measures of one particular PR program or activity to one or more others.

4. Measuring PR Outcomes

As important as it might be to measure PR outputs and outtakes, it is far more important to measure PR outcomes.

These measure whether the communications materials and messages which were disseminated have resulted in any opinion, attitude and/or behavior changes on the part of those targeted audiences to whom the messages were directed.

It is usually much more difficult and, generally, more expensive, to measure PR outcomes, and to some extent PR outtakes, than it is to measure PR outputs. This is because more sophisticated data-gathering research tools and techniques are required. Measuring PR outputs is usually a question of counting, tracking and observing, while for PR outtakes and PR outcomes, it is a matter of asking and carrying out extensive review and analysis of what was said and what was done.

Research techniques often used to measure PR outtakes and PR outcomes include quantitative surveys (in-person, by telephone, by mail, via fax, via e-mail, via the Internet, in malls, etc.) ... focus groups ... qualitative depth attitude surveys of elite audience groups ... pre-test/post-test studies (e.g. before-and-after polls) ... ethnographic studies (relying on observation, participation, and/or role-playing techniques) ... experimental and quasi-experimental research projects ... and multi-variate studies that rely on advanced statistical applications such as correlation and regression analyses, Q-sorts, and factor and cluster analysis studies.

5. Measuring Business and/or Organizational Outcomes

Whatever steps PR practitioners take to measure the effectiveness of what they, themselves, do in PR, it is imperative that they also take steps to seek to link their public relations accomplishments to the ultimate goals, objectives, and accomplishments of the organization as a whole.

What we are talking about here is seeking to relate PR outcomes to such desired business and/or organizational outcomes as increasing market penetration, market share, sales, and, ultimately, increasing an organization's profitability. It needs to be recognized that this is not easy to do. It requires a careful delineation of what the PR program seeks to accomplish in concert with what the organization as a whole seeks to accomplish. It also requires a good understanding about how and why the two processes are supposed to work together. When one has a good understanding of the impacts that are desired, as well as a good understanding of how the process is supposed to work, there are then many research design tools that can be employed to reliably and validly measure that impact.

For example, the subject of tying PR to sales is frequently discussed. Some trade publications offer response cards after specific articles have appeared in print. These offer very valuable "lead-generation" tools. With an effective "lead generation" system, those leads can frequently be tracked through to sales. However, it must be remembered that while PR may have generated the lead, the closure was, of course, heavily influenced by such items as the individual's need for or interest in that product in the first place, the quality of the products and services that are offered, the distribution channel, the availability of the product or service, the price, etc. All of these items, or variables, need to be taken into consideration when seeking to measure the effectiveness of what occurred.

Most organizations, be they business for profit, public sector governmental or non-profit groups and associations, nowadays take the position that PR objectives really do not have value, unless they further the goals of the total organization, or of its business units or sectors. It is most important, therefore, to integrate an organization's PR programs and goals with the strategies and objectives of the organization as a whole. Further, this requires that the practitioner understand what is critical to the organization overall and to its specific business strategies and plans.

Our communication objectives must be tied to business unit or central function operational objectives. These operational objectives are, or should be, behavioral. They should state who will change (customers, employees, suppliers, stakeholders, investors, management, etc.) in what way, by how much and when. In a results-based organization, the only result that matters is a change in behavior (market segment x bought more widgets; employee segment y became more productive; stakeholder segment z supported our environmental policy, etc.)

In a results-based organization, the business unit objective of behavioral change is stated as a Key Result. An achieved communication effectiveness outcome is one indicator of performance towards that result. Our communication program planning objective becomes a Performance Indicator statement in the business line document. We restate the same outcome as a measurable objective in our communication plan. Our objectives are then tied directly to business or organizational objectives.

GETTING SPECIFIC: STANDARDS FOR MEASURING PR OUTPUTS

There are many possible tools and techniques that PR practitioners can utilize to begin to measure PR outputs, but these are the four that are most frequently relied on to measure PR impact at the output level: Media Content Analysis … Cyberspace Analysis … Trade Show and Event Measurement … and Public Opinion Polls.

1. Media Content Analysis

This is the process of studying and tracking what has been written and broadcast, translating this qualitative material into quantitative form through some type of counting approach that involves coding and classifying of specific messages.

Some researchers and PR practitioners in the U.S. refer to this as "Media Measurement" and/or "Publicity Tracking" research. In the United Kingdom, the technique is often referred to as "Media Evaluation;" and in Germany as "Media Resonance." Whatever the terminology used to describe this particular technique, more often than not its prime function is to determine whether the key messages, concepts and themes that an organization might be interested in disseminating to others via the media do, indeed, receive some measure of exposure as a result of a particular public relations effort or activity.

The coding, classifying and analysis that is done can be relatively limited or far-reaching, depending on the needs and interests of the organization commissioning the research. More often than not, Media Content Analysis studies take into consideration variables such as these:

- Media Vehicle Variables, such as date of publication or broadcast … frequency of publication or broadcast of the media vehicle … media vehicle or type (that is, whether the item appeared in a newspaper, magazine, a newsletter, on radio, or on television) … and geographic reach (that is, region, state, city, or ADI markets in which the item appeared).

- Placement or News Item Variables, such as source of the story (that is, a press release, a press conference, a special event, or whether the media initiated the item on their own) … story form or type (a news story, feature article, editorial, column, or letter to the editor) … degree of exposure (that is, column inches or number of paragraphs if the item appeared in print, number of seconds or minutes of air time if the item was broadcast) … and the story's author (that is, the byline or name of the broadcaster.)

- Audience or 'Reach' Variables. The focus here usually is on total number of placements, media impressions and/or circulation or potential overall audience reached—that is, total readers of a newspaper or magazine, total viewers and listeners to a radio or television broadcast. The term "impression" or "opportunity to see" usually refers to the total audited circulation of a publication. For example, if The Wall Street Journal has an audited circulation of 1.5 million, one article in that newspaper might be said to generate 1.5 million impressions or opportunities to see the story. Two articles would generate 3 million impressions, and so on. Often more important than impressions is the issue of whether a story reached an organization's target audience group, by specific demographic segments. These data often can be obtained from the U.S. Census Bureau or from various commercial organizations, such as Standard Rate and Data Services. In addition to considering a publication's actual circulation figures, researchers often also take into consideration how many other individuals might possibly be exposed to a given media vehicle, because that publication has been routed or passed on to others.

- Subject or Topic Variables, such as who was mentioned and in what context … how prominently were key organizations and/or their competitors referred to or featured in the press coverage (that is, were companies cited in the headline, in the body copy only, in both, etc.) … who was quoted and how frequently … how much coverage, or "share of voice" did an organization receive in comparison to its competitors … what issues and messages were covered and to what extent … how were different individuals and groups positioned—as leaders, as followers, or another way?

- Judgment or Subjective Variables. The focus here usually is on the stance or tone of the item, as that item pertains to a given organization and/or its competitors. Usually tone implies some assessment as to whether or not the item is positive, negative or neutral; favorable, unfavorable or balanced. It is extremely important to recognize that measuring stance or tone is usually a highly subjective measure, open to a possibly different interpretation by others. Clearly-defined criteria or ground rules for assessing positives and negatives—and from whose perspective—need to be established beforehand, in order for stance or tone measures to have any credibility as part of Media Content Analysis.

"Advertising Equivalency" is often an issue that is raised in connection with Media Content Analysis studies. Basically, advertising equivalency is a means of converting editorial space into advertising costs, by measuring the amount of editorial coverage and then calculating what it would have cost to buy that space, if it had been advertising.

Most reputable researchers contend that "advertising equivalency" computations are of questionable validity. In many cases, it may not even be possible to assign an advertising equivalency score to a given amount of editorial coverage (for example, many newspapers and/or magazines do not sell advertising space on their front pages or their front covers; thus, if an article were to appear in that space, it would be impossible to calculate an appropriate advertising equivalency cost, since advertising could never ever appear there).

Some organizations artificially multiply the estimated value of a "possible" editorial placement in comparison to advertising by a factor of 2, 3, 5, 8 or whatever other inflated number they might wish to come up with, to take into account their own perception that editorial space is always of more value than is advertising space. Most reputable researchers view such arbitrary "weighting" schemes aimed at enhancing the alleged value of editorial coverage as unethical, dishonest, and not at all supported by the research literature. Although some studies have, at times, shown that editorial coverage is sometimes more credible or believable than is advertising coverage, other studies have shown the direct opposite, and there is, as yet, no clearly established consensus in the communications field regarding which is truly more effective: publicity or advertising. In reality, it depends on an endless number of factors.

Sometimes, when doing Media Content Analysis, organizations may apply weights to given messages that are being disseminated, simply because they regard some of their messages as more important than others, or give greater credence (or weight) to an article that not only appears in the form of text, but also is accompanied by a photo or a graphic treatment. Given that the future is visuals, organizations are more and more beginning to measure not only words, but also pictures.

It should be noted that whatever ground rules, criteria and variables are built into a Media Content Analysis, whatever "counting" approaches are utilized to turn qualitative information into quantitative form, it is important that all of the elements and components involved be clearly defined and explained up front by whoever is doing the study. The particular system of media analysis that is applied and utilized by one researcher should—if a second researcher were called in and given the same brief and the same basic criteria pertaining to the aims of the study—result in broadly similar research findings and conclusions.

2. Cyberspace Analysis

Increasingly, a key measure of an organization's image or reputation and of how that organization might be positioned is the chatter and discussion about that organization in cyberspace—specifically in chat rooms, forums and new groups on the World Wide Web. The same criteria used in analyzing print and broadcast articles can be applied when analyzing postings on the Internet.

What appears in print is frequently commented about and editorialized about on the Web. Therefore, one component of PR output measurement ought to be a review and analysis of Web postings.

In addition, a second output measure of cyberspace might be a review and analysis of Web site traffic patterns. For example, some of the variables that ought to be considered when designing and carrying out Cyberspace Analysis might include deconstructing "hits" (that is, examining the requests for a file of visitors to the Internet) … a review of click-throughs and/or flash-click streams … an assessment of home page visits … domain tracking and analysis … an assessment of bytes transferred … a review of time spent per page … traffic times … browsers used … and the number of people filling out and returning feed-back forms.

Best practices for this type of research are covered in "Measures of Success in Cyberspace," a paper authored by Katharine Delahaye Paine that is available from the IPR Commission on PR Measurement and Evaluation, www.instituteforpr.com; "Getting Started On Interactive Media Measurement," available from the Advertising Research Foundation, 641 Lexington Avenue, New York, NY 10022, and "Hits Are Not Enough: How to Really Measure Web Site Success," prepared by Interactive Marketing News and available from Phillips Business Information, Inc., 1201 Seven Locks Road, Potomac, MD 20854.

3. Trade Shows and Event Measurement

Frequently, the intent of a public relations program or activity is simply to achieve exposure for an organization, its products or services, through staging trade shows, holding special events and meetings, involvement in speakers' programs and the like.

For shows and events, obviously one possible output measure is an assessment of total attendance, not just an actual count of those who showed up, but also an assessment of the types of individuals present, the number of interviews that were generated and conducted in connection with the event, and the number of promotional materials that were distributed. In addition, if the show is used as an opportunity for editorial visits, one can measure the effectiveness of those visits by conducting a content analysis of the resulting articles.

4. Public Opinion Polls

Although most surveys that are designed and carried out are commissioned to measure PR outtakes and PR outcomes rather than PR outputs, public opinion polls are often carried out in an effort to determine whether or not key target audience groups have, indeed, been exposed to particular messages, themes or concepts and to assess the overall effectiveness of a given presentation or promotional effort. For example, conducting a brief survey immediately following a speech or the holding of a special event to assess the short-term impact of that particular activity would constitute a form of PR output measurement.

GETTING SPECIFIC: STANDARDS FOR MEASURING PR OUTTAKES

Just as there are many tools and techniques that PR practitioners can utilize to begin to measure PR outputs, there also are many that can be used to measure PR outtakes. Some of those most frequently relied on include surveys (of all types) … focus groups … before-and-after polls … and ethnographic studies (relying on observation, participation, and/or role playing techniques).

There are many books available that discuss and describe both qualitative and quantitative research techniques. Here are three that specifically discuss such techniques from a public relations perspective: "Using Research In Public Relations," by Glen M. Broom and David M. Dozier (Englewood Cliffs, NJ: Prentice Hall, 1990) … Primer of Public Relations Research," by Don W. Stacks (New York: The Guilford Press, 2002) … and "Public Relations Research For Planning and Evaluation," by Walter K. Lindenmann (available from the IPR Commission on PR Measurement and Evaluation, www.instituteforpr.com.)

Ultimately, one intent of public relations is to inform and persuade key target audience groups regarding topics and issues that are of importance to a given organization, with the hope that this will lead those publics to act in a certain way. Usually, this involves two different types of outtake measures: Awareness and Comprehension Measurements and Recall and Retention Measurements.

1. Awareness and Comprehension Measurements

The usual starting point for any PR outtake measurement is to determine whether target audience groups actually received the messages directed at them ... paid attention to them ... and understood the messages.

Obviously, if one is introducing a new product or concept to the marketplace for the first time—one that has never been seen or discussed before—it is reasonable to assume that prior to public relations and/or related communications activities being launched, that familiarity and awareness levels would be at zero. However, many organizations have established some type of "presence" in the marketplace, and thus it is important to obtain benchmark data against which to measure any possible changes in awareness and/or comprehension levels.

Measuring awareness and comprehension levels requires some type of primary research with representatives of key target audience groups.

It is important to keep in mind that Qualitative Research (e.g. focus groups, one-on-one depth interviews, convenience polling) is usually open-ended, free response and unstructured in format ... generally relies on non-random samples ... and is rarely "projectable" to larger audiences. Quantitative Research (e.g. telephone, mail, mall, internet, fax, and e-mail polls), on the other hand, although it may contain some open-ended questions, is far more apt to involve the use of closed-ended, forced choice questions that are highly structured in format ... generally relies on random samples ... and usually is "projectable" to larger audiences.

To determine whether there have been any changes at all in audience awareness and comprehension levels, usually requires some type of comparative studies—that is, either a before and after survey to measure possible change from one period of time to another, or some type of "test" and "control" group study, in which one segment of a target audience group is deliberately exposed to a given message or concept and a second segment is not, with research conducted with both groups to determine if one segment is now better informed regarding the issues than the other.

2. Recall and Retention Measurements

Traditionally, advertising practitioners have paid much more attention to recall and retention measurement, than have those in the public relations field.

It is quite common in advertising, after a series of ads have appeared either in the print or the broadcast media, for research to be fielded to determine whether or not those individuals to whom the ad messages have been targeted actually recall those messages on both an unaided and aided basis. Similarly, several weeks after the ads have run, follow-up studies are often fielded to determine if those in the target audience group have retained any of the key themes, concepts, and messages that were contained in the original advertising copy.

Although recall and retention studies have not been done that frequently by public relations practitioners, they clearly are an important form of outcome measurement, that ought to be seriously considered by PR professionals. Various data collection techniques can be used when conducting such studies, including telephone, face-to-face, mail, mall, e-mail, and fax polling.

When conducting such studies, it is extremely important that those individuals fielding the project clearly differentiate between messages that are disseminated via PR techniques (e.g. through stories in the media, by word of mouth, at a special event, through a speech, etc.) from those that are disseminated via paid advertising or through marketing promotional efforts. For example, it is never enough to simply report that someone claims they read, heard or saw a particular item; it is more important to determine whether that individual can determine if the item in question happened to be a news story that appeared in editorial form, or was a paid message that someone placed through advertising. Very often, it is difficult for the "average" consumer to differentiate between the two.

GETTING SPECIFIC: STANDARDS FOR MEASURING PR OUTCOMES

Some of the same tools and techniques that PR practitioners can utilize to begin to measure PR Outtakes—surveys, focus groups, before-and-after polls and ethnographic studies—also can be used to measure PR Outcomes. In addition, researchers designing and carrying out projects aimed at measuring changes in people's opinions, attitudes and behavior patterns also often rely on experimental and quasi-experimental designs, on multi-variate analysis projects, and on model building.

In addition to those works previously cited, two useful resources for qualitative and quantitative research techniques that can be used at the PR Outcome level are the Advertising Research Foundation's two documents: "Guidelines for the Public Use of Market and Opinion Research" and the ARF Guidelines Handbook: A Compendium of Guidelines to Good Advertising, Marketing and Media Research Practice. Both are available from the Advertising Research Foundation, 641 Lexington Avenue, New York, NY 10022.

Two different types of research are usually called for, when conducting public relations measurement and evaluation research at the outcome level: Attitude and Preference Measurements and Behavior Measurements.

1. Attitude and Preference Measurements

When it comes to seeking to measure the overall impact or effectiveness of a particular public relations program or activity, assessing individuals' opinions, attitudes, and preferences become extremely important measures of possible outcomes. It needs to be kept in mind that "opinion research" generally measures what people say about something; that is, their verbal expressions or spoken or written points of view. "Attitude research," on the other hand, is far deeper and more complex. Usually, "attitude research" measures not only what people say about something, but also what they know and think (their mental or cognitive predispositions), what they feel (their emotions), and how they're inclined to act (their motivational or drive tendencies).

"Opinion research" is easier to do because one can usually obtain the information desired in a very direct fashion just by asking a few questions. "Attitude research," however, is far harder and, often more expensive to carry out, because the information desired often has to be collected in an indirect fashion. For example, one can easily measure people's stated positions on racial and/or ethnic prejudice, by simply asking one or several direct questions. However, actually determining whether someone is in actual fact racially and/or ethnically prejudiced, usually would necessitate asking a series of indirect questions aimed at obtaining a better understanding of people's cognitions, feelings, and motivational or drive tendencies regarding that topic or issue.

Preference implies that an individual is or will be making a choice, which means that preference measurement more often than not ought to include some alternatives, either competitive or perceived competitive products or organizations. To determine the impact of public relations preference outcomes usually necessitates some type of audience exposure to specific public relations outputs (such as an article, a white paper, a speech, or participation in an activity or event), with research then carried out to determine the overall likelihood of people preferring one product, service, or organization to another.

Usually, opinion, attitude and preference measurement projects involve interviews not only with those in the public at large, but also with special target audience groups, such as those in the media, business leaders, academicians, security analysts and portfolio managers, those in the health, medical and scientific community, government officials, and representatives of civic, cultural and service organizations. Opinion, attitude and preference measurement research can be carried out many different ways, through focus groups, through qualitative and quantitative surveys, and even through panels.

2. Behavior Measurements

The ultimate test of effectiveness—the highest outcome measure possible—is whether the behavior of the target audience has changed, at least to some degree, as a result of the public relations program or activity.

For most media relations programs, if you have changed the behavior of the editor and/or reporter so that what he or she writes primarily reflects an organization's key messages, then that organization has achieved a measure of behavior change.

However, measuring behavior is hard because it is often difficult to prove cause-and-effect relationships. The more specific the desired outcome and the more focused the PR program or activity that relates to that hoped-for end result, the easier it is to measure PR behavior change. For example, if the intent of a public relations program or activity is to raise more funds for a non-profit institution and if one can show after the campaign has been concluded that there has, indeed, been increased funding, then one can begin to surmise that the PR activity had a role to play in the behavior change. Or, to give another example: For measuring the effectiveness of a public affairs or government relations program targeted at legislators or regulators, the desired outcome—more often than not—would not only be to get legislators or regulators to change their views, but more importantly to have those legislators and regulators either pass or implement a new set of laws or regulations that reflect the aims of the campaign. Behavior change requires some one to act differently than they have in the past.

More often that not, measuring behavior change requires a broad array of data collection tools and techniques, among them before-and-after surveys … research utilizing ethnographic techniques (e.g. observation, participation, and role playing) … the utilization of experimental and quasi-experimental research designs … and studies that rely on multi-variate analyses and sophisticated statistical applications and processes.

What is crucial to bear in mind in connection with PR outcome behavior measurement studies is that measuring correlations—that is, the associations or relationships that might exist between two variables—is relatively easy. Measuring causation—that is, seeking to prove that X was the reason that Y happened—is extremely difficult. Often, there are too many intervening variables that need to be taken into consideration.

Those doing PR outcome behavior measurement studies need to keep in mind these three requirements that need to exist in order to support or document that some activity or event caused something to happen: 1) Cause must always precede the effect in time; 2) there needs to be a relationship between the two variables under study; and 3) the observed relationship between the two variables cannot be explained away as being due to the influence of some third variable that possibly caused both of them.

The key to effective behavior measurement is a sound, well thought-out, reliable and valid research concept and design. Researchers doing such studies need to make sure that study or test conditions or responses are relevant to the situation to which the findings are supposed to relate, and also clearly demonstrate that the analysis and conclusions that are reached are indeed supported and documented by the field work and data collection that was carried out.

QUESTIONS THAT NEED TO BE PUT TO THOSE ORGANIZATIONS THAT COMMISSION PR MEASUREMENT AND EVALUATION STUDIES

Here are some of the key questions that those who commission PR measurement evaluation studies ought to ask themselves before they begin, and also the types of questions that those who actually carry out the assignment ought to ask their clients to answer before the project is launched:

1. What are, or were, the specific goals and/or objectives of the public relations, public affairs, and/or marketing communications program, and can these be at all stated in a quantitative or measurable fashion? (e.g. To double the number of inquiries received from one year to the next? To increase media coverage by achieving greater "share of voice" in one year than in a previous year? To have certain legislation passed? ... To enhance or improve brand, product, or corporate image or reputation?)

2. Who are, or were, the principal individuals serving as spokespersons for the organization during the communications effort?

3. What are, or were, the principal themes, concepts, and messages that the organization was interested in disseminating?

4. Who were the principal target audience groups to whom these messages were directed?

5. Which channels of communication were used and/or deemed most important to use in disseminating the messages? (e.g. the media ... word-of-mouth ... direct mail ... special events?)

6. What specific public relations strategies and tactics were used to carry out the program? What were the specific components or elements of the campaign?

7. What is, or was, the time line for the overall public relations program or project?

8. What is, or were, the desired or hoped-for outputs, outtakes, and/or outcomes of the public relations effort? If those particular hoped-for outputs, outtakes and/or outcomes could, for some reason, not be met, what alternative outputs, outtakes, and/or outcomes would the organization be willing to accept?

9. How does what is or has happened in connection with the organization's public relations effort relate to what is or has happened in connection with related activities or programs in other areas of the company, such as advertising, marketing, and internal communications?

10. Who are the organization's principal competitors? Who are their spokespersons? What are their key themes, concepts, and messages that they are seeking to disseminate? Who are their key target audience groups? What channels of communications are they most frequently utilizing?

11. Which media vehicles are, or were, most important to reach for the particular public relations and/or marketing communications activities that were undertaken?

12. What were the specific public relations materials and resources utilized as part of the effort? Would it be possible to obtain and review copies of any relevant press releases, brochures, speeches, promotional materials that were produced and distributed as part of the program?

13. What information is already available to the organization that can be utilized by those carrying out the evaluative research assignment to avoid reinventing the wheel and to build on what is already known?

14. If part of the project involves an assessment of media coverage, who will be responsible for collecting the clips or copies of broadcast materials that will have been generated? What are the ground rules and/or parameters for clip and/or broadcast material assessment?

15. What major issues or topics pertaining to the public relations undertaking are, or have been, of greatest importance to the organization commissioning the evaluation research project?

16. What is the time line for the PR Measurement and Evaluation Research effort? What are the budgetary parameters and/or limitations for the assignment? Do priorities have to be set?

17. Who will be the ultimate recipients of the research findings?

18. How will whatever information that is collected be used by the organization that is commissioning the research?

QUESTIONS THAT NEED TO BE PUT TO THOSE RESEARCH SUPPLIERS, AGENCIES AND CONSULTING FIRMS THAT ACTUALLY CONDUCT PR MEASUREMENT AND EVALUATION STUDIES

Here are some of the key questions that ought to be put to those who actually are asked to carry out a PR measurement and evaluation research project, before the assignment is launched:

1. What is, or will be, the actual research design or plan for the PR measurement and evaluation project? Is there, or will there be, a full description in non-technical language of what is to be measured, how the data are to be collected, tabulated, analyzed and reported?

2. Will the research design be consistent with the stated purpose of the PR measurement and evaluation study that is to be conducted? Is there, or will there be, a precise statement of the universe or population to be studied? Does, or will, the sampling source or frame fairly represent the total universe or population under study?

3. Who will actually be supervising and/or carrying out the PR measurement and evaluation project? What is, or are, their backgrounds and experience levels? Have they ever done research like this before? Can they give references?

4. Who will actually be doing the field work? If the assignment includes media content analysis, who actually will be reading the clips or viewing and/or listening

to the broadcast video/audio tapes? If the assignments involve focus groups, who will be moderating the sessions? If the study involves conducting interviews, who will be doing those and how will they be trained, briefed, and monitored?

5. What quality control mechanisms have been built into the study to assure that all "readers," "moderators," and "interviewers" adhere to the research design and study parameters?

6. Who will be preparing any of the data collection instruments, including tally sheets or forms for media content analysis studies, topic guides for focus group projects, and/or questionnaires for telephone, face-to-face, or mail survey research projects? What role will the organization commissioning the PR measurement and evaluation assignment be asked, or be permitted, to play in the final review and approval of these data collection instruments.

7. Will there be a written set of instructions and guidelines for the "readers," "moderators," and the "interviewers"?

8. Will the coding rules and procedures be available for review?

9. If the data are weighted, will the range of the weights be reported? Will the basis for the weights be described and evaluated? Will the effect of the weights on the reliability of the final estimates be reported?

10. Will the sample that is eventually drawn be large enough to provide stable findings?

11. Will sampling error limits be shown, if they can be computed? Will the sample/s reliability be discussed in language that can clearly be understood without a technical knowledge of statistics.

12. How projectable will the research findings be to the total universe or population under study? Will it be clear which respondents or which media vehicles are underrepresented, or not represented at all, as part of the research undertaking?

13. How will the research findings and implications be reported? If there are findings based on the data that were collected, but the implications and/or recommendations stemming from the study go far beyond the actual data that were collected, will there be some effort made to separate the conclusions and observations that are specifically based on the data and those that are not?

14. How will the data processing be handled? Who will be responsible for preparing a tab plan for the project? Which analytical and demographic variables will be included as part of the analysis and interpretation?

15. How will the research findings and implications be reported? If there are findings based on the data that were collected, but the implications and/or recommendations stemming from the study go far beyond the actual data that were collected, will there be some effort made to separate the conclusions and observations that are specifically based on the data and those that are not?

16. Will there be a statement on the limitations of the research and possible misinterpretations of the findings?

17. How will the project be budgeted? Can budget parameters be laid out prior to the actual launch of the assignment? What contingencies can be built into the budget to prevent any unexpected surprises or changes once the project is in the field or is approaching the completion stage?

DEFINITIONS OF SELECTED TERMS USED IN PR MEASUREMENT AND EVALUATION

Advertising Equivalency: A means of converting editorial space in the media into advertising costs, by measuring the amount of editorial coverage and then calculating what it would have cost to buy that space, if it had been advertising. Most reputable researchers contend that advertising equivalency computations are of questionable validity, since in many cases the opportunity to "buy" advertising in space that has been specifically allocated to editorial coverage simply does not exist.

Attitude Research: Consists of measuring and interpreting the full range of views, sentiments, feelings, opinions and beliefs which segments of the public may hold toward given people, products, organizations and/or issues. More specifically, attitude research measures what people say (their verbal expressions), what they know and think (their mental or cognitive predispositions), what they feel (their emotions), and how they're inclined to act (their motivational or drive tendencies).

Bivariate Analysis: Examination of the relationship between two variables.

Causal Relationship: A theoretical notion that change in one variable forces, produces, or brings about a change in another.

Circulation: Refers to the number of copies sold of a given edition of a publication, at a given time or as averaged over a period of time.

Communication Audit: A systematic review and analysis—using accepted research techniques and methodologies—of how well an organization communicates with all of its major internal and external target audience groups.

Confidence Interval: In a survey based on a random sample, the range of values within which a population parameter is estimated to fall. For example, in a survey in which a representative sample of 1,000 individuals is interviewed, if 55% express a preference for a given item, we might say that in the population as a whole, in 95 out of 100 cases, the true proportion expressing such a preference probably would fall between 52% and 58%. The plus or minus 3% range is called the confidence interval. The fact that we are using 95 out of 100 cases as our guide (or 95%) is our confidence level.

Content Analysis: The process of studying and tracking what has been written and broadcast and translating this qualitative material into quantitative form through some type of counting approach that involves coding and classifying of specific messages.

Correlation: Any association or relationship between two variables.

Correlation Coefficient: A measure of association (symbolized as r) that describes the direction and strength of a linear relationship between two variables, measured at the interval or ratio level (e.g. Pearson's Correlation Coefficient).

Cost Per Thousand (CPM): The cost of advertising for each 1,000 homes reached by radio or television, for each 1,000 copies of a publication, or for each 1,000 potential viewers of an outdoor advertisement.

Cross-Sectional Study: A study based on observations representing a single point in time.

Demographic Analysis: Consists of looking at the population in terms of special social, political, economic, and geographic subgroups, such as a person's age, sex, income-level, race, education-level, place of residence, or occupation.

Ethnographic Research: Relies on the tools and techniques of cultural anthropologists and sociologists to obtain a better understanding of how individuals and groups function in their natural settings. Usually, this type of research is carried out by a team of impartial, trained researchers who "immerse" themselves into the daily routine of a neighborhood or community, using a mix of observation, participation, and role-playing techniques, in an effort to try to assess what is really happening from a "cultural" perspective.

Evaluation: Determines the value or importance of a public relations program or effort, usually through appraisal or comparison with a predetermined set of organization goals and objectives. PR Evaluation is somewhat more subjective in nature, or softer, than PR Measurement, involving a greater amount of interpretation and judgment calls.

Experiment: Any controlled arrangement and manipulation of conditions to systematically observe specific occurrences, with the intention of defining those criteria that might possibly be affecting those occurrences. An experimental, or quasi-experimental, research design usually involves two groups—a "test" group which is exposed to given criteria, and a "control" group, which is not exposed. Comparisons are then made to determine what effect, if any, exposures to the criteria have had on those in the "test" group.

Factor Analysis: A complex algebraic procedure that seeks to group or combine items or variables in a questionnaire based on how they naturally relate to each other, or "hang together," as general descriptors (or "factors").

Focus Group: An exploratory technique in which a group of somewhere between 8 and 12 individuals—under the guidance of a trained moderator—are encouraged, as a group, to discuss freely any and all of their feelings, concerns, problems and frustrations relating to specific topics under discussion. Focus groups are ideal for brainstorming, idea-gathering, and concept testing.

Frequency: The number of advertisements, broadcasts, or exposures of given programming or messaging during a particular period of time.

Gross Rating Point: A unit of measurement of broadcast or outdoor advertising audience size, equal to 1 percent of the total potential audience universe; used to measure the exposure of one or more programs or commercials, without regard to multiple exposure of the same advertising to individuals. A GRP is the product of media reach times exposure frequency.

A **gross rating-point buy** is the number of advertisements necessary to obtain the desired percentage of exposure of the message. In outdoor advertising, GRPs, often used as a synonym for showing, generally refer to the daily effective circulation generated by poster panels, divided by market population. The cost per gross rating point (CPGRP) is a measure of broadcast media exposure comparable to the cost per thousand (CPM) measure of print media.

Hypothesis: An expectation about the nature of things derived from theory.

Hypothesis-Testing: Determining whether the expectations that a hypothesis represents are, indeed, found in the real world.

Impressions: The number of those who might have had the opportunity to be exposed to a story that has appeared in the media. Sometimes referred to as "opportunity to see." An "impression" usually refers to the total audited circulation of a publication or the audience reach of a broadcast vehicle.

Incidence: The frequency with which a condition or event occurs within a given time and population.

Inquiry Study: A systematic review and analysis, using content analysis or sometimes telephone and mail interviewing techniques, to study the range and types of unsolicited inquires that an organization may receive from customers, prospective customers or other target audience groups.

Inputs: (1) Everything that is involved upfront within the organization in the design, conception, approval, production and distribution of communications materials aimed at targeted audience groups. (2) Also, the research information and data from both internal and external sources that are applied to the initial stage of the communications planning and production process.

Judgmental Sample: A type of non-probability sample in which individuals are deliberately selected for inclusion in the sample by the researcher because they have special knowledge, position, characteristics or represent other relevant dimensions of the population that are deemed important to study. Also known as a "purposive" sample.

Likert Scale: Developed by Rensis Likert, this is a composite measure in which respondents are asked to choose from an ordered series of five responses to indicate their reactions to a sequence of statements (e.g., strongly agree … somewhat agree … neither agree nor disagree … somewhat disagree … strongly disagree).

Longitudinal Study: A research design involving the collection of data at different points in time.

Mall Intercept: A special type of in-person interview, in which potential respondents are approached as they stroll through shopping centers or malls. Most mall intercept interviews are based on non-probability sampling.

Market Research: Any systematic study of buying and selling behavior.

Mean: A measure of central tendency which is the arithmetic average of the scores.

Measurement: A way of giving a result a precise dimension, generally by comparison to some standard or baseline, and usually is done in a quantifiable or numerical manner.

Median: A measure of central tendency indicating the midpoint in a series of scores, the point above and below which 50 percent of the values fall.

Mode: A measure of central tendency which is the most frequently occurring, the most typical, value in a series.

Multivariate Analysis: Examination of the relationship among three or more variables.

Omnibus Survey: An "all-purpose" national consumer poll usually conducted on a regular schedule—once a week or every other week—by major market research firms. Organizations are encouraged to "buy" one or several proprietary questions and have them "added" to the basic questionnaire. Those adding questions are usually charged on a per-question basis. Also, sometimes referred to as "piggyback," or "shared-cost" surveys.

Outcomes: A long-term measure of the effectiveness of a particular communications program or activity, by focusing on whether targeted audience groups changed their opinions, attitudes and/or behavior patterns as a result of having been exposed to and become aware of messages directed at them.

Outgrowths: (1) The culminate effect of all communication programs and products on the positioning of an organization in the minds of its stakeholders or publics. (2) For some, the term used to describe the outtakes of a communications program activity (see that definition).

Outputs: (1) The short-term or immediate results of a particular communications program or activity, with a prime focus on how well an organization presents itself to others and the amount of exposure it receives. (2) For some, the final stage in the communications production process, resulting in the production and distribution of such items as brochures, media releases, web sites, speeches, etc.

Outtakes: (1) A measure of the effectiveness of a particular communications program or activity, by focusing on whether targeted audience groups received the messages directed to them … paid attention to the messages … understood or comprehended the messages … and retained and can recall the messages in any shape or form. (2) Initial audience reaction to the receipt of communications materials, including whether the audience heeded or responded to a call for information or action within the messages.

Panel Study: 1) A type of longitudinal study in which the same individuals are interviewed more than once over a period of time to investigate the processes of response change, usually in reference to the same topic or issue. 2) Also, a type of study in which a group of individuals are deliberately recruited by a research firm, because of their special demographic characteristics, for the express purpose of being interviewed more than once over a period of time for various clients on a broad array of different topics or subjects.

Probability Sample: A process of random selection, in which each unit in a population has an equal chance of being included in the sample.

Psychographic Analysis: Consists of looking at the population in terms of people's non-demographic traits and characteristics, such as a person's personality type, lifestyle, social roles, values and beliefs.

Q-Sort: A personality inventory introduced in the 1950's in which respondents are asked to sort opinion statements along a "most-like-me" to "most-unlike-me" continuum. Q-Sorting allows researchers to construct models of individual respondents' belief systems.

Qualitative Research: Usually refers to studies that are somewhat subjective, but nevertheless in-depth, using a probing, open-end, free-response format.

Quantitative Research: Usually refers to studies that are highly objective and projectable, using closed-end, forced-choice questionnaires. These studies tend to rely heavily on statistics and numerical measures.

Quota Sample: A type of non-probability sample in which individuals are selected on the basis of pre-specified characteristics, so that the total sample will have the same general distribution of characteristics as are assumed to exist in the population being studied.

Range: A measure of variability that is computed by subtracting the lowest score in a distribution from the highest score.

Reach: Refers to the range or scope of influence or effect that a given communications vehicle has on targeted audience groups. In broadcasting, it is the net unduplicated radio or TV audience—the number of different individuals or households—for programs or commercials as measured for a specific time period in quarter-hour units over a period of one to four weeks.

Regression Analysis: A statistical technique for studying relationships among variables, measured at the interval or ratio level.

Reliability: The extent to which the results would be consistent, or replicable, if the research were conducted a number of times.

Screener Question: One or several questions usually asked in the beginning of an interview to determine if the potential respondent is eligible to participate in the study.

Secondary Analysis: A technique for extracting from previously conducted studies new knowledge on topics other than those which were the focus of the original studies. It does this through a systematic re-analysis of a vast array of already existing research data.

Situation Analysis: An impartial, often third-party assessment of the public relations and/or public affairs problems, or opportunities, that an organization may be facing at a given point in time.

Standard Deviation: An index of variability of a distribution. More precisely, it is the range from the mean within which approximately 34% of the cases fall, provided the values are distributed in a normal curve.

Statistical Significance: Refers to the unlikeliness that relationships observed in a sample could be attributed to sampling error alone.

Survey: Any systematic collection of data that uses a questionnaire and a recognized sampling method. There are three basic types of surveys: those conducted face-to-face (in-person) … those conducted by telephone … and those that are self-administered (usually distributed by mail, e-mail, or fax.)

Univariate Analysis: The examination of only one variable at a time.

Validity: The extent to which a research project measures what it is intended, or purports, to measure.

Variance: A measure of the extent to which individual scores in a set differ from each other. More precisely, it is the sum of the squared deviations from the mean divided by the frequencies.

This booklet was first published in 1997 under the title, "Guidelines and Standards for Measuring and Evaluating PR Effectiveness." It was originally written by Dr. Walter K. Lindenmann, based on guidance, input and suggestions from a task force of PR practitioners, counselors, academicians and research suppliers that included the following individuals: Forrest W. Anderson … Albert J. Barr … Dr. Mary Ann Ferguson … Dr. James E. Grunig … Thomas Martin … Geri Mazur … Willard Nielsen … Charlotte Otto … Katharine D. Paine … David Silver … Kathleen Ward … Mark Weiner … and Dr. Donald K. Wright. The booklet was updated and revised in 2002 and given a new title, "Guidelines for Measuring the Effectiveness of PR Programs and Activities," to more accurately reflect its contents. The revised version is primarily the work of Dr. Walter K. Lindenmann, with input and suggestions from Fraser Likely.

6 Defining Components of a Public Relations Plan and Rules for Writing Them

Let's begin our study of winning plans and proposals by reviewing a whimsical presentation I like to call the "frog show." As you can see on the following page, it is titled, "A public relations plan to influence the behavior of a frog." The purpose of the show is to help clear your mind of the way you might think of writing the components of a plan and prepare you to think about what reviewers of plans and proposals would like to know from the components of a plan.

I have yet to name the frog character you are about to meet. However, you will get to know him quite well as he will appear repeatedly to remind you to resist voices from various sources telling you "this is how we do it here," or "in competition it is written this way," or "it won't be understood if you do it that way," or "never write it without this or that." Get to know the frog icon as a reminder that you are learning a new paradigm for writing proposals the way reviewers want to receive them, the way reviewers would find them easy to understand and approve, the way judges in competitions would love to recognize them as models that truly contribute to the growth of pride in a profession working diligently to earn its credentials.

It is a challenge to learn a new paradigm. It is easier if you are learning for the first time to write plans and proposals. It is more difficult if you have been following other, less effective patterns. Buckminster Fuller (designer, cosmologist, philosopher, mathematician, and architect who designed the geodesic dome) once said, "You can't change anything by fighting or resisting it. You change something by making it obsolete through superior methods." It is time for the profession to jettison its follow-the-rainbow approach to plan writing and replace it with a much sharper, prismatic paradigm for achieving results.

Enjoy the "frog show." I will rejoin you afterwards and we will turn whimsey into reality.

Case Six

A WHIMSICAL PUBLIC RELATIONS PLAN TO INFLUENCE THE BEHAVIOR OF A FROG

Problem

There is a problem. We have a frog that refuses to go back into its pond. The bank around the pond is wet and slippery and the safest time to take action would be in daylight hours. If we wait until after dark to get the frog back into the pond we run the risk of slipping, unseen, into deep water surrounded by a steep, slippery bank and no place to climb out. This problem calls for public relations–the practice of influencing behavior.

Situation Analysis

Our analysis of the situation is that the frog will not respond to instructions. We have tried over and over to tell the frog to jump back into the pond. First we tried a friendly, polite approach: "Would you please jump back into the pond?" Then we tried a firm approach, "We want you to jump back into the pond." Then we became frustrated and started shouting orders, "Get back into the pond!" Based on this failed experience, we could only conclude that the frog is stubborn. Not knowing what else to do, we decided to call on professional help–a public relations expert who knows how to influence behavior.

The Goal

The public relations expert accepted our challenge to influence the behavior of the frog. "The goal," she said, "is for the frog to be back in the pond." We said, "Yes, that's what we want."

Focus

"To achieve our goal, the focus of our effort must be on the frog," the PR expert said. "We must influence the behavior of the frog. The frog is our target."

Objective

According to the PR expert, an objective tells what must be done to achieve the goal and it must have three parts: 1) an action; 2) a receiver of the action; 3) and a certain behavior by the receiver that is expected as a result of the action taken. So the PR expert says that the objective should be: "To make the frog jump back into the pond before nightfall." The action is to make the frog jump. The receiver or target of the action is the frog. The desired result of the action is for the frog to jump into the pond before dark.

Strategy

The PR expert explains that we need a strategy because that tells how we will achieve our objective. "Our strategy," she says, "will be to lure the frog with a fly to get the frog back into the pond."

Tactic

The PR expert says to fully explain how we are going to carry out our strategy we will add specific tactics or activities to our strategy. She said, "Our tactic or activity, will be to lure the frog with a fly connected with a thread to a twig to lead the frog back into the pond.

Evaluation

The success of our public relations effort to influence the behavior of the frog will be determined by observing the frog back in the pond before nightfall.

Time Line

The PR expert said that our time line will include four steps: 1) preparing to connect a fly with a thread to a twig of an appropriate shape and length; 2) approaching the frog strategically; 3) beginning the luring operation before nightfall; 4) and causing a final leap into the pond.

Budget

A proposed budget from a PR agency includes an hourly rate for personnel, plus out-of-pocket expenses. The total cost of influencing the behavior of a frog is $745.00.

ESTIMATED BUDGET (Public Relations Agency Example)

Personnel Billing

Agency Staff	Rate/Hour	Estimated Hours/Day	Estimated Days	
Account Executive	110.00	2	1	220.00
Assistant AE	95.00	2	1	190.00
			Subtotal	410.00

Out-of-pocket Expenses

Photograph				120.00
Pictorial Report				200.00
Knife for cutting twig				12.00
Spool of thread				3.00
			Subtotal	335.00
TOTAL (for influencing the behavior of a frog)				745.00

FROM WHIMSEY TO REALITY ...

I am back, as promised. So, what did you learn from the frog story? It should have impressed you that a winning public relations plan can and should be written in clear, brief, direct human terms. Shortly, we will go from whimsey to reality and study a student plan for the campus organization, Center On Diversity and Community. But first it would be useful to become familiar with the planning process and basic format of a plan. You will see, also, that having a structure allows more time to concentrate on important work, such as research, measurement and creativity.

PLANNING PROCESS OVERVIEW

So far, we understand how planning relates to public relations, the challenges of the planning environment, and the importance of leading with integrity and planning with accountability. Now let's take a broad look at the planning process.

We said earlier that public relations is the practice of influencing behavior. Well, planning is the method by which behavior is to be influenced. A plan focuses on a problem, challenge or opportunity that would significantly benefit its sponsoring individual or organization. The subject of a plan could be the result of an organization's initiative or could arise as a result of circumstances beyond the organization's control. In either case, a plan is required to deal with the subject and derive benefits for its sponsor.

Planning begins with gathering information, first to understand the problem, challenge or opportunity, second to develop ways to accomplish the plan's goal, third to track and measure effectiveness in achieving the plan's goal. Planning efforts are likely to fail if you approach the task as a lone star, because effective planning requires a depth of knowledge and information gathering requires gaining the cooperation of many different sources.

One source of information, of course, is yourself and the knowledge you have acquired from your professional experience. Depending on the subject of your plan, you also will look within your organization to draw on the knowledge and background of other individuals. They can provide onsite expertise in law, marketing, product development, finance, sales, human resources, engineering, technology and other professional disciplines.

You will look to information sources outside your organization, such as industry trade associations, government agencies, non-government organizations, professional and service organizations, and you will tap other sources around the globe through the World Wide Web. Gaps in information will have to be filled and assumptions validated through informal (qualitative) or formal (quantitative) research recommended in the plan or conducted for development of the plan.

The information you gather must be assessed and funneled into development of the plan's situation analysis. From the analysis you should be able to: a) write a statement summarizing the problem, challenge or opportunity; b) establish a goal with compelling reasons for taking public relations actions to achieve it; c) decide what must be done to accomplish the goal, which is the role of objectives; d) determine the primary focus of the plan–people whose behaviors must be influenced to accomplish the plan's objectives; e) develop strategies with detailed activities to show how the plan's objectives are to be achieved.

The process of strategically influencing the behavior of individuals or groups of individuals must take into account all dimensions of communication as shown on the next page. The process requires careful development of what is to be communicated, selection of channels through which messages are to be conveyed, consideration for how the communication might become obstructed and/or filtered and regard for how messages will be received by the intended audience, depending on its disposition toward the message and its source.

A plan developer must decide how much of this process can be based on professional experience and intuition and how much should be based on formal or informal research. Another important part of the planning process is providing methods of evaluation for tracking and gauging the plan's progress as it is implemented and for measuring its ultimate effectiveness in achieving the plan's goal. The planning process includes development of a time line that provides an at-a-glance view of major preparatory steps and milestones leading to achievement of the plan's goal. Finally, a plan provides an estimated budget for its implementation.

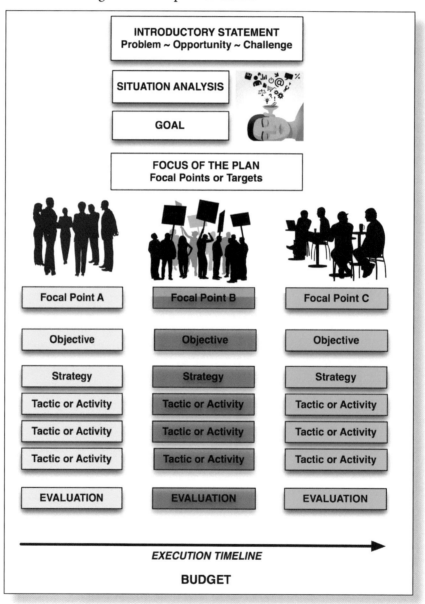

You Can Learn to Be the Idea Person

By Deborah Morrison, Ph.D.

Let's first clear up misconceptions: creativity—making ideas and using them well—belongs to everyone, in all job titles. It's a domain that spreads beyond art and writing and execution. To say you're creative simply can mean you make ideas. So say it. And most importantly, do it. Develop skills that let you be the idea person, ready to solve problems and engage your audience with bright ideas.

Professional creativity is an important tool for your work life. It grows across the broad sweep of public relations thinking and doing. As in advertising and other communication fields, public relations success relies on our ability as professionals to bring new approaches to problems at several different steps along the arc of a problem. This takes innovation, a bit of tenacity, maybe even some childlike fun along the way.

I see creativity as having three distinct stages to use in these professional communication situations. First, there are Generative Tasks, where our goal is to generate multiple possible solutions to a specific problem. Second, Developmental Tasks are opportunities to develop an idea to its fullest potential. And third, ideas are developed via Transformative Tasks, wherein the idea is polished and transformed into a product of value. Importantly, these are often team techniques to generate, grow and transform ideas as a dedicated cohort.

No matter the process stage, the point is this: creativity happens across the spectrum. It is not framed only by execution, but instead the romp of creative work happens in every stage and in every facet of communication situations. To give an idea of how this might work, let's briefly look at each stage of the creative process and understand how public relations ideas might be enhanced for Clean Air Awareness Day and its connection to a young audience. In each of the three areas, there are many techniques that might be used to great success. We'll use them here in a linear process, taking one idea and moving it through all three stages. But any of these stages might be used to deliver a solution to a problem. It's all in your ability to be nimble enough to try them out.

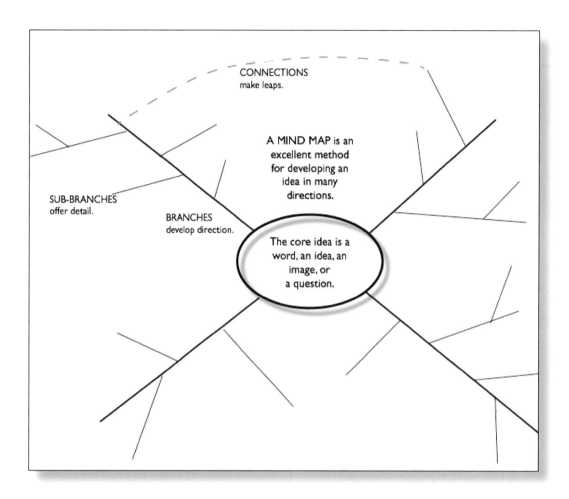

CONNECTIONS
make leaps.

A MIND MAP is an
excellent method
for developing an
idea in many
directions.

SUB-BRANCHES
offer detail.

BRANCHES
develop direction.

The core idea is a
word, an idea, an
image, or
a question.

Generative Tasks

In the generative stages, quantity means quality. These tasks usually are simple in nature—naming, finding associations and connections, using metaphors for communicating—and can be used for collecting many options for writing, design, messaging, or planning.

Brainstorming techniques might be used to name the event, to find unusual connections, or to find metaphors about clean air to be used in messaging and collateral materials.

A good example is the ABC approach using forced association. In this technique, a team lists out the alphabet on a whiteboard. One person writes down the team's answers as they list an answer to the problem using every letter of the alphabet. This is forced association because we're using the variable—What possibilities can we come up with for kids on Clean Air Awareness Day?—and forcibly connecting that problem to solutions that begin with each letter of the alphabet. Our goal would be to list specific ideas, no editing as we go. Everyone calls out possibilities and everything is written down. Our list might look like this:

A = apple   juice   animals   angels in the snow
B = blue sky   boxes with windows   big trees to climb   baseball   balloons   butterflies
C = coloring books   cookies   castles   circus   clouds   cotton candy

Each letter might get as many as 10 entries and from that long list, maybe a couple really stand out. The team decides on a handful they think unusual or especially interesting to develop further.

Developmental Tasks

This area of techniques and tasks centers on growing the idea and giving it some architecture. For this, we move out of the need for quantity and use approaches that can help build strong connections to support the idea.

One of the best developmental techniques is the Mind Map. A Mind Map can be a very simple image or it can be quite detailed and developed. A good Mind Map will begin in the center with a strong concept, question, or image. Three to five branches grow from that middle idea, each branch with sub-branches. The branches and sub-branches are labeled with words or short phrases, and each branch is somewhat parallel in thought to the others. The goal of a Mind Map is to develop those branches, some connecting to other branches to make rich connections, using words and small pictures to make the map interesting.

Mind maps should hold surprises at the end of drawing. Interesting connections, new ways of looking at certain areas or branches are part of the quest. The entire map should be seen as a possible solution. And interestingly, this technique can be accomplished either by a team or by an individual.

A Mind Map exercise using the idea "Imagination + Clean Air" might deliver some interesting directions. One branch might be about the concept of "invisibility" of clean air and ways kids can "see" it. Another branch might develop ideas on colors in a clean air world. A third branch might grow stories about clean air castles or a magic box with windows. And a fourth branch could be about animals and clean air ideas.

Of course, any branch could then be used to develop its own map with four branches. The development of ideas in this way is rich with possibility.

Transformative Tasks

The final stage of the creative process tasks focuses on transforming ideas into products of value. This usually centers on execution. A good writer or designer will explain that this is a final step and they've been using creative strategies to generate and develop possibilities from the onset of idea development.

And whereas the other stages depended on playfulness and fluency with making leaps and connections mentally, this stage and its techniques are often dependent on

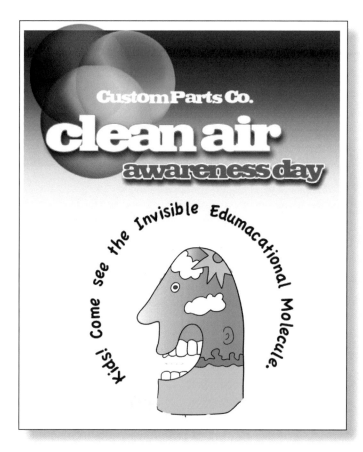

tools: good vendors (photographers and producers), software (Photoshop, InDesign, Flash, as examples), other members of the team. Though this stage is dependent on resources, the quality of a final product isn't defined by how much the budget is. Instead, it's how well you use the tools you have.

It's interesting to note also that the process may circle around and use generating and developing techniques throughout different stages of the problem. Maybe our team wants to think about different ways to deliver the message they've developed and goes back to ABC for a look.

It may be that our Clean Air Awareness Day example[1] grew a series of puppet shows for children with invisible characters living in clouds. A Mind Map was developed for each storyline. And then lists were generated about new places to tell our story. In the final stages, the idea had to transform into a real production: a script written, a puppeteer brought in, an event planned, giveaways produced. The success of the event depends on the quality of the ideas.

---

1 Author's Note: We can use this poster to illustrate the creative process described by Professor Morrison. Assume that words such as air pollution, dense, clear, visible, smoke, kids, education, molecules and others were brought forth in the Generative Tasks, that the opposing concepts of visible and invisible were tied together in the Development Tasks, that a fun illustration for awareness day was designed using an inexpensive computer program called The Logo Creator by Laughingbird Software, that a drawing of an invisible person was obtained free of royalties from iStockphoto.com, and a creative student, my Granddaughter Lindsey of middle school age, was recruited to make the tag line relate to kids, which she did by making up the word, ed-u-ma-ca-tion-al. I think we would have a poster that makes parents and kids think about clean air and Custom Parts Co. in distinctively new ways.

It may be that our idea generating, developing and transforming techniques offered a set of rich possibilities that moved youngsters and their parents to think of Clean Air in a new way, to help the world and the client in creative ways. For that, all you needed was a bright idea.

Deborah Morrison is the Chambers Distinguished Professor of Advertising at the University of Oregon's School of Journalism and Communication and a champion of creativity. Her latest book, with co-author Glenn Griffin, is Pure Process: Advertising's Top Brains Reveal How Big Ideas are Born (F+W Media, 2010). Her research and teaching focuse on the process and joy of making ideas.

CREATIVITY IN PUBLIC RELATIONS PLANNING

Public relations and creativity have certain characteristics in common. One is that both have eluded definition since their inceptions. Neither one has a single, authoritative perspective or definition. Research has identified more than 500 different definitions of public relations. As for creativity, the ways in which societies have perceived the concept have changed throughout history, as has the term itself. Despite the ambiguity and multi-dimensional nature of public relations and creativity, the two concepts are inextricably associated and, together, act as a powerful force in influencing human behavior.

Another common characteristic of public relations and creativity is that they are mental and social processes involving the generation of new ideas or concepts, or new associations of the creative mind between existing ideas or concepts. Both are fueled by the process of either conscious or unconscious insight. An alternative characteristic is that both are appreciated for the simple act of making something new or simply spawning something that had not been considered.

Intuitively, public relations and creativity would seem to be quite simple phenomena; however, both in fact, are complex and deliver quantifiable but never absolutely predictable outcomes.

So how does creativity manifest itself in public relations? This is such a sweeping question that books could be devoted to answering it. Let's narrow the focus to the application of creativity in the public relations planning process. Specifically, we will look at creativity as it applies to writing the 10 components of a public relations plan or proposal.

Introductory Statement

The introductory statement or summary of a plan is the plan developer's first opportunity to instill in plan reviewers confidence that the developer or the planning team has a solid grasp of the problem, challenge, opportunity or situation as a designer, a skilled agent of making things happen. Did you catch the key word "designer?" To be regarded at the start of a plan with the stature of a designer would be a high compliment to a plan developer because it would recognize the developer as a professional. Such confidence derives from introductory statements written in clear, concise, simple, coherent language. Errors in accuracy, omissions of facts, and abuses of plain English immediately undermine impressions of a plan developer's competence. It would not be an exaggeration to say that reviewers await plans with high expectations of right brain activity, genius or divine inspiration. Consider the introductory statement a handshake, first impression, connection of mutual respect. The introductory statement should cause a plan reviewer to think with confidence, "I know the task at hand and so do you."

Situation Analysis

What role does creativity play in a plan's situation analysis? The analysis is best presented in story form, right from the beginning, the way a situation has unfolded and led to the need for public relations action. What could be more creative than telling a story? You know what it means to embellish a story. Well, that's what needs to be done here. Describe the situation in detail and embellish the story with information that provides overall context, with research or recommendations for research that validates what is known or needs to be known, and a thoughtful analysis that provides a foundation for the other components of a plan. In-depth information here signals plan reviewers that you have full understanding of, strong interest in, and unquestionable commitment to the job at hand.

Goal

What about a plan's goal? How does creativity figure into developing a goal? At this point you go from analyzing to synthesizing–bringing all the pieces of the situation analysis together into a single, declarative statement. You have investigated. You have thought about the situation from every angle, and now you create a single goal. The study of creative thought underlying this synthesizing process belongs to the domains of psychology and cognitive science. Call it critical thinking, because an error in determining an appropriate goal would invalidate an entire plan or proposal. The goal is the rallying point for every component of a plan and can be assessed, ultimately, by asking, Did we achieve this state of being or condition or not?

Focus

Public relations plans focus on people. To determine the focal points or target audiences or publics of a plan requires a selection process. However, the process needs to be more than logical selection by association with the problem, opportunity, challenge or situation. The process can be made most effective by thinking intuitively about individuals, groups, and organizations and how they might be related to the subject of a particular plan. Using one's intuition in this way is a dimension of creativity. To adequately identify and describe a target of a plan requires the ability to place oneself in the positions of others, to see what others see, to feel the way others feel. Empathizing, which is what is being described, is the amazing human maneuver of mentally walking in someone else's shoes. To plan to influence the behavior of others you must know the subjects from the inside out.

Objectives

The objectives of a plan describe what must be done with the plan's target audiences or publics to accomplish the plan's goal. Another aspect of creativity comes into play in the writing of objectives. Creativity is an "assumptions-breaking process." Creative ideas are often generated when one discards preconceived assumptions and attempts a new approach or method that might even seem unthinkable to others. An objective, as you will learn later, has three components: 1) an action; 2) receiver of the action; 3) and a desired behavior of the receiver as a result of the action. The first component is one of a plan's most overlooked places for creativity. Typical of many objectives, the first component so often is an ordinary action, such as To inform, To convince, To provide, To educate. There are, of course, many creative ways to grab people's attention. Actions could be To surprise, To raise curiosity, To violate expectations, To disrupt a pattern, To create a gap of knowledge, To subvert a traditional schema, To tap into, To present consequences, To simulate, To inspire, To provoke. Think of it this way. What do you have to do to get your target audience to drop its ear buds and pay attention?

Strategies and Activities or Tactics

The strategy component of a plan is a creative platform. Strategies describe how objectives are to be accomplished; activities or tactics explain how the strategies are to be carried out. There are many different ways to develop strategies. One might be to learn from the successful lessons of others. Another might be to uncover, through research, ideas not thought of by others. Another might be to derive ideas from brainstorming sessions. In public relations, human behavior is influenced by strategic communication. Keep in mind; however, that what influences society's behavior has evolved over the years. People today are in search of meaning and purpose. To be effective, strategies must be more than a simple nudge from Point A to Point B. Strategies must have meaning to people in order to be influential. So when you are developing strategies, you must describe what must be done to make them influential. If your strategy is to entertain individuals with a dinner party, for example, it is essential to describe how you will make the dinner experience meaningful enough to influence your guests to react according to your strategy. Meaning and purpose are motivators and both can be leveraged with creativity.

On the following pages is a public relations plan initiated as a class exercise by students in the School of Journalism and Communication proposed for CoDaC, Center on Diversity and Community at the University of Oregon. CoDaC is an applied research center dedicated to advancing cross cultural dialogue, knowledge, skill, and awareness building, with an emphasis on academic communities within higher eduction. CoDaC works with individual faculty as well as campus units striving to become more multi-culturally inclusive and accessible. The plan is shown here as a model for teaching purposes.

A STUDENT INITIATED PUBLIC RELATIONS PLAN PROPOSED TO THE CENTER ON DIVERSITY AND COMMUNITY AT THE UNIVERSITY OF OREGON

Problem

The Center on Diversity and Community strives to promote racial, ethnic, and cultural diversity on the University of Oregon campus and in its surrounding communities. The center currently lacks sufficient resources to increase its visibility among faculty, students, potential university and corporate donors and surrounding communities about the universal benefits of diversity issues education.

Currently, some marketing challenges that the center faces include: limited financial resources, advertising and communication that is insufficiently tailored to multiple and specific audiences.

The center's executive committee recognizes the pressing need for a strategic public relations plan in its efforts to position the organization to fulfill its mission. Without the success that a plan could provide, which includes a financial development facet, the center could be seriously restricted in its ability to achieve its goals. The center is requesting assistance with these serious public relations problems.

Situation Analysis

In spring of 1999, a student publicly made a racially insensitive remark in a large University of Oregon classroom. A heated exchange ensued between the student and others attending the course, which spilled outside the class through violent threats and e-mails. The incident brought to light concerns of diversity and equity in classroom environments and throughout the University of Oregon campus. The incident led to an approximate 95-person sit-in at Johnson Hall. Students, faculty and staff demanded the administration address diversity issues on campus in a formal setting.

In the summer of 1999, the President's Office created an action staff to produce a Diversity Internship Program Report, a document describing how the University of Oregon could pro-actively address and promote diversity throughout the institution. Based on the report's findings, a research team was established.

The team developed a proposal for the Center on Diversity and Community, an interdisciplinary research center. Created in October 2001, the center promotes inquiry, dialogue, and understanding on issues of racial, ethnic and cultural diversity. The center considers cultural diversity to include such identity factors as socioeconomic status, sexual preference, nationality and language.

CoDaC offers competitive research grants and awards, diversity dialogue and facilitation training programs, public events and workshops, resource guides, and student internships. Its governing body is the executive committee that is composed of faculty, administrators, and student leaders. Executive committee meetings are held twice a term along with additional subcommittee meetings. CoDaC reports to the Office of the Vice President for Research and Graduate Studies and the Office of the Vice Provost for Institutional Equity and Diversity.

Currently, the center is funded by a one-time allocation from the Associated Students of the University of Oregon plus funds from the University of Oregon administration. Its marketing strategies use its Web site, e-mail lists, three-times-a-year newsletter, posters and flyers, campus announcements, UO media relations, announcements through local news outlets and Web sites, and display ads in the Eugene Weekly, Oregon Daily Emerald and The Register-Guard.

Goal

For the Center on Diversity and Community to be fully institutionalized as an essential, unique and authoritative resource for diversity education on the University of Oregon campus, and to be making greater regional and national impact.

Focus Of The Plan
Graduate Students

Many graduate programs require a research project. The grants offered by the center provide a financial resource for graduate students to complete such research. The completed research acknowledges the center as the funding source and serves as a promotion tool. These students participate in an annual Graduate Research Conference organized by the center.

Potential Corporate Sponsors

The center seeks to receive funding from corporations, specifically Northwest based and progressive-thinking national companies that value diversity and cultural competency. In an effort to continue the center's operations, the executive committee is seeking corporate or foundation sponsors. This target audience is important both because of its potential for funding the center and because many companies seek to increase diversity and cultural competency in the workforce. It is also the most time-consuming audience to research because, to be effective, contact must be made with senior management, one organization at a time, and any such relationship must relate closely both to the center's and the company's mission and values.

Undergraduate Students

The center is seeking greater visibility with undergraduate students. This audience comprises the majority of the university's population and can be viewed as the most impressionable of all target audiences. Some undergraduates could be experiencing their first meaningful encounter in a culturally diverse environment. The center strives to educate these students on diversity and cultural competency issues to encourage a positive college experience.

Faculty and Staff

The center seeks to improve its visibility with faculty as a resource for promoting and supporting their diversity-related research activities. The center also works with staff on increasing individual and organizational cultural competency.

Community

Despite successful public events and articles in the local press, many Eugene-area residents are not currently aware of the center's efforts, but could benefit from its programs and research. Greater knowledge and awareness of the center throughout the community would give more public emphasis to the program and would lead to more opportunities for obtaining sponsorships.

Potential/Current University Funding Sources

This audience is also important because it has a direct bearing on future funding of the center. The center provides its reporting offices with formal annual reports and informal reports on its activities and successes. Greater awareness of these results and reports may produce greater university funding sources, both current and potential.

A critical prerequisite to the recommendations contained in this plan is a suggestion to modify the organization's name. Currently, the center does not wish to change its name due to the recognition that it has accrued to date on campus and in the community, but it may consider doing so in the future if its mission were to undergo significant change. Potential funders and others unfamiliar with the organization might confuse "CODAC" with the Kodak brand. In order to clarify what the acronym signifies and to distinguish itself, the center has contemplated a change in printed appearance and logo from "CODAC" to "CoDaC." No name modifications or changes are suggested in this proposal.

Objective #1

To attract the interest of corporations and/or professional and business organizations that would like to raise their public profiles in the area of diversity and have them become active participants in and financial supporters of the Center on Diversity and Community.

Strategy

The center could better engage potential financial supporters through presentations to professional, business and civic organizations in the Eugene community and through personal contact with Oregon graduates who are employed by potential sponsors. We recommend implementing this strategy according the following:

1. Obtain from the Oregon Alumni Foundation the names of graduates who are employed currently by companies that the center has selected as potential financial supporters. Use graduates as "rainmakers" in helping the center establish relationships with the graduates' respective organizations and ultimately requesting financial support.
2. Call on selected graduates for assistance in arranging and possibly making a presentation to their respective companies.
3. For soliciting financial support from these organizations, develop a brochure of irresistible funding opportunities. The brochure would describe various ways to support the center in a range of marketable packages of opportunities with clearly defined forms of public recognition for the sponsors.
4. For example, one important area of funding would be for the design, production and special packaging of 1000 cast bronze mementos to be known as the center's Diversity Medallion, a gesture of recognition to be earned by individuals and organizations by volunteering time, talent and energy to embrace diversity. The medallion could have on one side a graphic symbol of the center and a slogan, such as a phrase borrowed with permission from the song, "Shed A Little Light," "We are bound together by the task that stands before us." On the other side could be the center's mission, "Men and women dedicated to promoting inquiry, dialogue and understanding on issues of racial, ethnic and cultural diversity." The role of the medallion will become clear as this plan unfolds. The sponsor that provides funds for the medallion could receive public recognition in the form of a credit line on each medallion, such as "Provided by The (Name) Foundation."
5. A range of funding opportunities from $100 to $100,000, each in an irresistible marketing package like the medallion with clearly defined public recognition of sponsors would be described in the center's brochure.
6. Expand the center's executive committee membership, or create a community advisory board, to include organizational memberships for professional, business and civic organizations in the Eugene community that would like to embrace diversity more openly.
7. Present each organization that joins the board with a membership plaque with the center's Diversity Medallion. The plaque could have a heading borrowed with permission from the song, "Shed A Little Light," that says, "There are ties between us, all men and women living on the earth, ties of hope and love."

8. Organizational board membership would require board member representatives of these organizations to host an annual presentation of the center to their respective organizations."

9. The presentations would be scheduled to be held during the week of the city "Diversity Walk," an annual commemorative event established by the Eugene City Council, which is described later in the plan.

10. The presentation would honor organizations for their support of diversity activities and would announce volunteer opportunities that would especially benefit from the joint participation of community and campus leaders.

11. Community leader participants could earn the center's Diversity Medallion for their efforts and involvement.

12. The center's fundraising brochure would be included in all presentations.

Evaluation

Success in achieving this objective will be based on total contributions received one year from the time the plan is launched.

Objective #2

To increase graduate student awareness of competitive research grants and conference opportunity available through the center so that more students participate in research on issues of diversity.

Strategy

We recommend that the center strengthen its appeal to graduate students through graduate-to-graduate briefings and through a special event. This strategy could be implemented as follows:

> Organize current graduate student grant recipients to undertake a series of graduate-to-graduate student briefings about the center and its research-funding opportunities. Make this outreach responsibility a requirement for every student who receives a grant in the future. It would be the responsibility of each grant recipient to inform through informal briefings all graduate students in the recipient's particular school of center activities throughout the grant recipient's period of center-sponsored research. As part of their participation in the Graduate Research Program, grant recipients would be given a certificate entitling each to receive a Diversity Medallion upon completion of their research.

Evaluation

Success in achieving this objective will be determined by the external support of the Graduate Student Research Award program, and by increased community attendance at the annual Graduate Research Conference.

Objective #3

To heighten interest among students in the center's undergraduate-focused programs and resources, so that more individuals participate in the organization.

Strategy

We recommend that the center heighten interest among undergraduates by communicating the benefits of participating in the organization frequently through multiple and familiar channels. Activities to consider are the following:

1. Publicize and fill openings for one or more credit-based internships in specific areas, such as public relations, Web site development, campus outreach, community outreach, faculty staff liaison, student group liaison, ASUO liaison and graduate student liaison and use this cadre of talent to produce promotional materials, such as brochures, newsletters and fliers. Each student that completes an internship would earn one of the center's Diversity Medallions.
2. Recruit, train and dispatch a dozen student volunteers who would like to develop their presentation skills as the center's ambassadors spreading word of the center's mission and events before large lecture classes in business, ethics, sociology, management—all areas of study, and before professional student organizations, such as the Society of Professional Journalists, American Marketing Association and business honors society. Students who make a certain number of presentations on behalf of the center would earn Diversity Medallions.
3. Develop a conspicuous presence for the center during the fall student orientation programs, perhaps in the form of a short workshop on conflict resolution or other skill-building activity related to diversity to educate students on diversity issues to encourage a positive college experience.
4. Partner with the appropriate organization for publicizing the up-coming dedication of the $1.5 million Longhouse being built on campus to represent student members of Native Americans throughout the Pacific Northwest. At an appropriate ceremony, present the leadership of the Longhouse with a piece of Native American art with the Diversity Medallion embedded in its design and publicize the presentation with a photo news release to all area media.

Evaluation

Success in achieving this objective will be determined by the following:

1. internship positions have been filled;
2. major events are regularly and successfully co-sponsored with other university organizations, as measured by attendance, event quality, and other factors;
3. student volunteers made an acceptable number of large class presentations on behalf of the center;
4. a center workshop has been established as part of the student fall orientation;
5. the center participated in the dedication of the Longhouse.

Objective #4

To raise the Eugene community's awareness of the center, its role and activities in the community and on campus, in ways that would motivate community members to get involved and participate in the center and its diversity-related events.

Strategy A

This objective could be accomplished by having the city establish an annual "Diversity Walk" for the greater Eugene area with proceeds contributed to the center for managing the event. This would require:

1. Making an informal inquiry of Councilman David Kelly, who represents the university area, to gage the interest in a possible council action to designate an annual "Diversity Walk."
2. If the inquiry receives a positive response, the center would work with Councilman Kelly to draft a council resolution establishing the annual event to promote diversity.
3. Council would pass the resolution and the day following the council meeting the mayor would announce the declaration at a special ceremony at city hall.
4. The center would manage the event for the city and receive some or part of the entry fees collected.
5. The center would be identified with the city on Diversity Walk tee-shirts that would be worn by all participants.

Strategy B

Another strategy for achieving this objective would be for the city of Eugene each year to honor an individual who deserves special recognition for promoting diversity in the community. This could be accomplished in the following manner:

1. The mayor and council would select and announce the "Citizen of the Year for Exemplary Efforts in Promoting Diversity."
2. The mayor would decorate the individual with a Diversity Medallion suspended from a ribbon and placed on the honoree in the manner of an Olympic medal presentation. (Some medallions would be produced with an eye through which a ribbon could be passed.)
3. This would be an award made jointly by the center and the city.
4. The honoree would become a special ambassador to the center, would be featured in the center's annual report, and would have a portrait photo displayed at the center.

Evaluation

Success in achieving this objective will be based on completing preparations for the events, conducting the actual events and assessing by sign-ups and field observation participation of community residents in the center's activities.

Objective #5

To motivate university faculty and staff to take an interest in and actively support the center and its mission on campus and in the community.

Strategy

One way to accomplish this objective would be to enlist the cooperation of the U.S. Ambassador to the United Nations to personally encourage University of Oregon faculty and staff to advance the cause of diversity among all people for the benefit of world peace. The letter would be sent to all faculty and staff members with a cover letter from the university president that would endorse the ambassador's message and urge individuals to advance diversity on campus by participating in the center's activities and earning a Diversity Medallion. Prior to this communication the university president would be awarded a Diversity Medallion in a publicized ceremony. This strategy would require the following:

1. Discuss the proposal with the university president.
2. Discuss the president's endorsement and proposal with the ambassador's staff.
3. Draft a letter for the ambassador's review, approval and signature addressed to University of Oregon faculty and staff.
4. Draft a cover letter for the university president.
5. Follow distribution of the ambassador's letter one week later with a letter from the center referring faculty and staff to the center's new Web site with a link to a

screen with specific ways in which faculty and staff could support the center and earn a Diversity Medallion for their contribution.

Evaluation

Success in achieving this objective will be based on distribution of the ambassador's letter and sign-ups by faculty and staff in the center's activities for earning Diversity Medallions.

Objective #6

To communicate to potential and current university funding sources the achievements the center has made toward its goal so that donors will see progress and be motivated to provide or continue to provide financial support.

Strategy

This objective would be accomplished through an annual survey with results published in an annual report to be distributed to potential and current university funding sources. The strategy would require:

1. An on-line campus climate survey developed and conducted by the center. The survey would be publicized and participation would be encouraged by enabling students who answer several questions to qualify for a drawing in which the winner would receive textbooks free for one quarter.
2. Survey findings would be published by the center in a news release.
3. The center's intern cadre would prepare a by-lined op-ed piece for the director discussing the campus climate survey results and its implications to be submitted in two different versions, one to the Oregon Daily Emerald and the other to The Register-Guard.
4. The survey results would be included in an annual report published by the center and delivered and discussed in one-on-one visits with the center's current and potential university funding sources.

Evaluation

Success in achieving this objective will be determined by completing the survey and annual report, communicating the center's accomplishments to potential and current university funding sources and spot checking feedback from these sources through informal conversations.

TIME LINE

Activities	Target Execution Date
Research name change	
Prepare publicity materials	
ANNOUNCE NEW OR MODIFIED NAME	Martin Luther King Jr. Week 2004
Develop internships and student executive board positions	
Prepare publicity materials	
SELECT INTERNS	Martin Luther King Jr. Week 2004
Identify UO alumni rainmakers employed by potential financial supporters	
Develop fundraising brochure	
Identify potential title sponsor to finance production of diversity medallions	
LAUNCH FUNDRAISING CAMPAIGN	March 2004
Organize meeting of grant recipients	
BEGIN SCHEDULE OF GRADUATE-TO-GRADUATE BRIEFINGS	March 2004
Train cadre of ambassadors to make presentations to student classes	
BEGIN SCHEDULE OF AMBASSADOR PRESENTATIONS	March 2004
Enlist cooperation of U.S. Ambassador to the United Nations	
Coordinate with university president's staff	
Send Ambassador letter w/president's cover letter to faculty	
SEND FOLLOW-UP LETTER TO FACULTY	March 2004
Plan workshop on conflict resolution for student orientation	
CONDUCT WORKSHOP DURING STUDENT ORIENTATION	Orientation Week 2004
Research opportunity to partner in Native American Longhouse dedication	

TIME LINE (continued ...)

Activities	Target Execution Date
PARTICIPATE IN LONGHOUSE DEDICATION	TBA
Plan meeting with Eugene mayor to discuss possible "Diversity Walk"	
Obtain city resolution for "Diversity Walk"	
MANAGE 'DIVERSITY WALK' FOR CITY OF EUGENE	Martin Luther King Jr. Week 2005
Develop on-line campus climate survey	
CONDUCT CAMPUS CLIMATE SURVEY	Martin Luther King Jr. Week 2005
Plan and produce annual report	
PUBLISH ANNUAL REPORT	Martin Luther King Jr. Week 2005
Coordinate with university president's staff	

Evaluation

This plan is written to enable evaluation in two areas: performance and effectiveness. It has a Progress Tracking Report to be issued on a specified schedule to gauge performance in implementing the plan. It has objectives written to enable measurement to judge the plan's effectiveness in accomplishing it's goal. Following is a recap of objectives and means of evaluation:

Objective #1

To attract the interest of corporations and/or professional and business organizations that would like to raise their public profiles in the area of diversity and have them become active participants in and financial supporters of the Center on Diversity and Community.

Evaluation

Success in achieving this objective will be based on total contributions received one year from the time the plan is launched.

Objective #2

To increase graduate student awareness of competitive research grants and conference opportunity available through the center so that more students participate in research on issues of diversity.

Evaluation

Success in achieving this objective will be determined by the external support of the Graduate Student Research Award program, and by increased community attendance at the annual Graduate Research Conference.

Objective #3

To heighten interest among students in the center's undergraduate-focused programs and resources, so that more individuals participate in the organization.

Evaluation

Success in achieving this objective will be determined by the following: internship positions have been filled; major events are regularly and successfully co-sponsored with other university organizations, as measured by attendance, event quality, and other factors; student volunteers made an acceptable number of large class presentations on behalf of the center; a center workshop has been established as part of the student fall orientation; the center participated in the dedication of the Longhouse.

Objective #4

To raise the Eugene community's awareness of the center, its role and activities in the community and on campus, in ways that would motivate community members to get involved and participate in the center and its diversity-related events.

Evaluation

Success in achieving this objective will be based on completing preparations for the events, conducting the actual events and assessing by sign-ups and field observation participation of community residents in the center's activities.

Objective #5

To motivate university faculty and staff to take an interest in and actively support the center and its mission on campus and in the community.

Evaluation

Success in achieving this objective will be based on distribution of the ambassador's letter and sign-ups by faculty and staff in the center's activities for earning Diversity Medallions.

Objective #6

To communicate to potential and current university funding sources the achievements the center has made toward its goal so that donors will see progress and be motivated to provide or continue to provide financial support.

Evaluation

Success in achieving this objective will be determined by completing the survey and annual report, communicating the center's accomplishments to potential and current university funding sources and spot checking feedback from these sources through informal conversations.

ESTIMATED PUBLIC RELATIONS AGENCY BUDGET

For the 10-week period January 5 to March 12, 2004

Staff	*Hours*	*Rate*	
Account executive	30	75.00	2,250.00
Account coordinator	30	65.00	1,950.00
Secretary	40	50.00	2,000.00
General manager	5	150.00	750.00
Subtotals	105		6,950.00

Out-of-pocket Expenses	
Publicity materials	600.00
Production of fundraising brochures	1,000.00
Production of presentations materials	450.00
Production of workshop materials	300.00
Subtotal	2,350.00
TOTAL	9,300.00

Progress Tracking Report (example)

Objective/Audience	Activity	On schedule On target On budget	Behind schedule Off target Over budget	Completed
Objective #1 Donors	Names	�		
	Rainmakers		■	
	Brochure	�		
	Memberships	�		
Objective #2 Graduate Students	Briefings			■
Objective #3 Undergraduate Students	Internships	�		
	Ambassadors	�		
	Workshop		■	
	Longhouse	�		
Objective #4 Community Residents	Inquiry		■	
	Response	�		
	Resolution	�		
	Event	�		
	Tee-shirts	�		
	Award	�		
	Ceremony	�		
	Center/City	�		
	Honoree	�		
Objective #5 University faculty and staff	President	�		
	Ambassador		■	
	Letter Ambassador		■	
	Letter President		■	
	Web site			■
Objective #6 Donors	Survey	�		
	Annual report	�		

SILVER ANVIL AWARD CAMPAIGN PROFILES
From whimsey, to reality, to practice ...

We have taken our orientation on planning from whimsey, to reality. One more step will give us a look at plans developed by professional practitioners. On the following pages, you will find five plans that were among those recognized with Silver Anvil Awards from competition sponsored by Public Relations Society of America. Review the profiles. Copy the worksheet on the following page for each campaign summary and use the form to note your comments and questions for further study and discussion.

Silver Anvil Award summaries were printed with permission from:

Public Relations Society of America

The Icon of Best Public Relations Practices

The Silver Anvil, symbolizing the forging of public opinion, is annually awarded to organizations, which have successfully addressed contemporary issues with exemplary professional skill, creativity and resourcefulness. In the 60-plus year history of the Silver Anvil Awards, more than 1,000 organizations have been recognized with Silver Anvils for excellence in public relations.

Silver Anvil Awards recognize complete programs incorporating sound research, planning, execution and evaluation. They must meet the highest standards of performance in the profession.

WORKSHEET FOR STUDYING AND DISCUSSING PROFESSIONAL PUBLIC RELATIONS PLANS

Use this form to note your comments and questions about the components of the plan summary.

Summary or introductory statement	
Situation analysis	
Research	
Goal	
Focus or target audiences	
Objectives	
Strategies	
Activities or tactics	
Execution timeline	
Evaluation	
Budget	

 Public Relations Society of America

Product #: 6BW-0913A04

Format: Campaign Profile-A two-page summary of a Silver-Anvil Award winner, addressing research, planning, execution and evaluation.

Title: Allstate Insurance Company Southeast Region Employee Engagement Strategy

Silver-Anvil Award Winner

Allstate Insurance Company, **2009**

Summary: 2009 Silver Anvil Award Winner – Internal Communications – Business (Fewer Than 10,000 Employees)

Allstate's Southeast Region created an Employee Engagement Committee (EEC) to improve employee engagement, to focus on driving a cultural shift through grassroots communication, and to increase positive responses on an employee engagement survey. As tactics, this committee introduced employee events including: community workdays, a regional library, Bring Your Child to Work Day, and Lunch and Learn sessions. The team was successful in leading an overall positive engagement shift and contributed to moving Southeast regional employees from 2nd tier agreement levels ("agree") to top line agreement ("strongly agree") on engagement index questions.

Full Text: BACKGROUND:

Allstate introduced a new initiative to align its employees around its vision for the future. Since this rollout would require a culture change throughout the company, Allstate's leadership asked Allstate regional leaders to implement engagement plans in all 14 of Allstate's operating regions. Allstate's Southeast region is headquartered in Atlanta, and the Southeast Assistant Field Vice President contacted Allstate's Corporate Relations (CR) internal communications consultant for assistance. Since highly engaged team members are usually informal opinion leaders within an organization, the Southeast leadership team saw the need to engage employees to drive this cultural shift from a grassroots level to augment this culture change initiative. Although this employee engagement project initially began to assist with the initiative implementation, it expanded to become a vehicle to drive overall employee engagement. The primary goal was to increase employee engagement as measured by EEC surveys and annual Quality Leadership Measurement Survey (QLMS) results.

RESEARCH:

Primary Research
The employee focus group, which later evolved into the EEC, was the primary research vehicle to help the region determine how best to align the region with Allstate's updated vision and to increase employee engagement. This group was made up of 12 non-managerial employees, and care was taken to ensure diverse representation. A pre-focus group meeting survey was conducted with all committee members.

The EEC examined variety of topics:
a) what engagement means to employees,
b) what is the current perception of employee engagement within the region, and
c) how do regional employees feel that they could improve engagement.

Specific questions were geared toward what is defined as an "Engagement Index" to measure an employee's connectedness to the company, willingness to exert extra effort, and desire to remain with the organization.

Highlights of the survey—confirmed by discussion—included opportunities within the areas of:

o Career development:
Less than 70% of group felt that the company and region were interested in advancing their career development. Further group discussion in this area revealed interesting point—not all development has to lead to advancement. A number of members, while most comfortable in their current position, consider the opportunity to branch out, learn and grow as development. This point also led to the idea that there is business value (via engagement) in assisting with emotional / life development of employees as well.

o Work / life balance:
General discussions with the group revealed a desire to incorporate family into work life during occasional events.

The statement was shared that people naturally become more connected to one another when they can get to know the person outside work. The region did not have integrated activities where employees could interact outside the work environment (such as intramural sports, or community projects).

o Communication regarding company programs / services:
Many employees were not aware of existing programs and offerings the company already has in place to support employees.

Secondary Research:
Allstate surveys its employees yearly via a QLMS to gauge overall employee satisfaction with the company work environment, and this data was used to serve as a baseline for measurement of regional efforts to improve engagement and identify potential opportunity areas.

Outside Research:
A number of web / periodical articles were researched before beginning focus group. The best conversation-starter article was a Wall Street Journal article that outlined activities of highly engaged companies. Web research was used in order to prepare CR representative for task ahead and to use as pre-read for focus group to spark conversations, thoughts, and ideas.

PLANNING:

The creation of the EEC was an idea that resulted from the extensive research phase. For example, one of the companies mentioned in the Wall Street Journal article employed a similar entity. Focus group findings, reinforced by QLMS data, pointed to certain opportunity areas which would be the main focus of the EEC with a target audience of regional employees and regional leadership:
o Employee development (including career, emotional, and life development)
o Communication regarding existing programs and offerings the company already has in place to support employees, as well as enhanced 2-way communication to allow EEC members to advocate for Company initiatives while also providing anonymous, real-time feedback to regional leadership without formal surveys.
o Esprit de Corps: Promote, encourage, create, and execute activities that promote connectedness and interconnectedness among Southeast Regional employees

The general plan was that a CR consultant, armed with findings from the QLMS and focus group, would present the proposal to Southeast Region leadership to allow for formal creation of the EEC. The CR consultant would serve as committee chair and liaison between leadership and EEC with an approved budget of $14,000.

This EEC offered a unique measurement challenge because Allstate's Southeast regional employees already had strong numbers on engagement index questions. For example, the region scored in the low 90th or high 80th percentile on majority of questions such as 93% favorable response to question Q.29: "Considering everything, how would you rate your overall satisfaction with Allstate?" The EEC goal was to make employee engagement even stronger—as measured by QLMS and compared with 2007 level used as baseline.

The opportunity areas (lower scores from 2007) included:
o Q.38—How would you rate Allstate as a company to work for compared to other companies (83% said either 'above average' or 'one of the best'—this represented a 9% drop from 2006)
o Q.28—If the choice is mine I will be working for Allstate in 3 years (82% favorable)
o Q.21—How do you rate your overall benefits program (84% favorable)
o Q.16—I feel I am paid competitively for the work I do (61% favorable)

Goals: 5% top line movement across all engagement index questions and to improve all questions identified as EEC opportunity areas.

EXECUTION:

With the permission of regional leadership, the EEC was formed. The committee:
o Developed a set of bylaws to govern operation.
o Formed sub-committees with chairs acted as team leads for committee initiatives.
o Promoted committee with theme "Everyone Counts" and logo.
    o Secured time in each quarterly regional meeting to discuss committee activities/projects
    o Collaborated with other regional committees such as Well & Fit fitness and Helping Hands volunteerism committees
o Rolled out committee initiatives such as book clubs, regional blog, regional library, lunch and Learns, Quarterly Community Work Days, and Bring Your Child to Work Day.

EVALUATION

The EEC contributed to positive 2008 SE regional employee engagement results. There were no 2008 decreases from 2007 survey levels with any of the employee engagement index questions; instead, the team led an overall positive engagement shift and contributed to moving Southeast regional employees from 2nd tier agreement levels ("agree") to top line agreement ("strongly agree") on engagement index questions.

WORKSHEET FOR STUDYING AND DISCUSSING PROFESSIONAL PUBLIC RELATIONS PLANS

Use this form to note your comments and questions about the components of the plan summary.

Summary or introductory statement	
Situation analysis	
Research	
Goal	
Focus or target audiences	
Objectives	
Strategies	
Activities or tactics	
Execution timeline	
Evaluation	
Budget	

 Public
Relations
Society of
America

Product #: 6BW-0901D02

Format: Campaign Profile-A two-page summary of a Silver-Anvil Award winner, addressing research, planning, execution and evaluation.

Title: Spike & Biscuit Rebrand The Charleston Animal Society

Silver-Anvil Award Winner

Charleston Animal Society, Rawle Murdy, **2009**

Summary: 2009 Silver Anvil Award Winner – Community Relations – Associations / Nonprofit Organizations

The non-profit John Ancrum Society for the Prevention of Cruelty to Animals (JASPCA) struggled with an overcrowded facility, virtually no name recognition and a poor community profile. Rawle Murdy helped the JASPCA redefine its image and raise community awareness of its mission and new location. The campaign rebranded the organization, increased visitation, boosted adoptions and educated area residents on issues like spaying/neutering by building buzz through a fun, interactive presidential election between a dog and cat. The campaign successfully repositioned the Charleston Animal Society as a positive force in the community culminating in a record number of adoptions in 2008.

Full Text: SITUATION ANALYSIS:

When the John Ancrum Society for the Prevention of Cruelty to Animals (JASPCA) prepared to open a new $11 million center, it faced a tough reality. Although the non-profit group had found good homes for great animals for more than a century, it was virtually unknown in the greater Charleston, S.C. community. Recognizing the new center as a landmark opportunity, Rawle Murdy volunteered to help JASPCA leadership redefine its image and raise community awareness of its mission. The ensuing pro bono campaign set out to increase visitation, boost adoptions and educate area residents on messages like the importance of spaying/neutering.

RESEARCH:

Rawle Murdy set out to uncover why pet owners historically have not turned to JASPCA. We conducted our own primary research by surveying 100 locals, conducting on-the-street interviews, and speaking with vets and pet store owners. Secondary research involved mining the Internet for historical information and local message boards for opinions, as well as reviewing JASPCA's historical data and comment cards.

This research indicated Charleston County residents barely knew the JASPCA existed. An estimated one in three locals owned a pet, but most either adopted them through rescue centers and newspaper ads or purchased them at pet stores and breeders. The few familiar with the JASPCA believed it was an old, run down, dirty "kill" shelter for diseased and unwanted animals. In fact, this non-profit has been the place for Charleston animals in need of care since 1880. No animals are turned away…ever – a strong point of differentiation from other local shelters. Moreover, many mistook the center as a government-funded facility when it actually depended on private donations.

PLANNING:

Rawle Murdy's challenge was to create a campaign that didn't use the guilt strategies commonly employed by animal shelters nationwide to drive adoptions and donations. We worked closely with JASPCA staff to identify business goals and communication objectives that would drive the strategic campaign and effect meaningful change

Business goals:
1) Build positive credibility
2) Boost the number of animal adoptions.
3) Educate the public on the importance of spay/neuter and other JASPCA messages.

Rawle Murdy recommended changing JASPCA's name to the much more identifiable Charleston Animal Society (CAS). We then shook up its approach to public outreach, using humor and irreverence in messaging and collateral.

Through research we knew the target audiences were:
1) Local animal lovers who have adopted or purchased pets elsewhere, supported other organizations, were

unfamiliar with JASPCA or have supported JASPCA in the past and needed to know about the upcoming name change.
2) Pet-related businesses.
3) Veterinarians.
4) Media.

The public relations objectives were to:
1) Establish consistent messaging to tell the positive story and build excitement.
2) Identify 1-2 speaking opportunities or public engagements each month where CAS could demonstrate community leadership.
3) Secure 5-7 local placements prior to and 5-7 post the new center opening.
4) Plan and execute a grand opening event.
5) Identify 5 key pet-related businesses for potential partnerships.

Rawle Murdy's awareness strategy contained four essential elements:
1) Build buzz and entertain locals through a fun, interactive political campaign tapping into the current climate (S.C. was an early presidential primary state).
2) Intrigue people to seek more details online.
3) Stage a mock presidential election between a dog and a cat.
4) Spread CAS key messages via candidates' platforms on a continuous basis instead of a one-time re-naming and center opening announcement. The Public Relations Budget was $19,207 with an equal amount donated in time. Paid media and production vendors doubled our limited budget by matching the spend 2:1 across the board.

EXECUTION:

In late 2007 and early 2008, the U.S. presidential candidates and primaries transfixed Charleston. In the midst of this chatter, we unleashed the CAS's rebranding campaign. With our tongues firmly planted in cheek (and a nod to Stephen Colbert), we offered up two additional candidates for President, Spike the Dog and Biscuit the Cat. (See enclosed DVD containing news release with embedded audio file of candidates). These two CAS alumni — both successfully adopted into loving homes — on November 27, 2007 announced their respective candidacies for President of the newly-renamed Charleston Animal Society and its new center for animals.

The intensive, four-month public relations campaign served up a political race, mimicking and spoofing storylines playing out in national headlines. Through the combination of public relations, community relations, social media, paid media and grassroots strategies, word spread quickly.

Each candidate developed platforms (Spike: Adoption and Animal Rights. Biscuit: Healthcare and Owner Education). Weekly updates from each campaign announced key endorsements, introduced new campaign commercials and sometimes even alleged dirty tactics. They candidates made public appearances and mobilized the College of Charleston vote with a campus information booth. Political posters were displayed in more than 100 stores and restaurants, and campaign collateral hit 75 local veterinarians, kennels, groomers, and pet stores – both at the start of the campaign and again before Election Day/Grand Opening. Biscuit's spokes-human the CAS Director of Outreach garnered exposure for Biscuit's campaign on her weekly radio and TV appearances, while Spike's spokes-human CAS Board of Directors Chairman used his influence to gain local mayoral endorsements. Rawle Murdy supported both efforts by "scratching up" Biscuit and Spike endorsements from numerous key community leaders.

The spikeVSbiscuit.org Web site was the hub for campaign details and information, linking to the candidates' diaries on Facebook, campaign commercials on YouTube, and to charlestonanimalsociety.org for building construction updates and campaign contributions. As word continued to build, profiles on Catster and Dogster emerged, and the weekly YouTube videos were distributed via eNewsletter, news releases and virally. Billboards, print ads, interactive media and radio traffic sponsorships also helped leverage the public relations effort.

The ensuing buzz was unlike any the area—and the country, it soon became clear—had seen from a non-profit marketing campaign before. Media covered the hype, community leaders took sides and citizens began donning campaign buttons. A reporter from The New York Times—among many outlets that covered the race was among the first to call the morning after the final poll, eager to find out who won. Rawle Murdy planned to have a third-party candidate enter the race as a "dark horse" candidate, but that happened naturally when Hissy the Snake jumped in and called a local radio station. Several bunnies were write-in candidates on Election Day.

The new center for animals opened on March 8, 2008, with local leaders, elected officials and the Charleston community pouring in to show their support and adopt pets in record numbers. A small army of Rawle Murdy and CAS volunteers hosted center tours, games and pet fashion shows while supporters donated free refreshments. During the grand opening ceremony, which Rawle Murdy wrote and produced, Spike was declared the winner and first ever President of the Charleston Animal Society by 86 votes, out of a total 3,780 votes. The crowed cheered when he graciously invited Biscuit to serve as Vice President, and again when staff, community leaders, animals and their guardians together pulled a giant dog toy (instead of cutting a ribbon) to officially open the new center.

EVALUATION:

We measured the success of the campaign by:
1) Adoptions compared to 2007.
2) Media hits and key and the presence of key messages
3) Social media penetration: Daily voting on Web site; Web site click throughs and page views; Facebook, Catster, Dogster friends; YouTube viewing of candidate videos; opens on eNewsletters.
4) Fulfilling PR objectives. The entire campaign revitalized the center with an ongoing brand, successfully positioning the Charleston Animal Society as a positive force in the community.

Adoptions:
CAS had record-breaking adoption numbers for the opening weekend – 29 adoptions on Saturday and 13 on Sunday. CAS had 82 more adoptions in March 2008 than from the March prior. In April, that number increased to 114 more than the year before. In 2008, 4,407 animals were saved compared to 3,944 in 2007 – a 12% increase and a 22% increase from 2006!

Media Hits:
38 print, radio, TV and online media hits were secured ?almost three times the goal with an estimated ad equivalency value of $297,486. And more importantly, all stories included messages related to the name change, the organization's mission, the services available to the community and the need for support.

Social Media Penetration:
The spikeVSbiscuit.org pages were viewed more than 10,000 times, and traffic to the Charleston Animal Society Web site increased a sustained 100,000+ monthly visitors year over year, surging to more than 680,000 hits in March 2008. More than 268 people signed on as "friends" of Spike or Biscuit on their respective Facebook pages, and a "Vote for Spike!" fan group even formed. Campaign commercials posted to YouTube racked up more than 4,300 views. Over the course of the campaign, a total of 3,780 online votes were cast.

We surpassed all five objectives
1) messaging/build excitement;
2) public engagements;
3) media placements;
4) grand opening event and
5) relationships with key pet businesses.
In the ultimate compliment, the New York ASPCA which announced Charleston as the only city in the nation to be awarded a special grant in 2008? "borrowed" the pet presidential race concept and is currently staging its own version.

WORKSHEET FOR STUDYING AND DISCUSSING PROFESSIONAL PUBLIC RELATIONS PLANS

Use this form to note your comments and questions about the components of the plan summary.

Summary or introductory statement	
Situation analysis	
Research	
Goal	
Focus or target audiences	
Objectives	
Strategies	
Activities or tactics	
Execution timeline	
Evaluation	
Budget	

 Public Relations Society of America

Product #: 6BW-0911B03

Format: Campaign Profile-A two-page summary of a Silver-Anvil Award winner, addressing research, planning, execution and evaluation.

Title: Putting Lessons Learned to Work: Managing Communications After a Campus Shooting - Northern Illinois University Office of Public Affairs, 2008

Silver-Anvil Award Winner

Northern Illinois University, **2009**

Summary: 2009 Silver Anvil Award Winner – Crisis Communications – Government

Shortly after 3 p.m. on February 14, 2008, a gunman burst onto the stage of a large NIU lecture hall and began firing into an audience of nearly 150 undergraduates. Within three minutes, six people (including the gunman) lay dead, and 19 others were injured. In the minutes, hours and days that followed, NIU Public Affairs successfully managed all aspects of crisis communications, from emergency alerts, news conferences and message development to media relations, event management and speechwriting. One year later, campus, community, media and professional audiences call NIU's response exemplary. More importantly, the university has emerged from crisis with its reputation as a safe and caring institution intact, without threat of legal action, and inspired by an increase in applications from prospective students.

Full Text: SUMMARY

Shortly after 3 p.m. on February 14, 2008, a gunman burst onto the stage of a large NIU lecture hall and began firing into an audience of nearly 150 undergraduates. Within three minutes, six people (including the gunman) lay dead, and 19 others were injured. In the minutes, hours and days that followed, NIU Public Affairs successfully managed all aspects of crisis communications, from emergency alerts, news conferences and message development to media relations, event management and speechwriting. One year later, campus, community, media and professional audiences call NIU's response exemplary. More importantly, the university has emerged from crisis with its reputation as a safe and caring institution intact, without threat of legal action, and inspired by an increase in applications from prospective students.

RESEARCH

The terrorist attacks of September 11, 2001 prompted NIU President John Peters to call for increased attention to campus emergency preparedness. To that end, NIU Public Affairs staff attended crisis communications workshops, participated in teleconference seminars and read books and articles by crisis communications experts, including "Crisis Communications: A Casebook Approach" by Kathleen Fearn-Banks; "Crisis-Proof Your Organization" by James E. Lukaszewski; and "Basic Guidelines for PIOs" by the Federal Emergency Management Administration, or FEMA. Information and best practices prescribed in those publications and presentations greatly informed revisions to NIU's crisis communications plan in the first half of this decade, as did departmental participation in development of a campus-wide Emergency Operations Plan and mock disaster drills.

The Virginia Tech shootings in April 2007 stunned the higher education community, eliciting even greater calls for campus preparedness. NIU Public Affairs worked hard to glean lessons from Virginia Tech: NIU's webmaster spoke with her Virginia Tech counterpart to learn new web communication techniques; the department head attended a national higher education meeting at which Virginia Tech administrators shared lessons learned; and Public Affairs staff participated in an exhaustive, line-by-line review of the Virginia Tech Review Panel report. The NIU crisis communications plan enacted on February 14, 2008 was greatly informed by the collective wisdom of the aforementioned experts, as well as the generosity of our counterparts at Virginia Tech.

PLANNING

Based on what they had learned through practice, research and consultation other university peers, NIU's crisis communications planning included the following objectives:

o Provide emergency alert information as quickly as possible to students, faculty and staff -- no time for meetings prior to first alerts

o Keep all audiences (particularly students and parents) as widely informed as possible throughout crisis
o Use website to provide updates to all audiences – including news-hungry media
o Treat news media as partners – they have communication tools necessary to reach primary audiences
o Maintain institutional credibility through maximum timely disclosure
o Manage the message: Victims and their families are our first priority
o Reestablish/reinforce reputation as safe and caring campus community

In the months leading up to February 14th, 2008, NIU's crisis communications plan was tested twice: First, a late August downpour caused flooding that required total campus-evacuation on the day before the fall semester started. A second and more serious incident occurred in December when a racially-charged threat was found in a residence hall bathroom and repeated on a website, necessitating a one-day campus closure. In both instances, NIU Public Affairs successfully enacted its crisis communications plan and updated its procedures based on lessons learned.

One such modification bears special attention: A review of website traffic following the December threat revealed the need for additional server space to handle unusually large visitor spikes. Six new servers were purchased and dedicated to website support – a move that took on special significance during the February 14 crisis, when website traffic numbered in the millions.

EXECUTION

o First emergency alerts (web, email, voicemail, hotline) completed at 3:20, less than fifteen minutes after shooting (plan required only simple authorization from president, no meeting or discussion required prior to initial alerts)
o Website quickly became " information central," with automatic repostings to Facebook
o Arranged and presided over six news conferences, the first at 5:30 p.m., less than 2 ½ hours after last shot was fired; 200 - 300 reporters and photographers were present at each
o Participated in hourly meetings of president's crisis management group; led message development and spokesperson preparation
o President positioned as "public face" of university; messages of sympathy, caring and determination developed
o Established media center in Altgeld Hall (administration building); auditorium used for formal briefings fully equipped with multiple feed boxes and other technology for broadcast media; also opened up two large conference rooms near auditorium, enabled wi-fi access in each, and regularly supplied food and drinks for media
o Worked with building services and campus police to facilitate parking of 25+ satellite trucks nearby
o Streamed all news conferences and subsequent events live on Internet
o Facilitated dozens of individual interviews with president, police chief and other spokespersons during first 48 hours; Assistant Vice President for Public Affairs also served as spokesperson; greatest attention on local and regional media who cover NIU regularly
o Created and distributed campus maps, graphics, logos, photos, biographies of victims, b-roll footage, etc.
o Worked closely with counterparts at Kishwaukee Hospital and with coroner on release of information about victims (did not release names of wounded, though many came forward and identified themselves to media)
o Prepared talking points, speeches, letters, all-campus emails, etc. Originated use of "Forward, Together Forward" motto (a line from the NIU fight song) as symbol of healing and recovery
o Participated in planning of memorial service on February 24; more than 12,000 people attended
o Created memorial website with application that allowed visitors to leave messages of condolence and hope
o Continued to manage media and messages throughout following year, culminating in one-year anniversary observance on February 14, 2009

EVALUATION

One year later, NIU is a stronger and more unified campus than ever before. Much of that strength derives from positive assessments –both internal and external – of the university's crisis response.

o The Illinois Governor's Task Force on Campus Security issued a report praising NIU's response, singling out the Office of Public Affairs for excellence in crisis communications.
o The U.S. Department of Homeland Security commissioned a report on the NIU incident in which crisis communications is likewise held up as exemplary.
o The Chicago Tribune called NIU's response "textbook crisis management," and praised the institution for "transparency and candor."
o NBC Nightly News with Charles Gibson named NIU its "Person of the Week" for its handling of the crisis and the resolve of its campus community to not let an act of violence define the university.
o Applications from prospective students continue to rise, and only 19 of 300+ students directly affected by the shooting left the university.
o NIU Public Affairs staff are in demand as speakers and consultants for other universities developing crisis plans
o No lawsuits have been filed in connection with the February 14, 2008 shooting.
o Spontaneous (and unsolicited) gifts for scholarships and memorials total more than $1 million.

WORKSHEET FOR STUDYING AND DISCUSSING PROFESSIONAL PUBLIC RELATIONS PLANS

Use this form to note your comments and questions about the components of the plan summary.

Summary or introductory statement	
Situation analysis	
Research	
Goal	
Focus or target audiences	
Objectives	
Strategies	
Activities or tactics	
Execution timeline	
Evaluation	
Budget	

 Public
Relations
Society of
America

Product #: 6BW-0902C17

Format: Campaign Profile-A two-page summary of a Silver-Anvil Award winner, addressing research, planning, execution and evaluation.

Title: Brown Goes Green: Telling The UPS Environmental Story

Silver-Anvil Award Winner

UPS, Fleishman-Hillard, **2009**

Summary: 2009 Silver Anvil Award Winner – Reputation / Brand Management – Business – Companies With Sales Over $10 Billion

With 99,000 vehicles logging 2 billion miles a year, UPS has a considerable carbon footprint. And the company is transparent in reporting its emissions – the data is supplied in the UPS Corporate Sustainability Report. Further, when businesses ask for data about emissions associated with the packages UPS delivers for them, the company supplies the data. It was the skyrocketing number of these requests that created the need for an aggressive communications program showing that "Brown Goes Green." The program's nearly 500 media placements totaling 97.5 million impressions reached UPS customers, who increasingly asked to benchmark their environmental programs against UPS's

Full Text: OVERVIEW:

With more than 99,000 delivery vehicles logging 2 billion miles a year, not to mention the world's ninth-largest airline, UPS has a considerable carbon footprint – especially when you consider that it delivers 15.5 million packages and documents globally each day. And the company is absolutely transparent in reporting its carbon emissions – the data is supplied in the annual UPS Corporate Sustainability Report. Further, when businesses ask for data about carbon emissions associated with the packages UPS delivers for them, the company gladly supplies the data.

It was the skyrocketing number of these requests that generated the need for a more aggressive communications program to inform customers that UPS is extremely focused on reducing excess emissions. And by turning up the volume on this story, a greener picture of UPS would emerge – a company with sophisticated technologies and a relentless 101-year focus on operational efficiency and sustainability. A company continually challenging itself to be more efficient, more responsible, and more sustainable.

With this in mind, UPS and Fleishman-Hillard created a sustained 2008 communications campaign to weave together nine discreet programs into a single tapestry of green hues. It was an effort to show how "Brown Goes Green."

RESEARCH:

The most authoritative voice in any company is not that of the CEO – it's the customer's voice. In 2007 and early 2008, UPS began to see an increase in the number of requests from key business customers for data about the carbon footprint associated with UPS's delivery of their packages. Research showed that, in the first quarter of 2008, the number of such customer requests increased 243 percent. This trend continued throughout 2008, with full-year customer requests growing 237 percent compared with 2007. Clearly, UPS's environmental programs were becoming increasingly important to customers and to UPS's bottom line.

PLANNING:

This rise in customer interest in UPS's environmental impact illustrated the need for a program to showcase the ways UPS minimizes that impact. The PR channel was identified as a key way to reach customers and the broader public with messages about UPS's environmental stewardship. While UPS for some time had been communicating its environmental stewardship, there clearly was a need to turn up the volume with an aggressive media relations program in 2008. The keys to success would be to develop provable green messages, strategically target the right media, and deliver "out-of-the-box" thinking. The program spanned nine UPS environmental stories and news announcements throughout 2008, with each illustrating UPS's commitment to operating the most efficient delivery network and, by doing so, reducing its environmental impact.

Objectives:
o Position UPS as a company committed to environmental responsibility by showcasing initiatives with positive environmental impacts that are measurable
o Highlight the technologies UPS uses to be more efficient and reduce its environmental impact.

Target Audiences:
o Current and prospective UPS customers.
o Investors, employees, and UPS stakeholders.
o Third parties such as non-governmental organizations.
o Elected and appointed public officials.

Budget: While UPS prefers that budget details not be disclosed, 20 percent of Fleishman-Hillard's 2008 professional services budget for UPS was allocated to this effort.

EXECUTION:

Beginning in early 2008 and lasting through November, the team aggressively pursued media coverage of nine green stories. The key was identifying solid proof points that showed how UPS minimizes its environmental impact, enabling UPS's stories to be heard above the din of other green stories.

A look at the nine stories:
1) UPS Avoids Left Turns To Reduce Emissions:
To minimize its environmental impact, UPS deploys a high-tech route-planning system to reduce the number of miles driven. The key is minimizing left turns, which require drivers to idle at intersections to wait for traffic to pass, burning excess fuel and generating excess emissions. The team aggressively pitched this story to top media in connection with Earth Day 2008. Research conducted by UPS provided statistics showing that the "no left turns" initiative:
o Shaves nearly 30 million miles a year from routes – enough miles for more than 60 round-trips to the moon.
o Reduces emissions by 32,000 metric tons of CO_2 – the equivalent of removing 5,200 passenger cars from roadways for an entire year.
o Saves 3 million gallons of gas annually.

2) UPS Deploys Eco-Friendly Vehicles:
Targeting media in a California city with some of the nation's worst air quality might seem strange for a delivery company seeking positive environmental coverage, but it was part of an intensive print, broadcast, and online media blitz as UPS rolled out compressed natural gas (CNG) vehicles in Dallas, Atlanta, and five cities in California in March 2008. This announcement helped showcase UPS's alternative fuels vehicle (AFV) fleet – the largest private fleet in the transportation industry.

3) UPS Places World's Largest Hybrid Vehicle Order:
A May 2008 news release announcing the world's largest hybrid vehicle order was not finalized by UPS until 5 p.m. the day before the announcement. To generate a burst of national media coverage on announcement day and spark additional interest, the team offered an exclusive to USA Today for use in its Money section briefs column. That placement helped fuel the next day's aggressive national media outreach.

4) UPS Reduces Idling To Save Emissions:
Similar to the "no left turns" initiative, UPS deploys sophisticated telematics technology to monitor vehicle performance. UPS discovered that reducing idling during the delivery day can reduce emissions. In fact, idling a medium-duty gasoline vehicle for five minutes a day can emit as much as 300 pounds of CO_2 a year. In the end, the company helped drivers reduce idling by 24 minutes a day. Armed with these statistics, the team aggressively pitched the story.

5) UPS Paperless Invoice Makes Going Global Greener:
In June 2008, UPS unveiled a new product to help customers more easily conduct global trade – and do so without having to generate as much paperwork as normally required when goods cross borders. Garnering coverage of this product would not only help UPS generate revenue but also showcase the company's environmental commitment because research showed that the product saves about two pallets of copy paper per year and about 150 toner cartridges.

6) UPS Delivers For Solar Car Race Team:
Solar cars depend on the weather to run, so targeting USA Today's "The Weather Guys" for a story about UPS engineers helping University of Kentucky students build a solar car was spot on.

7) UPS Takes Cool Approach To Data Center Efficiency:
Even in its data centers, UPS strives to reduce energy use. And the energy-efficiency innovations at a UPS data

center were perfect angles for pitching and a byline article.

8) UPS First To Purchase Hydraulic Hybrid Vehicles:
A request for "out-of-the-box" strategies to optimize a traditional news conference led the team to a partnership with a respected environmental Web site – TriplePundit.com. The Atlanta media event in October 2008 was broadcast live on TriplePundit.com, which also sent one of its bloggers to Atlanta for the event. In addition to announcing UPS's purchase of hydraulic hybrid vehicles, the event also featured a panel discussion with executives from UPS and hydraulic hybrid innovators Eaton Corp. and Navistar, as well as a U.S. Environmental Protection Agency representative.

9) UPS Adopts Paperless Printing Solution:
In November 2008, UPS announced a new technology that enables package handlers to scan barcodes and print package-handling instructions directly onto packages, eliminating paper labels. Attached to the wrist, this device saves UPS 1,338 tons of paper a year and enabled UPS to end 2008 on a solidly green note.

EVALUATION:

Customers responded positively. The UPS Customer Solutions Group reported a jump in 2008 in the number of requests from companies asking to benchmark their green programs against UPS's programs, as well as an increase in requests for help from UPS on their own environmental initiatives. Meanwhile, aggressive media relations generated nearly 500 placements and 97.5 million impressions.

Here's a look at the success of each initiative:

1) UPS Avoids Left Turns:
A deluge of "no left turns" coverage began with an April 2008 placement in Parade, the nation's largest consumer magazine with a Sunday circulation of 32.2 million. In the wake of the Parade story, UPS began fielding daily calls from other media wanting to cover the story. In total, the Parade placement generated 110 major print, broadcast, and online placements, including "The CBS Early Show," USA Today, and, astoundingly, a second Parade placement in July 2008. Total impressions: 76.9 million.

2) UPS Deploys Eco-Friendly Vehicles:
Key placements included the Sacramento Business Journal, the Los Angeles Business Journal, FresnoBee.com, and The Business Journal in Fresno. Total impressions: 928,000.

3) UPS Places Hybrid Vehicle Order:
Customers opening their USA Today on May 13, 2008, read a brief in the Money section on UPS's hybrid vehicle order, sparking national coverage by The Associated Press, The Wall Street Journal, and others. Total impressions: 7.8 million.

4) UPS Reduces Idling:
"Brown Continues Getting Greener," announced TriplePundit.com about UPS's reduced idling initiative. This and other stories netted 281,000 impressions.

5) UPS Paperless Invoice:
Coverage on Forbes.com, CNNMoney.com, USAToday.com, BusinessWeek.com, and elsewhere generated 1.2 million impressions.

6) UPS Delivers For Solar Team:
The USA Today "Weather Guys" posted a story and a UPS video about the project, as did top environmental sites TriplePundit.com, GreenerAssets.com, and others. Impressions: 402,000.

7) UPS Takes Cool Approach To Data Center:
Top green outlet Environmental Leader featured a UPS byline article, while TriplePundit.com published a substantial article.

8) UPS Purchases Hydraulic Hybrid Vehicles: The news conference attracted national attention from CNN, CNN.com, The Associated Press, and Bloomberg. And the live Webcast was viewed on TriplePundit.com by 1,100 online visitors. Total impressions for all coverage: 6.3 million.

9) UPS Goes Paperless:
Results included coverage in 71 outlets and 3.7 million impressions. Notable placements: The Associated Press, Reuters, TreeHugger.com, and the Atlanta Journal-Constitution.

10) UPS Issues Sustainability Report, Wins Awards:

Finally, UPS in 2008 issued its fifth Corporate Sustainability Report and earned these green honors: EPA's SmartWay Excellence Award; Dow Jones Sustainability North America Index; Working Mother "Best Green Companies for America's Children"; Uptime Institute Green Enterprise IT Award; Alternative Fuel Institute's Green Fleet Award; and Supply & Demand Chain Executive's Green Supply Chain Award.

WORKSHEET FOR STUDYING AND DISCUSSING
PROFESSIONAL PUBLIC RELATIONS PLANS

Use this form to note your comments and questions about the components of the plan summary.

Summary or introductory statement	
Situation analysis	
Research	
Goal	
Focus or target audiences	
Objectives	
Strategies	
Activities or tactics	
Execution timeline	
Evaluation	
Budget	

 Public
Relations
Society of
America

Product #: 6BW-0901B26

Format: Campaign Profile-A two-page summary of a Silver-Anvil Award winner, addressing research, planning, execution and evaluation.

Title: The New UTC: Building Community Support for a $1 Billion Shopping Expansion and Revitalization

Silver-Anvil Award Winner

Westfield, Southwest Strategies, **2009**

Summary: 2009 Silver Anvil Award Winner – Community Relations – Business Services

Westfield hired Southwest Strategies in 2003 to develop and implement a comprehensive community relations program to build support for the company's proposed $1 billion expansion and renovation of its UTC shopping center in San Diego. The project, dubbed "The New UTC," includes three new department stores, 150 boutiques, eight new restaurants, two food courts, a new movie theater, a transit center and 250 residential units. After nearly five years of hard work with the San Diego community, the San Diego City Council voted 7-to-1 to approve The New UTC, making it one of the largest privately financed development projects in the history of San Diego.

Full Text: OVERVIEW

Southwest Strategies (SWS) was hired by Westfield Corporation in 2003 to develop a community relations program to advocate the public and develop build support for the company's proposed $1 billion expansion and renovation of its UTC shopping center in San Diego. To proceed, Westfield needed to secure a vote of approval from the San Diego City Council. The project, dubbed The New UTC, would add three new department stores, 150 specialty shops, up to eight new restaurants, two food courts, a new 14 screen movie theater, a $22 million transit center, 10 acres of solar power on parking garages and 250 housing units to the existing site. The New UTC would be one of the largest privately financed development projects in the history of San Diego.

RESEARCH

SWS initially recommended a comprehensive research program to better understand the community's perception of the existing shopping center, as well as to help identify potential messages that would resonate with the public. Previous efforts to develop a message platform were unsuccessful because the company's message was fragmented. As a result, a more focused effort was developed, which was comprised of four parts. Ultimately, this resulted in more than 1,000 personal contacts with shoppers, local residents, business owners, elected officials and key opinion leaders. Each is described below:

o Key opinion leader audit
SWS interviewed 20 elected officials and key opinion leaders to get a perspective from those who shape policies and make decisions in San Diego. The results were crucial in developing the right kind of information for opinion leaders. Smart growth, infrastructure and traffic were top issues of concern for this group.

o Public opinion survey
Various concerns emerged from telephone interviews with more than 400 San Diegans throughout the City. This target audience was far more concerned with entertainment options and specific stores that might be offered at the new shopping center. Participants also expressed concerns about increased traffic and how the development would impact the quality of life in surrounding neighborhoods.
o Dial session/focus group
SWS also worked with Westfield to coordinate an enhanced focus group with a handheld dial that allowed participants to measure their support or opposition to specific issues in real-time by turning the device in different directions. Through this session, Westfield learned that shoppers and other important audiences wanted a "green" shopping center that used sustainable materials and designs.
o Parent survey
Nearly 300 parents at the UTC playground were also interviewed. The purpose was to determine how Westfield could improve amenities for local families. The most common response was more shaded areas for parents.

To address the results of the research, four distinct messages were developed. They were....
The New UTC:

1) represents the evolution of a place that is casual, yet sophisticated;
2) integrates environmentally friendly practices and sustainable designs;
3) boosts the regional economy by creating jobs and generating tax revenues; and
4) preserves the convenient, hassle-free nature of the shopping center.
Using this information, SWS developed a targeted community relations program.

PLANNING

Due to the sheer size of the project, SWS recommended that Westfield secure third-party support both locally and regionally. Local support would be particularly important given that many of Westfield's neighbors had previously expressed concerns about the projected increase in traffic and degradation of their quality of life resulting from the project. In addition, opponents would quickly seize on the idea that approving this project would set a bad precedent for the community, allowing other developers in the surrounding areas to seek major expansions of their properties. As a result, Westfield and SWS agreed on a plan to identify, educate and mobilize credible third parties that would be able to reinforce the project messages (or strengths). It was also decided that project support would be measured by collecting signed support cards and letters of support in favor of the project. Plan details are below.

Objective
SWS initially established a goal of identifying 2,000 support cards (500 neighbors) from San Diegans and securing endorsements from influential regional organizations.

Strategy
Recognizing the project would face stiff local opposition, SWS set out to "break even" with local neighbors, while winning the support of regional leaders.

Target audiences
UTC shoppers, neighbors, key opinion leaders, regional organizations, San Diego City staff, the San Diego City Planning Commission and the San Diego City Council were all audiences.

Materials
In conjunction with Westfield, SWS developed a number of materials. These included a project Web site, presentation boards, a PowerPoint presentation, fact sheets, direct mail pieces, brochures, and regular e-Blasts.

Budget
The overall budget for this public affairs program was $300,000.

III. EXECUTION

SWS started by creating a comprehensive database that allowed the team to segment project supporters by City Council districts. The database was also designed to track those supporters willing to write letters to key decision-makers and those willing to testify at critical public hearings. Community relations tactics used include:

o Community presentations –
SWS conducted more than 50 presentations with homeowners groups, trade associations, civic organizations, labor unions and neighborhood groups.

o Direct mail
Westfield and SWS developed and distributed three separate direct mail pieces with tear off response cards aimed at local residents.

o The UTC Experience
Westfield opened the UTC Experience, an interactive design studio and lounge with project renderings and a project model, which was open seven days a week at the shopping center.

o Strategic partnerships
As noted, the Westfield/SWS team also determined early on that forming strategic partnerships with key regional organizations could also play a role in demonstrating widespread support for the project. Realizing that projected traffic from the expansion was a potential area of vulnerability for Westfield, SWS encouraged the company to seek the support of the Metropolitan Transportation System (MTS) and the San Diego Association of Governments (SANDAG), the two regional government agencies responsible for transportation planning in San Diego. Forging a unique partnership with MTS and SANDAG, Westfield agreed to provide nearly two acres of the shopping center to accommodate a state-of-the-art $22 million transit center. This deal resulted in support from both MTS and SANDAG and helped neutralize criticism from opponents about increased traffic.

o Key groups that ould reinforce the project messages

In terms of generating support from key groups that could reinforce the project messages, SWS took the unusual step of approaching organizations that typically steer clear from development proposals. For example, the American Lung Association wrote a letter of support because of the project's focus on transit, sustainability and solar power. The United States Green Building Council also supported The New UTC in part because of water conservation and on site affordable housing.

o Media relations campaign

Westfield and SWS also engaged in a media relations campaign that started with the launch of the final project design in August 2007. The launch, intended to focus on the "green" elements of the project, was covered by every major television station in the region, and the headline in the largest print publication read, "UTC to go Green." The successful launch served as a media catalyst that resulted in numerous positive stories leading up to public hearings, editorial board support from the largest newspaper in the region and several favorable opinion-editorials from local residents.

o e-Blast and letter writing campaign

Finally, an aggressive e-Blast and letter writing campaign in support of the project was launched in the weeks leading up to the final City Council vote. The Westfield/SWS team also met personally with each of the eight City Councilmembers, delivering copies of signed support cards (tracked in our master database) from constituents in each of their districts.

IV. EVALUATION

On July 29, 2008, after nearly five years of hard work, the San Diego City Council voted 7-1 to approve The New UTC. The approval represents one of the largest land development projects ever supported in San Diego's history. SWS easily exceeded its objective in terms of support, identifying more than 3,000 from San Diegans (and more than 800 from neighbors within one mile of the shopping center). In addition, more than 500 letters and e-mails were sent to each City Councilmember, and more than 200 people attended the public hearing and wore green t-shirts in favor of The New UTC.

SWS also secured the support of virtually every influential regional group in the County, including the Asian Business Association, the San Diego Housing Commission, the San Diego County Taxpayers Association, the San Diego County Parent Connection, the San Diego Cinema Society, the San Diego Regional Chamber of Commerce, the San Diego Regional Economic Development Corporation, and the San Diego Chapter of the California Restaurant Association.

The wide-ranging support sparked one City Councilmember during the final hearing to say, "The UTC project is not only a model for how to build a project in San Diego, it is a prototypical example about how to run a community relations campaign in favor of a development project."

Public Relations Society of America © 2009

WORKSHEET FOR STUDYING AND DISCUSSING PROFESSIONAL PUBLIC RELATIONS PLANS

Use this form to note your comments and questions about the components of the plan summary.

Summary or introductory statement	
Situation analysis	
Research	
Goal	
Focus or target audiences	
Objectives	
Strategies	
Activities or tactics	
Execution timeline	
Evaluation	
Budget	

RULES FOR WRITING COMPONENTS OF A PUBLIC RELATIONS PLAN

I have taken you on a trip from whimsey to reality to established practice to raise your interest in writing public relations plans and proposals. My hope is that this orientation will focus your attention on the challenge of influencing behavior through strategic communication, and that appearances of the yet-to-be-named frog icon throughout the rest of this chapter will remind you that regardless of the complexity of the challenge, your plans should be written in clear, brief, direct, human and well-defined terms.

There is much more to learn about writing plans that have potential to produce results and win approval. If, from what you have read so far, developing and writing plans seems like something you would enjoy doing on your own or with a team, and you believe you have the motivation, basic background, creative energy and skills necessary to learn to influence behavior effectively, I am confident that you are ready to pursue the art of writing winning plans.

I have 30 years of experience influencing behavior through strategic communication and it is abundantly clear from my work that writing winning plans requires structure. That's why I have developed rules for writing each component of a public relations plan. Critics are quick to claim that rules stifle creativity. However, you will discover just as quickly how structure frees up creativity and provides just the right places to showcase it. So to critics who might say that writing by rules is a cookie-cutter approach to public relations that inhibits creativity, I say that plans written by the rules produce irresistible "cookies" that sell!

1. Writing the Introductory Statement

Public relations plans are presented formally or informally, verbally or as written proposals.

Writing the plan in a conversational style is appropriate for all forms of presentation. You will find that in the industry, plans and definitions of their parts vary from organization to organization, from public relations agency to agency. It's not the lack of standardized form, but rather the lack of definition that does a great disservice to the profession. The model plan presented has 10 clearly defined components. We will look at each one from the plan reviewer's perspective, from the person responsible for authorizing funds to implement a plan.

A PR plan begins with a statement summarizing a problem, challenge, opportunity or situation which, when addressed with public relations activity, would in some significant way benefit the organization you work for or that you have as a client.

This part of the plan should be headed Problem, Challenge, Opportunity or Situation. It is best **not** to include the word "statement" in the subhead. The introduction is important to plan reviewers because it tells in capsule form what the situation is and why public relations actions should be seriously considered.

The statement should be written after information has been gathered and the situation has been analyzed.

A public relations plan is aimed at influencing behavior, so the statement must focus on communicating with people. It should show clearly that a situation exists that warrants public relations action and an allocation and expenditure of resources. The statement is a call to action.

To test your statement, ask yourself if a reviewer of your plan would easily recognize the significance of a situation and understand why taking public relations action would benefit the organization.

Rules for Writing the Introductory Statement

1. Label the statement as a problem, challenge, opportunity or situation without including the word statement.
2. Write the statement in a conversational style briefly stating a situation that requires public relation action.
3. Begin the statement by identifying the nature of the situation, for example, "There is a problem ... We have a challenge ... XYZ has an opportunity ... or, We have a situation ..."
4. Present the introductory statement in a storytelling manner, briefly describing what has developed and reached a point requiring public relations action.
5. The statement should provide a compelling argument for taking action, but must stop short of suggesting a solution or course of action.
6. The statement must be complete and accurate, but must not be judgemental or place blame.

Example of an Introductory Statement
Problem

Industrial Products, Inc. started planning a plant expansion and discovered that a large lagoon on the construction site contains hazardous material. The lagoon has to be cleaned out and closed before plant expansion work can begin. Closing the lagoon will be in the public eye and will raise questions, especially about people seen working in hazardous materials safety suits. If everyone who sees the activity—news media, community residents, employees, local government representatives, and others—is left to speculate about what is seen, the community could become unnecessarily alarmed.

Media reports could exaggerate health risks and call the company's reputation into question. The general public could pressure government for information and public meetings about the project. Local government officials could delay issuing permits for expansion. Employees could become outraged about earlier potential exposure of their families to health risks.

We don't want anyone to become alarmed unnecessarily. We don't want expansion plans to be delayed because needed modernization is already costing the company money and inadequate capacity is causing the company to lose market share. This clearly is a potential public relations problem with serious consequences that must be addressed.

Exercise 1.   *Introductory Statement*
Using the rules for developing an introductory statement, write a problem statement using ONLY the information provided in the following case summary.

Tasty Products Tries For Distinction

It used to be that food processors could market products for their good taste. Today it is evident that people are more interested than ever before in their health and fitness. When they shop, they want to know what products will do to them, and more importantly, what they will do for them. Health claims on products have an influence on buying decisions. Tasty Products figured that when you have a product that is not only great tasting, but also naturally nutritious, it makes sense to promote the natural health benefits. The company wanted to put a health claim on its Ultra Fine orange juice. It wanted to spotlight the fact that Ultra Fine orange juice contains potassium. The mineral potassium is found in orange juice. The company wanted to point out that in clinical trials potassium has been shown to reduce the risk of both high blood pressure and stroke. Tasty Products petitioned the Food and Drug Administration (FDA) to carry the health claim about potassium on its Ultra Fine orange juice label. The company spent months researching and writing the petition and working with FDA employees on drafting the claim's language. The petition was accepted. Now Tasty Products can market the potassium health benefit claim. But so can any juice producer tout the benefits of having potassium in its orange juice. Tasty Products wants to use the health claim, but has to keep other orange juice producers at bay.

2. Writing the Situation Analysis

The second component of a public relations plan is the situation analysis. Why is this component of the plan important to plan reviewers? The analysis is important to reviewers because it assures them that you have a complete and accurate understanding of the situation from which to develop a plan. The manner in which the analysis is written gives reviewers evidence of your depth of knowledge, the breadth of your experience, your level of professionalism, your understanding of the organization and its needs, the seriousness of your commitment to addressing the situation, and your overall understanding of public relations.

In developing a situation analysis, it is important to consider all aspects of the situation and to gather and record information necessary to provide an in-depth understanding of the problem, challenge or opportunity. The analysis should be a focused investigation of internal and external factors necessary to achieve a level of understanding that will identify areas requiring further study and possible research and that will support effective strategic planning.

Be judicious in preparing the analysis. Collecting and assembling everything that could possibly relate to a situation, including volumes of peripheral information that might be useful for other purposes and conducting broad-based communication audits that might or might not contribute to addressing a situation could be seen by reviewers as a costly, overindulgent, unnecessary use of resources.

For the analysis to be a useful component of a public relations plan, it should organize and convey information in a familiar, easy-to-understand manner. What better way could there be to describe a situation than to do what comes naturally, that is, tell a story?

To tell a story in this regard is to describe a series of happenings which, when related or connected, enables others to grasp the significance of a problem, challenge or opportunity. It is up to you in your storytelling to enable others to sift through events, understand how and why they occurred and what part they played in creating the situation under study.

Storytelling allows you to describe the development of a situation from its origin to its current state based on a thoughtful review of explicit, as well as tacit information. In other words an analysis will involve hard evidence as well as unseen influences and factors difficult to evaluate. It will be necessary to decide to what extent you can rely on intuition to form an analysis and to what extent it will be necessary to conduct and/or recommend primary or secondary research to help validate your "story" of how the problem, challenge or opportunity surfaced. Research to be recommended and/or conducted could be, for example, in the form of in-depth interviews, focus groups, field observation, tabulating telephone calls, postal mail and electronic mail, surveys, content analysis.

Example of a Situation Analysis
Situation Analysis

A totally unexpected merger and acquisition announcement came over the financial news wires at 5:05 p.m. on Friday, Oct. 17, 20xx. Neither of the companies involved had done any prior planning for communicating to stakeholder groups. The announcement was a complete surprise to everyone. The corporate announcement was written by an outside investment banking company and its public relations firm. Currently,

Rules for Writing the Situation Analysis

1. The situation analysis is more than a report of known facts; it is your analysis of the situation. So present the information you have as you understand it and include recommendations for further investigation (informal or qualitative/formal or quantitative research) into areas that you believe require clarification or verification.

2. Write the analysis in a conversational style as though you are explaining your assessment of the situation to your client or employer.

3. Present your analysis in a storytelling format—begin at the beginning and tell how the situation developed and reached a point requiring public relations action.

4. The analysis should provide a compelling argument for taking action.

5. The analysis should be forthright about problems, weaknesses and mistakes, but must not be judgemental or place blame.

6. The analysis must not include solutions or suggestions for dealing with the situation; however, it should provide a strong argument for public relations action.

communication plans are being prepared—this particular one, is for employees of both organizations. Following is an analysis of the situation.

The surprise merger announcement put employees of Tall Coffee Shops, Inc., in a face-to-face quandary over job security with employees of Grande Coffee Shop Corporation. At this time, one day after the announcement, employees have no idea what is planned for the merged organization for the near or long term. Beyond hearing some broad statements relating to corporate strategy, finance and management and how combining the two companies can help finance and enable Grande Coffee to grow in size and value in a highly competitive industry, employees have no idea how the pieces of the merger are going to fit together and, more specifically, how their jobs will be affected.

Employees of the two companies have been pleased with the way their respective employers managed the local shops, provided opportunities for individual advancement and competitive pay. Both companies provided clear visions for employees about their respective missions and goals. A vision of the merged company has yet to be provided. The former visions of each company must be replaced quickly with a common vision so employees can see light at the end of the tunnel.

Executive officers of both companies know that employees are worried that this corporate action could be like a merger of banks, which for some, created an excuse for closing branch offices and cutting jobs. After all, there's no reason to have Tall Shops in proximity to Grande Shops. Executives know there will be short-term pain and will have to decide whether to hide it or try to balance potential negatives by describing the long-term payoffs for everyone.

Based on lessons learned about mergers and employee communication from MCI, British Telecom, IBM, Lotus, BellSouth, LG Electronics, UPS, Martin Marietta, GE and others, the companies realize that the chief executive officers of both entities should champion a common vision and take an active role in articulating it to employees and the news media. It is common knowledge that messages in a merger acquisition must be consistent.

The CEO of Grande Coffee, the acquiring company, knows and acknowledges to staff members that she buries herself in her work and is seldom seen by employees. She says the perception employees have of her is probably that what's most important to her are investors. Research makes clear that in times of uncertainty employees want a lot of "face time" from the CEO and need to be treated with the same intellect and attention given to shareholders, customers, and the media.

There is no empirical data to show that mergers and acquisitions, in any way, guarantee benefits. There is evidence to show that mergers and acquisitions produce unanticipated, and often, undesirable consequences. With respect to employees, it is important to focus on retaining an organization's human capital, which represents a large part of its intellectual capacity and abilities. A major bank in an acquisition, ignored its wealth of human capital by neglecting to assure its most valued employees that they were important to the success of the organization and that their jobs were secure. Consequently, the bank lost many of its most valuable employees who took jobs with other banks.

Referring to employees as a valuable "asset," as so many executives do, puts employees into a category with copy machines, computers and water coolers. Experienced professional communicators know that employees will not get behind the broad strategy of a merger and acquisition until they know how the merger is going to affect them personally. They must be able to function as participants, not as victims or powerless players. In a merger process, employees can feel like the corporate culture is under siege. They can feel like things are out of control. Suspicions, even a degree of paranoia get heightened. There is enormous ambiguity. Employees must be made to feel that their interests are being well represented.

Companies that have worked through a merger know that a constant effort must be made to monitor traditional and new media channels of communication and clear up blurred impressions. Experienced companies know how important it is to constantly revise main messages to respond to criticisms and misinformation. They know how vital it is to help all stakeholder groups keep things in perspective. For example, instead of talking about becoming a $43 billion corporation and fourth largest telecom corporation in the world, MCI in response to criticism started to point out that, although it would be big, MCI would have only six percent of the market.

Establishing and maintaining two-way communication with employees and all stakeholder groups is essential. Even if there is nothing new to provide, management must stay in close touch with its constituents and reassure them that they will get straightforward information as soon as it is available.

This is a quick analysis of the situation. There is a body of knowledge to draw on in the public relations profession that makes it possible to develop an employee communication plan solidly based on the challenges and successes realized by companies that have gone through the merger and acquisition process. This plan is based on the successes of others.

Exercise 2.   *Situation Analysis*

Based on the rules for developing a situation analysis, read the case overview below and describe what additional information you would want to have to do a thorough analysis of the situation. Include in your critique recommended informal or formal research that you think should be conducted to verify certain information or suppositions or to shed more light on the situation.

Shelter Association Pursues Housing For The Homeless

Homeless individuals (mostly men) lived and searched for food on land along the riverbank in downtown Berryton. However, in 1998 the area came under rapid change with the development of expensive homes, a science museum and an arena.

The Berryton Relocation Task Force was formed by the Shelter Association, a provider of homeless services, to help homeless men who were threatened with being displaced from the riverfront property.

The task force studied the situation and conducted public meetings. It came up with a five-year plan proposing to locate 500 apartments for homeless men throughout the county, building a shelter in an inner-city neighborhood and a facility for alcoholic homeless men. The idea was to reduce homelessness and have the permanent housing and support services replace a variety of emergency shelters.

The plan faced significant challenges. Affordable housing hasn't been popular anywhere in the country, not even Franklin County which is more tolerant than many other counties. NIMBYism (opposition by nearby residents to a proposed building project, especially a public one, acronym for Not In My Back Yard) is common. People are not inclined to want to live next door to formerly homeless men, many of whom have mental illnesses and addictions. Shelter Association doesn't know what to do to win acceptance of the plan and to successfully raise money for an unpopular effort.

3. Writing the Goal

The next component of a plan is the goal. Why is a goal important to plan reviewers? It is important because the goal in a public relations plan has four functions.

One function is to provide a vision of a desired position or condition. A plan should have one ultimate aim. All of a plan's objectives should be directed toward achieving the plan's goal. The goal can be specific to the public relations task, for example: for XYZ to be trusted by the community for its safe use of chemicals. Or it can relate to broader organization aims that require plans from other functions, such as human resources, marketing and finance, for example: for XYZ to be merged with ZYX with the support and understanding of all stakeholders.

Another function of a goal is to provide a target on which to organize resources. A goal gives followers of a plan a point of reference on which to center their efforts.

Rules for Writing the Goal

1. A plan should have one goal.
2. The goal should be written in a single sentence.
3. The goal should be distinguished by use of the present infinitive phrase "to be," responding to the question, What do you want the ultimate condition or state of being to be as a result of having executed the public relations plan successfully? (Example: For the medical center to be serving 50 additional patients.)
4. The goal should describe a desired ultimate condition or state of being as though it has been achieved. (Acceptable: For XYZ to be operating as a recognized leader in its field. This is written as though the company has arrived at a new level of esteem—a new state of being. It would be unacceptable to write as a goal, for XYZ to become a recognized leader in its field, because that leaves XYZ in its current unrecognized position or state of being—trying to become a recognized leader.)
5. A goal should not tell what must be done for it to be achieved. That is the role of an objective. (Unacceptable: For XYZ to raise $15 million to expand the hospital. That is an objective describing what must be done to accomplish the ultimate goal—to be serving 50 more patients in a new addition to the hospital. The goal should be evidence that a plan's objectives have been successfully completed.
6. A goal should not tell how it is to be achieved. That is the role of a strategy. (Acceptable: For XYZ to be a trusted member of the community with its use of hazardous chemicals. Unacceptable: for XYZ to be a trusted member of the community with its use of hazardous chemicals by communicating its safety record.)

It enables them to set their sights on what is to be the overall result of the combined efforts of all contributors to the plan. A goal should use the present infinitive "to be" to distinguish this targeting function. What follows "to be" should be stated as though the position or condition has been achieved. Examples: The goal for XYZ is to be a recognized leader in its field. This goal clearly rallies an organization's resources around making it a recognized leader in its field.

Another function of a goal is to provide verification that the plan is focused correctly. By stating the goal, plan developers can demonstrate to plan reviewers that the plan focuses on the correct priority. For example, if the client's goal is for XYZ to be viewed as an essential, unique and authoritative resource for diversity education on the university campus and in the greater community, the goal would not be focused correctly if it were stated: For XYZ to be a well-funded campus organization. Directly stated, when a client's goal calls for everyone to be eating BigMacs, plan developers had better not be writing about Chicken McNuggets. That may sound exaggerated, but sometimes client or employer instructions are not followed explicitly or overlooked entirely and the experience for them is exasperating because they are putting up major resources to accomplish a specific job that is important to them.

Another function of a goal is to provide a measurement of success. When a desired condition or position is evident as stated in the goal, a plan's objectives have been met. In other words, the fact that a certain condition or position now exists is evidence that the plan's objectives have been achieved successfully. Let's say, for example, the goal is for a hospital to be serving 50 more children. When the hospital is, in fact, serving 50 more children, that is proof or evidence that the plan's objective (i.e. to raise $20 million for hospital expansion) has been successfully achieved.

So the goal of a public relations plan has four functions—it provides a vision, a target, verification and measurement.

Examples of Acceptable and Unacceptable Goals
Note how easily and incorrectly goals get combined with objectives and strategies.

Unacceptable: "To provide eligible families with a smooth transition from Island Health Offspring to Children's Health Insurance Program."
Reasons: It begins with the infinitive "To," which the rules reserve for beginning objectives. It does not include the present infinitive phrase "to be" followed by an ultimate vision, state of being, or desired condition.
Acceptable: For eligible families to be receiving increased benefits from the Children's Health Insurance Program, having made a smooth transition from Island Health Offspring.

Unacceptable: The goal of the Clean Teeth campaign is to heighten awareness about the importance of tooth brushing.

Reasons: The statement is set off with the infinitive "to," which the rules reserve for beginning objectives. It does not include the present infinitive phrase "to be," which the rules reserve for introducing a goal—a desired condition or state of being. It does not tell whose awareness is to be heightened. The scope of the goal is not defined; the campaign was launched in Gumsport, but apparently intended to target audiences globally.

Acceptable: For people around the world to be more aware of the importance of brushing teeth.

Unacceptable: To have the public adopt natural garden care by changing certain gardening behaviors.

Reasons: It does not include the present infinitive phrase "to be," which the rules reserve for introducing a goal—a desired condition, state of being, ultimate vision. The phrase "to have the public adopt natural garden care" tells **what** must be done, which is the role of an objective. The phrase "by changing certain gardening behaviors" tells **how** something must be done, which is the role of a strategy.

Acceptable: For male homeowners, ages 25 to 54 in the Garden Gateway area, to be using natural gardening practices.

Unacceptable: For ABC Company to become accepted as an economic partner in the community by participating in local service clubs.

Reasons: It does not contain the present infinitive phrase "to be," which is necessary to introduce a desired condition, state of being, ultimate vision. "To become accepted" tells **what** must be done, which is the role of an objective. And "by participating in local service clubs" tells **how** to do something which is the role of a strategy.

Acceptable: For ABC Company to be operating in the community as a full-fledged economic partner.

Unacceptable: For Children's Hospital to raise $100,000.

Reasons: Raising $100,000 is not the vision, the desired state of being or condition. Raising $100,000 is **what** must be done to achieve the vision, which according to the rules is the role of an objective. The vision or goal is for the hospital to be serving more patients.

Acceptable: For Children's Hospital to be serving 25 more patients in a new wing of the hospital.

Unacceptable: For XYZ, Inc. to be closing one assembly plant.

Reasons: Closing one assembly plant is not the ultimate vision, goal or state of being. It is **what** must be done to achieve the goal or vision which, according to the rules, is the role of an objective.

Acceptable: For XYZ, Inc. to be operating more competitively having closed one assembly plant.

Examples of Acceptable Goals

1. For X to be recognized nationally for its expertise in nubyonics.
2. For employees to be accepting greater financial responsibility for their health benefits.
3. For customers to be relying on X for its technical expertise and creative solutions.
4. For X to be merged with Y and the new organization vigorously pursuing a common mission.
5. For X to be relocated with a minimal amount of confusion.
6. For (person) to be a sought after expert in launching new ventures.
7. For X to be recognized by the community as a leader in economic development.
8. For employees to be satisfied with the measures taken to ensure their safety relative to the new hazardous materials operation.
9. For X to be serving 50 more patients.
10. For (country) to be supportive of adding a new industry to its economy.
11. For the community to be satisfied with the level of public participation afforded by X on the proposed energy project.
12. For X to be expanding its operation with the support of local and state governments.
13. For X to be regarded by subscribers as the authority on health issues.
14. For X to be seen by potential employers and experts in public relations planning.
15. For X to be increasing membership at a rate of 10 percent a year.
16. Fox X to be approaching strike issues with open communication with Y.
17. For members of X to be making appearances on TV shows around the world.
18. For all students of X to be supported by individual sponsorships.
19. For X to be the most popular Web site for information about Y.
20. For consumers of X to be the preferred customers of Y.
21. For wind surfers throughout the world to be aware of Hood River on the Columbia River as one of the most popular locations for the sport.
22. For X to be regarded as the most popular wine-tasting festival in the Pacific Northwest.
23. For artisans of the Columbia River Gorge to be discovered by and publicized internationally for their unique creations.
24. In the acquisition of X by Y, for all employees to be fully supportive of the merger.
25. For the new comet-like logo to be seen by employees as a more progressive representation of the organization's identity than the old logo that was fondly referred to as the "flying meatball."

Exercise 3.   *Goal*

Explain why the goals in the following article would not be acceptable according to the rules and write one goal for the museum that would be acceptable.

The Great Museum of Natural History

Museums have to work hard to attract interest and visitors. The Great Museum of Natural History is no exception. However, it decided to break out of the low-attendance crowd by adding a planetarium. It was a $6.9 million project. The museum launched a PR campaign. It had two goals: generate publicity that would position the museum as a world-class institution, and boost revenue through increased attendance.

The museum set up a promotion team of PR professionals and representatives from local TV, radio stations and newspapers. It used its member resources to help publicize the grand opening of the Space Planetarium. A media teaser campaign was also launched that used puzzles and electronic postcards to visually convey the planetarium's design. Media events for the planetarium were sold out. The campaign was a complete success with all attendance goals exceeded, planetarium shows sold out for the first three months and the museum positioned as a learning center.

4. Writing the Focus of a Plan

The focus of a public relations plan, without exception, should be on people because public relations is the practice of influencing behavior through strategic communication. Practically speaking, a plan could not be implemented without the engagement of people. A plan must focus on influencing the behavior of people to achieve the plan's goal. The focus of a plan could be on one individual, on individuals comprising an organization or segment of an organization, on individuals comprising an audience or an entire public. Focal points of a plan could be a labor leader, the management of a labor union, members of a nation's trade unions. Focal points could be a business, community, activist, student or government leader. They could be the management of a public, private, non-profit, government or non-government organization. Focal points of a plan could be employees or members of organizations. They could be community residents, journalists, industry analysts, potential investors. A plan could have multiple focal points, but each one must be treated separately.

Example of a Focal Point or Target Audience of a Plan
Following is a description of a target audience written by a student team:

Parents of Apple Elementary School Children
Parents of students at the neighboring Apple Elementary School are among the most concerned audiences about the use of chemicals at WafferMakers, Inc. Parents are

concerned for the safety of their children and want to be assured that the wafer plant operation near the school is not a risk to their children's health or safety. Many of these parents are already highly emotional about the situation and want their questions answered immediately. Parents regard WafferMakers as a good corporate citizen and up until this time were unaware of the company's use of many hazardous chemicals. They are members of the local community and it is important to make sure that they trust and continue to be supportive of WafferMakers, Inc.

Exercise 4. *Focus of a Plan*

Based on the rules for describing the focus of a plan, explain why it would be helpful to plan reviewers to have more than just a list of entities identified as subjects or targets of a plan as shown here:

The ABC Transport System Key Target Audiences:

- Landowners
- Local elected officials
- Community leaders
- Media

Rules for Writing the Focus of a Plan

1. A public relations plan must focus on people. (For example, This plan focuses on active and latent patrons of the theater.) Plans focus on people because the engagement of people is required to achieve a plan's goal.
2. People who are at the focus of a plan may be referred to as focal points. Use of the term focal point is appropriate when there is a need to focus the plan on an entity, such as executive management, without having to refer to it as a "target." (For example, Our own management is one focal point of this plan.) The terms target, target audience, target public, also may be used.
3. In writing the focus of a plan, list the main focal points or targets.
4. Describe why each entity is a focal point or target of the plan.
5. Tell what each entity knows about the subject of the plan.
6. Describe the disposition of each entity toward the subject of the plan.
7. Describe the disposition of each entity toward the originator of the plan.
8. Provide demographics of each entity that are particularly relevant to the plan.
9. Write about each entity separately; do not combine entities.

- State elected officials, regulatory/admin staff
- U.S. Senators, Reps & staff from 6 states
- Fed regulators
- Rural/farm groups

5. Writing Objectives

Objectives tell plan reviewers what actions must be taken with subjects of the plan to achieve a plan's goal. More than one objective usually is needed to achieve a goal. There must be one objective for each focal point or target audience of a plan.

An objective is distinguished by starting it with the infinitive "To," and must contain three parts: 1) an action to be taken; 2) receiver of the action (e.g. focal point, target audience); and 3) a behavior that is desired of the receiver as a result of the action taken.

Let's look at examples of an objective's three components.

The first component of an objective describes an action that must be taken to achieve a plan's goal, for example, "to inform about a company's skyrocketing costs of medical insurance."

The second component identifies a receiver of the action. Who do we want to inform about the company's skyrocketing costs of medical insurance? The receiver of the action should be one of the focal points or target audiences of the plan, in this case employees. A plan's objectives always focus on people because implementing a plan requires the engagement of people and public relations is the practice of influencing human behavior through strategic communication. When an objective is written without a receiver of the action, it is like focusing on a ghost. This exasperates plan reviewers because they want to know whose behavior is to be influenced to achieve the objective.

The third component tells what behavior is desired of the target audience as a result of the action taken, for example, "be willing to accept an increased share of medical insurance cost."

A complete objective would be "To inform employees about the company's skyrocketing costs of medical insurance so that they are willing to accept an increased share of the cost."

Action	To inform about the company's skyrocketing costs of medical insurance
Focus or Target	employees
Result	willing to accept an increased share of the costs for medical insurance
Objective	To inform employees about the company's skyrocketing costs of medical insurance so that they are willing to accept an increased share of the cost.

Rules for Writing an Objective

1. An objective must tell what must be done to achieve a plan's goal.
2. An objective must begin with the infinitive "To ..." to distinguish it as an objective.
3. An objective must focus on people because in public relations nothing can be accomplished without some form of human engagement.
4. There should be one or more objectives for each of a plan's focal points or target audiences.
5. An objective must state an action to be taken with a particular group of people and a reason for the action, which could be called the objective's purpose or desired outcome.
6. An objective must be written to enable measurement. Measurement is enabled by the third part of an objective–a desired measurable outcome. The first part of an objective is an action, the second part is a receiver of the action, and the third is a desired measurable outcome as a result of the action. For example, the measurable desired outcome of the objective, "To inform parents of safety measures that are in place so they feel there is no danger in sending their children to school on Monday," would be that parents send their children to school on Monday, which could be measured by school attendance records.
7. An objective should not state a means of measurement; that should be included in the evaluation provision for an objective (e.g. EVALUATION This objective can be measured with attendance records of the number of children who attend school on Monday).
8. An objective may contain a critical deadline or milestone; however, scheduling details are best left for inclusion in a plan's execution time line.
9. An objective should not claim to have the ability to single-handedly influence areas over which it has partial control, such as sales, productivity and stock value. It would be dishonest to guarantee a target, such as a 15 percent increase, or claim total credit for reaching a target in areas influenced by many other factors. It would be proper to "assist with," or "contribute to" a particular target.

It is the third component of an objective that most often is omitted, which is a crucial error because it is this component of an objective that enables measurement. An objective, for example, might be stated "To provide the media with information." This

Figure 2. List of Objectives by Component Parts

1) One action that must be taken with a target audience or public in order for an objective to contribute toward the achievement of a plan's goal

To accom-modate	To diffuse emotion	To instill	To reconcile
To address	To educate	To mobilize	To recruit
To advise	To enlighten	To negotiate	To reduce
To alleviate	To explain	To offer	anxiety
To apprise	To focus	To organize	To restore
To assure	To forecast	To orient	To reveal
To attract attention	To generate interest	To pique	To sensitize
To change	To heighten	To placate	To share
To com-municate	interest	To present	confidence
To compile	To honor	To prove	To show
To convey	To improve	To provide opportuni-ties	To simplify
To describe	To increase knowledge	To raise awareness	To stimulate interested pet owners
	To inform	To recognize	

2) Target audience or public whose participation is necessary to accomplish the objective

analysts	environmental activists	local elected officials	service providers
backpackers	executives of non-profits	local news media	shareholders
bankers	farmers	news media	special interest groups
chamber of commerce	fashion editors	parents	suppliers
college students	government regulators	physicians	talk show hosts
commissioners	government representatives	product partners	teachers
community leaders	high school students	professional organizations	trade press
council members	homeowners	program directors	U.S. Repre-sentatives
customers	investors	prospects	U.S. Senators
development council	landowners	residents	veterans
educators	lawyers	seniors	voters
employees		service clubs	

3) A behavior that is desired of the target audience or public as a result of the action taken.

accept	donate	leave alone	report
apply	e-mail	march	accurately
approve	empathize	participate	seek
assemble	enroll	petition	sell
attend	experience	play	sing
believe	help	promote	start
buy	insist	publicize	stop
capitulate	invest	question	support
contact	investigate	recommend	sympathize
contribute	join	reconsider	travel
demand	keep	reject	trust
demonstrate	lead		try

is not measurable because it does not tell what the media is expected to do as a result of having been provided information.

Action	To provide information
Focus or Target	media
Result	What's the desired result???

The reason for providing the media with information cannot be simply assumed. It must be stated. Reviewers who are paying the bill to have a plan implemented want to know what outcomes to expect from every objective. For example, reviewers would be expected to ask, "Why are we spending money to provide the media with information?" To answer the question, an objective must provide a desired behavioral outcome. For example, "To provide the media with newsworthy material so that journalists take an interest in publishing articles and that their reports can be based on complete and accurate information." Articles published can be measured in terms of number and content quality.

Action	To provide information
Focus or Target	media
Result	interest and reports based on complete and accurate information
Objective	To provide the media with information so they take an interest in publishing articles and that the reports can be based on complete and accurate information.

An objective must be achievable, as well as measurable. It must aim at a result that is possible to achieve cost effectively. An objective can include a deadline or time frame. However, the sequencing of activities is best left for inclusion in the plan's time line. If an objective includes a milestone or benchmark to be achieved, developers of the plan must have complete control of all factors required to reach the benchmark. A public relations plan, for example, should not contain a sales target of, say a 10 percent increase, unless the plan developers have total control over all factors that affect sales. A plan developer would not want to be held accountable for something over which he or she has only partial control.

An objective stops short of telling how something must be done. That is the role of a strategy. So a writer must resist the temptation to include in an objective a phrase, such as "… by holding a news conference;" that tells how, for example, an objective would be accomplished and is the role of a strategy.

Examples of Acceptable and Unacceptable Objectives

Unacceptable: "Work on many levels of the problem simultaneously to deliver a 'cannon shot' impact that is deep and long lasting."
Reasons: This is gobbledygook; it is totally meaningless to plan reviewers.
Unacceptable: Generate publicity that strongly links Box of Snaps with baseball and highlights new 'prize inside' series.
Reasons: An objective must focus on an audience and it must start with the infinitive "To." An objective must include a desired outcome or change in behavior by the intended audience. In this case there is no target audience, nor is there any indication of what the writer of the plan wants the implied audience to do as a result of the publicity. Also, plans should take advantage of lessons learned from research on persuasion. A reviewer of this objective might ask, "Have you taken into account that research has shown that messages, especially those presented through the public media, are quickly forgotten if they are not at least moderately reinforced by repetition and that repetition is useful for keeping ideas in the public mind?"
Acceptable: To generate publicity that in the minds of Major League Baseball fans strongly links Box of Snaps with baseball and raises an interest in the new "prize inside" series so that more fans buy Box of Snaps.

Unacceptable: Promote each member of Smith's family of digital audio players through individually tailored campaigns to maintain market share of at least 30 percent.
Reasons: This objective does not begin with the infinitive "To." It has no target audience. "Through individually tailored campaigns" tells how the objective is to be accomplished which is the role of a strategy. Most importantly, public relations is a staff function and has no direct control over marketing—certainly not over all of the many factors necessary to promise a market share of 30 or any percent.

Unacceptable: Collect $5 million in contributions by conducting a capital fund drive.
Reasons: The statement does not begin with the infinitive "To." No audience is specified. No time frame is specified. The phrase, "by conducting a capital fund drive" tells how something is to be accomplished which is the role of a strategy.
Acceptable: To convince targeted donors to pledge by Dec. 1, 200X, a total of $5 million for expansion of the XYZ Medical Center.

Unacceptable: To fully inform the news media about the incident.
Reason: No desired outcome is indicated. What is expected of journalists if they are fully informed of the incident? In other words, what does the organization want journalists to do as a result of fully informing them?
Acceptable: To fully inform the news media about the incident to help ensure that their news reports are complete and accurate.

Exercise 5. *Objectives*
Study the objectives in the following article. Explain how the objectives would be written according to the rules.

To help promote Charmin Ultra, Procter & Gamble conducted a traveling road show. An 18-wheel semi-truck trailer was converted into a "commode on the road" with 27 private bathrooms. The facilities had hardwood floors, sinks with running water, uniformed attendants and Charmin Ultra toilet paper.

Teaser promotions were sent to local media in advance of each appearance of the Potty Palooza. They included T-shirts with "Potty Palooza 2002. … It's Loo-La-La on the front; on the back was a U.S. map and stars marking each stop on the tour. The shirts were compressed and shrink-wrapped into the shape of an 18-wheel trailer. Press releases were sent to local media two days before each festival or fair's opening day. A media alert invited the press to visit the Potty Palooza. The main objectives were to get at least 30 million media impressions, secure at least 30 aired segments on TV news and to drive trial and sales of Charmin Ultra. The objectives were surpassed, with more than 62 million media impressions, more than 45 b-roll news hits, three national news stories plus print and TV coverage in all local market stops. Also, research showed a 14 percent increase in Charmin sales among consumers who used the Potty Palooza. Budget for the program was $300,000 and the agency was Manning, Selvage & Lee.

6. Writing Strategies

The next component of a plan is the strategy. Why are strategies important to plan reviewers? They are important because strategies describe how you will achieve your plan's objectives. Reviewers want to assess your methods for achieving objectives, the creativity behind your methods, the feasibility and practicality of your methods, and your knowledge of applying the fundamentals of persuasion in influencing behavior.

Every objective must have a strategy that describes how, in concept, the objective is to be achieved. More than one strategy might be necessary to accomplish an objective. A strategy must be realistic; it must take into account the amount of time, energy, personnel, expertise and financial resources available for its implementation. A strategy can state key themes or messages to be reiterated throughout a campaign.

This component is the plan's stage for creativity. It is a plan's platform on which to showcase imaginative approaches to problems, opportunities, challenges and all manner of diverse situations. If you don't think of yourself as creative, think again. My experience is that creativity is thinking of something that has not been thought of by others. In most cases, it has not been thought of by others because they have not had or taken the time to thoroughly investigate–research–a situation. To a plan reviewer, failure to come up with creative ideas is failure to study a situation in earnest.

When developing a strategy, you will strengthen what you propose by basing it, where possible, on lessons learned by others in the profession. You will find commonly known facts about persuasion in Figure 4 on page 183.

The strategy component provides a plan developer with an opportunity to educate plan reviewers on communication and persuasion. For example, it might be appropriate in a strategy to explain how the seed of an idea becomes a conviction to act as shown in Figure XX below. It is wise to review each of your strategies and ensure that they are in line with the profession's experience. As mentioned earlier, this is your opportunity to educate plan reviewers so, where applicable, include in your strategy a reference such as, "experience in the profession has shown that ..." Do not refer to a particular experience unless it is totally appropriate to the situation. And be sure not to propose a strategy that is contrary to professional lessons learned, unless you can provide a solid rationale for the recommendation.

Examples of Acceptable and Unacceptable Strategies

Unacceptable: The campaign strategy is a simple message for the campaign that could be conveyed through all mediums: "When it comes to keeping your water features clear, count on Barley Bob." Bob is an honest country boy who chews on barley and is spokesperson for the campaign.

Reasons: The strategy, according to the rules, must explain how an objective is to be accomplished. In this statement, the explanation is vague. It says, "The campaign strategy is a simple message ..." A strategy may contain and explain the use of a particular message and may include the description of a character to deliver the message. However,

Rules for Writing a Strategy

1. A strategy should describe how, in concept, an objective is to be accomplished. More than one strategy could be required to accomplish a single objective.
2. A strategy may include an explanation about the use of persuasive techniques based on lessons learned through research; however, research findings should not be included unless they apply specifically to the situation.
3. A strategy may include a discussion of messages or themes.
4. A strategy is the place in a plan for creativity—a platform for presenting ideas that plan reviewers have not considered.
5. A strategy should be described in broad terms with details left to be covered as activities or tactics.

this strategy falls short of explaining the strategic use of the message and the campaign character. According to the rules, a strategy must explain how an objective is to be accomplished and activities, in bulleted or numbered form, should provide an elaboration of details. A strategy should take into account lessons learned by public relations professionals. A plan reviewer might ask, for example, "Have you taken into account experience that has shown that humor sometimes can generate a liking for the message source, but can backfire if the audience thinks the use of humor is a manipulative device?"

Acceptable: We will accomplish [Objective #1] by communicating through a variety of media a message for people to "Count on Barley Bob to keep water features clear." The message promoting the use of barley to keep ponds and other water features free of algae the natural way will come from Barley Bob, the campaign's spokesperson. Research has shown that humor can be effective if it seems natural and not contrived. Bob is a friendly and believable character who delivers the natural care message with a hint of humor. The message from Bob will be conveyed to the region's homeowners through six different activities.

Unacceptable: "Develop key messages and create benefit-focused materials that set a celebratory tone."
Reasons: This is gobbledygook and is totally meaningless to plan reviewers.

Unacceptable: "Invite parents to an informational meeting."
Reasons: There is nothing strategic about this action. There is not sufficient detail to instill confidence that this strategy will accomplish its objective. There is no attempt

to use this opportunity to educate plan reviewers on the techniques of persuasion or communication methods or to elaborate with a message theme or other details.

Acceptable: Contact parents by phone and provide compelling reasons why it is important for them to attend an informational meeting on Jan. 1, 20XX. Enlist volunteer parents to make the phone calls to give credibility to the communication. Have parent callers make note of feedback from the calls and have them try to confirm attendance of parents they contact in order to get an estimate of the total number likely to attend the meeting. Have callers stress that "No cases of this health problem have been detected and that the purpose of the meeting is to inform parents how to protect their children from becoming susceptible to the problem."

Exercise 6.   *Strategies*

Based on the rules, write a strategy for the case below. Use only the information provided in the case summary and stop short of listing the details (activities) of how the strategy is to be carried out.

T.T. Cottonfield LLC Media Campaign

Off-balance sheet financing is what got Enron in trouble. So you can appreciate how any company that provides off-balance sheet financing could easily be associated with such scandalous behavior. T.T. Cottonfield is a leading provider of net-lease financing, a traditional form of off-balance sheet financing. The company worried that when the Enron scandal hit that all forms of off-balance sheet financing would be discredited and considered invalid. The company decided to go on the offensive by launching a media campaign designed to differentiate the company's net-lease financing from Enron's use of special-purpose entities. T.T. Cottonfield wanted to capitalize on the high media interest by educating investors and corporate executives about the advantages of net-lease financing and promoting the company as the best firm to provide such financing.

The company, together with Dice, Dice & Rice, Inc. arranged a luncheon with journalists from The Wall Street Journal, Fortune, Dow Jones, Bloomberg and others.

The company created advertisements highlighting its financial capabilities aimed at executives whose companies held synthetic leases.

The company produced an acquisitions brochure that was distributed to senior-level corporate executives.

As a result of these efforts, T.T. Cottonfield was able to complete more than $1 billion in net-lease transactions in 2002, a new record for the company and more than double its 2001 results.

Figure 3. Factors to Consider in Communicating Strategically

Influencing behavior through strategic communication requires that a message be received, noticed, understood, believed, remembered and acted upon. The sender of a message must focus on message development, source and channel selection, exposure, navigation around obstacles and through cognitive filters. The following factors should be considered in planning strategic communication.

Source	The source of the communication should be someone who is familiar to the intended audience or public, who is trusted, considered knowledgeable and credible and who normally is looked to for information.	Familiar Trustworthy Knowledgeable Credible
Message	In developing a message, a sender should know what's on the intended target's mind and should try to align the message with existing attitudes. The sender should know what the intended audience or public talks and thinks about and how the receiver converses with peers so that the message can be written in familiar language as part of the receiver's natural routine. Content of the message must be clear, appropriate, meaningful, memorable, understandable and believable. The message should get the receiver involved using triggers—reasons or incentives for the receiver to act on the message, in other words telling what's in it for the intended audience if it responds as requested. The behavior requested must be within the intended audience's ability to perform or learn to perform.	Aligned Language Clear Appropriate Meaningful Understandable Memorable Believable Appealing Beneficial Triggers Ability
Channels	The message should be sent through one or more channels that are familiar to and relied upon for information by the target audience or public. Selection of channels must be accurate. The channels must be adequate to convey the message completely and accurately. Redundant use of channels may be necessary to penetrate or circumvent communication barriers.	Familiar Adequate Redundant Accurate

Figure 3. Factors to Consider ... (*continued ...*)

Exposure	Day of week, time of day and frequency with which the message is communicated are important factors in determining message exposure.	Timing Frequency
Obstacles	To be effective, communication of the message must overcome obstacles, such as noise, clutter and competition.	Clutter Noise Competition
Cognitive Filters	Communication of the message must penetrate a receiver's thinking process, passing through cognitive filters of attitude, culture, experience, affiliations and needs.	Attitude Culture Experience Affiliations Needs
Target	The intended receiver could be an individual, group of individuals or a larger audience or public. To be effective, strategic communication must be noticed, understood, believed, accepted, remembered and acted upon.	Noticed Understood Believed Accepted Remembered Acted Upon

7. Writing Activities

An activity or tactic is what puts a strategy into action. Why is the activity component of importance to plan reviewers? It's important because activities provide the details of a strategy and reviewers want to assure themselves that they concur with the ways in which strategies are to be carried out.

More than one activity is usually required to implement a strategy. Typically, activities include the use of communication tools, such as podcasts and news releases, along with various actions and events. (See examples of communication tools in Figure 5 on page 185.) However, a plan developer must resist the temptation of throwing out a list of communication tools to solve a problem, meet a challenge or take advantage of an opportunity. For example: "We can solve this problem with two brochures, a poster and a fact sheet." There are many factors to consider in communicating strategically to influence behavior. See Figure 3 on page 179.

Avoid beginning activities with communication tools. It is always better to emphasize a strategic step rather than the vehicle that will be used to implement it. See the following illustration.

Strategic Activity is Emphasized (better)	Communication Tool is Emphasized
Generate interest and excitement about the sponsorship among reporters with a message from Bobby Apple and views of him racing in past competitions by sending them a short, specially produced communication on video or CD.	Send a video to all targeted media outlets to generate excitement about the sponsorship with a message from Bobby Apple and scenes of him racing.
Entice the media to interview Bobby Apple and photograph the show car at the Los Angeles Convention Center during the annual car show by sending them a media advisory loaded with photo op ideas.	Send a media advisory that entices the media to interview Bobby Apple and see the team's show car at the Los Angeles Convention Center during the annual car show.
Announce XYZ's sponsorship of the Indy race car team with attention-grabbing quotes from driver Bobby Apple in print and video news releases.	Send a print and video news release announcing XYZ's sponsorship of the Indy race car team with attention-grabbing comments from driver Bobby Apple.

Every tool must be used correctly by itself and in conjunction with other activities. It would be incorrect, for example, to use a news release in place of a media alert to announce a news conference. A plan developer must realize that plan reviewers at the senior level, for the most part, are not professional public relations practitioners. It is likely, for example, that they would not know a white paper from a position paper, a tip sheet from a fact sheet or a news conference from a news briefing. So when an activity calls for the use of a communication tool, you must describe what the device is as well as its purpose.

Activities should not be a list of routine logistical chores, such as "picking up donuts for the meeting," "copying and mailing letters," "renting a car," etc. Plan reviewers are interested in strategic details.

Also, activities should be comprehensive so that the plan developer does not unwittingly shift the job of development to the reviewer. For example, when an activity is described simply as, "Hold a meeting of faculty members who teach courses related to diversity," it raises questions of, Hold a meeting where? When? How many faculty members? How would they be identified? What courses do they teach? How would the meeting be conducted? By whom? For what purpose? Providing answers to these questions is the job of the plan developer.

In summary, activities should provide reviewers with a detailed strategic sequence of moves necessary to carry out a strategy.

Rules for Writing Activities (or Tactics)

1. Activities are detailed steps to be taken to carry out a strategy.
2. Activities should not be a to-do list of logistical chores (e.g. reserve a meeting room, order coffee, bring name tags, etc.)
3. Activities should not be a skeleton list of communication tools (e.g. brochure, news release, backgrounder, etc.); each communication tool must have a stated strategic purpose and must be employed in the correct manner.
4. Activities should begin with a strategic move, rather than a communication tool or vehicle.
5. Activities should provide complete information; they should not burden plan reviewers with unanswered questions.

Exercise 7. *Activities or Tactics*

The following activities are unacceptable according to the rules. Make up details and write them so they are acceptable according to the rules.

Unacceptable:

- arrange a phone bank for parent callers
- assemble callers
- provide refreshments

Examples of Activities Written by a Student Team

Provide a company phone number for employees to call to receive information and ask questions about the company's downsizing activities. The phone number will be activated on Sept. 18, 20xx, and will be deactivated Dec. 31, 20xx.

Managers and supervisors will establish, or in most cases reaffirm their open-door policy so employees will be more inclined to approach management with questions about the company's downsizing activities. The open-door policy will be implemented Sept. 20, 20xx, and will continue indefinitely.

The company will provide the most current downsizing information in monthly employee newsletters or memos. To increase employee confidence, included will be success stories of laid-off workers who have found new jobs outside the company. The first newsletter or memo will be sent to employees Oct. 31, 20xx, and will be published monthly through Jan. 31, 20xx.

Figure 4. Commonly Known Facts About Persuasion

<u>Sources</u>

1. People are strongly and quickly influenced by people they feel they can trust and believe.
2. People give even more credence to someone whose opinions are repeated by respected others.
3. People don't take seriously what they hear from people they don't trust, but over time they may recall what was said and forget who said it.

<u>Message Structure</u>

5. It's usually best to make your argument first, refute opposing arguments, and restate your position, depending on the complexity of the subject.
6. The last word is the one most likely to be remembered, especially with less educated people.
7. It's more effective to give both sides of an argument than to give one side, especially with educated audiences.
8. A one-sided argument might change attitudes initially, but the effect may fade when another side is heard.
9. People who hear both sides of an argument are likely to maintain a position even when other arguments are heard later.
8. It's more persuasive to state a conclusion than to expect people to draw their own.
9. Repetition keeps issues in the public eye. Messages, especially in the media, are quickly forgotten if they're not reinforced.

<u>Message Content</u>

10. People listen to what they like and ignore what they dislike.
11. People pay attention to messages that favor what they believe and ignore those that don't.
12. People interpret things the way they think; they see what they want to see.
13. People remember what they consider to be relevant and forget the rest.
14. People remember things that support what they believe.
15. Facts and emotional appeals are more effective than either one alone.
16. Messages aimed at the interest of a target audience are likely to get attention.
17. Trying to incite fear, guilt, or other negative emotions, or to issue threats are likely to turn people away.

Figure 4. Commonly Known Facts About Persuasion (*continued ...*)

18. The use of fear is more effective when combined with suggesting how to avoid it.
19. Fear can affect how people think, but not necessarily how they act.
20. Humor can win the hearts of an audience and alienate people if it seems manipulative.

<u>Media</u>

21. Face-to-face communication is more effective in changing minds than communication through various types of media.
22. Verbal communication conveys less but is more readily accepted than written communication.
23. Public media are more useful in reinforcing existing attitudes than in changing attitudes.
25. Print media produce more comprehension, especially with complex issues, than broadcast media.
26. Broadcast media are more attention-getting than print media.

<u>Audience</u>

28. People with low self-esteem are more influenced by unsupported messages and fear appeals than people with higher self-esteem.
29. People with high self-esteem are more likely to be persuaded by well substantiated messages.
30. People who make a commitment are likely to resist changing their minds afterward.
31. People who actively participate in making decisions are likely to retain changes in attitude over the long term.

Managers and supervisors will recognize and reward employees for both their accomplishments and their efforts in this time of transition. Employees want to work for an organization and in a department that is successful, and they need something back in return. They need to know how they are doing: whether they are succeeding or failing, are average or exemplary, and what they can do to improve when improvement is needed. Receiving awards helps employees know that their work is appreciated. Awards will be given on a case-by-case basis to recognize individual and sometimes group effort. There will be no starting or ending dates. Recognition will be publicized in the aforementioned newsletter.

Figure 5. List of Communication Tools

Actuality
Alerts—Internet
Annual meeting
Annual report
Archive video
Archived Webcast
A-roll
Background video
Backgrounder
Biographical
  sketch
Blog
Booklet
Briefing paper
Broadcast news
  release
Brochure
B-roll
Bumper sticker
Buzz
Byliner
Card stacking
Case history
Chat rooms
Circular
Closed circuit TV
Collateral
  publication
Commentary
Communication
  audit
Communication
  meeting
Contingency
  statement
Corporate profile
Cover letter

Dashboard
Demonstration
Direct mail
Door hanger
Editorial
Editorial board
  briefing
E-mail alert service
E-mail campaign
E-mail pitch
E-mail survey
E-newsletter
Episodic framing
E-tour
Event
Exclusive story
Expert news
  source
Facebook
Fact sheet
Factoid
FAQ
Fax, broadcast
Fax, on demand
Feature, business
Feature,
  educational
Feature,
  personality
Feature, trend
Infographics
Information kit
Insert and
  enclosure
Instant messaging
Interview – print
  media

Interview – radio
Interview – TV
Intranet
Leak
Letter
Letter pitch
Letter to editor
Media advisory
Media alert
Media interview
Media tour
Memento
Memo
Message board
Mission statement
MySpace
NetBriefing
News briefing
News kit
News release
Newsgroup
  seeding
Newsgroups
Newsletter
Newswire
Online media
  room
Online newsroom
Op-ed
  commentary
Opinion actuality
Organization
  profile
Personality profile
Phone pitch
Photo caption
Photo news release

Figure 5. List of Communication Tools (*continued ...*)

Pitch for radio talk
  show
Pitch for TV
  coverage
Pocket points
Podcast—audio
  and video
Position paper
Poster
Prepared
  statement
Presentation
Print publication
Printcast
Product profile
Product review
Public Service
  Announcement
  – radio
Public Service
  Announcement
  – TV
Publicity event
Publicity photo
Q & A
Quarterly earnings
  statement
Questionnaire
Report
Rolling one-on-
  one
Safety meeting
Satellite media
  tour
Search engines
Social media

Social responsibil-
  ity report
Speakers' bureau
Speech
Spokesperson tour
Streaming video
Syndicated service
Talk show
Testimonial
Testimony
Tip sheet
Tours
Town hall meeting
Trend story
TV stand-up
  interview
Twitter
Video news release
Video
  teleconferencing
Virtual conference
VO-BITE
Voice mail
VO-SOTs
Web conference
Web monitoring
Web news
  conference
Webcast – audio
  presentation
Webcast – full
  feature
Webcast – video
  presentation
White paper
YouTube

8. Writing the Execution Time Line

The execution time line is a schedule of all activities in a plan. The time line is important to reviewers because it provides a visual—at-a-glance—sequence of actions showing how long each will take to implement. Timing has a major bearing on the success of a plan, so it is essential to schedule each activity or tactic to know exactly when one needs to begin in order to be completed on time. Plan reviewers see the time line as an orchestration of activities or tactics that must be conducted with precision because they know that one of weaknesses of executive management in recent times has been initiating plans and failing to supervise them through to completion. Time for each activity must be allotted accurately not only for a plan to succeed, but to show plan reviewers what is involved in preparing to achieve certain milestones. It is unlikely that a plan reviewer

would know how much time is necessary to research a speech, design a Web site, write, review and clear a news release, or produce a white paper. In addition to showing dates, preparatory activities and milestones, a time line could provide a place for assigning responsibilities so that it is perfectly clear who is expected to execute each activity or tactic. The time line could be in the form of a table, critical path diagram, Gantt chart or even a calendar. See sample time lines on pages 188–191.

Exercise 8.   *Execution Time Line*

Develop a time line for an elegant dinner party celebration. Use your imagination to provide details of the event.

Execution Time Line Table

Date	Preparation	Execution
July 8	Conduct plant closure planning meeting; review business rationale and approve Q & A	
July 12	Notify manager of Cyber of plant closure	
July 15	Meet with Cyber plant manager to discuss business issues relative to closure	
July 17–19	Conduct three-day work session with human resources director and Cyber plant manager (review operational shut-down plan and timetable; identify core staff; develop retention plan; approve communication plan; discuss government regulations; approve news releases; review employment information; develop employment assistance; finalize security arrangements; approve contingency plan)	

July 26	Notify all plant managers by phone of Cyber plant closure; Notify all functional managers of Cyber of closure; Have customer mailings ready; Deliver by courier information kits to division managers	
July 27	Have information kits ready for sales representatives, sales managers and service center managers	
July 28	Follow up with Cyber functional managers Notify district sales managers by phone	
July 29		**Plant Closure Announcement** • Inform service center managers • Inform Cyber supervisors • Conduct meetings with Cyber employees • Inform community (hand-deliver news release to local media) • Inform sales representatives by phone • Inform Cyber customer service reps in face-to-face meeting • Notify employees of relocation opportunities • Distribute news release to corporate personnel • Transmit news release to state wires via BusinessWire • Distribute letter from CEO to all employees • Call community opinion leaders • Call or fax local and state officials • Notify key suppliers by phone • Fax news release to trade press • Mail letter and news release to customers • Mail letters and news release to suppliers • Period Following Announcement • Follow up on all communication to ensure complete and accurate understanding by all audiences.

A **TIME LINE** may be shown in a variety of forms, such as a flow chart (right). The critical path chart (below) shows preparatory work below the time line and the main event above the line. Another version could be showing behind-the-scenes work below the line and activities in public view above the line, or preparatory work below the line and milestones (stages of progress) above the line

July 8

Conduct plant closure planning meeting—review business rationale and approve Q & A

July 12

Notify manager of Cyber of plant closure

July 15

Meet with Cyber plant manager to discuss business issues relative to closure

July 17–19

Conduct three-day work session with human resources director and Cyber plant manager (review operational shut-down plan and timetable; identify core staff; develop retention plan; approve communication plan; discuss government regulations; approve news releases; review employment information; develop employment assistance; finalize security arrangements; approve contingency plan)

July 29

Plant Closure Announcement
- Inform service center managers
- Inform Cyber supervisors
- Conduct meetings with Cyber employees
- Inform community (hand-deliver news release to local media)
- Inform sales representatives by phone
- Inform Cyber customer service reps in face-to-face meeting
- Notify employees of relocation opportunities
- Distribute news release to corporate personnel
- Transmit news release to state wires via BusinessWire
- Distribute letter from CEO to all employees
- Call community opinion leaders
- Call or fax local and state officials
- Notify key suppliers by phone
- Fax news release to trade press
- Mail letter and news release to customers
- Mail letters and news release to suppliers
- Period Following Announcement
- Follow up on all communication to ensure complete and accurate understanding by all audiences.

July 26

Notify all plant managers by phone of Cyber plant closure

Notify all functional managers of Cyber of closure

Have customer mailings ready

Deliver by courier information kits to division managers

July 28

Have information kits ready for sales representatives, sales managers and service center managers

July 27

Follow up with Cyber functional managers

Notify district sales managers by phone

9. Writing The Evaluation

Public relations plans and proposals should be written to enable evaluation in two ways: performance and effectiveness. Simply: Did the plan implementor do what the plan implementor stated he or she would do? How effectively was it done?

Performance

A plan reviewer wants a regular means of assurance that a plan is being implemented the way it was proposed—every strategic step executed on schedule, on target and on budget. The plan reviewer knows that the implementor of a plan cannot guarantee results, but can be and should be held accountable for performance. Plan implementors must be careful to promise to deliver only what they totally control and that is their own performance. They are expected to execute a plan to the best of their ability, but because they do not have control over every factor that can affect a plan's outcome, they cannot guarantee results.

Plan developers and implementors should provide reviewers with means to monitor progress and performance in the execution of a plan with a Progress Tracking Report.

Rules for Writing the Evaluation

1. Show that the plan is written to enable evaluation in two areas: performance and effectiveness.
2. Include after the plan's execution time line a Progress Tracking Report to show reviewers they will receive, on a specified schedule, an at-a-glance visual to see that activities of the plan are on schedule, on target, on budget and completed.
3. Explain how each objective is to be measured. Following each objective > strategy(ies) > activities sequence, add EVALUATION. The entry could read, "Success in achieving this objective will be determined by …" (explain the means of measurement). Example:

   Evaluation
   Success in achieving this objective will be determined, informally, based on feedback supervisors receive from employees indicating employee understanding and support of a need to change communication procedures.

4. Position the main Evaluation component of the plan after the plan's Execution Time Line and before the Progress Tracking Report. The component could be shown as follows:

Rules for Writing the Evaluation (*continued ...*)

EVALUATION

This plan is written to enable evaluation in two areas: performance and effectiveness. It has a Progress Tracking Report to be issued on a specified schedule to gauge performance in implementing the plan. It has objectives written to enable measurement to judge the plan's effectiveness in accomplishing it's goal.

It is optional to include in the evaluation section a recap of objectives and evaluations that would enable reviewers to concentrate on studying, together, the indicators to be used in determining the value of a plan. Example:

OBJECTIVE 1—(employees)   **OBJECTIVE 2—(residents)**

EVALUATION   **EVALUATION**

5. Use means of measuring that are timely, cost-effective, practical, credible, accurate, verifiable. and founded on the "Guidelines For Measuring The effectiveness Of PR Programs And Activities" by Dr. Walter K. Lindenmann and published by the Institute for Public Relations. See page 76.
6. Write plans that promise performance, perform on research, stand up to measurement and reflect the Code of Ethics espoused by Public Relations Society of America.

The report can provide an at-a-glance visual check to see that activities of the plan are on schedule, on target, on budget and completed or not. Every plan should contain a Progress Tracking Report. Once a template is formed, the report can be updated easily and submitted to reviewers on paper or electronically as frequently as desired. See a sample Progress Tracking Report on page 194.

Effectiveness

The relative effectiveness or value of what is done in public relations is determined by measurement. PR measurement involves assessing the success or failure of specific PR programs against predetermined objectives.

More specifically, PR measurement is a way of giving a result a precise dimension, generally by comparison to some standard or baseline and usually is done in a quantifiable or numerical manner. That is, when we measure outcomes, we should come

PROGRESS TRACKING REPORT (example)				
Objective/ Focus	Activity	On Schedule On Target On Budget	Behind Schedule Off Target or Over Budget	Completed
1	Conduct company meeting			■
Employees	Issue weekly progress reports	▨		
	Distribute PCB fact sheet			■
	Open employee hotline	▨		
	Memo to employees on safety			■
2	Distribute door hangers		■	
Residents	Conduct town meetings	▨		
	Open community hotline		■	
	Publicize cleanup program	▨		
3	Call press conference			■
Media	Distribute media fact sheet			■
	Have experts at conference			■
4	Schedule milestone meetings		■	
Government	Send information packets		■	
	Conduct tours		■	
	Send follow-up letters	▨		
	(DATE)			

up with a precise measure, for example: number of persons convinced to participate, to contribute, to attend, to accept, to reject, to follow, to respond, etc. Because public relations is not an exact science, and because a plan implementor does not have total control of all factors that influence results, public relations practitioners must be mindful not to claim total credit for results, such as increasing sales, improving productivity, and raising stock values. It is important to the profession and to the practitioner to make legitimate claims about "supporting," or "contributing to" outcomes that are obviously the result of multiple factors, along with public relations actions. Boastful, unsubstantiated claims of success serve only to undermine the credibility of the profession and when observed should heighten the profession's resolve to adhere to the Code of Ethics espoused by the Public Relations Society of America.

Writing plans based on solid research and written to enable measurement are products that distinguish professionals in this field. Every practitioner, to be a true professional, must have a fundamental knowledge of how value is established in public relations. The place to begin in acquiring such background is reading the Gold Standard Paper from the Commission on Public Relations Measurement & Evaluation, titled, Guidelines For Measuring The Effectiveness of PR Programs And Activities," by Dr. Walter K. Lindenmann and published by the Institute for Public Relations. Access to this paper is closer than you might know; turn to page 76.

Exercise 9.   *Evaluation*
Based on the rules for developing the evaluation component of a plan, explain how the entry below could be improved.

Evaluation

The public forum on February 29 was well attended (300 people). Initial questions regarding the problem shifted to broader questions regarding health policy and were directed to the present officials. The center was not the main focus as before. Media coverage on February 30 and March 2 reported on the forum as well as the court findings of no wrongdoing … and for the first time in months, things got quiet. The hot line recorded 10 phone calls-many from customers wanting reassurance that their warranties remained unchanged. Employees who had born the brunt of angry customers were acknowledged with a series of appreciation events, including a pancake breakfast served by the president. Further, anecdotal feedback from community leaders was positive and the quick resolution of negative media coverage were great indicators of initial success. The topic, which held the attention of the media and community for nearly four months has entirely dissipated.

10. Writing The Budget

The budget is of paramount interest to reviewers. One of the quickest ways to have a plan rejected is by proposing a budget that is out of line with the organization's resources. An experienced plan developer will gather the insights necessary to present a budget appropriate to the organization. It is much better to present a budget that is on target than to present one that is out of the ballpark and will require major modifications, even elimination of some creative strategies, to be acceptable. With public relations, communication objectives can be accomplished in many different ways at different levels of expense. Developing a plan within a particular budget is one of the responsibilities of the plan developer.

A proposed budget should be developed from one of two positions. One position is that you represent a public relations firm or agency and your plan is for a client. The other position is that you are an employee of an organization with responsibility for public relations and your plan is for your employer. You must use a budget format that is appropriate for your position.

Let's look first at a budget format for a plan developed by a public relations agency. The budget should have two parts: 1) time billing for agency personnel and 2) billing for out-of-pocket expenses.

For time billing, you must estimate the amount of time required by agency personnel to carry out the work of your plan. The lead person on an agency account usually is the account executive. So most of the work will be done by an account executive and an account coordinator, account assistant or assistant account executive. A certain amount of administrative/secretarial work usually is required also.

Time for personnel more senior to the account executive might be included for their particular expertise or experienced counsel. For a highly complex plan time might be budgeted for an account supervisor who would be responsible for managing the use of additional expertise and services, such as various forms of research. Following are typical public relations agency hourly billing rates for use in developing a budget for case exercises in this book.

Public Relations Firm or Agency Hourly Billing Rates

President, General Manager, PR Director	$200
Vice President	$150
Account Supervisor	$125
Senior Account Executive	$100
Account Executive	$90
Assistant Account Executive	$85
Account Coordinator, Account Assistant	$75
Secretary	$60

Next your budget should show out-of-pocket expenses. These are expenses the agency would incur or contract for on behalf of the client, such as photography, graphic design, opinion research, media monitoring, long distance phone charges, photo copies, printing, etc. So an estimated budget from an agency should have two components, time billing for personnel and billing for out-of-pocket expenses. Suggested formats:

ESTIMATED BUDGET (PR Agency)

Time Billing				
Agency Staff	Rate/hour	Est. hours/day	Est. days	
			Subtotal	
Out of Pocket Expenses				
			Subtotal	
			Total Estimated Budget	

Rules for Writing the Budget

1. Use the correct budget format–PR Agency or Company
2. A proposed budget from a public relations agency must show time billing for personnel and out-of-pocket expenses.
3. An estimated budget by an organization's public relations function must show only extraordinary expenses–those not covered in an annual department budget.
4. Proposed budgets should be affordable to an organization.
5. Budget items should be self-explanatory.
6. Budget figures must be aligned on a decimal point.

Next let's look at a budget format for a plan that you, as the person responsible for public relations, would develop for your employer. One major difference between this budget and one developed by a public relations firm is that time for work done by you and various staff members is already accounted in salaries and some of the expenses shown in the plan, such as photography, might already be covered in your organization's annual public relations budget. So, in this position, the budget should show only items or services for which you must request authorization for additional funding.

The budget format for a plan developed by company public relations personnel should be as follows, and is easily set up using the table function in your word processor.

ESTIMATED BUDGET (Company)

Expenses		
	Estimated Total Expenses	

Exercise 10. *Budget*
Develop a proposed budget from a public relations agency for pitching a client's appearance on Hello America. Consider accounting for time to develop the pitch, including researching the client's subject, creating and producing visuals for the client (e.g. charts, photographs, etc.), writing briefing notes for the client, TV monitoring service, and other details using your own imagination.

On the following pages are planning worksheets to copy and use in rough drafting public relations plans and proposals for cases in Chapter 7.

PLANNING WORKSHEETS
(Copy worksheets for drafting plans for cases in Chapter 7.)

INTRODUCTION (Summary of problem, challenge, opportunity or situation.)

SITUATION ANALYSIS (Start from the beginning. Tell as a story. Do not repeat the introduction.)

GOAL (Express in one sentence.)

FOCUS (target audiences, target publics, focal points)

PLANNING WORKSHEETS
(Copy this worksheet for each objective of your plan.)

FOCUS (One focal point, target audience or public for each objective.)
OBJECTIVE (What must be done with one focal point of the plan to accomplish the plan's goal?)
STRATEGY (How the objective will be accomplished.)
ACTIVITY OR TACTIC (Detailed steps to implement the strategy.)
ACTIVITY OR TACTIC (Detailed steps to implement the strategy.)
ACTIVITY OR TACTIC (Detailed steps to implement the strategy.)
ACTIVITY OR TACTIC (Detailed steps to implement the strategy.)
ACTIVITY OR TACTIC (Detailed steps to implement the strategy.)
EVALUATION (By what means the objective will be measured.) Success in achieving this objective will be determined by (explain means of measurement)…

PLANNING WORKSHEETS

Execution Time Line

Insert Time Increment	Preparation	Milestone

PLANNING WORKSHEETS

Evaluation

This plan provides for evaluating performance and effectiveness. Performance is shown with a Progress Tracking Report at a scheduled interval of time, such as weekly, biweekly, monthly, etc. The report appears at the end of the plan. A means of measurement to determine effectiveness is shown with each objective.

ESTIMATED BUDGET (Use the correct budget form)

(For a PR agency includes time billing for personnel and out-of-pocket expenses.)

Time Billing				
Agency Staff	Rate/hour	Est. hours/day	Est. days	
			Subtotal	
Out of Pocket Expenses				
			Subtotal	
			Total Estimated Budget	

ESTIMATED BUDGET (Use the correct budget form)

(For a company or nonprofit organization includes extraordinary expenses not covered in an annual budget.

Expenses		
	Estimated Total Expenses	

7 More Public Relations Cases: Problems, Opportunities, Challenges

This section of the book features more real world case situations with compelling needs for public relations action. Each case is presented in a different manner, such as a role play of a meeting, a contract for services, a transcript of private meetings, field notes by an account executive. Each case has a team assignment to develop a public relations plan, and individual team member assignments to provide written elements in support of a plan, such as a news release, briefing notes for a TV show or pocket point cards.

No solutions are offered for the cases because, realistically, in public relations, there are different ways to address situations effectively.

Names of people, companies, organizations are fictitious, while cases are actual experiences.

Case Seven
Social Media

UNCHARITABLE BLOGGERS?

This case is based on provocative questions about philanthropy and the nonprofit sector courageously raised by Dan Pallotta in his book, UNCHARITABLE How Restraints On Nonprofits Undermine Their Potential. Dan Pallotta founded Pallotta Teamworks, the company that invented the AIDS Rides and Breast Cancer 3-Day events, which raised over half a billion dollars and netted $305 million in nine years—more money, raised more quickly for these causes than any known private event operation in history. 182,000 people participated in the events. The company had more than 350 full-time employees in 16 U.S. offices, was the subject of a Harvard Business School case study, and fundamentally re-invented the paradigm for special event fundraising in America.

Dan Pallotta argues that society's nonprofit ethic acts as a strict regulatory mechanism, that it denies the nonprofit sector critical tools and permissions that the for-profit sector is allowed to use without restraint (e.g., no risk-reward incentives, no profit, counterproductive limits on

Against Change

"People who want to work in the nonprofit world should be more interested in the good they do than in the money they can make."

"Charities should not take risks. They are taking risks with earmarked funds. They should be cautious."

"Charities do not have the luxury to think about the future. Donated money should be spent immediately to alleviate the suffering of others."

"Charities should not waste money on expensive advertising. It is money that could otherwise go to the needy."

"Charities should not make mistakes. A mistake means a charity is wasting money and waste is immoral."

"Charities should maintain a low overhead percentage. This is the only way to know that any good is being done. Low overhead is moral. High overhead is immoral."

For Change

"If we allow charity to compensate people according to the value they produce, we can attract more leaders of the kind the for-profit sector attracts, and we can produce greater value."

"The more that charities take calculated risks, the better the chance that they will break new ground."

"The more we allow charities to invest in the future instead of only the current fiscal year, the more they will be able to build the future we all want."

"Advertising builds consumer demand. The more that charities are allowed to advertise, the better they can compete with consumer products for the consumer's dollar, and the more money they can raise for the needy."

"The more mistakes a charity makes in good faith, the faster it will learn and the quicker it will be able to solve complex problems. This is the only path to solving problems—one must 'fail upward.'"

"A charity's overhead percentage doesn't give you any data about the good it is doing in the world. If charities focused more on solving the world's problems than on keeping overhead low, more of the world's problems would be solved."

Excerpted from Dan Pallotta, *Uncharitable: How Restraints on Nonprofits Undermine their Potential.* Tufts, 2008. Reprinted with permission from the publisher.

compensation, and moral objections to the use of donated dollars for anything other than program expenditures). While the for-profit sector is permitted to use the tools of capitalism to advance the sale of consumer goods, the nonprofit sector is prohibited from using any of them to fight hunger or disease. The argument is illustrated by bloggers on the next page.

This irrational system, Pallotta explains, has its roots in 400-year-old Puritan ethics that banished self-interest from the realm of charity. The ideology is policed today by watchdog agencies and the use of "efficient" measures, which Pallotta argues are flawed, unjust, and should be abandoned. By declaring our independence from these obsolete ideas, Pallotta theorizes, we can dramatically accelerate progress on the most urgent social issues of our time.

Team Assignment

Your assignment in this case is to assume that your PR agency team has agreed, on a pro bono basis, to assist the organizer of a marathon run whose upcoming event could become the center of a fire storm of discussion among bloggers over society's ethics for nonprofits. The organizing charity wants to proceed with the marathon that is just three months away, but is afraid that negative cyberspace buzz about the use of donated funds could undermine participation in the event and the reputation of the organizing charity.

The issue being debated among bloggers was sparked by the marathon organizer's use of advertising, hiring of a highly experienced event coordinator, decision to risk rallying participants to a first-of-its-kind

event for the town, above-average administrative cost for the event, and investment in event logistical equipment to be used in future marathons. Your job is to keep a cyber fire storm from developing and undermining the potential fundraising success of "Run For The Little Ones."

The purpose of this case, based on actual events, is to provide an experience in developing a public relations plan for working with the new media in addressing a public relations problem.

Background

A charity we will call The Society For Little Children, has organized a three-day marathon run we will call "Run For The Little Ones." Three months before the event, the charity enlisted the pro bono support of your public relations agency. While the charity is operating within legal bounds, it has pushed the envelope on what the public regards as ethical and moral behavior for nonprofit and philanthropic endeavors.

The charity is using some of the tools, such as advertising, that are freely available to the for-profit sector, but frowned upon by the public for use by nonprofits. The charity's use of advertising, hiring of a highly experienced event management company, taking the risk of rallying participants to a first-of-its-kind event for the town, above-average administrative cost for the event, and investment in event logistical equipment to be used in future marathons is beginning to be debated among bloggers as shown on the previous page. The controversy has not, as yet, appeared in the traditional media.

The charity is concerned that becoming the center of a fire storm of discussion among bloggers over society's ethics for nonprofits is going to reduce participation in the event and damage the reputation of the charity. Your job is to quickly quell the negative cyber buzz and prevent undermining of the potential fundraising success of "Run For The Little Ones."

The event is expected to attract about 500 participants, who are expected to raise $1.6 million in donor contributions. Expenses in support of participants for three days and two nights are estimated to be $275,000. Expenses for marketing and raising awareness of the event are expected to be about $112,000. Fee for an event coordinating company will be $140,000. The contribution remaining for direct charitable service would be about $1,073,000 or 67 percent of total funds donated. Because of the nature of the event, there is no other way to significantly reduce expenses.

Individual Writing Assignments

Each team member is to complete a different one of the following items that might or might not be included in the design of your plan.

1. Develop a social media news release announcing that "Run For The Little Ones" is expected to raise more than $1.5 million based on early registrations. Include links to items, such as reports, backgrounders, financial statements, that would help quell the developing negative cyber dialogue.

2. Write a persuasive e-mail message to area bloggers involved in the nonprofit, for-profit discussion, inviting them to an informational

meeting with the charity's director (make up name) to discuss their concerns about the charity's use of funds.

3. Write an e-mail news release to editors of the traditional area media announcing that "Run For The Little Ones" is expected to raise more than $1.5 million based on early registrations and calling their attention to the social media news release on the charity's Web site.

4. Using the Internet, research information about how the performance of nonprofits is to be judged and write, with a reader-grabbing headline, a compelling blog of about 150 words in favor of giving nonprofits more latitude in using the tools available to for-profit organizations in planning, promoting and implementing fundraising events.

5. Write a memo from the charity's president to staff members calling their attention to the growing debate among bloggers about nonprofit organizations' use of donated funds, how the charity and its marathon run could become the center of a fire storm of negative publicity on the Web and in the traditional media, and stating a policy directive that no one but the director is to engage in the discussion online or with the traditional media because even personal comments by employees could be reported as statements by the charity.

6. Describe the electronic tools that could be used in creating a digital dashboard for monitoring the debate on the Internet over the use of donated funds by nonprofit organizations.

7. Create in diagram form a crisis communication page for the charity's Web site. Include buttons or links that take visitors to information that would be responsive to criticisms of the charity identified in Assignment Details. This would not be titled a "crisis communication" page because it isn't a crisis yet, and you don't want visitors to see the situation labeled a crisis. Use an appropriate title. Show how you want this gateway to information to look and what you want it to include.

ARTICLE: CHARITABLE DECISION-MAKING MADE EASIER AND MUTUALLY BENEFICIAL

There comes a time with many companies when the task of making charitable contributions gets to be more of a headache than a gratifying gesture of goodwill.

Decision-making becomes inconsistent and untimely. Objectives become obscure. Requests from not-for-profit organizations pile up. Record keeping gets haphazard. And if the situation continues, grant giving loses its community relations effectiveness.

When such a condition develops, it becomes readily apparent that corporate contributions must be managed like every other business function.

By managing corporate contributions effectively, the task of making donations becomes easier and mutually beneficial.

Here are four reasons why managing corporate contributions makes the task of making donations easier.

One reason is that a company provides grant seekers with guidelines that enable them to qualify or disqualify their organizations as potential recipients.

Guidelines, for example, might specify that a company consider only proposals originated by organizations residing in communities in which the company has an operation.

Guidelines might specify that a company does not fund organizations whose services are duplicated by government agencies.

A second reason is that a company makes known to grant seekers the extent to which it is willing to support certain areas of interest.

It is not necessary for a company to indicate dollar limits. For example, a company might indicate levels of funding by stating that it would like to "recognize," "reward," "support," or "invest in" youth programs. It might define "recognize" as "A modest investment in the recognition of an idea or person that might bring superlative returns in terms of community awareness and support."

A third reason the task of making donations becomes easier when contributions are managed is that a company specifies the format in which requests must be submitted.

By specifying a format, a company ensures that proposals will be a quick read for reviewers. Companies might, for example, specify that submissions be limited to a certain number of pages, that type faces be a certain size, that the text contains no jargon, that budgets are kept to one page with self-explanatory line items.

A fourth reason is that a company requests from grant seekers certain information that enables company reviewers to expedite their evaluations of proposals.

A company might, for example, ask for a statement of an organization's goal, mission and beliefs to ensure that what is being proposed is true to the organization's fundamental purpose.

By managing corporate contributions effectively, the task of making donations becomes easier and mutually beneficial.

Here are three ways that managing corporate contributions makes donating funds mutually beneficial?

One way is that a company funds only proposals that are of particular interest to it. In other words, the company establishes preferred areas of giving.

On one hand, a company might express an interest in funding proposals related to youth programs or health maintenance, music or culture and the arts, education, people needs, senior citizens, free enterprise and/or family values.

On the other hand, a company might advise that it is not interested in funding national health organizations, endowments, capital fund drives or operating expenses.

A second way is that a company funds only potentially successful activities and shares in the recognition.

A company might request that grant seekers organize proposals in terms of a goal, objectives, activities, schedule and budget, so that it can evaluate its potential for success from a management perspective.

A third way managing contributions makes donating funds mutually beneficial is that a company seeks assurance that whatever it supports will have lasting value, thereby providing continuing benefits to the company's employees, their families and members of the community in which they work.

In this regard, a company would question the sustainability of an organization's proposed activity. Does the proposal contain adequate provisions for organizational change, new mechanisms and public involvement to sustain change?

So, to manage corporate contributions effectively a company needs to establish guidelines for grant seekers, prescribe a format for proposals, request evaluative information from qualifying organizations, reveal its areas of preferred giving, assess a proposal's potential for success, and select funding opportunities that have lasting value.

It is important to consider that managing corporate contributions should facilitate charitable giving and not restrain the potential of nonprofit organizations. In the private sector we compensate people according to the value they produce. We take calculated risks to improve our chances of breaking new ground. We invest in the present, but more importantly in the future. We use promotional tools to increase business. We allow ourselves to learn from mistakes. We know that it takes money to make money. We must afford nonprofits the same benefits if we are to facilitate charitable giving.

By managing corporate contributions effectively, the task of making donations becomes easier and mutually beneficial.

Case Eight
Community
Relations

CONTAMINATED LAGOON

This is a case of a contaminated lagoon. Plans were being made for the expansion of Industrial Products Inc. in Douglas, U.S.A., when management discovers that a lagoon on plant property is contaminated with hazardous chemicals. The hazard must be removed before plant expansion work can begin. Industrial Products decides that it does not have the expertise necessary to handle public communication regarding the hazardous waste site cleanup and calls on the public relations staff of corporate headquarters for assistance. A staff member is dispatched to meet with the management of the subsidiary operations in Douglas.

Details of the case unfold in a dialogue between the headquarters public relations staff person, Kelly O'Connel, and management staff at Douglas. The conversation is in the form of a classroom/professional workshop role play. More detail is available in Kelly O'Connel's handwritten field notes that follow the script. The article titled, "Community relations can facilitate corporate growth" provides a broad perspective on the value of good community relations.

Team Assignment

Your team assignment is to develop a public relations plan for closing the contaminated lagoon. You and your team are staff members of the headquarters public relations department of Rockover, Inc., owner of the subsidiary operation, Industrial Products, Inc., located in Douglas, U.S.A. The goal of your plan, stated by the operations manager, is for Industrial Products, Inc. to be expanding its facilities with minimal delays from the lagoon closure.

Individual Team Member Assignments

Each team member is to complete a different one of the following items that might or might not be included in the design of your plan.

1. Write a statement to the news media to be used only if reporters inquire about the project.
2. Write the script for a podcast by the plant manager to be accessed from the plant's Web site.
3. Write a memo from the manager of human resources to employees responding to their health and safety concerns with regard to the contaminated lagoon.
4. Write a Q & A for management personnel to use in discussing the cleanup project with people within or outside the company.
5. Write a letter to government representatives (David Hall, mayor, or Randy Don, county

commissioner) apprising them of the project so they are prepared to answer questions from their constituents.
6. Write a fact sheet on the cleanup project with construction scheduling information. (See field notes.)
7. Write a one-page backgrounder exclusively on the subject of PCBs. Provide information that would be useful to journalists, not to chemical engineers.
8. Write a pocket point card for management (all levels through supervisor) with information on both sides with talking points about the lagoon project.

ROLE PLAY
Cast

Narrator
Kelly O'Connel - PR Assistant
Bob Elwood - PR Director
Sam Seabert - Operations Manager
AJ Detweiler - Production Manager
Jordan Slagel - Environmental Engineer
Terry Trobaugh - Safety Manager
Sharon Duncan - Administrative Assistant
Case Dilena - Manager, Human Resources

Public Relations Department
Rockover, Inc., Corporate Headquarters

(Public Relations Assistant approaches Public Relations Director for assignment)

Kelly O'Connel - PR Assistant

Good morning.

Bob Elwood - PR Director

Hi Kelly. Ready to work?

Kelly O'Connel - PR Assistant

(Not knowing what to expect)
I'm ready!

Bob Elwood - PR Director

That's good. I'd like you to make a plane reservation to Douglas, U.S.A. They're expecting you for a meeting tomorrow morning.

Kelly O'Connel - PR Assistant

(Clearly caught off guard ...)
Douglas! Who's expecting me?

Bob Elwood - PR Director

(Privately amused by her reaction, but totally confident that she can handle the job)
I would have handled this myself, but I've got a speech to write for the chairman.

Kelly O'Connel - PR Assistant

So who's the meeting with?

Bob Elwood - PR Director

The manager of Douglas Operations and members of his staff.

Kelly O'Connel - PR Assistant

What's it about?

Bob Elwood - PR Director

A lagoon. They have to deal with it before they can proceed with their expansion plans.

Kelly O'Connel - PR Assistant

(Half joking.)
A lagoon needs public relations?

Bob Elwood - PR Director

You need to hear the whole story firsthand. The lagoon is contaminated.

Kelly O'Connel - PR Assistant

Are they worried about publicity?

Bob Elwood - PR Director

That's part of it.

Kelly O'Connel - PR Assistant

What else are they worried about?

Bob Elwood - PR Director

Employees. Sorry, I've got to see the chairman.

Kelly O'Connel - PR Assistant

I'll make the reservations.

At an altitude of 37,000 feet heading for Douglas.

Kelly O'Connel - PR Assistant

(Musing to herself ... I can't believe this ... My first assignment ... A polluted lagoon ... That's all right. I can do this.)

Conference Room, Douglas Operations

Kelly has been introduced; meeting is under way.

Sam Seaberg - Operations Manager

Thanks for coming Kelly. We were making plans to expand our operations. In the process we discovered that we have a polluted lagoon. We need to be undertaking the expansion with minimal delays from the lagoon closure. That's our goal.

Jordan Slagel - Environmental Engineer

(Interjecting)
We tested sediment in the bottom of the lagoon and found a significant concentration of PCBs. PCBs are ... (pause)

Kelly O'Connel - PR Assistant

(Interrupting)
I know. Polychlorinated biphenyls (by-fee-nals). Not very friendly to people. I did some quick research before I left headquarters. So how did the PCBs get into the lagoon?

AJ Detweiler - Production Manager

We think it happened years ago with the old forming operation. They mixed water from the lagoon with a petroleum based lubricant for cooling. The water was recycled back into the lagoon. PCBs probably floated to the bottom and settled into the sediment.

Kelly O'Connel - PR Assistant

(Mentally starting to shape a message ...)
So, we can say that the pollution isn't the result of any of our current operations, but that we're taking full responsibility for cleaning it up.

Sam Seaberg - Operations Manager

Yes. And it will be closed. The lagoon will be closed as part of our overall plant expansion plan.

Kelly O'Connel - PR Assistant

What do you mean, closed?

Jordan Slagel - Environmental Engineer

It will be lined and used as a storm water retention basin.

Kelly O'Connel - PR Assistant

How big is this lagoon?

Jordan Slagel - Environmental Engineer

Surface size of the lagoon is about 37,000 square feet.

Kelly O'Connel - PR Assistant

That's a small lake.

Sharon Duncan - Administrative Assistant

(Abruptly interjecting in a tattle-tale tone of voice.)
It used to be a picnic area for employees. With tables ... And benches, and ...

Kelly O'Connel - PR Assistant

(A dreaded thought occurred. Were employees exposed? She interrupts Sharon.)
Don't tell me ... A place where families could play in the water? Are employees at risk?

Casey Dilena - Mgr., Human Resources

No. Fortunately, the lagoon has always been fenced off. We're confident that no one is at risk. But employees might not be easily convinced of that.

Jordan Slagel - Environmental Engineer

PCBs are heavy. They don't float. They're in the sediment, not the water.

Kelly O'Connel - PR Assistant

(Thinking to herself: I wonder how assured I would feel as an employee who worked for 10 years or more around a hazardous waste site.)
Where is the lagoon?

Sharon Duncan - Administrative Assistant

(She exclaims in her tattle-tale tone of voice.) That's easy! Don't ya know. It's in plain sight of the whole world!

Casey Dilena - Mgr., Human Resources

Get a grip, Sharon. (pause) It's behind the finishing and forming operations. Unfortunately drivers coming into town in the morning look directly at it from City Expressway. You could read a billboard in the time it takes to pass by.

Terry Trobaugh - Safety Manager

The lagoon will be designated a hazardous materials area and workers will be wearing hazardous materials suits.

Kelly O'Connel - PR Assistant

You mean … moon suits?

Terry Trobaugh - Safety Manager

They do look like space suits.

Kelly O'Connel - PR Assistant

(Thinking to herself–we've got a lot of communicating to do.)
Who knows about this situation?

Sam Seaberg - Operations Manager

The state Department of Environmental Resources.

Kelly O'Connel - PR Assistant

The media?

Sam Seaberg - Operations Manager

No, not yet.

Kelly O'Connel - PR Assistant

What about employees?

Sam Seaberg - Operations Manager

No. When they do, the long-time veterans are going to be concerned. They'll remember the picnic grounds.

Sharon Duncan - Administrative Assistant

(Admonishing the company.)
You bet they will! They'll remember all right!!

Kelly O'Connel - PR Assistant

I would think so. Not the best place to eat hotdogs.

Sharon Duncan - Administrative Assistant

(Emotionally charged, she exclaims)
Listen, Kelly. Just the mention of toxic chemicals and some people will go into orbit! Know what I mean? Do you know what I mean!!

Kelly O'Connel - PR Assistant

What about government? City and county officials? Do they know?

Sam Seaberg - Operations Manager

No. And there's a potential problem. We don't have the best working relationship with local and county government. It's not bad. It's just that ... Well, we just don't have one and we need their support to get construction permits on schedule.

Kelly O'Connel - PR Assistant

When is work supposed to start on the lagoon?

Jordan Slagel - Environmental Engineer

May 15th.

Kelly O'Connel - PR Assistant

Today is May 1st. We have precious little time to do a lot of communicating.

AJ Detweiler - Production Manager

(Grumbling about headquarters involvement ...)
What's the big deal? It's not like we're into a meltdown. Why do we need public relations? The facts will speak for themselves. All's we need to do is get the contractor in here and get the job done.

Sam Seaberg - Operations Manager

Not so fast, AJ. Let's think about this. Douglas is about to discover that it has toxic waste on the edge of town. Rush hour drivers coming into town are going to see workers in moon suits. Veteran employees are going to be fearful of possible health hazards to themselves and their families.

Local and county officials could get flooded with phone calls from residents wanting to know what's going on. And who knows how the media is going to play this.

AJ Detweiler - Production Manager

(Grousing to himself about getting PR involved and unable to keep to himself ...)
Come on, Sam. We've been a good company to work for, for years. I don't know why people have to meddle in our affairs.

Sam Seaberg - Operations Manager

(Realizing that some people are more sensitive about public relations than others, Sam ignores AJ's comment and turns to Kelly)
Kelly, we obviously need some help from the PR Department.

Kelly O'Connel - PR Assistant

I'm here to help, Sam. Could we take a few minutes to go over the plan so I have an idea of what's ahead?

Sam Seaberg - Operations Manager

Sure. We hired BBEO Remediation and Construction Company to close the lagoon.

AJ Detweiler - Production Manager

(Straightening up and trying to be a constructive participant.)
It's a Jersey company. They have experience in cleaning up hazardous waste.

Jordan Slagel - Environmental Engineer

The state Department of Environmental Resources is overseeing the cleanup.

AJ Detweiler - Production Manager

Our engineers and BBEO staff have a detailed closure plan. First the water will be pumped out of the lagoon.

Jordan Slagel - Environmental Engineer

It will be treated, tested and discharged into a connecting stream. The sediment will be excavated from the bottom of the lagoon. It will be pressed through a filter to get rid of excess water. Then it will be tested and stored in sealed containers.

Kelly O'Connel - PR Assistant

What happens to the containers?

Jordan Slagel - Environmental Engineer

They'll be loaded on a train and taken to a regulated disposal site. We'll cover the area with a liner and it will be used as a storm water retention basin.

Terry Trobaugh - Safety Manager

The entire work area will be fenced in. Only authorized workers will be allowed access to the site. There will be strict safety rules. Workers will have to wear protective gear that will be cleaned and properly disposed of daily throughout the process.

Kelly O'Connel - PR Assistant

(Testing the accuracy of what she thought she heard …)
So we can say the water will be pumped out, tested and discharged into a connecting stream. The polluted sediment will be excavated, stored in leak-proof containers and shipped by rail to a regulated disposal site. The area will be lined and used as a storm water retention basin.

Sam Seaberg - Operations Manager

That's correct Kelly. The project will take about six to eight weeks. After BBEO brings in its heavy equipment, the area will be closed. No company equipment will be used. Workers will wear protective suits, gloves, boots and respirators that will be cleaned or disposed of each time they leave the site.

Kelly O'Connel - PR Assistant

Is there any health risk to people around the site?

Jordan Slagel - Environmental Engineer

The chemicals are in the sediment, not in the water. PCBs are not airborne, so there's no chance of contact with employees or plant visitors or area residents.

Kelly O'Connel - PR Assistant

(Thinking to herself: Employees will wonder, if there's no risk, why do workers have to wear moon suits? I need to know more about PCBs, like what are the effects of PCBs on people? She thumbs through her notes … Sam hands her a project schedule …)
Sam, how will closing the lagoon affect your expansion plans?

Sam Seaberg - Operations Manager

The project might delay our plant expansion work. But it's essential that we clean things up properly, and safely.

The meeting adjourns. Kelly returns to headquarters to draw up a PR plan.

Work schedule Kelly received from Sam.
The plan has three phases:

1. Mobilization and site preparation; BBEO brings and sets up equipment; start date May 15, finish date May 24
2. Site remediation activities; lagoon dewatering starts May 25, finishes June 16; sediment removal starts June 1 and finishes Aug. 9; belt press dewatering starts Aug. 8 and finishes Aug. 23; post-removal sampling starts Aug. 24 and finishes Aug. 30; preparation for structural backfill starts Aug. 31 and finishes Sept. 4
3. Demobilization and closeout activities, removal of temporary facilities and controls starts Sept. 5, finishes Sept. 11; demobilization starts Sept. 12 and finishes Sept. 13; closeout meeting Sept. 20.

Kelly's Initial Research Notes

PCBs or polychlorinated biphenyls are a class of compounds consisting of two benzene rings joined together at one carbon on each ring ... the rings are then substituted with one to 10 chlorine atoms. ... developed in 1929 they have been used as electrical insulating fluids, fire-resistant heat transfer and hydraulic fluids, lubricants and as components in elastomers, adhesives, paints, pigments and waxes. ... PCBs were very attractive in industrial use because they are non-volatile, non-flammable, chemically stable and good electrical insulators. Because PCBs are very stable, they do not break down in the environment; therefore they are environmentally unsuitable. ... in 1976 Congress enacted the Toxic Substance Control Act (TSCA), which required the Environmental Protection Agency (EPA) to establish rules regarding PCBs. ... production ceased in 1977. ... in 1979 the EPA published the PCB ban rule which prohibits the manufacturing, processing, distribution in commerce and use of PCBs except in a totally enclosed manner. Concentrations of PCBs 50 parts per billion or over fall under EPA regulations, and must be disposed of under EPA guidelines. ... PCBs can affect the body if inhaled, swallowed or there is contact with the eyes or skin. ... they may cause irritation of the eyes, nose, and throat and an acne-like skin rash. ... they may also cause liver disorders which would result in such effects as fatigue, dark urine, and yellow jaundice. ... studies on laboratory animals showed the chemicals caused liver, reproductive and gastric disorders, skin lesions and tumor.

* * *

Notes on meeting with Operations Manager Sam Seaberg and staff, Industrial Products, Inc., Douglas, U.S.A. subsidiary of Rockover, Inc. May 1.

What is the situation at Douglas?

We were in the process of planning plant expansions Discovered that a small lagoon on our property was polluted

How small?

A lagoon approximately 37,114 square feet in surface size

Where?

Located behind the finishing and forming operations

What kind of pollution?

Tested sediment in the bottom of the lagoon; found a significant concentration of PCBs (polychlorinated biphenyls) The PCBs likely entered the lagoon as a result of the old forming operation. ... the water was mixed with a petroleum-based lubricant for cooling. ... the water was then recycled back into the lagoon. ... PCBs likely floated to the bottom and settled into the sediment The lagoon will be closed as part of the overall plant expansion plan. It will be lined and used as a storm water retention basin.

Did the company dump PCBs in the lagoon?

The PCBs are not a result of any of our current operations. We're taking responsibility for cleaning and closing the lagoon

Possible quote: "The pollution is not a result of any of our current operations at the plant. But we will take full responsibility for cleaning it up."

Note to self: What are PCBs? Research [later: PCBs or polychlorinated biphenyls are a class of compounds consisting of two benzene rings joined together at one carbon on each ring. ... the rings are then substituted with one to 10 chlorine atoms. ... developed in 1929 they have been used as electrical insulating fluids, fire-resistant heat transfer and hydraulic fluids, lubricants and as components in elastomers, adhesives, paints, pigments and waxes. ... PCBs were very attractive in industrial use because they are non-volatile, non-flammable, chemically stable and good electrical insulators.]

Is this a health hazard to employees? Or to area residents?

The chemicals are settled in the sediment They're not in the lagoon water. There's no possibility of contamination to any plant employees or visitors, according to plant staff members. The PCBs are not airborne; there's no chance of contact The situation poses no danger to plant employees or residents

Possible quote: "Although we are dealing with hazardous waste, we want to assure the public there is no danger to residents, plant employees or to the surrounding environment. Our primary concern is to have this project done in the safest manner possible."

What are the best ways to communicate with employees?

The plant operates three shifts: 1) 7 a.m. to 3 p.m.; 2) 3 p.m. to 11 p.m.; and 3) 11 p.m. to 7 a.m. On each shift employees are given a 20-minute lunch break. Supervisors conduct safety meetings every day at the beginning of each shift. Supervisors also conduct communication meetings once each month. The plant manager talks to employees quarterly by shift. The most effective ways to communicate with employees are 1) through supervisors; 2) by weekly newsletter; 3) by monthly video tape; and 4) by closed circuit TV. Sometimes project teams are formed with a leader selected by each team. Supervisors oversee and coach the teams.

Note to self: Why are PCBs a problem? Is there a legal limit? What are the effects of PCBs on people? [Research later: Because PCBs are very stable, they do not break down in the environment; therefore they are environmentally unsuitable. … in 1976 Congress enacted the Toxic Substance Control Act (TSCA) which required the Environmental Protection Agency (EPA) to establish rules regarding PCBs. … production ceased in 1977. … in 1979 the EPA published the PCB ban rule which prohibits the manufacturing, processing, distribution in commerce and use of PCBs except in a totally enclosed manner. Concentrations of PCBs 50 parts per billion or over fall under EPA regulations, and must be disposed of under EPA guidelines. … PCBs can affect the body if inhaled, swallowed or there is contact with the eyes or skin. … they may cause irritation of the eyes, nose, and throat and an acne-like skin rash. … they may also cause liver disorders which would result in such effects as fatigue, dark urine, and yellow jaundice. … studies on laboratory animals showed the chemicals caused liver, reproductive and gastric disorders, skin lesions and tumors.]

So how did the PCBs get there?

The lagoon has been used as part of our overall water management plan and has never been used for the disposal of any industrial chemicals or wastes In the 1960s and 1970s, the lagoon water was used for cooling baths in the old forming operations We believe the contaminants were released when the cooling water was recycled back into the lagoon The forming operation has since been relocated and an oil/water separator has been installed; so there is no danger of further contamination

We can say tests of the lagoon sediment revealed the presence of PCBs (polychlorinated biphenyls) … that company engineers believe the lagoon was contaminated during the 1960s and 1970s when its waters were mixed with a petroleum-based lubricant for cooling metal in the old forming facility … that this facility has been closed for 14 years, so there is no danger for further contamination. The lagoon was constructed in 1959 to be used as cooling water for molds in the old metal forming operations. This was discontinued in 1981 when forming operations moved. The lagoon is currently used as fire water for the sprinkler system and also for the discharge of cooling waters from the current forming operation.

What's the plan to deal with the situation?

The company hired BBEO Remediation and Construction Company to close the lagoon This New Jersey based company has experience in cleaning hazardous waste, including PCBs The state Department of Environmental Resources (DER) is overseeing the cleanup Work will begin May 15 to clean the lagoon

Our engineers and BBEO personnel have developed a detailed closure plan The water will first be pumped from the lagoon. It will be treated, tested and then discharged into a connecting stream The sediment will then be excavated from the bottom of the lagoon It will be filter pressed to remove excess water, tested, stored in sealed containers and removed by rail for disposal The area will then be lined and used as a storm water retention basin

Possible quote: "Work is scheduled to begin May 15 to clean the lagoon. ... the area will be closed, and strict access and safety guidelines will be followed during the project. ... workers will be wearing protective gear which will be cleaned and disposed of daily throughout the process. ..."

So we can say the water will be pumped, treated, tested and then released. The polluted sediment will then be excavated, stored in leak-proof containers and removed by rail for disposal. The area will then be used for storm water retention.

Let's go over the plan once more.

BBEO Remediation and Construction has been contracted to close the lagoon. ... they have previous experience in dealing with PCBs. ... work will begin May 15. ... the project is expected to take six to eight weeks. ... after bringing in their equipment (no company equipment will be used) they will close off the entire area. ... only select BBEO and company personnel will be permitted to enter the cleaning site. ... workers will wear protective suits, gloves, boots and respirators which will be cleaned and/or disposed of each time they leave the closed zone surrounding the lagoon. ... the water will be pumped, treated and released into a connecting stream. ... the sediment will then be excavated, filter pressed to remove excess water, tested, stored in sealed containers and removed by train for disposal. ... the area will then be lined and used for storm water retention.

Will this operation present any kind of safety hazard?

The closure plan includes strict safety guidelines Throughout the project, access to the lagoon site will be allowed for authorized BBEO and company personnel only. All equipment, materials and safety gear will be either cleaned or disposed of immediately after use.

Do employees know about all of this?

Employees are not yet aware of the discovery of PCBs in the lagoon.

Who knows about it outside the company?

We are working with the state Department of Environmental Resources, but county and city government officials don't know about the discovery yet

What kind of relationship does the company have to city and county government?

Distant, at best. We need their cooperation to complete permits for our expansion plans. But we haven't done much in the way of building relationships. They're going to get a lot of questions from the public.

How's that?

The lagoon is visible from the City Expressway that leads into the city People working on the site will be wearing "moon suites" or hazardous materials protective gear and will be seen especially during rush hours by people entering and exiting Douglas.

The plan has three parts or phases:

1. mobilization and site preparation—that's when BBEO brings and sets up equipment (start date May 15; finish date May 24)
2. site remediation activities—lagoon dewatering starts May 25 and finishes June 16; sediment removal starts June 1 and finishes Aug. 9; belt press dewatering starts Aug. 8 and finishes Aug. 23; post-removal sampling starts Aug. 24 and finishes Aug. 30; preparation for structural backfill starts Aug. 31 and finishes Sept. 4.
3. demobilization and closeout activities—removal of temporary facilities and controls starts Sept. 5 and finishes Sept. 11; demobilization starts Sept. 12 and finishes Sept. 13; and there will be a closeout meeting Sept. 20.

Will taking care of lagoon slow down the plant expansion work?

Possible quote: "The project might slow plant expansion work, but that will be resumed right after the lagoon is closed." Also: "Our expansion plan is important and will give a boost to the local economy. But our first interest is cleaning up the lagoon." [could expand on this]

When all of this gets communicated who is going to field questions?

Casey Dilena, Manager of Human Resources (717) 393-9433.

ARTICLE: COMMUNITY RELATIONS CAN FACILITATE CORPORATE GROWTH

Community relations—how much is enough? Chief executives of companies, especially those striving to grow in difficult economic times, should know the answer to this question.

Senior managers today are running their organizations lean, mean and fast. Like astronauts, they are bearing on targets and defying the odds of colliding with the unexpected.

Little do some leaders realize that effective community relations is low-cost insurance for keeping their companies from colliding with the unexpected and incurring potentially crippling costs.

By establishing effective community relations, executive managers facilitate corporate growth.

How does effective community relations facilitate corporate growth?

One way is by giving managers in the communities in which they operate the credibility they need to deal with and recover quickly from a crisis situation.

This is particularly important to managers in charge of plants that use substances that pose a potential threat to the health and safety of people residing near manufacturing/production plants. Plant mangers with effective community relations programs are visible participants in local affairs and trusted spokespersons and representatives of their respective organizations.

Unknown managers from unknown facilities with unknown risks have no credibility with community residents in a crisis situation. The consequences of a poorly managed crisis can paralyze an operation by restricting operating permits, plant modifications and expansion plans.

Another way effective community relations facilitates corporate growth is by giving executive managers foresight into matters affected by public policy.

Manufacturers around the world are learning that long-term contracts for power, for example, are not absolute entitlements. They are learning that public opinion can effect contract power rate changes, as well as the future supply of electricity. Taxes, transportation, education are among other major public policy areas never to be taken for granted.

Managers who are well connected with the communities in which they operate are not likely to be blind-sided by public initiatives. Instead, they are welcomed as participants in the public policy making process. Statesmanlike collaboration with lawmakers and regulators usually results in acceptable policy with sustainability, in contrast to high-handed power plays that eventually cave in to the public interest in one way or another.

By taking an active part in government processes, an executive manager can have an influence on shaping public policy and regulations as they affect a particular facility.

Another way effective community relations facilitates corporate growth is by affording executive managers flexibility. Well-managed facilities with effective community relations do not have to fear the threat of labor activities and various adverse external pressures.

Public support can provide extraordinary management flexibility and access to resources when residents of a community value a facility in terms of its economic contribution in wages, taxes and local purchases, and in terms of its respect for human values and the quality of life.

So effective community relations facilitates corporate growth by giving managers in the communities in which they operate the credibility they need to deal with and recover quickly from a crisis situation; by giving executive managers foresight into matters affected by public policy and welcoming their participation in the public policy making process; and by affording executives extraordinary management flexibility.

By establishing effective community relations, executive managers facilitate corporate growth.

Case Nine
International Art Exhibit Promotion and Volunteer Recruitment

Kazuho Hieda "Sacred Waterfall and Mist"

日本画 **NIHONGA**

INTERNATIONAL ART EXHIBIT PROMOTION

This is a case of promoting the premier showing of Nihonga art in the United States. The exhibit comprises a world-class collection of 50 contemporary works of Japanese masters. Showing of the exhibit was arranged by the mayor of Townsville, U.S.A. for the purpose of promoting greater understanding of the Japanese culture in a community attracting businesses based in Japan.

To the Japanese, Nihonga exemplifies the solidly traditional merged with the new. The name "Nihonga," essentially means Japanese style of painting, as distinguished from Chinese style or Western style, and describes a blend of graphic style from the Chinese with the Western-influenced use of perspective. The imagery shown in the exhibition illustrates how the Japanese are able to reconcile old and new, to adapt a traditional discipline to embrace new ideas.

For this case, you are to assume that your public relations firm has competed for and won a contract with Townsville, U.S.A., for services to promote attendance at the exhibit, community involvement in three exhibit programs, and recruit volunteers to help operate the exhibit. Details of your work on this case are contained in a contract with the city of Townsville, U.S.A. Additional information follows the city contract, including articles about how to attract and retain volunteers.

Team Assignment

Your team assignment is to develop a public relations plan that meets the specific requirements of the contract between your public relations firm and Townsville, U.S.A. —to promote attendance at the exhibit and community involvement in three exhibit programs, and recruit volunteers.

Individual Team Member Assignments

Each team member is to complete a different one of the following items that might or might not be included in the design of your plan:

1. Write for the town a news release announcing that Townsville U.S.A. will host an exhibit of Nihonga art. See case information for dates, cost of admission and other details. Assume that visitors to the exhibit will receive a designer-type ticket with a large souvenir portion to be retained that features a Nihonga painting, that they will be greeted and guided through the exhibit by one of more than 150 docents trained by Townsville Art Museum Director Ron Hawkins, shown a five-minute video tape and given a four-color brochure about Nihonga art.

2. Write instructions to a Web designer for an event page featuring the Nihonga exhibit. Include an outline of content and through what electronic devices it is to be made available to visitors.

3. Write a post of at least 150 words to the city's event blog recruiting volunteers to serve as docents (knowledgeable tour guides) for the exhibit. See the article titled, "How to Attract and Retain Volunteers," on page 239.

4. Write briefing notes for Mayor David Green to use in talking about the exhibit of Nihonga art on a local television talk show. Prepare the mayor's notes in the form of sound byte responses to questions in the order they are most likely to be asked by a talk show host. Answers should be short and conversational. Every response should work to entice people of all ages to see the exhibit and participate in exhibit activities. Responses should be organized with labels so that topics are easy to spot.

5. Write a letter of invitation from the mayor to major donors. Assume that the mayor decides to precede the public opening of the exhibit with an exclusive dinner (paid for by private sources) and a private showing of the exhibit for 16 donors who made major contributions in support of the exhibit. The event is an expression of gratitude from the mayor on behalf of the town so use your imagination to describe in the letter an elegant affair in terms of location, guest transportation, menu, entertainment and, of course, the private presentation of Nihonga art.

6. Write a persuasive letter for Mayor David Green's signature to superintendents of public school districts

encouraging them to make Nihonga Classroom Experience programs available to schools (kindergarten thru 12th grade) throughout their respective districts. The president's letter must have compelling reasons for superintendents to use the programs, including bus tours to the exhibit.

7. Write a script for a podcast exclusively on Nihonga art, drawing on Internet sources for information.

8. Write a news release for Townsville to announce that it is accepting applications for volunteers to be trained to serve as docents for the exhibit. The release should center on quotes from the mayor that present this volunteer experience in irresistible terms. For ideas on what motivates people to volunteer their time and energy, see the article on page 239. The city needs to recruit 150 docents to staff the exhibit. Volunteers are required to complete training provided by the Townsville Museum of Art. It will include five, one-hour lectures on Nihonga art, instruction on the correct approach to conducting tours and a bibliography of readings. The cost of training will be covered by the law firm of Swallow, Finch and Robin, one of the exhibit's major sponsors. For their service, docents will receive commemorative gold pins in the form of the Japanese alphabet characters for "Nihonga."

9. Write a radio news actuality promoting the exhibit.

ROLE PLAY
Cast

Narrator
Clarissa, Vice President
Katie, Account Executive
Danielle
Abby
Robert
Hilary
Chad
Erin
Kelsey
Zoe
Elizabeth
Zachary
Sara
Amanda
Stephanie

PR Firm's Conference Room

Members of the account team assigned to the Nihonga program and other staff members assemble in the PR firm's conference room for a preliminary information dump on the new account assignment and prepare for the first client meeting with Mayor David Green.

Clarissa - V.P.

Let's go over our plan for tomorrow's meeting with the mayor. Close the laptops. I want your full attention.

Katie - A.E.

(asserts herself)
So what does the mayor expect?

Clarissa - V.P.

OK Let's start from the top. We won the contract from the city. Now we need to

make absolutely sure that we understand the assignment.

Danielle - Coordinator

It's spelled out in the contract.

Clarissa - V.P.

Yes, but it's important to think about what the mayor is asking for and what we can realistically deliver. Abby, you did some preliminary research.

Abby

There's no question, Townsville's growth in the past three years has come from an increasing Asian population. About a 22 percent increase: 5600 to 7000.

Clarissa - V.P.

The city is developing relationships with in-coming Japanese firms faster than townspeople are developing relationships with their new Asian neighbors. It's this growing culture gap that concerns the mayor.

Robert

And he wants to use the arts to bring everyone together.

Clarissa - V.P.

Yes, and not just the arts. He's bringing to Townsville a world-class, first-of-its kind

exhibit. He has managed to put Townsville on the premiere, international showing of Nihonga art.

Hilary

How did he manage that?

Clarissa - V.P.

One of the Japanese companies here is half-owner of the art collection.

Conference room door opens, receptionist/ secretary enters and hands Clarissa a note.

Clarissa - V.P.

It was the mayor. He says we need to talk tomorrow about a news conference to announce the exhibit.

Chad

The media will love this. The project is loaded with "firsts."

Clarissa - V.P.

What do you have?

Chad

Well, it's the first of its kind ever assembled. It will be shown for the first time in Tokyo, Yokohama, Osaka, and Nagoya. Townsville will be its premier showing in the United States that will launch its premier showing in Europe–London, Paris and Barcelona. It's the first major activity our town has had with its sister, Japan City.

Erin

So our job is to promote the exhibit

Clarissa - V.P.

That's just part of it. I want everyone to read the contract with the city very carefully. Who has a copy?

Kelsey

I have one.

Clarissa - V.P.

Read assignment number one.

Kelsey

Number one. That our agency will promote (exclusive of the use of paid advertising) exhibit attendance among people of all age groups throughout the Greater Townsville Area That we will secure publicity about the exhibit and prepare all of the materials necessary to work with the news media, such as a fact sheet, backgrounder, and news announcements. And that we will work with Townsville staff and elected officials on all questions or issues involving the exhibit event.

Clarissa - V.P.

Thanks, Kelsey. So, how far do we go with the promotion?

Zoe

Just Greater Townsville. Why not the region? Or national media?

Clarissa V.P.

Good question. What's the mayor's main objective?

Elizabeth

To address a situation in Townsville.

Clarissa - V.P.

Exactly. What about contract Item #2? Zachary, answer your e-mails later, please.

Zachary

Sorry. What was the question?

Clarissa - V.P.

What is the second part of our assignment from the city?

Zachary

We're supposed to get the community to participate in three programs: Nihonga Artists on Location; Nihonga Classroom Experience; and Nihonga Town Seminars. Should I read each one?

Clarissa - V.P.

No. But everyone needs to read the details before our meeting with the mayor tomorrow.

Sara

The third part of the assignment is right here—to help the town recruit about 1500 volunteers as tour guides, gift shop keepers, program coordinators, and others to assist with the exhibit.

Clarissa - V.P.

Thanks, Sara.

Amanda

I just read two good articles about recruiting volunteers.

Clarissa - V.P.

Why don't you make copies for everyone, Amanda? Let's see. Yes, Stephanie.

Stephanie

The contract says that we are to help the town recruit volunteers. Does that mean just publicizing volunteer opportunities? Or do we have to get names?

Clarissa - V.P.

I like that. You think like an attorney. Danielle talked about that with the mayor's assistant.

Danielle

I did and here's what they want. It's not just publicity. The mayor wants a campaign to get people to sign up to help. We need to rely on some good research about what entices people to volunteer. The city estimates that 1500 volunteers will be needed to setup and operate the exhibit. We need to incite a recruitment epidemic!

Clarissa - V.P.

That's something to think about. OK, let's get ready for our meeting with the mayor. Danielle, you just did that volunteer recruiting campaign for the Red Cross. You can be the project leader on the volunteer recruitment campaign. CHAD, put together a checklist on setting up a news conference that we can show to the mayor tomorrow.

Meeting adjourns.

Contract

This is a contract between Townsville U.S.A. and (Your Public Relations Firm) by which your firm agrees to provide certain public relations services to Townsville in connection with an exhibit of Nihonga art.

WHEREAS, Townsville will be host to an exhibit of Nihonga art from July 1, through September 14,

WHEREAS the exhibit was assembled and offered for display by Japan City, sister city to Townsville,

WHEREAS this collection of 50 contemporary Japanese paintings in traditional style—known as Nihonga—will be shown for the first time in Tokyo, Yokohama, Osaka and Nagoya then on to its premier showing in the United States at Townsville, launching its world tour that will include London, Paris and Barcelona,

WHEREAS this first of its kind collection assembled by a sister city and provided by masters of the art is seen by citizens and officials of Townsville as an effective way to promote greater understanding and appreciation of the Japanese culture in a town that is growing faster in its relationships with businesses on the Pacific Rim than in its personal relationships among citizens of communities with an increasing Asian population,

WHEREAS to prevent the widening of a culture gap, citizens and city officials set as their objective the showing of a world-class exhibition of Nihonga art in Townsville as a stimulus for local residents, and people throughout the area, to learn more about the history, customs and national character of Japan,

WHEREAS the public of which 50,000 visitors are expected, will be able to view the Nihonga art from 10 a.m. to 6 p.m., daily at the Townsville Arts Center,

WHEREAS for the exhibit event to be the success that it should be, it has been and will be necessary to contract with a public relations firm to promote attendance and community involvement in the exhibit, and recruit volunteers, and (Your Public Relations Firm) is qualified and willing to provide such services

NOW, THEREFORE
IT IS HEREBY AGREED AS FOLLOWS:

1. That (Your Public Relations Firm) will promote (exclusive of the use of paid advertising) exhibit attendance among people of all age groups throughout the Greater Townsville Area, securing publicity about the exhibit, preparing all of the materials necessary to work with the news media, such as a fact sheet, backgrounder, news announcements and cooperating with Townsville staff and elected officials on all questions or issues involving the exhibit event and public relations.

2. That (Your Public Relations Firm) will generate community involvement in the exhibit specifically by promoting three educational programs:
   • Nihonga Artists on Location

- Nihonga Classroom Experience
- Nihonga Town Seminars

each of which is described in the Attachment to this contract.

3.   That (Your Public Relations Firm) will help the town recruit approximately 1500 volunteers as tour guides (docents), gift shop keepers, program coordinators and others to assist with the exhibit.

For services under this agreement, extending from this contract date to September 14, (years intentionally omitted), (Your Public Relations Firm) will present Townsville with invoices and proper vouchers, documenting time spent on such services at standard public relations rates for total compensation not to exceed $100,000, plus documented out-of-pocket costs not to exceed 10 percent of such professional fee. Major promotional items, such as direct mail pieces, video productions, classroom materials, are to be presented separately and will be approved as funding sources are secured. (Your Public Relations Firm) is to begin its work by providing Townsville with a public relations plan for promoting attendance for the exhibit and community involvement in the three aforementioned educational programs and for helping the city recruit 1,500 volunteers to help with the exhibit. The plan should include a proposed budget. Major promotional items should be shown as line items marked "TBF" (To Be Funded) in place of a cost estimate.

DATED this 10th day of December.

TOWNSVILLE, U.S.A., a municipal corporation

By: _____

David Green
Title: Mayor

_____

T. Tom Plumb, Town Clerk
By April Rostkemper, Deputy Town Clerk

_____

(Your Public Relations Firm)

Approved as to form:

_____

Alfred A. Apple, Town Attorney
ATTACHMENT

Contract
Attachment A

Nihonga Artists On Location

Townsville Museum of Art will host the visit of four Nihonga artists. The purpose of this program is to give people an opportunity to converse, informally, (through an interpreter) with students of Nihonga, to learn about the history of the art, the painting techniques used, and about the way in which the artists select and approach their work.

The student artists will be in residence for six weeks beginning the second week in June. The artists' programs will include workshops and demonstrations of painting techniques; informal discussions with American artists; visits with educators and summer workshop students; studio time for the artists to work on a current or new painting and for visitors to observe; and time for the artists to produce artwork of their own to take back to Japan, possibly inspired by the greater Townsville environment. The schedule will be developed cooperatively between the artists and the museum staff member responsible for the Nihonga Artists On Location program.

Nihonga Classroom Experience

The Nihonga Classroom Experience is a student lesson using Japanese art to generate interest in learning more about Japan—its culture, history and national heritage. Lessons are being prepared for students in three groups: ages 4 to 6; 7 to 11; and 12 to 18. Instruction packets for each age group will contain a teacher's lesson guide, appropriate classroom activities, video, Nihonga brochure, all enclosed in a program folder imprinted with a sponsor's name. Instruction packages could be available to all public school buildings. The classroom program will have a potential audience of 55,000 children.

Curriculum units for the classroom lesson and summer workshops are being developed, professionally, as follows:

Purpose: To promote a better understanding of the Japanese people—their customs, culture and national heritage.

Curriculum units: designed for children of ages ranging from 4 to 6 years; 7 to 11 years; and 12 to 18 years. Each unit will include three activities. Individual activities will take one to three hours each. These activities will include the following components that emphasize instruction and content that promote greater understanding of the Japanese culture.

    I. Instructional Components
        A. Goals and objectives.
        B. Good, clear directions so that non-specialist teachers can readily translate the materials.

C. A range of activities that appeals to different learning styles.

D. Activities that stress collaborative learning.

E. Activities that foster higher level thinking skills.

F. A concluding activity that engages students in evaluation of their own work and/or their peers' work.

G. List of materials - specific.

II. Content Components

A. A general background and history of the activity as it relates to the Japanese culture, as expressed, for example, in Nihonga.

B. Introduction to the appropriate Japanese words that relate to the activity.

C. A geographical orientation to the activity, i.e. Where in Japan does this activity take place/originate?

D. An introduction to stories, music, dance, art, drama, and/or games of Japan that enhance the activity.

E. An exploration of Japanese life surrounding the activity, i.e., Where would students find this—at home? In school?; For what age group is it appropriate.

Each curriculum unit will be packaged in folders appropriate for each grade level and will be used during the Nihonga children's workshops, as well as in regular classrooms. A curriculum director has been retained to develop the lessons, to provide in-service training for area teachers, and to help with summer workshops.

Nihonga Town Seminars

The Nihonga Town Seminars will be designed to introduce mature students and adults to a broad range of subjects. They include: Tea Ceremony; Japanese Cuisine; Japanese Flower Arranging; Raising of Koi; Bonsai Demonstration; Myths & Customs of Japan; Japanese/American Woman; Kimono Demonstration/Fashion Show; and Japanese Business Etiquette.

Each seminar will be presented by a qualified leader. There will be a different seminar each Monday evening at the Townsville Art Museum, and possibly other locations, during the exhibition. There will be 6 to 8 seminars in the series.

Additional funds are being sought to enhance the stature of the seminar series by featuring a Nihonga artist for one of the sessions.

Each of the seminars will be video taped for use by colleges and universities, civic and professional organizations.

The following sources have been contacted for help in identifying qualified seminar leaders:

Japan American Society
International Examiner

Asian Arts Council
Council General of Japan (state office)
California Institute of the Arts
School of Music and the Arts
San Francisco Art Institute
United States International University
Western State College
World Affairs Council
Japan-American Society (state office)
University of Washington
Regional art institutes
Regional art museums
Academy of Art College San Francisco
California State University Los Angeles
Pacific Northwest College of Art
University of Southern California
University of California
University of Hawaii
Others

Notes about Nihonga art

... a technique whose roots extend back more than a thousand years.

... a term created in the 19th century to distinguish traditional Japanese painting methods from Western-influenced art

... often synonymous with art of the past

... incorporates time-honored materials, such as silk, rice-paper, ground semi-precious mineral, gold and silver leaf

... employs only materials fully derived from natural sources (brushes, paper, Chinese ink, mineral pigment and animal glue)

... paintings retain close harmony with nature

... the technique has become one of the principal art forms of Japan

... one distinctive feature of this medium is the subtle control of detail that it allows— fine variations in line thickness and nuances in color attainable in Nihonga require painters to maintain close observation of their subjects

... once seen, paintings remain in the heart, create a feeling of internal peace that originates with the painter's own clear conception of the subject

... rock pigments come from natural minerals; hues differ according to the fineness of the grains

... Nikawa (glue) is used to affix pigments to silk or paper on which artists paint

… the eginu silk used in Nihonga is woven from unglossed raw silk strands—there are three or four different types of silk material, graded by strand thickness

… large number of types of paper are used in Nihonga—choice of a particular type depends on personal preferences and an artist's intentions for the painting

… a wide variety of brushes in many sizes is used and broadly classified into brushes for drawing lines and brushes for coloring

… another distinguishing feature is the use of gold and silver foils

… artist usually begins by sketching a rough image

… more difficult to convey a lifelike subject in Nihonga than with oil painting

… subject matter classified broadly into landscapes, flowers and birds, and the human figure

… landscape paintings traditionally referred to in Japan as sansui-ga or paintings of mountains and water

… there are paintings of the kacho-ga, or flowers and birds genre generally have flowers and birds as their themes

… there are kaki-ga, only flowers, and sochu-ga, with butterflies or other insects instead of birds

… the genre also includes paintings of animals as well as birds

… figure painting is in portraits and bijin-ga, or images of famous beauties

… Nihonga artists look beyond the surface of their subject

… have a reverence toward nature

… appreciate the inherent beauty of nature in themes they portray

ARTICLE: START A RECRUITMENT EPIDEMIC
How to Attract and Retain Volunteers

Does your organization rely heavily on the use of volunteers? If so, are you finding it more difficult to maintain a full complement of them? Perhaps it's time for your organization to start a recruitment epidemic. By creating such an epidemic you should be able to attract and maintain volunteers at a consistent level.

What is a recruitment epidemic? I created the phrase by borrowing from the term "epidemic," as popularized by Malcolm Gladwell in his best-selling book "The Tipping Point." I define a recruitment epidemic as a phenomenon in which an individual has an exceptional volunteer experience that results in feelings of joy and gratification that the individual feels compelled to share. The volunteer speaks to others with contagious enthusiasm that infects and motivates them to pursue the same experience. The cycle repeats itself in the form of an epidemic, demonstrating that the best recruiters are satisfied volunteers. Interestingly enough, we don't see such epidemics in our local communities because conditions must be right to spark an epidemic.

Why do you need to start an epidemic? The main reason is that lifestyles have changed dramatically and individuals' discretionary time has become a precious commodity. Lack of time was the most common reason given by respondents (45.6 percent) for not volunteering, according to a supplement to the September 2005 Current Population Survey (CPS) by the Bureau of Labor Statistics of the U.S. Department of Labor.

Recent studies of our community at the University of Oregon conducted by five student teams clearly indicated lack of time as a deterrent to volunteering, while also indicating no lack of interest or desire to participate in volunteer activities. This means that organizations must work even harder to attract and retain volunteers. In fact, organizations should generally elevate volunteerism in their hierarchy of social responsibilities because it's a material factor in the strength of the nation.

However, there is cause for hope. About 65.4 million people volunteered through or for an organization at least once between September 2004 and September 2005, according to the CPS survey. In fact, boosted by greater teen participation, the number of Americans who volunteer hit a 30-year high, according to a December report by the Corporation for National and Community Service, which has tracked volunteer rates since 1974. It found 27 percent of adults currently giving to their communities, up from 20.4 percent in 1989. Teens age 16 to 19 increased most, with 28.4 percent volunteering compared with 13.4 percent in 1989.

Creating the right conditions

Many organizations launch recruitment efforts with an advertising or PR campaign when, in fact, content volunteers seem to be the most effective force. According to the CPS survey, only two in five volunteers became involved with the main organization for which they did volunteer work on their own initiative. Almost 43 percent were asked to volunteer, most often by someone in the organization.

We don't see recruitment epidemics because of another missing condition. It has to do with context or the environment in which an organization operates. The context of an organization (i.e., how people treat each other, the norms and values they share, the way they relate to people outside the organization) is shaped by the executive director. It's the head of an organization whose policy direction fashions the organization and makes volunteers feel at home, respected and appreciated.

Once accountability for volunteerism is established, then it is necessary to ensure that policies for its engagement are effectively managed. Volunteerism is not something for an executive simply to recognize and relegate to the human resources or PR department. In their book "Execution," Larry Bossidy and Ram Charan maintain that delegation of responsibilities to others with no executive follow-through or oversight has been one of the greatest management pitfalls in recent times. An executive manager must see that an organization has the discipline necessary throughout the process to get things done.

Another reason for lack of success is due to a lack of resources — having in place all that enables a volunteer to have an exceptional experience.

First and foremost, a volunteer's time must be put to good use. Assignments should be well-defined, interesting and relevant to a volunteer's personal interests and needs. They should give individuals an opportunity to accomplish something. Volunteers want to see direct results from their personal efforts.

What a volunteer needs

An exceptional volunteer experience has several important elements:

- A job description stating tasks to be done, work standards, measurements and reporting relationships.
- A job title for résumé use
- Introduction of volunteer to staff
- Job orientation
- Work area and tools to operate

- List of co-workers with job titles, phone numbers, and reasons why they are important to the volunteer
- Important publications and documents to read
- A conversation about how assignments contribute to the volunteer's professional goals
- Periodic critiques of the volunteer's performance
- Notes of praise that the volunteer could include with a résumé

The experience should provide a volunteer with meaningful recognition that exceeds a mere thank-you note. A word of encouragement or praise for something specific is powerful, as are grateful comments from someone served.

A volunteer experience can offer personal growth, giving people a chance to learn new skills, develop additional capabilities and discover more about themselves.

A volunteer experience can be a valuable outlet for developing relationships. It can be a place for meeting new friends and provide a feeling of belonging and an opportunity for making social connections.

Remember, the recruitment epidemic increases by word-of-mouth and enables an organization to attract and maintain an adequate complement of volunteers.

Case Ten
Media
Relations

CHARLIE ZURLOCK

This case is a challenging exercise in media relations. Working with the mass media in seeking publicity or responding to their interests is a major function of public relations. This case requires more than establishing and maintaining a good working relationship with the media. It involves counseling a company owner, whose lack of understanding of how to work with the media, has resulted in an unending saga of negative publicity.

The challenge is to educate the client on the basics of media relations, take immediate steps to end the negative publicity, provide the client with measures that will begin to restore and establish external relationships that will serve to reduce the chances of generating negative publicity in the future.

The case also involves addressing relationships with government and with company employees. Details of the case unfold in a script, which can be used as a classroom or professional workshop role play, to show how the company got into an adversarial relationship with a newspaper reporter. Additional case materials appear after the script. For a broad perspective on media relations see the article on page 256 titled, "What is a media strategist?"

Team Assignment

Charlie Zurlock, owner of Custom Parts Co., has hired your team, a local public relations agency, to help with a situation created by his company's poor handling of media relations that is tearing down the reputation of his family-owned business in his home community. Charlie is used to telling people what to do within his organization. However, he has yet to learn that his authority does not extend to the media or to any level of government, as you can see by his demands of your agency.

He said, "I want you to put an end to the negative publicity we're getting and see to it that it never happens again. I want you to set state government straight on this health issue. And I want you to keep my employees from getting overly excited about so-called health risks in the workplace." Charlie believes that the media can be controlled, that state government can be told what should or should not be investigated, and that employee relations is a matter of giving everyone a Starburst glazed ham for the holidays.

Your team must develop a public relations plan for Charlie Zurlock that is responsive to his objectives. However, the plan must provide for educating Charlie in the basics of media, government and employee relations. In the situation analysis of your plan, you must identify the company's shortcomings in dealing with the health issue, but the rules for writing the analysis are clear about not being judgemental or attributing blame to individuals or to the company. Consulting in public relations requires firm but tactful criticism and advice.

Individual Team Member Assignments

Suppose that your agency decides that the company's management of relationships requires special guidance to raise standards and, as part of your plan, you offer guidelines. Each team member is to complete a different one of the following items that might or might not be included in the design of your plan.

1. Draft for Charlie a memo to employees establishing guidelines governing the company's working relationship with the news media. The memo should explain how the company is to work with the media and how employees should respond to inquiries from journalists. Because this is intended to be general company policy, there should be no reference to the company's current situation with the media. See Random Thoughts About Working With the Media on page 251 as a resource for writing this memo. Select only a few points that help shape your proposed guidelines for Charlie. (Use memo format– From: Charlie Zurlock To: All Employees Re: You And The News Media)

2. Draft for Charlie a memo to his staff about how the company is to work with all levels of government– local, county, state and federal. See Random Thoughts About Working With Government as a resource on page 252 and select only a few points that help shape your proposed guidelines for Charlie. (Use memo format—From: Charlie

Zurlock To: Management Staff Re: Working With Government)

3. Develop a backgrounder on "effective employee communication." Use Internet sources to include some of the latest research on how today's employees want to be treated. See Random Thoughts About Effective Communication Among Individuals on page 253 as a resource. The backgrounder might be used by your PR firm in counseling Charlie.

4. Draft a memo from you, as head of the account team, to Custom Parts management providing guidance on how to discuss matters of risk with employees and the community. The memo should point out that there are some basics they should know in order to communicate matters of risk without getting people upset. See Random Thoughts on Communicating Matters of Risk on page 254. (Use memo format— From: (Your Name) To: Custom Parts Management Re: Talking About Risk)

5. Draft an outline of contents for a new company Web site and provide reasons for what is proposed.

6. Draft a media advisory addressed to editors and news directors (of print and broadcast media) calling their attention to an up-coming event commemorating the start-up of new environmental control equipment at Custom Parts, Inc. and launching of the company's new program, "Clean Air Awareness." You make up the details for writing the advisory that must answer the journalist's Ws–Who? What? When? Where? Why" and describe an irresistible photo/video opportunity (photo-op) for the media.

7. Draft an e-news release announcing the hiring by Custom Parts Inc. of a director of public relations. Assume that you are the new director. Make up the details of the announcement to include job experience, professional awards, education and major job responsibilities. Write two quotes from you as the new director that would be especially appreciated by local journalists. In other words, write something about wanting to work with reporters as partners.

8. Develop an information sheet providing an overview of the state's environmental protection agency. It is to be used to brief Charlie and his staff on the agency's director, the director's views on air quality (from testimony on the Web site), the agency's mission and goals specifically related to clean air, key staff members and other background to promote a better understanding of working with the government role toward common goals. For purposes of illustration use any state's environmental protection department.

ROLE PLAY

Cast

Narrator
Secretary - Dorothy
Reporter - Student's Name
Plant Engineer - Robin Jackson
Director, Department Of Ecology
Jessica Murray
Owner - Charlie Zurlock
State Physician - Dr. Emerson
Human Resources Secretary
Nancy White
Director, Human Resources
Dan Peopleton

Newsroom

A reporter lifts the telephone receiver. Calls Custom Parts Company. Asks for the owner. Secretary answers.

Secretary

Charlie Zurlock's office, this is Dorothy. How can I help you?

Reporter

Hello Dorothy. This is (your name) with the MESSENGER. I'd like to speak to Mr. Zurlock about your pollution problem.

Secretary

(Instructively) Mr. Zurlock said if anyone calls about that citation, they should talk to our plant engineer. Would you like me to transfer you to her line?

The reporter, somewhat concerned about the owner's refusal to speak to the media about environmental health and safety, agrees to talk to the plant engineer.

Reporter

Yes. What's his name?

Secretary

(Boldly correcting the reporter …)
HER name is Jackson. Robin Jackson. Just a minute please.

Phone rings. Robin Jackson answers.

Plant Engineer

(Sounding annoyed.)
Hello. Robin Jackson here.

Reporter

Hello, Ms. Jackson. This is (your name) with the MESSENGER. Your title, is it plant engineer?

Plant Engineer

That's right. What do you want?

Reporter

I'd like your reaction to the Department of Ecology's announcement. The agency said it appears that five out of every 10,000 people living around your plant stand a good chance of getting cancer.

Plant Engineer

(Defensive; takes a shot at D-O-E)
There are plenty of ways that government bureaucrats can interpret its data. We've conducted our own health studies of our workers. There's been no increased incidence of cancer.

Reporter

(Aggressively interjecting)
But the D-O-E …

Plant Engineer

(Interrupts; tries to impose the results of a "company-paid" study that has yet to be completed; tries to minimize the health risk) Listen. We just launched a new study. And we are predicting that by year-end, the findings will show that our emissions pose no more risk than smoke from a cigarette in an auditorium.

Aghast! The reporter thinks: this engineer must have a crystal ball! She knows the results of a study before it's conducted. Wonder how much the company is paying to get the findings it wants.

Reporter

If you're so sure your emissions are harmless, why did the D-O-E target your operation for an impact study?

Plant Engineer

(Attempts to sidestep the issue; takes another shot at D-O-E; points finger at other companies)
They're picking on us because we're nearby. We're just on the outskirts of town, you know. Practically under their office window. Hey look, we're not the only plant around here with emissions. The other plants like ours are tuned into this issue. You can bet on that! Sorry, I've got to take another call.

Reporter, irritated with having been cut off, calls Jessica Murray, director of the state's Department of Ecology.

Reporter

(Feeds back to the state Department of Ecology what the Custom Parts engineer said about the pollution fine and about the D-O-E.)

Hello, Jessica, this is (your name) with the MESSENGER. I tried to talk with Custom Parts about the pollution citation and fine that it got from you. The plant engineer, Robin Jackson, disagrees with you. She says their emissions pose no health risk. She implied that your agency is manipulating the data. She said the D-O-E is picking on Custom Parts because the plant is conveniently close to your offices.

Upset with the accusation that her government agency is lazy and manipulative, the department head strikes back with a sweeping unsubstantiated, but quotable opinion.

Director Department of Ecology

I think we're going to be able to show that emissions from that plant, and every one like it, pose a substantial health threat.

The reporter ends the call to the state Department of Ecology and calls Custom Parts, this time getting through to the owner, Charlie Zurlock.

Reporter

Hello, Charlie Zurlock?

Owner

Yes, this is Zurlock.

Reporter

I'm (your name) with the MESSENGER. I'm doing a story on your plant and yesterday's announcement by the state Department of Ecology. I talked earlier with your engineer, Robin Jackson. But I have a few more questions.

Owner

Get on with it. I've got a busy schedule.

Reporter

(not about to be rushed)
The state Department of Ecology thinks it's going to be able to show that emissions from your plant, and plants like it, pose a substantial health risk to employees and people living around your plant. Exactly how much toxic material is your plant emitting?

Ignoring the public's legal right to know about toxic emissions, the owner hesitates, then responds …

Owner

(Clears throat …)
I can't recall the amount. Even if I could, I wouldn't want to tell you.

Reporter

(Disgusted with the owner's arrogance)
Aren't you even a little concerned that your emissions might be endangering the health of your own employees and the community?

Owner

(Tries to minimize the risk)
I'm telling you … Our emissions are no more harmful to the human body than smoke from a wood-burning stove.

Reporter calls the state's Department of Health and reaches the state physician.

Reporter

Hello, Dr. Emerson. I'm (Your Name) with the MESSENGER. I just spoke with the owner of Custom Parts Company. He claims that their emissions are no more harmful than smoke from wood-burning stoves How harmful do you think the effects really are?

Not pleased to hear the company minimize a health risk, the physician offers an unsubstantiated, but quotable opinion and refuses to let the company off the hook.

State Physician

I think there is occupational exposure at the plant causing more cases of cancer. At this point, I can't tell you what it is— whether it's the emissions or other toxic chemicals. But I am working on a lot of different possibilities.

Reporter

You mentioned the increased incidence of cancer. How many cases have been reported?

Physician offers opinion based on hearsay which is quotable.

State Physician

Over the past several years, I've heard of at least nine workers at the plant who had cancer of the blood-forming organs. But this information came to me by word of mouth.

Reporter calls Custom Parts and this time, for some unknown reason, is referred to the Human Resources Department. A secretary answers.

Human Resources Secretary

Human Resources. Nancy White speaking.

The reporter tries to speak to the owner.

Reporter

I would like to speak to Charlie Zurlock. I'm (Your Name) with the MESSENGER. I'm doing a story on your plant. We understand that at least seven employees at the plant have been diagnosed with cancer of the blood forming organs over the past several years. I'd like Mr. Zurlock to confirm this.

Human Resources Secretary

(Acting as though she is an authorized spokesperson for the company)
Well, I'd like to help. But we have NO COMMENT.

Reporter

I'd like to speak to Mr. Zurlock.

Human Resources Secretary

No way, José

Reporter is upset with the brush-off. Calls state Department of Ecology and describes the company's arrogance.

Reporter

Hello, Jessica? This is (Your Name) at the MESSENGER. We spoke earlier about the Custom Parts plant. I'm not getting much cooperation from them. I understand that your agency has ordered the company to do emission studies to determine the possible threat of cancer to employees and those living near the plant. How severe is the threat of cancer?
The head of D-O-E offers the strongest statement yet of unsubstantiated, but quotable opinion.

Director, Department of Ecology

The risk of getting cancer to employees and people outside the plant could be substantial.

Reporter tries once again to reach Charlie Zurlock.

Director, Human Resources

Hello, Dan Peopleton, Human Resources.

Reporter

I'm (Your Name) with the MESSSENGER. We're doing a story on your plant. I am trying to reach the owner, Mr. Zurlock. According to the state Department of Ecology, your plant's emissions are jeopardizing the health of workers and community residents. I need to know more about that.

The director of Human Resources also thinks he has psychic powers and predicts the results of a study yet to be done, then takes a shot at state government.

Director, Human Resources

Sure, I'll be happy to comment. We're confident that at year-end our research will show that any cancer cases were not caused by working at the plant. Hey look, Clark Kent, if you want some advice, don't pay much attention to the D-O-E. They haven't done a thorough job of studying our emissions.

[End]

BACKGROUND
Custom Parts Company

Custom Parts Company is located in Capital City, U.S.A. It produces custom parts for industrial machines using steel, titanium and various carbon composite materials. It employs 231 people. The workers, about 198 people, are members of a union, represented by the All Trades Council. CPC is privately owned by the Zurlock family and run by Charlie Zurlock. Its products are marketed throughout the United States. The company is not involved in the local community, except for Charlie's wife Helen who is a major donor to and board member of the Women's Association.

The company has been in operation for 28 years and has a record of eight citations by the state Department of Ecology (DOE) for air pollution. The DOE doesn't make a special effort to publicize its fines unless the subject of a fine fails to cooperate and adhere to environmental regulations. On March 1, 20XX, the DOE cited Custom Parts Company for exceeding toxic emission limits once a week since the beginning of the year. DOE fined the company $20,000 and mandated that an independent study be conducted on a voluntary basis, at the company's expense, of worker health and of the health of residents living within two miles of the plant. It is true that the company had excursions of toxic emissions once each week from the beginning of the year to the end of February. No excursion lasted more than 10 minutes, but each time expelled more than two tons of fowl-smelling particulate matter into the air. The emissions were big in volume and highly visible. It's true that the company has not been responsive to the government.

New control equipment has been ordered, but for some reason not in time to meet regulatory deadlines. It has not as yet arrived and no one seems to have even an estimated delivery date. Meanwhile, company engineers have tried to fine-tune existing controls, but the effort has not produced consistent results. The company maintains that the worker environment is absolutely free of any health risk. However, the company is in the process of hiring an independent laboratory, True-Test Labs, Inc., to conduct a health study of employees and local residents. It is true that the company does not have a perfectly clean record for environmental control. However, Charlie has updated the company's pollution control equipment, once in 1970 at a cost of $2 million and again in 1990 at a cost of $6 million. Employees are loyal to the operation, not because of the Starburst glazed ham their families get from Charlie and his wife each year, but because their skills are specialized and limited to Charlie's operation. In other words they couldn't get work anywhere else.

The local newspaper was informed of the citation and fine in a news release issued by the DOE. The reporter contacted the company for a statement. The reporter talked with several different people (refer to classroom/professional workshop role play) who seem to have an adversarial attitude toward state government and newspaper reporters. Reports of the company's alleged cancer-causing emissions have alarmed employees and have resulted in two weeks of negative publicity for the company. Employees feel, "Just because Charlie says it's safe doesn't mean nothin'."

A Charlie Zurlock Family Business

Random Thoughts About Working with the News Media

Employees are largely responsible for the reputation of an organization ... A company's reputation makes qualified people want to come to work and stay with an organization. ... Reputation has an influence on customers' buying decisions. ... A reputation contributes to investor decisions in buying stock. ... Financial institutions that loan money for business development are influenced by a borrower's reputation. ... Government officials are more likely to treat an organization fairly and journalists are more likely to write accurately about an organization if the name is respected. ... A good reputation helps an organization to be a welcomed part of the communities in which they operate. ...

Employees help form an organization's reputation because to outsiders, employees are the organization. ... How employees feel about the organization and what they say about it are the basis of attitudes others hold toward the organization. ... In going about their daily work or personal activities, employees represent a powerful influence on their employer's reputation. Employees may have occasion at one time or another to speak with a representative of the news media.

It's important to bear in mind that to the media, employees are the organization. ... Whatever an employee says could easily be broadcast or printed as a statement from the employee's employer. Some organizations have guidelines for employees if they are contacted by any of the media (newspapers, magazine, radio, TV). They might include telling employees to immediately refer all contacts by the media to a designated spokesperson. ... This enables an organization to gather any necessary information and respond promptly to media inquiries. ...

Responses to the media usually require some research, review of information by appropriate individuals, including an organization's attorney, and clearance by executive management to release the information to the media. ... Media requests must be acted on promptly because reporters are usually working against tight deadlines; they often need specific information quickly. ... A neglected press call could mean losing an important opportunity for comment or clarification of an issue. ...

Some guidelines discourage employees from engaging in idle conversation with reporters because the journalists decide what is quotable and what is not. ... Some guidelines stress that complete and accurate information is best given by an organization's spokesperson. ... Some guidelines say that if it has been determined by the organization that it is appropriate for an employee to engage in an interview with the media that it is essential for the interview to be monitored by another organization representative who can listen to the conversation and help ensure that there is an accurate interpretation and understanding of information discussed.

Random Thoughts About Working with Government

Organizations want to have effective working relationships with local, county, state and federal government officials—elected representatives, as well as government agency personnel. Well run organizations debate issues on the basis of their merits and will not engage in any combative behavior over any matter with government. ... They make an effort to become acquainted with and helpful to government representatives who have an interest in various aspects of business—from health and safety to environmental control. They tour government representatives through their operations, meet with them in their offices to discuss current business issues and problems, particularly those involving government measures or need for them. ...

They attend or send a representative to public hearings on public policy relating to the organization's interests. ... They offer to testify at hearings on matters of particular concern. ... They encourage employees to serve on business committees, local boards, commissions, civic groups, etc. ... Where appropriate, they invite officials to make presentations (e.g. a public safety director or fire chief might be asked to be on hand to mark a new record of consecutive no-accident days; environmental protection agency officials might be invited to start up a new piece of recycling equipment). ...

Well run organizations encourage communication with government that fosters mutual understanding and respect. ... They welcome government officials for first-hand inspections of operations and to meet employees on the job. ... They host government representatives for meetings with management to discuss issues and, at the same time, apprise them of the organization's contributions to the local and regional economies—number of people employed; average annual payroll; products manufactured; annual sales revenue and how it is allocated for supplies, rent, depreciation, payroll; state and local taxes paid; property tax and personal income taxes paid by employees; uses made of profits for plant improvements, new equipment, research, employee benefits, aid to schools, hospitals and other local organizations and causes; special local programs and services provided, such as day care, diversity training, continuing education; participation in community improvement projects; employee benefits provided; plant environmental problems and cleanup efforts; amount of energy consumed in daily operations and energy-saving measures implemented; safety and health standards in the operation; new protective equipment facilities or technology; security standards used for plant protection; utility requirements for water and sewage, waste disposal; employees who serve on local boards and commissions, etc.

Well run organizations expect managers to be current on issues of public policy affecting the organization. ... The organization is expected to be an active participant in the public policy process—in other words when regulations or laws are being considered the organization wants to take an active part in discussing and debating points of interest to help shape policy that is fair, practical and cost-effective. ...

This means the organization will be alert to the potential effects of proposed legislation and determine a course of action; determine if others are getting involved or if the organization must take the initiative; identify supporters and opponents of a proposed measure; make personal contact with elected representatives to express a position and present the organization as a source of information; consider offering to testify at hearings about how an action will affect the welfare of the organization, employees and community; develop support from other political bodies; inform employees of legislation that would affect their well-being and consider enlisting their aid in contacting elected representatives; monitor day-to-day developments so that the company's action will be absolutely relevant. Well run organizations are interested in early identification of issues of importance. ...

When appropriate, the organization will reach out to organizations with common interest in an issue to form a coalition so as to speak with a stronger voice in getting a message across to government officials. ... The organization will join and support organizations whose charter is to represent and lobby for public policy that supports the responsible growth and development of business. ... The organization will host visits with government representatives to set the stage for mutual understanding between us and our representatives on a continuing basis. ... Facility tours initially tell government officials that an organization is a member of his or her constituency; it also helps government representatives to know and understand an operation. ...

Follow-up is important–efforts must be made to ensure that government officials continue to be aware of an organization's operation. ... Notes of thanks reemphasizing key points made during a visit should be sent. ... Remaining questions should be answered. ... Interest in an elected official's or regulatory representative's activities should be expressed. ... Request to be put on mailing lists should be made. ... Organization members who accompanied representatives on a visit should express interest in keeping in contact with them. ... Copies of photographs taken of government visitors with employees, a plant or office manager, labor leaders and others during the visit, along with copies of newspaper or plant newsletter articles detailing the visit should be sent to visitors. ... A well run organization continues to inform government representatives of key activities and continuing challenges, and concerns about up-coming legislation ...

Random Thoughts About Effective Communication Among Individuals

What does it mean to have effective communication among individuals? It means showing respect for each other regardless of position. ... It means recognizing individuals as intelligent, well-meaning and responsive. ... It means sharing information about all areas of an organization and its interests so everyone is informed. ... It means talking to each other in an informational rather than judgmental way … It means being in the loop–getting information on a regular basis. …

Effective communication is two-way and two-way communication in an organization must be encouraged. … Effective communication among individuals requires a team orientation. Job-oriented dialogue among team members is essential for achieving productivity goals and high quality standards. Effective communication among individuals also means frequent face-to-face meetings … It means talking and thinking about communication. … It means planning together and executing plans with precision. … It means everyone striving to be clear, direct and open with each other. … It means revealing the bad and celebrating the good. … It means accepting responsibility for mistakes and providing plans to correct them. … It means pricking the fat balloons of pomposity and telling it like it is … It means rejecting the notion that there is power in hoarding information. … It means nurturing the notion that having common knowledge about an organization makes work meaningful. …

Effective communication among individuals means challenging each other to be knowledgeable enough to be good ambassadors of an organization who can provide complete and accurate information to others. … It means being completely truthful. … It means sharing information about an organization's outlook, future plans, policies and practices affecting daily work, about challenging local and regional issues, employee benefits, how an individual's work fits into the big picture, personnel changes, where and how an organization's products and services are used, where the organization stands on issues affecting its industry, about cash flow and the bottom line, what competitors are doing, activities in other parts of the organization. It means cultivating genuine working relationships that provide a sense of security. … Effective communication among individuals means listening to understand and letting others know that it is OK to show compassion.

Random Thoughts About Communicating Matters of Risk

A red flag should pop up in your mind when you, as a public relations practitioner, have to communicate to others matters of risk to human health, safety and the environment. Risk communication is a special area of expertise based on a body of knowledge developed by individuals and organizations that have invested major resources in studying the dynamics of how risks are perceived and how citizen outrage can be avoided when sensitive subjects are raised to a plane of public discussion. I had the privilege and pleasure of working on several risk communication projects with the nation's preeminent risk communication consultant, Peter M. Sandman, a Rutgers University faculty member since 1977. A wealth of information can be found on Dr. Sandman's Web site: <www.psandman.com>. He founded the Environmental Communication Research Program (ECRP) at Rutgers in 1986 and was its director until 1992. During that time ECRP , now called the Center for Environmental Communication, published more than 80 articles and books on various aspects of risk communication, including separate manuals for government, industry, and the mass media.

I have learned that there are four especially important factors to keep in mind when communicating matters of risk.

One is that people are more receptive to receiving information about risk to their health or safety if the communication comes from a familiar source. The source must be trustworthy and have the good sense and compassion to recognize people's feelings and address them before getting to the facts of the matter.

Another factor is control. People feel uncomfortable and threatened by risks over which they

seem to have no control. People today know they are entitled to be made aware of any serious threat to their health, their safety and their environment. Such threats are viewed not only as wrong, but morally wrong. Emotions intensify if these threats are controlled and/or imposed by someone else. One way to provide control in a risk situation is to invite oversight by an established authority, such as a government agency or, for example, a public fire and rescue unit.

Another factor is answering questions. When it comes to personal risks, people

want all of the answers, not just some or those considered most important. In other words, if a person is in a public meeting, for example, and is discussing a matter of risk, it is imperative that the individual stay as long as necessary to answer every question, respectfully, down to what might seem unimportant and trivial. It is equally important to find out what is of greatest concern to people, because a risk can be perceived in many different ways

and it is essential to focus accurately on the concern that is upper most in mind.

One other factor of importance in discussing matters of risk can be referred to as evidence. Does the person discussing risk have credibility. Is want the individual is saying backed by evidence. It would not be effective for a company executive, for example, to assure community neighbors of their safety

if the executive's company has a long and continuing record of industrial injuries and accidents. In discussing risk the source of the information must have a credible basis from which to speak.

ARTICLE: WHAT IS A MEDIA STRATEGIST?

Working with the media is a complex and demanding job. People in the public relations profession who have responsibilities in media relations take this aspect of the job in their stride. It would be rare to find a reference in their job descriptions to performing six functions of a "media strategist." And yet that's what they do and they deserve recognition for doing it effectively.

When a person says he or she has responsibility for the media, most people think that involves issuing news releases and answering press calls. However, if someone were to create the job of media strategist, I believe it would have, among others, six important functions, each requiring knowledge of new and traditional media and a full range of skills–from monitoring, planning and writing messages.

Six key functions of a media strategist would be:

1. originates news by knowing media interests and how to develop information to capture them;
2. works comfortably with traditional and new media;
3. addresses the news–responds to reports and inquiries by knowing how to take a position as an information source, knowing what to say and how to say it;
4. diffuses situations before they become news or Internet fire storms by recognizing potential issues in advance and using conflict resolution and accommodation measures to resolve them;
5. disseminates news by knowing how to prepare information and arrange for its instant distribution;
6. corrects erroneous reports by knowing how to approach information sources and present accurate information.

Many public relations practitioners starting a new job have an opportunity to shape the job according to their individual skills and the needs of their respective organizations. Often that entails drafting or editing a job description. Should that be your good fortune consider including the six key functions of a media strategist.

Case Eleven
Hospitality
Event
Planning

INDYCAR RACING

This case is an introduction to sports marketing with a focus on auto racing, the most popular sport in the world. It provides insights to corporate sponsorships of IndyCar Racing League teams and to how businesses participate in and profit from these high profile activities. In professional sports, there are essentially athletes, owners and fans. However, as you get into a particular activity, such as Indycar racing, things get more complicated. There is the racing team owner, the driver, the crew, the title sponsor and secondary sponsors (usually corporations); there are fans, at large, and corporate fans to include employees, customers, suppliers, investors; and there are the general media plus the business, financial, sports and trade print and broadcast press.

All of these interests surround the sport in a complex configuration of relationships and are drawn to it by an incredible aura of competitive excitement. The distinctions between these groups are basic and straightforward. Spectator sports generate about $60 billion in revenue annually, a clear indication of the tremendous involvement they draw from both business and consumers. Corporations purchase billions of dollars worth of sports-related products annually, commonly in the form *of advertising and sponsorships. Managing a title sponsorship can become a public relations responsibility with requirements similar to managing a multi-million-dollar business. This case is your opportunity to explore the hospitality event planning facet of sports marketing by seeing what your team can do with the title sponsorship of an IndyCar Racing League (IRL) team.*

Team Assignment

Chief Executive Officer Daria Malone has just signed a contract for Severe Clear to be title sponsor of an IndyCar racing team. Malone has always taken great pride in the strength of the company's relationships with customers. For the coming year, she wants to make a social connection with customers and, at the same time, make a lasting impression on them about the company's creative, customer-centered use of advanced technology. The company, Severe Clear, Inc. is a leader in cleaning, sanitizing, food safety and infection control products and services. Malone has a personal interest in auto racing and, especially, in the way that IndyCar racing requires teamwork, precision and the creative use of advanced technology to be a winner. She would like from the company's public relations department a hospitality event plan to be used at each race of the Indy Car season, except for the Indianapolis 500 which is to be planned separately. Details of the assignment are provided in the case role play.

Individual Writing Assignments

For this case, each team member is to complete a different one of the following items that might or might not be included in the design of your plan.

1. Write a colorful, 100-word description of your IndyCar racing team's driver to be used by a speaker to introduce the driver at a hospitality event.

2. Write in stellar terms (200 words) a description of your IndyCar racing team, its record of accomplishments and how a race car team relates to Severe Clear's business to be used on the company's Web site and in various program materials.

3. Write a 150-word business rationale to justify the investment in sport marketing by Severe Clear, Inc. Include the total number of customers and the sales regions to be influenced by the sponsorship. Base the rationale on comments made in the role play by CEO Daria Malone.

4. Write an electronic news release announcing that Severe Clear has decided to sponsor an IndyCar racing team. It must include two quotes of meaningful substance from CEO Daria Malone.

5. Write a response to a letter from a Severe Clear stockholder who criticizes the company's investment in sponsoring a race car team and would like the money used to pay dividends to investors. Use a factitious name for the stockholder.

6. Assume that after each race, Severe Clear sends an e-mail to guests it

has hosted at a track announcing who took the top three positions, providing a few race highlights, and re-enforcing their connection with the company. Write the message using any past IRL race for details and assume that your team took first place on the podium.

7. Draft and storyboard a video podcast for internal use introducing the company's IndyCar team and driver and stimulating employee interest in the sponsorship.

ROLE PLAY
Cast

Narrator
Daria - CEO
Christina
Chris
Maria
Ali
Nickie
Rachel
Joshua
Justin
Marissa
Ruth
Babe
Caitlin
Amanda
Richelle
Amber
Becky
Kristen

Executive Conference Room

CEO DARIA Malone has called a meeting with the company's public relations department to make an assignment. Some staff members from sales, marketing and product development also are in attendance.

Daria - CEO

Good morning. I have an assignment that I think you are going to find interesting. Severe Clear has signed a contract to be the title sponsor of an IndyCar racing team. It will be a two-year investment. We have strong relationships with our customers. However, I would also like to have a strong social connection with our customers. And I believe we can do that with our sponsorship of an IndyCar racing team.

Our drive to grow and exceed customer expectations is fundamental to this company. I think our customers would be even more impressed if we met with them, socially, to showcase our innovative use of advanced technology. Now I don't mean putting products on display like we do in a trade show. I mean surprising customer guests at each race with an entertaining dinner show extravaganza that incorporates some of our newest products and services to make a lasting, overall impression that we are a leader in applying advanced technology for their businesses.

Christina

What specifically would you like us to do?

Daria - CEO

I would like your PR team to prepare a hospitality event plan. I want it to be implemented at every venue of the IRL racing season, except the Indy 500, which we will plan separately.

Chris

I just found the IndyCar site [www.IRL.com]. So you're talking about hospitality at 15 races?

Daria - CEO

Yes—generally the same format for each one. I want to include a reception and business dinner and show the evening before race day. That's when I want the company to make a lasting impression on them about our creative use of advanced technology to serve their needs.

Maria

Would that be for about 50 customers, plus company hosts?

Daria - CEO

Yes, about 50 customers and 15 company hosts for the dinner. We will have some executives from headquarters, including me, plus our sales/service representatives from or near each venue. On race day we will have 50 customers each with an additional guest, plus the same 15 company hosts. So, about 115 people total on race day.

Ali

We launched nearly 40 products and services this year. Which ones do you want to use in this hospitality plan?

Daria - CEO

Remember, now. I want a show, not a display of individual products. But let's go ahead and talk about products and services that could be highlighted in the show. One product that must be included is our revolutionary utensil-washing sys-

Transporter with awning that forms a hospitality area.

tem. Nickie, you've been working on that. Describe it for us?

Nickie

The Sperge is revolutionary! This system gives restaurants better control of their utensil-washing process. We can download operating data from the Sperge controller that can be processed and analyzed. The results can show restaurants how to reach higher levels of efficiency and reduced utensil-washing costs. We can also use the results to show how the Sperge reduces a restaurant's environmental impact. Is that cool, or what!

Daria - CEO

I would also like to focus on the Severe Clear Hand Check Program. You know, in North America alone, more than two million health care patients get health care-related infections every year. Hand hygiene is the single most effective method for preventing these infections. Our program enables hospitals and health care facilities to comply on a consistent basis with federal hygiene regulations. So, we need to include the Hand Check Program. (pause) Let's see, Justin, I also want to include your new product for the food and beverage industry.

Justin

Yes! The Scruitiniser! We're just launching this system. This is awesome! Imagine getting excited about a sanitation system! This product cleans up salmonella on poultry product surfaces. Not completely. But dramatically. And you know what else? The solution can be reconditioned and used over and over again. That saves water, energy and labor. And it complies with federal regulations on using it more than once. Awesome! Just awesome!

Daria - CEO

I have to comment on your enthusiasm, Justin. It's part of our culture. We have talented high-potential people, like Justin, in every area–from R & D to sales. We work in an environment of spirit, pride, determination, passion and integrity. That's what drives results for our customers. It's the lifeblood of our company. Yes … well, there are two other products to include in our social relationship-building effort.

Pace cars take special guests on the track before.

Rachel

What about Sanitair? We're introducing this new sanitizing agent next month to the dairy, beverage and food processing industries.

Daria - CEO

Yes! Excellent example of our innovative R & D.

Rachel

It's also registered with the EPA as a disinfectant for farms, poultry operations and animal care facilities

Marissa

Hey! What about the new bed bug treatment protocol?! That's brand new from the Nuisance Elimination Department. It's already cutting downtime by 25 percent for our hospitality customers. N E D also has an improved version of the AirWatch unit. It uses a lot less energy to catch even more flying pests.

A country western theme party before an Indianapolis 500 race.

Hospitality area referred to as the chalet, usually within a short walking distance to track seating.

Daria - CEO

I'd say that we have more than enough innovative examples for a great dinner show! We've always given our sales and service reps the technology and support they need to help our customers run clean, safe operations. Now we're going to add another dimension of support with our hospitality event program.

Ruth

So, you want our PR team to develop a special hospitality event plan using our new Indy car sponsorship. And you want the centerpiece to be a dinner show extravaganza our customers will never forget.

Daria - CEO

Yes. Here's what I have in mind: ... a reception, dinner and dinner show extravaganza the evening before race day for 50 customers and 15 company hosts ... on race day, there will be time for the 50 customers and their respective guests to use their credentials to explore the track ... have a continental breakfast at the transporter ...

tour of the team's motor coach. We would probably want to use the area covered by the awning from the motor coach for serving lunch and having customers socialize with the team owner ... maybe getting an informal chalk talk from the driver about his strategy for the race.

I want to see in your plan a detailed description of the dinner show extravaganza concept. When you are thinking about show themes, you need to connect with how IndyCar racing requires teamwork, precision and the creative use of advanced technology to be a winner.

Babe

What about during the race?

Daria - CEO

For the race, we will have a chalet. It's a private, covered, hospitality area with food and beverages. During the race, guests can go back and forth between reserved stadium seats and the chalet. They are only about 100 feet apart. There will be live TV coverage of the race in the chalet.

Joshua

I assume that our sales and services reps will provide guest lists in each of the 15 cities. Do you want only customers and company hosts at the dinner? Can guests come to the race with an associate, spouse or friend? And what's our budget?

Daria - CEO

Only customers and company hosts at the dinner. This is a business meeting. Yes, customers may bring one associate, spouse or adult friend to the race. No children under the drinking age. As for budget, the motto we live by is, if we're going to do it, we're going to do it right. That's your budget.

Meeting With CEO Adjourns

CEO Exits. PR staffers gather briefly

Caitlin - PR Manager

Well, team. Now we are hospitality events planners for the 20XX IndyCar racing season. We need to do some preliminary research. We need to know more about our team and driver. We need to know what hospitality opportunities we have to work with in the sponsorship contract. Let's divide up the work, take three days for research and regroup to begin planning.

Conference Room - PR Department

PR team meets after researching sponsorship contract provisions and race track hospitality features and opportunities.

Justin

I checked out the IRL Web site. I still need to make a list of the 15 cities that are race venues. I also got a bio of our driver and background on the team.

Amanda

What about the dinner before race day? I started to research restaurants and hotel facilities.

Dara

We don't have to be so traditional. We could have dinner catered. …maybe in an old car museum or some sports facility.

Richelle

What do we know about "transporters?"

Amber

They are large trailers, usually with two compartments–one above, one below. Get this. A hydraulic device lifts a race car to the upper compartment. There's room for two cars. Below is a machine shop where mechanics can make repairs to parts. Some transporters have an awning on one side to form a hospitality area. … or a place where the pit crew can take a break. Here's a picture …

Becky

I checked on motor coaches. The team usually has one. Some race car drivers have their own.

Kristin

Another feature at each track is the chalet. … the private hospitality area with food and beverages. During the race, guests can leave a private section of the stadium and walk less than 100 feet over to the chalet, which has live TV coverage of the race. Sponsors also have theme parties.

Joshua

Don't forget the pace car! We can offer a few of our very special guests rides around the track in one of the pace cars. The drivers can treat guests to some impressive speeds.

Justin

I found out that most teams make two or three pit passes available to guests … No more than three at a time, even during the race. Some teams give guests a personal device that lets them listen to the owner and driver talk to each other during the race.

Christina

It's customary for a driver to give a kind of chalk talk to guests. The driver shows the track on a board and explains the strategy for the race–how turns must be taken, how certain unsafe drivers have to be dealt with or avoided. This is not a contact sport like NASCAR. The engines in these cars are so expensive that many are leased from manufacturers. The cars go more than 200 miles an hour. There's no front bumper, guys. The driver's toes are about eight inches from the front tip of the car.

Ali

Something else we can use are show cars. Teams have a couple of these. They are actual racing cars, but without engines. They can be used for display in lobbies, outdoor parties, country clubs, shopping malls. There is usually a team representative on duty, who might let people sit in a car or have their picture taken in or next to the car. On very special occasions, the driver might make an appearance and pose with people for pictures and sign autographs.

PR team meeting wraps up.

Race car on hydraulic lift that hoists it to the upper chamber of the transporter. Bottom compartment is a machine shop for making minor repairs.

Stefan Johansson Motorsports Profile

Introduction to Motorsport

Motorsports is the fastest growing sport in the world. It is watched, in person or on TV, by more people than any other sport including soccer. Motorsports exudes glamour and drama and is unquestionably, the ultimate sports and entertainment spectacle. It is the pinnacle of high-tech, state-of-the-art machines and the challenge of man to control them.

That challenge has fascinated us for many decades. Throughout that time, as today, the drivers are revered for their bravery, athletic ability, charisma and truly are the personalities that make the sport so special. The result of this fascination with speed and spectacle is that motor racing draws a highly desirable demographic profile. The most recent trends show an increase in the number of women and families attending the races and watching at home. Due to its reach and effectiveness, motorsports has become, in its own right, one of the worlds premier and most desirable marketing properties. Worldwide, the popularity of racing has skyrocketed over the last five years. This dramatic growth has resulted in the development of new racing series as well as race facilities, which in turn, has brought more racing to more people and created new fans.

Without a doubt, the popularity of the sport has been assisted by the dramatic increase in televised coverage of racing events. All the major networks broadcast racing and in addition channels such as SKY, Eurosport, ESPN, Fox Sports Network, ESPN2, Sports Channel, Speed Vision and TNN are firmly dedicated to carrying races as well as the multitude of race related shows. Motorsports enjoys participation by a wide variety of supporters. Long gone are the days when racing was solely supported by automotive companies and related products. Race weekends are attended by the who's who of international and US business as well as celebrities from other sports and entertainment forums.

Today, companies from all disciplines support this sport for a variety of business reasons. Consider the wide spectrum of products and services provided by the companies that participate in racing. Why are they here? Simply because they are meeting and exceeding their marketing and business goals through a motorsports platform. Motorsports allows a company to break through the marketing clutter with creative promotions that reach a very targeted audience. Whether its launching a new product, increasing name recognition, vying for the fiercely product loyal race fan base, or business-to-business reasons, companies are receiving a return on their investment which keeps them coming back year after year. This Executive Summary outlines what JOHANSSON MOTORSPORTS ("JMS") is all about? It further explains the benefits of a properly executed motorsports marketing program and delineates our teams role with its marketing partners. Reviewing this book should prove entertaining, but most importantly, it will leave you with a better understanding of how and why motorsports so effectively builds business and drives sales.

Ameritech, Anheuser-Busch, Bell South, Beecham Braun, Casa Fiesta, Casino Queen, Coca-Cola, DKNY, Duracell, First Alert, Gatorade, GE Capitol, Gillette, Hewlett Packard, Holiday Inn, Kleenex, Lanier, Marathon, Mercedes Benz, Microsoft, Mobil 1, Motorola, Nextel Omega, Planters, PPG, Sears.

Genesis of Stefan Johansson Motorsports

For over two decades, Stefan Johansson has been one of the top drivers in the world of international motorsports. He has been successful in Formula One, IndyCar and Le Mans style sports cars, recently winning both the 1997 12 Hours of Sebring (Ferrari) and the 24 Hours of Le Mans (Porsche). He again drove for Porsche in the 1998 24 Hours of Le Mans and in other international endurance events. Throughout his career, Stefan has driven for some of the most prestigious teams and manufacturers in the world including:

Ferrari, McLaren, Porsche, Mercedes, Toyota, Nissan and Mazda. Over the years he has accumulated a superlative degree of knowledge and experience regarding race team operations as well as technical issues. Stefan remains very active with his driving career and is constantly evaluating opportunities to use his experience and knowledge about the sport. One such avenue is in fulfilling his ambition to own and run his own race team. In this manner, he brings to JMS over 20 years of racing experience. Stefan has a clear picture of what he desires in his team. To this end, he is instrumental in all facets of the team from choosing drivers to designing the team's headquarters in Indianapolis. Detail oriented, Stefan stays in touch with everything and allows little to pass by. When not overseeing the team or tending to his own racing career, Stefan is something of a Renaissance man with interest in art, design, business and music. accomplished painter with several He is an accomplished painter with several exhibitions under his belt.

In design his talent runs the gamut from creating all the watches for his H III watch company to the furniture for the race shop and logos for his products. His business acumen focuses not only on his US based businesses such as his European style in-door go-karting track in Indianapolis which is currently under nation-wide partnership offering, but also on international concerns. Well liked in the racing and business community,

Stefan is key in generating world wide business contacts which continue to expand the JMS networking portfolio.

Goals and Objectives

JOHANSSON MOTORSPORTS goal is to establish itself as the premier team in every category in which it participates. This includes not only the results on the race track, but also off the track. To accomplish this JMS has assembled a group of the most competent and talented personnel available in the business. Today, every effort continues to be made to select the best people in their particular field. In this quest, JMS searches for top talent from around the world, as it sees these people as an essential investment in the Team's future. Additionally, only first rate equipment and tools are provided to the Team so that it can perform its tasks at peak levels. Presentation of the Team and its members is meticulous with every effort being made to adhere to the Team's philosophy and goal of being the most professional presented company in the business. The same holds true for the Team's home base.

JMS is headquartered in a 15,000 square foot state-of-the-art race factory located on Gasoline Alley in Indianapolis, Indiana. The facility design clearly expresses the Team's philosophy and goals. As the showcase of JMS it was important in its design that the facility incorporate the same attention to detail as that which is the focus on the Team itself. Outside of the practical nature of the facility, its second purpose is to create a confidence in all who visit, that JOHANSSON MOTORSPORTS is absolutely the best the racing industry has to offer. All of this is combined to forward the main objective of JMS which is to win every race and championship in which it participates.

The focus of each team member is to put forth every possible effort to achieve this goal. In turn this attitude will give JMS's drivers the confidence that every time they get into the car, they will have the best prepared equipment at their disposal. The motor racing platforms for JMS to implement its goals and objectives shall include, but not be limited to, the Le Mans 24 hour race, the American Le Mans Series and the European Le Mans Series. Currently JMS focuses on Le Mans style racing with the ALMS series. This series offers premier venues, highly desirable demographics and of course, intense competition.

Motor Racing Series ALMS

Every year millions of spectators, broadcast viewers and listeners from around the globe focus on the Sarthe region of France to witness a 24-hour motor racing event that dates back to 1923. The 24 Hours of Le Mans tests both man and machine in what is arguably the world's most prestigious automobile race. In an effort to expand upon the rich history and tradition of the 24-Hours of Le Mans, the Automobile Club de l'Ouest (ACO), organizers and rights holders for the trademarks and rules for the 24-hour race, agreed to license their internationally famous brand name and rules to successful businessman and entrepreneur Donald E. Panoz. In addition to the licensing rights, the ACO agreed to grant pre-qualifying exemptions for the 24-Hours of Le Mans each year to three class winners in each of the three major territories (Americas, Asia and Europe).

This represents nine of a total of twelve prequalifying exemptions for the 48-car starting field. Such an incentive is sure to attract major teams and manufacturers from around the world. With these rights, Panoz founded the American Le Mans Series in 1999 with an eight-race schedule. In 2000, the schedule has been expanded to 12 races; eight in the United States, one in Canada, 2 in Europe and the season finale in Adelaide, Australia.

Each race will have a minimum purse of $200,000 with ten percent of each purse going to the privateer fund to be distributed at the end of the season. Prize money from the race purses is distributed exclusively among privateer teams. Our domestic and international television and Internet distribution is unprecedented in American sports car racing history.

American Le Mans Series

In a survey of American Le Mans spectators held by Peter Honig Associates:

- Almost 30% of fans planned nearly a year in advance to attend race events
- Sports cars, followed by Formula 1 and IndyCars are the most popular types of racing. At a lower level is a second group led by Stock cars/ NASCAR racing, followed by drag racing, sprint car racing, other stock car racing, midgets and trucks.
- Nearly 80% of those interviewed liked all three classes of cars in the same race. This is true for those whose favorite racing is sports car racing as well as those favoring IndyCar and Formula1.
- The cars are the stars! Most fans rank seeing the cars they are interested in, together with passing and speed attributes as the number one point in racing. Manufacturer participation is next most important, followed by driver interest.
- Avid fans, those attending more races and stock car fans are most likely to be 35 or older and be married.
- Sports car fans are more likely to be college educated and have higher incomes than stock car fans.
- Many of the world's most prestigious sports car brands intend to compete in the Le Mans series; BMW, Panoz, Chrysler, Viper, Corvette, Cadillac, Porsche, Ferrari, Bentley, Volkswagen and Audi.
- The Le Mans Series license is worldwide, and has been granted up to 9 prequalifying exemptions for the Le Mans 24 Hour event.

Sebring Speedvision	28.9 Million
Fox Sports Net	54 Million
Charlotte NBC	28.9 Million

Speedvision	100.8 Million
Silverstone Speedvision	28.9 Million
Fox Sports Net	54 Million
Nurburgring Speedvision	28.9 Million
Fox Sports Net	54 Million
Sers Point Speedvision	28.9 Million
Fox Sports Net	54 Million
Mosport NBC	28.9 Million
Speedvision	100.8 Million
Texas NBC	28.9 Million
Speedvision	100.8 Million
Portland NBC	28.9 Million
Speedvision	102.2 Million
Atlanta Speedvision	28.9 Million
Fox Sports Net	54 Million
Laguna Seca Speedvision	28.9 Million
Fox Sports Net	54 Million
Las Vegas Speedvision	28.9 Million
Fox Sports Net	54 Million
Australia NBC	102.2 Million

The Motorsports Marketing Platform

A motorsports marketing partnership provides a company with an opportunity to become a part of the fastest growing and the most popular sport in the world. Motorsports provides brand awareness and customer loyalty unlike no other sponsorship venue. Jim Schiemer, CART Racing Program Manager for Shell puts it best, "[motorsports] has become one of the leading spectator sports in the country with growing media attention given to the drivers, the teams and the sponsors, building enhanced brand awareness and increased customer loyalty for those companies involved." The importance of Schiemer's remarks become more apparent when one considers that in a competitive consumer market, a brand associated with motorsports will win the business over another, all other things being equal, when the customer has an interest in motorsports.

It is widely accepted that on average, 65% of race fans consciously purchase the products and services of the companies that sponsor motorsports. This is a compelling statistic when one considers that a full 30% of any cross section of the general public expresses a strong interest in motorsports. Motorsports is a powerful multimedia marketing platform which a company can use to communicate its desired image. A motorsports partnership provides a company access to tens of millions of potential customers in the United States and hundreds of millions world wide that fit within that company's demographic profile.

Corporate hospitality and entertainment programs are other ways a company can benefit from a motorsports program. Again, Schiemer states that, "Shell hospitality is a way to put your best foot forward for dealers and jobbers, or potential new customers. They can meet the drivers and team members, and experience the excitement of getting a first-hand look behind the scenes in the pits and garages."

Marketing Partner Growth Objectives

JOHANSSON MOTORSPORTS has a vision focused on the future. JMS knows that in order to develop a solid long term relationship with a company, it takes time for that entity not only to understand the many benefits that a motorsports marketing platform can provide, but just as important, how that platform can efficiently and effectively be used to attain its goals. Without this understanding, a marketing partner may not be able to justify expending the resources required to continue its affiliation with our Team. JOHANSSON MOTORSPORTS is looking for marketing partners who will grow with the Team. JMS provides an option to marketing partners to start in American Le Mans Series racing as a way to "get its feet wet" without spending a tremendous amount of marketing resources.

During such an introduction into motorsports, a company can learn how to maximize this multimedia marketing platform to accomplish its goals. Whether its to sell more product, develop business relationships or build a strong corporate image, this can be accomplished through motorsports. But the bottom line is knowing that JMS wants to grow with its marketing partners so that each will understand the needs and abilities of the other, thus developing a win/win relationship.

The Motorsports Marketing Partnership

It is important to note that before JMS begins any program with its marketing partners, an exhaustive analysis of that partner's needs is completed. As with racing, a strong marketing partnership is won back at the workshop and office with proper planning and preparation. The planning and preparation does not end when the season begins since we view the relationship with our marketing partners as an ongoing process. We continuously evaluate the program to ensure that our marketing partners are achieving their goals, maximizing their involvement and continually benefiting from the opportunities that arise through their participation with JMS. In this manner, special attention is focused on the following:

- Clearly Defining Objectives
- Creating a Cost Effective Program
- Establishing Guidelines for an Effective Program
- Delineating an Internal Communication Policy

- Monitoring Program Effectiveness on a per venue basis
- Evaluating Potential Opportunities
- Assisting in the Development of a Total Promotional Package
- Determining Media Strategies
- Continuously Planning and Evaluating Program.

It is JMS's goal to offer our marketing partners much more than simply placing their logo on a winning car. Beyond the above and upon implementation, the focus with our marketing partners becomes two-fold: First, to maximize a company's marketing resources; and Secondly, to create measurable results–new or increased business.

Maximizing marketing resources is JMS's way of assisting a company to create a motorsports program using the least amount of that company's market dollars. JMS's approach creates an opportunity for a company to become involved with the Team without having to increase it marketing and advertising budgets. JMS knows how to identify potential synergistic partners and how to maximize their benefit as a "cooperative" marketing partner. This is accomplished through forming strategic alliances with a company's vendors, suppliers, franchises the media and other companies.

This leveraging of relationships increases the effectiveness of a company's marketing resources and results in generating "free" marketing dollars as well as improving relationships with the company's cooperative marketing partners. Measurable results of a motorsports marketing program come from the forming of new business relationships and/or the increase in sales of products or services. JMS provides to a marketing partner access to its global portfolio of business partners and relationships. This proves effective in generating new business both domestically and abroad.

Benefits of the Motorsports Marketing Partnership

Motorsports is the number one sport in attracting corporate sponsorship dollars, with 25% of all sponsorship money being directed to racing. Why? Because it allows a company to break through the marketing clutter with creative promotions that reach a very targeted audience. Motorsports brings to a company a broad market. Involvement alone will generate millions of impressions for a marketing partner. In order to maximize its involvement, JOHANSSON MOTORSPORTS will assist a company in the development of any race related merchandising program, which could include but are not limited to:

- Promote a sponsor supplement with a major racing magazine designed to build lists and establish a company as a major brand name in motorsports.
- Develop a sweepstakes series that is designed as a self funding promotional program to build lists and generate floor traffic.

- Provide show cars, again designed to increase floor traffic and to be used as a general promotional tool.
- Assist in the development of a marketing partner's team fan club as a promotional tool designed to build lists and loyalty.
- Assist in the development of a marketing partner's team direct mail program. The goal of this program is to build a loyalty/affinity program based on developing a lifestyle list.
- Assist in development of authentic sponsor team merchandise. The goal of this program is to build loyalty and impressions.
- Deliver race weekend event marketing programs for a company to use as VIP hospitality to build trade relations and top-of-mind awareness on the part of the buyer and distribution channel executives. This type of sports based entertainment can avoid the anti-gratuity policies many companies have.

Business-to-Business Sales

Many of the business-to-business objectives apply equally well to the business-to-consumer process. The potential marketing benefits that accrue from the association with a race team can be focused on maximizing specific business-to-business relationships and audiences. These audiences are:

- Potential customers
- Existing customers
- Trade press, media and market opinion makers
- The company's employees and families
- The company's vendors There are many marketing and hospitality programs that can be developed to:
- Build a competitive and leading edge image
- Create product and/or market distinction
- Crack hard to reach accounts in a neutral environment
- Trigger buy decisions
- Reward customer loyalty Enhance relationships and promote bonding with key accounts
- Build a distinct identity with the trade media
- Drive morale and team building
- Build distinct commercial sales programs with a
- Use the JOHANSSON MOTORSPORTS facilities as an unusual and dramatic customer demonstration, reference and/or meeting site.

Stefan Johansson has been a key part of many of the world's top
racing series in a storied driving career and has now cast his lot with
the Champ Car World Series as he joins the Bridgestone Presents
The Champ Car World Series Powered by Ford with a new two-car
team. Johansson began his major-league driving career in 1983
with the Spirit/Honda Formula 1 squad and earned his first World
Championship points in 1984 while with Toleman. He earned
podium finishes for Tyrrell and Ferrari and gave the Onyx team its
first podium in 1988. He moved to Champ Cars in 1992 with Tony
Bettenhausen and made 73 starts, earning four podium finishes in
five seasons. He launched his Dayton Indy Lights team in 1997 but stayed in the cockpit,
racing sportscars, winning the Sebring 12 Hours and the 24 Hours of Le Mans in 1997. He
was also the European champion of the American Le Mans Series. Johansson currently lives
in Indianapolis with his wife Gabriela and children Clara and Stefan Jr.

Article Courtesy of Stefan Johansson Motorsports

Case Twelve
Public School
Emergency
Response

VIOLENCE AT SOUTH COUNTY HIGH

School districts have a responsibility to develop crisis plans. However, the range of traumatic events that districts experience has increased significantly over the years from temporary disruptions to highly publicized events. Educators are greatly challenged to obtain the training needed to deal effectively with today's diverse range of crisis situations. While many schools have plans to deal with the unexpected, their plans must employ more than a top administrator and a small response team. Today's problems require broader involvement—all members of the school community. They require the involvement of outside support services, from fire and rescue to professional counseling. They require plans with provisions to meet the physical and psychological needs of individuals in every stage of a crisis situation—from trauma through recovery.

This is the case of a peaceful school environment that unexpectedly exploded with emotions, taking administrators, faculty, staff, parents and even many students by surprise. The role play that follows will lead you through a dramatization of what actually happened. A high school principal who had no training in crisis management or communication tried unsuccessfully to deal with a mounting crisis that led to a gathering of more than 600 parents who were fright-ened for their children's safety, highly upset over the principal's mismanagement of the situation and who attempted to take control of solving the problem.

Team Assignment

In this case your team will be a school district's public relations staff. The class role play contains all the case details. After conducting the class role play, we will turn back the clock and assume that the parent meeting had not been called. Your assignment is to develop for the principal a crisis communication plan for recovering from unanticipated incidents. If your team decides that a parent meeting should be part of your plan, but with certain alterations, that is permissible. Stay within public relations responsibilities and remember that safety, training, policy enforcement, building operation and maintenance are human resource functions at the high school and district levels and thus, should not be included in your communication plan. Your challenge begins when the principal calls the Public Relations Department at school district headquarters and asks for your assistance in making an immediate recovery from unexpected incidents. He has not asked for a 6- or 12-month recovery plan. When you meet with the principal at the high school, the principal says, "We have a serious situation and I think I should call an emergency meeting of parents this weekend. This is overwhelming. I'm not trained for this. I

just want the high school operation to be back to normal as quickly as possible."

To turn things around you will have to focus not only on the situation, but on two important dimensions of leadership—courage and trust. The case provides an opportunity to show how your team would support a leader, the high school principal, in ways that would strengthen his courage to stand up and do what's right. It also provides an opportunity to show how your team would support the principal in ways that would enable him to regain the trust that people would want in order to let a leader, the principal, guide them through a difficult situation.

Individual Writing Assignments

Each team member is to complete a different one of the following items that might or might not be included in the design of your plan. It is up to you to decide what the content should be for each element.

1. Write opening remarks (2-minute duration, 250 words) for the high school principal to make in appropriate tone (attitude toward the subject) and voice (personality) before a student assembly that would establish a climate for everyone to be able to work through the school's racial unrest in a sensible manner.

2. Write a letter from the principal of South County High School to parents explaining the unexpected incidents and using key principles of risk communication to assure them that the situation is under control.

3. Write remarks (2–3 minute duration, 250–350 words) for the South County High School principal to use in explaining to the local newspaper's editorial board what happened, why, and how the situation is being managed.

4. Write a memo from the high school principal to faculty and staff to be placed in mailboxes in time to be read Monday morning that explains what happened, why it happened, how the situation is being managed, and how to handle questions from students, parents, others and the media.

5. Write a script for the principal to use in recording a podcast recapping recent unrest and appealing to students to embrace diversity.

6. A question and answer sheet for school faculty and staff to use in responding to queries by anyone interested in the current situation. The sheet should cover what happened, why it happened, how it is being managed.

7. A phone script to be read by a school secretary with a message from the principal to leaders of South County High's Parent Teacher Organization to meet with him to discuss what happened, why it happened and how it is being managed.

8. A segment of remarks (long enough to do the job) for the principal to use in advising leaders South County High's Parent Teacher Organization what they could tell parents that would help them keep their children safe at school. For content, search the Internet for "violence in schools" and related subjects.

ROLE PLAY
Cast

Narrator
Sally Edwards (Parent)
Tom Edwards (Parent)
Nadel Harper (Parent)
Paul Burdick (High School Principal)
Irritated Parent No. 1
Irritated Parent No. 2
Irritated Parent No. 3
Irritated Parent No. 4
Irritated Parent No. 5
Irritated Parent No. 6
Irritated Parent No. 7
Clark Cantwell (Reporter)
Rose (Teacher)
Ellen (Teacher)
Alex (Science Teacher)

Narrator

A stream of several hundred cars flows into the parking lot at South County High. Doors slam shut, one right after another, as parents leave their vehicles and head for the walk to the auditorium. A journalist asks an officer to reposition her patrol car and turn on the strobe lights for a more dramatic camera shot. Tom Edwards and his wife Sally are among the parade of parents.

Sally Edwards - Parent

Tom, I'm worried. We've never been called like this to attend a meeting. (pause) Oh, my, an "emergency" meeting they said on the phone! (pause) Tom!!

Tom Edwards - Parent

(Trying to be reassuring ...)
Now, Sally, let's not jump to conclusions. It's probably just a precaution.

Sally Edwards - Parent

Precaution!!

Tom Edwards - Parent

Calm down, dear. It's probably about some party that got out of hand.

Sally Edwards - Parent

Get real Tom. It's not about six-pack shenanigans down on the Chattahoochee. These days it's about hostage-taking, sniper attacks, murders, terrorists and bombings. (pause) Oh my, Tom!!

Narrator

The Edwards reach the auditorium entrance with others. No one is at the door to meet the anxious visitors, which adds to an already empty feeling in the pits of nervous stomachs. Tom Edwards takes a seat, turns his head to the left and is eye to eye with Nadel Harper, another parent.

Tom Edwards - Parent

Hello. I'm Tom Edwards. This is my wife Sally.

Nadel Harper - Parent

(Looks with a raised eyebrow …)
Hey!

Tom Edwards - Parent

(Speaks again to Nadel …)
Do you know what this is about, Nadel?

Nadel Harper - Parent

(gossipy voice)
Well this is what I heard from Gloria and Trudy Shonemocker …

Sally Edwards - Parent

(To her husband in a hushed voice …)
Wha'd she say, Tom? Wha'd she say!

Tom Edwards - Parent

(To his wife …)
She must be the school gossip, bless her heart.

Narrator

In the South you can say whatever bad things you want about a person as long as you follow it with "ain't he special" or "bless her heart" as Edwards said, "She must be the school gossip, bless her heart." Principal's finger thumps over the sound system. (Tap the mic several times.) It's more an expression of nerves than a test of the microphone. Thump. Thump … Thump. The high school principal speaks …

Paul Burdick - Principal

(Staring not at the audience of 600 parents, but down at notes on the podium …) Several years ago, we established a program for diversity in our school …

Sally Edwards - Parent

(Talking loudly to her husband, Tom …) He could have at least said hello. He makes us come to this meeting at nine o'clock on a Sunday morning and doesn't even acknowledge that we're here.

Paul Burdick - Principal

(Continuing his remarks …)
Included in our diversity program were students, faculty members, administrators …

Narrator

An irritated parent STANDS to address the high school principal …

Irritated Parent No. 1

(Assertively interrupts the speaker …)
Paul darling, would you mind just telling us why we are here?

Irritated Parent No. 2

(Also interrupting, assertively …)
Yes! What's the big emergency? What's this all about?

Paul Burdick - Principal

(Raising his eyes slightly; not looking very far into the audience …)
Yes, I'm getting to that. (PAUSE) Last Wednesday, a boy, 19 years old, who is not a student, drove into the parking lot in a pick-up truck flying two Confederate flags. His name is Jack Sanders. He got out of the truck, and for no apparent reason,

mumbled something and assaulted an Afro-American student. He entered the school wanting to reclaim his jacket that he gave to a girlfriend, a student at South County. The girlfriend gave the jacket to another student who saw a Ku Klux Klan patch on the jacket and cut it off. Before Sanders could find his jacket, he was escorted off the campus and arrested for assault.

Irritated Parent No. 3

(Interrupting the principal …)
So what's the big emergency, Paul?

Paul Burdick - Principal

Yes, I'm getting to that. That incident on Wednesday started students talking about race, freedom of speech, about wearing a KKK or any patch, about the boy being apprehended and sent away from the school.

Narrator

The principal fidgets with the microphone … (Tap mic …)

Paul Burdick - Principal

(thump, thump, thump)
Thursday morning, we discovered random acts of vandalism around the school.

Irritated Parent No. 4

Like what? What kind of vandalism?

Paul Burdick - Principal

Yes. (PAUSE) Well, 62 bird feeders were found glued solid to a paint bench in wood shop. In the "home ec" room the door to a refrigerator was glued shut, and so were the doors to all of the storage cabinets. Thursday afternoon we had some trouble during band. Students got into another argument.

Irritated Parent No. 5

What kind of trouble, Paul? We didn't give up a Sunday morning for nothing. What exactly happened in the band room?

Irritated Parent No. 6

(Shouting out …)
I'll tell you what happened! I heard from Nadel that a tuba got thrown out a window. A trombone was wrapped around someone's neck … nearly strangled him. A student got struck in the head with an oboe and was taken to the hospital.

Irritated Parent No. 7

(Interrupting, excitedly …)
I heard teachers and two parents just stood and watched. That's when Jamie got hit in the head with the oboe …

Irritated Parent No. 1

(Interrupting …)
My daughter said she ran down to the office to call home … she said they wouldn't let her use the phone … said it was school policy …

Paul Burdick - Principal

Listen up now, and let me tell you what happened in the band room. An argument over free speech started among several

students. That's not true about the tuba or the trombone. There was no damage.

Irritated Parent No. 2

What about the oboe?

Paul Burdick - Principal.

One girl did get bumped in the head with an oboe, but it wasn't a serious injury and she was not taken to a hospital.

Irritated Parent No. 3

(Shouts out two questions that shock the audience ...)
What about the gun reports? Are you going to tell us about the gun reports?

Sally Edwards - Parent

(She screams ... gasps repeatedly for air ... calls to her husband ...)
Tom! Oh, Tom, dear! They've got guns!

Paul Burdick - Parent

Yes. I'm getting to that ... I mean, no, I wasn't going to bring that up. We checked those reports thoroughly and found no basis for them. Believe me. No guns. Now let me finish telling you what happened. By Friday, it was pretty intense around here. So in the morning I told students that I would like to meet with anyone who would like to talk about their feelings and what was causing the unrest. About 60 students met with me at the back of the cafeteria. There were some heated exchanges among several students. The meeting ended about 1 p.m. As students moved into the main part of the cafeteria where about 1,000 students gather for lunch, someone let out a very nasty racial slur. That led to shouting, pushing and shoving. Two male students

started punching each other. A girl tried to break up the fight and her arm was broken. She was taken to the hospital. One of our staff members called 911 and the police came and were able to calm things down. Now you have the whole story. I'd like to introduce Jeri Johnson, my secretary, who will collect questions. I would like those of you who have questions to write them on a slip of paper. We will pick out the most important ones to answer because we can't answer every question.

Irritated Parent No. 4

(Barking at the principal ...)
NO! We're not going to do that!
And YES, you ARE going to answer questions. We are staying until every one of our questions is answered!

Irritated Parent No. 5

I'm not sending my child to school until I know exactly what's behind all this and that it's safe for my child to be in school!

Irritated Parent No. 6

(Interjecting ...) So what's the plan, Paul? How is the school going to deal with this? What are you going to do to make this place safe for our children?

Paul Burdick - Principal

Yes. I'm getting to that ... That's why I called this meeting. We used a phone tree to notify everyone. I know we didn't offer a reason for the meeting. I hope that didn't alarm anyone. (PAUSE) We are thinking about banning any clothing that disrupts education. We are also planning to have security personnel, and city police visible and in uniform, and two metal detectors at the main doors.

Irritated Parent No. 7

(Interrupting …)
How many entrances are there?

Paul Burdick - Principal

There are six.

Irritated Parent No. 7

Then we want SIX metal detectors!

Irritated Parent No. 1

(With an expression of disgust …)
There doesn't seem to be any plan.

Irritated Parent No. 2

(Stands up …) If you don't have a plan, we'll give you one. So, here's the plan, Paul. We want every measure necessary to secure the safety of students. We want an 800 help line for any student who is troubled about anything. We want to review the dress code. I'm sure many of us parents are willing to volunteer to …

Paul Burdick - Principal

I appreciate that … We also want to involve the students in helping to solve this problem.

Irritated Parent No. 3

(Interrupting …)
That's the LAST thing we need. This is for ADULTS to straighten out …

Irritated Parent No. 4

I don't agree with that …

Clark Cantwell - Reporter

Excuse me, Mr. Burdick. I'm Clark Cantwell from the Spotlight News. I would like to know …

Paul Burdick - Principal

(Interrupts …) I'm sorry Mr. Cantwell. The press wasn't invited. This is, well it's a private meeting with parents.

Clark Cantwell - Reporter

You can't be serious! A private meeting? At a public school? With parents! A student riot! You might not want to answer my questions, but you can be sure that every comment made today will be in tomorrow's paper.

Narrator

The meeting finally adjourns after nearly three hours of emotionally-charged dialogue. Parents feeling frustrated and upset are leaving the auditorium. Small groups gather outside talking. The Edwards walk toward the parking lot …

Sally Edwards - Parent

So, we're called to an emergency meeting, given no useful information on the phone OR at the meeting.

Tom Edwards - Parent

This is shocking! There was no indication of any kind of festering problems. It's the largest high school in the district. Students come from up-scale suburban neighborhoods.

Sally Edwards - Parent

Everyone seemed to be getting along. What's the minority population, John?

Tom Edwards - Parent

About 10 percent, I think.

Sally Edwards

Paul Burdick doesn't do very well under pressure. I thought he was going to have a heart attack.

Tom Edwards - Parent

He tried to avoid telling us about the incidents. He went on and on about diversity. He ducked the gun reports. He tried to duck the press.

Sally Edwards - Parent

Worst of all he didn't address our biggest concern–safety.

Tom Edwards - Parent

I thought his action plan was … Well, it wasn't even a plan … He didn't have a plan!

Sally Edwards - Parent

What about the way he tried to control questions! He says write down your questions and we'll pick the ones we want to answer.

Tom Edwards - Parent

Where was the district? I can't believe no one came from the district. Where was the superintendent?

Sally Edwards - Parent

Probably at the WaffleHouse.

Tom Edwards - Parent

(Closing the car door …)
Heads are going to roll, Sally. Heads are going to roll.

Sally Edwards - Parent

We're not sending our daughter back until this mess is straightened out.

Tom Edwards - Parent

Yes Dear. That's for sure!

Narrator

Standing in a hallway near the auditorium are three teachers talking about the meeting and wondering if any parents are going to let their children go to school on Monday.

Rose - Teacher

This is a mess. I don't know what's going to happen on Monday.

Ellen - Teacher

I'd say we're all a little short on facts.

Alex - Science Teacher

Does anyone know exactly what happened? How accurate are these stories? Is that true about the fight in the band room?

Ellen - Teacher

I'm in the room next door. Things have been kicked up a notch.

Rose - Teacher

Why didn't Mr. Burdick anticipate what parents were going to ask? Why the big emergency meeting? Seems like we could have taken the initiative to head off the rumors. We still could. Parents are begging for some plan of action.

Alex - Science Teacher

I'd like to know more about pressure behind all this pent up emotion. What's forcing the steam out of the volcano? What's happening at the core? Is a really big eruption eminent?

Ellen - Teacher

Poor Mr. Burdick. He's no coward. But he let fear get the best of him instead of letting it bolster his courage. He needs to step up to the tough questions, be more open with people. He was so nervous he didn't see how desperately parents wanted him to talk about keeping their kids safe.

Rose - Teacher

No question. He missed an opportunity. The school has to be more responsive. There are too many unanswered questions for parents, for us, for the students. Parents trust Burdick. He's always shown respect and compassion for everyone. He just needs to be clear, to give everyone a chance to work on the problem.

Alex - Science Teacher

Well, he had better be quick about it. This mountain is puffing steam. The magma is moving …

Ellen - Teacher

It's not like the district to get so caught off guard. Knowing the superintendent, there will be an action plan on the table before anyone sleeps tonight.

Rose Teacher

I think you're right. We'll see details on building security, notification procedures, intervention. There will be an investigation of the current issues, open forums for kids and parents and individual counseling. I know this superintendent. She's thorough. We'll have a plan that let's everyone know that the problem is being managed.

Alex - Science Teacher

I hope you're right. I'm telling you, the mountain is …

Ellen - Teacher

That's enough about the volcano, Alex.

Rose - Teacher

Oh, what do you expect from a science teacher?

Alex - Science Teacher

I'm serious. This is earth shaking.

DISCUSSION POINTS

Situation

- Called emergency meeting
- Addressed broad issues
- Tried to minimize the incidents
- Ducked gun reports
- Overlooked priority concern–safety
- Offered inadequate immediate action
- Tried to control discussion–censor questions
- Tried to ignore the press
- Did not insist on parent/student involvement in solution
- School district headquarters offered no support, physical presence

Crisis Communication Principles

- Tell it all
- Tell it fast
- Tell it truthfully
- Take charge
- Own up to responsibilities
- Lay out immediate action steps
- Validate actions
- Determine who needs what
- Address everyone's concerns
- Assist the media
- Communicate frequently, regularly

Risk Communication Principles

- Provide information from a trusted source
- Source must have a record of credibility
- Address emotion first, then risks
- Answer ALL questions
- Ignoring even one of the four principles above could ignite outrage.

Case Thirteen
Crisis Preparedness

ARE YOU PREPARED?

This case is presented as a role play written to enable participants in a class or workshop to experience what it feels like to witness a crisis. The case is based on an actual experience; however, the names are fictitious.

A crisis situation develops at a manufacturing plant that necessitates a series of conversations between Ted Robbins, the plant manager, and Dave Hollings, public relations director located at company headquarters several states away. Hollings also confers with his staff assistant, Jill Peters.

I recommend that the role play be conducted twice: once for participants to get a sense of what it is like to be a PR person working a crisis situation; and again to study the case exercises.

After the role play, read CRISIS: By The Rule Of Advanced Engagement *to learn the difference between crisis preparedness, crisis management and crisis communication; then follow the instructions to develop a model Crisis Code of Conduct.*

Team Assignment

For this case, it is important to experience how quickly an incident or accident can occur and realize the necessity of having plans and policies in place ahead of time. As you read or conduct the case role play, think of how useless it would be for a company to have a policy mandating the all news media calls and incidents or accidents are to be handled only by headquarters personnel. After conducting the role play, once to feel the experience of witnessing a crisis, and again to study aspects of the case, read CRISIS: By The Rule of Advanced Engagement to learn the difference between crisis preparedness, crisis management and crisis communication. Learn what an organization can do to be prepared for a crisis. Then, as a team, develop a Crisis Code of Conduct. Follow the instructions to complete the model Crisis Code of Conduct presentation, making collective decisions on which principles to include in the code. When the presentation is complete, have one person on the team read it aloud and determine how well it provides an overall behavioral framework that would enable individuals, intuitively, make good decisions in a crisis situation. If your model seems too logistical, go back and replace your entries with broader principles that would serve to establish a culture, rather than a what-to-do checklist.

Individual Writing Assignments

Each team member is to select a different one of the following writing assignments to complete:

1. Write a news statement for the media. Keep it short, but complete, factual and detailed with exact times. Assume victims' families have been notified and make up fictitious names for the victims.
2. Write for the plant manager's signature a message to be conveyed electronically to plant employees describing the accident and measures that will be taken to prevent future occurrences, that is, there will be a thorough investigation and the company's safety committee will develop procedures for working more safely with nitrogen.
3. Describe what tools you would use to monitor comments about the accident in the social media and what you would do to correct erroneous reports.
4. Assume that you are head of the public relations department and you are responsible for PR coordinators at 12 company locations. Write a message to be conveyed electronically apprising the field coordinators of the accident and reminding them of the proper procedure is for handling this type of crisis situation. Based on the role play, you decide what the policy should be.
5. Write a brief discussion about the pros and cons of letting reporters and photographers tour and photograph the accident site.

6. Write a memo from the PR director to the plant manager providing suggestions for following up the accident with the victims' families, employees, emergency service personnel and the immediate community.

7. The media would have appreciated a fact sheet about the company and mostly about the manufacturing plant where the accident occurred. Describe what information reporters would have wanted on the fact sheet. Exclude any references to the accident.

ROLE PLAY
Cast

Narrator
Plant Manager Ted Robbins
PR Director Dave Hollings
PR Staff Assistant Jill Peters

Inside Manufacturing Plant

Plant Manager Ted Robbins calls public relations director at company headquarters

Plant Manager Ted Robbins

This is Ted Robbins at the North Fork plant. Is Dave there?

PR Director Dave Hollings

Yea, Ted. What do you need?

Plant Manager Ted Robbins

We could have a fatality to report. There's a man lying at the bottom of one of our storage tanks. We called 911.

PR Director Dave Hollings

Do you have a name?

Plant Manager Ted Robbins

Not yet. We think he works for a contractor that was purging the tank yesterday. I'll get right back. Huck, our safety supervisor, is here.

Plant manager ends call abruptly. Less than five minutes pass and another call from North Fork

PR Director Dave Hollings

This is Dave. (silence) Hello?

Plant Manager Ted Robbins

Dave this is Ted. (long pause) We have two fatalities.

PR Director Dave Hollings

Ted … (louder) Ted … What's going on?

Plant Manager Ted Robbins

Our safety supervisor is dead.

PR Director Dave Hollings

Do you have help? Are the paramedics there?

Plant Manager Ted Robbins

(long pause) Sorry, Dave.

PR Director Dave Hollings

Take your time. Take a couple deep breaths.

Plant Manager Ted Robbins

The medics are here. Both bodies are out of the tank. They didn't have a chance.

PR Director Dave Hollings

What happened?

Plant Manager Ted Robbins

An outside contractor was hired to clean out a storage tank. They were purging it with nitrogen. Listen, Ted, I ... We've got a crowd of reporters ...

PR Director Dave Hollings

They must have picked up on the emergency calls ... Call me as soon as you can.

PR Director Dave Hollings turns to staff assistant, Jill Peters.

PR Director Dave Hollings

Jill, do some quick research. See what you can find about purging enclosed spaces with nitrogen.

Staff Assistant Jill Peters

OK

PR Director Dave Hollings

Also check on any accident related incidents.

Plant manager calls Dave Hollings, PR director

Plant Manager Ted Robbins

Dave, I'll give you a brief account of what happened.

PR Director Dave Hollings

Excuse me, Ted. What about the media?

Plant Manager Ted Robbins

We're OK, so far. We've withheld the names of both men. I've already broken the news to Huck's wife. They have six children, Dave.

PR Director Dave Hollings

What have you told the media?

Plant Manager Ted Robbins

Sketchy details: two men dead, one employee and one outside contractor, industrial accident, paramedics arrived 6:58 this morning, unable to save the victims.

PR Director Dave Hollings

Ted, the safety supervisor!?

Plant Manager Ted Robbins

That's what's impossible to explain ... I'll call you right back ...

PR Director Hollings puts down the phone and looks up at Jill Peters ...

Staff Assistant Jill Peters

A rapid release of nitrogen gas into an enclosed space can displace oxygen. That represents an asphyxiation hazard. I have an example with the first space shuttle launch in 1981. Have time?

PR Director Dave Hollings

Make it brief.

Staff Assistant Jill Peters

Two technicians were exposed to a pure nitrogen atmosphere in an enclosed area around the engines inside the shuttle. Both died.

PR Director Dave Hollings

So why do you need nitrogen around the engines?

Staff Assistant Jill Peters

The nitrogen is used to drive out the oxygen present in normal air. That lessens the chance of a fire or explosion in the engine area. The deaths were caused by a lack of oxygen.

PR Director Dave Hollings

How often can that possibly happen?

Staff Assistant Jill Peters

Nitrogen asphyxiation hazards in industry killed 80 people from 1992 to 2002. Forty-two involved contractors. According to this government bulletin, every year people are killed by breathing air that has too little oxygen. Seventy-eight percent of the air we breathe is nitrogen gas, so many people think that nitrogen isn't harmful. But, as the bulletin points out, nitrogen is safe to breathe only when it's mixed with the right amount of oxygen.

PR Director Dave Hollings

And you can't smell oxygen or nitrogen.

Staff Assistant Jill Peters

If the concentration of nitrogen is too high and oxygen too low, the body becomes oxygen deprived and asphyxiation occurs.

PR Director Dave Hollings

They must have died instantly.

Phone rings. Plant Manager Ted Robbins calls PR director.

Plant Manager Ted Robbins

Dave, we're going to have to release a statement.

PR Director Dave Hollings

OK. We read some background on nitrogen asphyxiation. So tell me about the actions of the two men.

Plant Manager Ted Robbins

The outside contractor cleaned one of our storage tanks. Purged it with nitrogen. That was yesterday afternoon. This morning, sometime before 6:45 an employee from the contract service firm apparently came to finish the job. Must have forgotten about the nitrogen, climbed through a hatch on top of the tank and went down a ladder. Paramedics think he died instantly. At about 6:45 one of our employees reporting for work noticed that the safety tape around the tank had been unfastened and the hatch was opened. He climbed to the top of the tank, looked into the opened hatch and saw the victim lying at the bottom. He called to him, then ran to my office to get me. I called 911 and I talked to you on the way to the tank.

PR Director Dave Hollings

What about Huck?

Plant Manager Ted Robbins

Huck got to the tank while you and I were talking and the rescue unit was coming. According to other employees he went to the top of the tank, saw the man, went right into the tank to investigate. When I got there, workers were shouting that Huck was in the tank. The rescue crew was on the scene at 6:58.

PR Director Dave Hollings

I can't believe this. Huck has been safety supervisor there for how many years?

Plant Manager Ted Robbins

... 15 years.

PR Director Dave Hollings

Whatever made him ...

Plant Manager Ted Robbins

We'll never know, Dave. How do we explain his actions to his family ... I'm feeling sick ... (pause) Everyone is going to wonder what kind of safety management we practice ...

PR Director Dave Hollings

How did the rescue workers get them out of the tank.

Plant Manager Ted Robbins

They followed a procedure. One guy started down through the hatch using an oxygen mask. His partner handed him the respirator once he was in the tank. A person couldn't fit into the hatch wearing oxygen tanks. They did everything possible. Pronounced both men dead.

PR Director Dave Hollings

Did the contractor have any warning signs about nitrogen in the tank?

Plant Manager Ted Robbins

No. Just the yellow safety tape in a circle around the tank.

PR Director Dave Hollings

In some quick research we found a commonly used danger sign that reads: "This building contains air purged enclosures. Check for adequate oxygen before entering. Authorized personnel only." Did the contractor post signs?

Plant Manager Ted Robbins

Isn't it ironic that one of the most important commercial uses of nitrogen is to improve safety. It doesn't react with other materials. In fact it's used to purge flammable or toxic material prior to opening equipment for maintenance. No. No signs were posted.

PR Director Dave Hollings

That's what the contractor was doing for you–purging the tank of another gas so it could be cleaned for another use.

Plant Manager Ted Robbins

Yes.

PR Director Dave Hollings

I'll have a statement for you shortly. Company attorney has been alerted. He'll be calling you.

Plant Manager Ted Robbins

What about the media?

PR Director Dave Hollings

You can use the statement for media calls. We'll publish a news release from here.

CRISIS: BY THE RULE OF ADVANCED ENGAGEMENT

"Crash the West Wing!" to the Secret Service means there is imminent danger and to lock down that part of the White House. "Code Blue!" to doctors and staff signals a medical emergency. "Scramble!" to Air Force personnel means to immediately dispatch jet fighters." In each of these situations, an order is given for specific, previously defined behavior. People in these situations then do what they have been trained to do and everyone involved and/or observing has confidence that things are being managed.

How is it that in such crisis situations people, on command, shift quickly and smoothly into an emergency mode and follow a precise set of sequential steps that bring the crisis to a turning point? The answer is that organizations, certainly emergency services, have a preparedness strategy that is integral with their operations strategies. In other words, preparedness is an operational priority. That is not the case for most organizations when it comes to crisis situations.

A bullet from a high-powered sniper rifle pierces a window and produces a sharp-sounding snap as it barely clears heads in the boardroom. Does everyone present automatically shift into an emergency mode and follow a precise set of predetermined steps. Or does the incident result in chaos with the chief executive, once secure, looking to legal counsel for advice and asking the public relations executive to bring in the crisis communication plan?

Preparedness is not an operational priority for most organizations and therein lies a problem. Most companies have several layers of management. Strategic management is the highest of these levels in the sense that it is the broadest–applying to all parts of the organization–while also spanning the longest time horizon. It gives direction to corporate values, corporate culture, corporate goals and corporate missions. Under this level there are business-level competitive strategies and functional unit strategies. All or-

ganizations-for-profit and not-for-profit are vulnerable to crisis situations, yet very few have preparedness as an established functional strategy. That is why, in most cases, when a crisis situation occurs it gets treated, functionally, as an unwanted distraction, rather than the way an unexpected

A crisis is not the time to be arguing about whether to behave for the court of law or the court of public opinion, as though they are mutually exclusive.

challenge would be treated in the pursuit of financial, production, human resource, sales and marketing and R&D goals. Without a preparedness strategy that guides behavior in a crisis situation, an organization turns to checklists, manuals and sometimes even to the stupid mistakes of peers, which Warren Buffet refers to as the "institutional imperative."

Government sources estimate that more than 32 million workers are exposed to 650,000 hazardous chemical products in more than three million American workplaces, that each day an average 16 workers die in the U.S. from injuries on the job, that more than 1.2 billion pounds of toxic pesticides are used annually in U.S. agriculture and are responsible for more than 300,000 illnesses and 1,000 deaths in the farm worker community each year. There are shooting sprees, product failures, financial disasters, explosions, natural disasters and many other threatening situations.

Despite the looming risks, surveys continue to show that less than half of the organizations that should have crisis plans actually have them, that most plans have never been tested and when crises occur 90 percent of the crisis time is spent debating how and what to communicate.

A crisis is not a time to circle the wagons and draw down the blinds—a time to isolate the management of a problem and shut down communication. It's a time to move the organization to a higher level within its governance framework.

Wouldn't chief executives like to have confidence that operational practices were in place that would enable them to assess, act and communicate in a crisis situation as readily as they are able to manage a production problem? I am not minimizing the challenge of managing a crisis situation. However, I am saying that an organization can develop, with professional public relations assistance, business practices that will provide a framework for dealing effectively with the unexpected. In many cases, it is difficult to get senior management to focus on crisis planning. (Read Barriers to Crisis Planning on page 300.)

Typically, the public relations practitioner says to the employer or client:

"You should have a crisis communication plan."

Typically, the employer or client responds:

"I can handle it when the time comes."

Is that familiar to you? How do we reconcile the two views?

One way is to approach the subject from the chief executive's perspective, rather than the communicator's perspective. Consider that crisis work has three dimensions. The public relations practitioner typically approaches the work emphasizing only one dimension–communication. The other two dimensions are crisis management and preparedness. It's far more meaningful to a CEO to talk about preparedness, first, then crisis management, and then crisis communication. It's a matter of looking at the big picture first, then the details. The first question to ask senior management: "Is your organization prepared for a crisis? If not, isn't it time to think about what your organization must do to establish and maintain an optimal state of preparedness?"

This approach of talking first about preparedness and then about communication would engage the interest of the head of an organization because it covers the full scope of crisis work, that is, being prepared to manage and communicate in a crisis. Let's follow through on this.

Once we have executive attention on the subject, we would need management to give preparedness the same priority as the organization's over arching operating strategies.

The goal, or desired ultimate condition, would be for [name of organization] to be at an optimal state of preparedness.

The objective, or what must be done to achieve the goal, would be to give management an organizational preparedness framework so that it could expeditiously recognize, contain, and/or resolve any occurrence that could adversely affect an organization's viability and thrust its management of the situation into public view.

The strategy, or how the objective is to be achieved, would be by making preparedness an integral operations strategy.

Few organizations have preparedness strategies that are integral with their operations. Most organizations do have operational strategies that describe how they are

Situation Team: essential part of a preparedness strategy.

THE RULE OF ADVANCED ENGAGEMENT is that individuals who must work together in a crisis situation must agree in advance to operate on mutually acceptable principles embodied in a Crisis Code of Conduct.

going to accomplish their respective missions. These strategies center on various factors, such as productivity, sales, service, and financial performance. They give consistent direction to day-to-day operations. When a problem develops in any of these areas it is resolved through the normal operating strategies.

However, when a difficult situation develops that could thrust the organization's management of the situation into the public spotlight, most often the problem is placed in isolation. Then a few senior people spend time debating over what to say and whether it's more important to perform for a court of law or for the court of public opinion. Things would go a lot smoother if organizational framework were in place to handle situations of crisis potential–if a preparedness strategy were in place with activities to implement it. Such a framework could be developed with certain activities.

One activity would be to establish a Situation Team. I prefer the designation Situation Team because it would be best for individuals to say, "We have a situation," and to let the Situation Team assess an issue's crisis potential. There's enough workplace stress today without having people prejudge issues and shout "We have a crisis! Activate the Crisis Management Team!" Selection of team members would be at the discretion of the chief executive. It should be a small operating group that represents areas of particular relevance to preparedness. To convene the group, the chief executive would say, "We have a situation." That command, spoken by the CEO or any member of the executive staff, would signal team members to drop everything and assemble to assess a special situation. Note that the command, "We have a situation," calls for an immediate assessment; it does not prejudge the nature of a situation and label it a crisis as would be the case if the command were, "We have a crisis!" One important principle that the team must respect is that it is functioning not in isolation but on behalf of and with the support of the entire organization. The team must encourage two-way communication so that others in the organization with crisis management or communication responsibilities can offer as well as receive information.

The next activity for implementing the strategy would be requiring that individuals who know they must work together in a crisis situation agree in advance to operate on a mutually acceptable set of principles embodied in a Crisis Code of Conduct. Individuals with crisis work responsibilities would be required to review with each other principles that relate to their working relationship and hammer out agreement on those that might be contentious in a crisis situation. This collaboration I refer to as The Rule of Advanced Engagement.

Another activity for implementing a preparedness strategy would be for the Situation Team to assess situations with integrity, considering all perspectives—organizational, individual, social and environmental. The aim would be to align the team's thinking on the matter with the thinking of each of its constituencies or stakeholder groups. The strength of an organization's integrity is determined by the strength of its relationships and the values it shares with those affected by its conduct. When an organization openly assesses a situation in the context of relationships, its judgment is most likely to earn the trust of its stakeholders, as well as their respect for the organization's embrace of a holistic view toward accountability. The organization, in other words, is viewed as doing what is socially responsible.

The next activity would be for the Situation Team, in formulating recommendations to the chief executive, to make decisions on courses of actions that are aligned with the organization's core values. Decisions are easier to make when they are guided by core values.

The sample list of core values taken from dozens of organizations, shown on page 306, reveals that most core values relate to "bottom line" returns, rather than to the safety and health of people and the quality of their environment. The key here is to ensure that an organization has core values that relate specifically to preparedness.

When an organization knows clearly what it stands for, it can rely on those values to guide and shape its decisions in a crisis situation. Values must be clear, simple and easy to understand. Values not only facilitate decision-making, but align people in addressing a crisis situation with energy and dedication. When people are focused with purpose on a difficult situation, they will work tirelessly toward an appropriate resolution. Critical decisions backed by core values are respected by all stakeholders as a display of an organization's true strength. Core values for preparedness should become part of an organization's culture from which communication should flow naturally, especially in a crisis.

There is a natural attraction for others to want to work with and be identified with an organization that takes pride in the strength of its preparedness for the unexpected, especially in today's world of uncertainties, insecurities and faltering leadership.

Another activity for implementing a preparedness strategy is for the Situation Team to communicate its course of action, once it has been approved by the chief executive. Consider the enormous spectrum of communication needs in a crisis–between board members and the chief executive, between the chief executive and investors and the public and the media, between management and employees, between sales and customers, between management and volunteers, between purchasing and major suppliers, between executive management and operating units, between employees and their communities, between technicians and government regulators, between operating units and local opinion leaders.

This is a typical breakdown area for many crisis communication situations because of debates over what should or shouldn't be communicated, to whom, in what manner and when. With a preparedness strategy this shouldn't be a problem because The Rule of Advanced Engagement requires members of the Situation Team to agree in advance on a set of principles for communicating in a crisis.

The preparedness strategy would not be complete without activities to keep the strategy alive and energized. One way to do that is with a scheduled recurring activity. For example, the Situation Team might conduct an Annual Preparedness Forum. A recurring event would cycle the strategy to keep it current and top of mind. The forum might last for a month as a function added to existing activities, such as employee safety meetings and other established activities. The month might be September, which is National Preparedness Month. Every support and operating unit of an organization would be accountable for brainstorming potential crisis situations, discussing ways to reduce their potential for occurring, and categorizing which ones should be handled locally, such as a fatal accident, and which ones should be handled by senior management, such as a product recall. Activities would be given high visibility for a month, but vigilance would be required always.

This participatory approach of including everyone in implementing the strategy would make employees aware of the strategy, the organization's readiness for its use, and most of all, would signal the entire organization that preparedness for a crisis situation has the same high priority as the organization's over arching operational strategies. The forum would serve as an educational experience in crisis management and an exercise in building the strength of an organization's culture.

From the forum could be derived the top five or six crisis situations that could develop for a particular organization. Every functional area of an organization–finance, planning, sales, marketing, human resources, production–would then decide how its respective unit could contribute to reducing the risk and supporting the organization in carrying out its preparedness strategy should a crisis occur. The strategy would include the development of specific competencies required to reach a state of optimal preparedness.

To be supportive of an organization during a crisis situation, every member of every unit must know and understand the organization's preparedness strategy. If support and operations units do not participate in the preparedness strategy, the most that can be expected during a crisis is for them to carry forth with their day-to-day routines and simply be spectators. Support and operations units could be an invaluable resource to the Situation Team by anticipating questions from stakeholder groups to functioning as communication channels directly to stakeholders with approved information.

Many organizations convince themselves that in a crisis it is best to lock down communication for the entire organization, turn all stakeholders into spectators and have a handful of executives make all of the assessments, decisions and messaging. Truthfully, is any chief executive capable in every situation to know the information needs of all of an organization's stakeholder groups—board, investors, financial community, employees, customers, suppliers, media, community? A preparedness strategy could marshal for the chief executive assistance from throughout an entire organization to provide multiple levels of invaluable intelligence, resources and skills.

When members of an organization can say, "We're prepared," and mean it, the organization gets an infusion of synergistic strength to manage and communicate with a natural confidence. An organization's culture is strengthened when all employees can articulate a common theme, "We're prepared," and when all of its stakeholders can articulate the same theme: "They're prepared." Turning to a common theme, based on integrity, core values and principles can strengthen the bonds of collaboration and welcome broader accountability and teamwork, thereby making full use of all of the organization's competencies in a challenging situation. A preparedness strategy is solid framework for collectively addressing an unexpected situation, a health, safety or environmental threat, a natural disaster, a criminal or civil investigation–any occurrence that could adversely affect an organization's viability.

To enable employees of an organization to understand and support preparedness, the strategy can be embodied in a Crisis Code of Conduct. The presentation in the following pages shows framework for a model code that could be customized for any public, private or nonprofit organization.

A crisis can occur any place at any time. It can happen with a public, private or not-for-profit organization. A crisis can be real or perceived, both subject to enormous positive or negative consequences because a crisis is not only a time of great danger, but a turning point usually with an opportunity to influence outcomes.

While trade journals abound with articles on crisis management and communication, it's the general public that has "written the book" on what is expected of organizations in a crisis and it is by the public's book that organizations are judged on how well or how poorly they manage crises. This book contains lessons learned in meeting the public's expectations for managing and communicating in crisis situations.

BARRIERS TO CRISIS PLANNING

To develop an effective proposal for a crisis plan or crisis communication plan, it is helpful to understand what many chief executives of organizations know and think about this type of planning.

- Many executives have great confidence in their own ability to manage a crisis situation and see little need to spend time and money on contingency planning.
- Crisis communication is an area in which many leaders have little training and therefore find it difficult to assess proposals for crisis communication plans with much self-confidence.
- While crisis communication professionals are available, some executive leaders with little background in the field feel uncomfortable putting their personal reputation and that of their entire organization in the hands of someone else.
- Crisis communication can mean to some executives taking problem solving away from organizational processes and isolating it in closed session planning.
- Because many leaders see communication as more of an art than a science and that some of their peers have failed publicly in its use, they are insecure in taking crisis planning initiatives.
- Crisis communication planning and training exercises can seem to executive leaders to be overly complex, excessively costly in time and money, and of questionable value in actual application.
- Crisis communication can seem to some leaders to be a shallow exercise in how to act in the public eye.
- Many leaders are uneducated in communicating risks to human health and safety and realize they can blunder into causing public outrage with a single statement, so they keep their distance from the subject, or don't realize they need to be educated in communicating risk.
- Crisis communication can seem incomplete to leaders—being just one of several ingredients essential to achieving a full state of preparedness.
- A leader's reticence toward crisis communication is most likely knowledge based rather than attitude centered.
- Some leaders have been embarrassed before their boards of directors for spending extraordinary sums on shelved crisis plans, manuals, checklists and drills or for retaining outside expertise that fails to justify exorbitant fees.

CREATE A CRISIS
CODE OF CONDUCT

Use this presentation template to develop a model Crisis Code of Conduct. The purpose of the code is to establish behavioral norms that become integral with an organization's culture. You will feel as though more than the specified number of principles should be included in each crisis area; however, the code is not a how-to instruction manual. It comprises key principles which, together, provide an organization with a certain way of thinking in a crisis situation. This exercise is best done in teams to allow debate and discussion in selecting what the team considers to be the most important principles to feature. Begin by inserting the name of an organization in the adjacent frame.

Continue by following the instructions adjacent to each frame.

See the insert after page 314 for how your Crisis Code of Conduct can be produced as a quick reference pocket card or display on mobile phones.

Enter the name of the organization for which you are developing the code.

Crisis Code of Conduct

The Crisis Code of Conduct provides not a checklist, but a behavioral framework to enable _____ to expeditiously recognize, contain, and/or resolve any occurrence that could adversely affect our viability and thrust our management of a situation into public view.

We believe it is the process used to achieve preparedness that creates the value of a crisis management or communication plan and that the plan is most effective under the direction of a code of conduct.

Our crisis code of conduct provides:

- A guide to behavior
- Broad application to diverse situations
- An intuitive way of thinking about what's right to do
- A mind-set that is easily assimilated into our culture
- Behavioral principles easily refreshed and sustained

Preparedness

Preparedness is a responsibility of every employee of _____.

Preparedness is an integral part of our organization's culture.

Our preparedness strategy has the priority of our principal operating strategies and is embodied in this Crisis Code of Conduct.

Integrity

We assess difficult situations with integrity.

We consider all perspectives—organizational, individual, social and environmental.

We align our thinking with the thinking of all of our stakeholder groups.

We embrace a holistic view toward accountability.

Core Values

Our core values clearly and simply express what we stand for and we rely on these values to guide our actions in a crisis situation.

When we align ourselves with our core values it gives us energy and a sense of dedication to do what's right in resolving a situation.

We know that critical decisions backed by core values are respected by all stakeholders as a display of an organization's true strength.

*From the list of core values on page 306, or from your own thoughts, insert two more of what you consider to be the most important crisis **core values** for an organization. You may replace the sample with your own selection.*

We know that when preparedness based on core values becomes an integral part of an organization's culture, that decision making is facilitated and communication in a crisis flows naturally.

One of our core values for preparedness is, **employees always have a right to know the truth in a timely manner.** [sample]

Another core value is, _____.

Another core value is, _____.

Rule of Advanced Engagement

Our preparedness strategy requires that we have a Situation Team. The team's job is to assess difficult situations and recommend courses of action to the chief executive.

It also requires members of the team, especially, to follow the Rule of Advanced Engagement—know who they must work with in a crisis situation and agree in advance to work together according to the principles contained in our Crisis Code of Conduct.

*From the list of crisis leadership principles on page 307, or from your own thoughts, insert two of the most important principles of crisis **leadership**. You may replace the sample entry with your own selection. Express the principle in a single phrase or sentence with no further explanation.*

Crisis Leadership Principles

Our leader will:
• put the safety and mental disposition of people first and equipment second [sample]

• _____
  _____

• _____
  _____

*From the list of crisis **management** principles on page 308, or from your own thoughts, insert of the most important principles of crisis management. You may replace the sample entry with your own selection. Express the principle in a single phrase or sentence with no further explanation.*

Crisis Management Principles

The Situation Team will:
• assess situations with integrity, aligning its thinking with the thinking of all stakeholder groups [sample]

• _____
  _____
  _____

• _____
  _____
  _____

*From the list of crisis **communication** principles on page 308, or from your own thoughts, insert two of the most important crisis communication principles. You may replace the sample with your own selection. Express the principle in a single phrase or sentence with no further explanation.*

Crisis Communication Principles

- We will meet all communication needs, internally and externally fast, accurately and honestly. [sample]

- _____
  _____
  _____

- _____
  _____
  _____

*From the list of crisis **media relations** principles on page 312, or from your own thoughts, insert two of the most important media relations principles. You may replace the sample with your own selection. Express the principle in a single phrase or sentence with no further explanation.*

Crisis Media Relations Principles

- We will treat reporters as partners. [sample]

- _____
  _____
  _____

- _____
  _____
  _____

*From the list of crisis **spokesperson** principles on page 310, or from your own thoughts, insert two of the most important spokesperson principles. You may replace the sample with your own selection. Express the principle in a single phrase or sentence with no further explanation.*

Crisis Spokesperson Principles

- We will be visible, accessible, and seek to provide answers to all questions. [sample]

- _____
  _____
  _____

- _____
  _____
  _____

We're Prepared!

A Strategy to Refresh & Sustain

We will keep our preparedness strategy alive and energized.

We will conduct a recurring event to cycle the strategy and keep it current and top of mind.

We will conduct an annual Preparedness Forum during September, National Preparedness Month.

Annual Preparedness Forum

The forum will show that preparedness has the same high priority as the organization's over arching operational strategies.

Members of every operations and support unit will participate.

Situations of crisis potential will be identified and their risk reduced.

Every functional area of our organization—finance, planning, sales, marketing, human resources, production—will determine how its respective unit will contribute to reducing risk and support the organization in carrying out its preparedness strategy.

List of Core Values

Following are examples of core values expressed by many different organizations. For preparedness to be an effective integral operations strategy it is important to have core values that relate not only to the "bottom line," but to the health and safety of people and their environment.

above-and-beyond
 efforts
accuracy
act with urgency
be a tough competitor
benefits
build trust
care about each other
challenge status quo
cleanliness
collaboration
communicate
 honestly
communicate openly
communicate with
 compassion
communication
complete job first
 time
coordination
courtesy
customer-driven
 quality
customer orientation
customer service
decisiveness
compassion for each
 other
respect for each other
development of
 people
discipline
display integrity
diversity

do what's right
effective use of space
efficiency training
embrace change
empowerment
encourage, reward
 risk taking
environment
ethics
fairness
great place to work
grow profitably
help people develop
honest
innovation
integrity
integration
involvement
job security
knowledge
learn from success,
 mistakes
listen to all ideas and
 views
maximum use of time
measurement
orderliness
pay program
physical skills
provide opportunity
 for growth
punctuality
pursue excellence
putting clients first

quality of product
quality of service
quality of work
recognition
reliability
respect
respect for others
results orientation
risk taking
safety
service to society
speed
support each other
sustained speed
systemic functioning
team recognition
teamwork
training
trust
walk in shoes of
 customers
widespread
spontaneous
 recognition
work for, care about
 team success
expect accuracy
act with urgency
communicate openly
 and honestly
encourage innovation
foster job security
learn from success,
 mistakes

personal growth	commit to safety	provide cutting-edge
professional growth	encourage teamwork	training
demand reliability		

CRISIS LEADERSHIP PRINCIPLES

1. We will tell it all and tell it fast. The public will judge our company, in part, by how quickly we respond to an emergency.

2. We will assess and address "situations" as quickly as they are suspected, known or anticipated.

3. We will base decisions on our core values.

4. We will own up to responsibilities. It is fool-hearty to think that anyone can get away with minimizing the seriousness of a situation, especially in today's world of electronic communication. Some lawyers are reticent about admitting guilt and accepting responsibility for a situation out of concern that it will be used against a company. However, refusing to own up to obvious responsibilities could adversely affect the attitude of a jury. One chief executive said, "My law department tells me that we are not responsible for this situation, but we're going to act as though we are."

5. We will show that "We get it." We will pay attention to how people feel. We will try to understand the stresses people are under and figure out how to help manage them. We will be sensitive to the point that nothing is normal in a crisis situation and that communicating in usual ways might not be adequate.

6. We will treat the media as partners. We will be accessible to the media and do what we can to help them do their work, including educating them on issues.

7. We will have a single spokesperson.

8. Our leadership will be visible and in charge immediately. We will show people that we are managing the situation—to reduce the threat or speed recovery. We know that if the community, its families, or individuals let their feelings of fear, anxiety, confusion and dread grow unchecked during a crisis, they will begin to feel hopeless or helpless. A reasonable amount of fear is OK. But instead of striving to "stop the panic" and eliminate fears, we will help people manage their fears and set them on a course of action, which will help them overcome feelings of hopelessness and helplessness.

9. We will be honest and open. We're not protecting people by holding back information or avoiding a bigger problem by keeping information away from people. Any information is empowering; uncertainty is more difficult to deal with than knowing

a bad thing, and people are prepared to go to multiple sources for information. The truth will always emerge, one way or another.

10. We will devote special attention to victims and their families.

11. We will always try to do what's right. We will make every effort to align our actions with social responsibilities and our core values.

12. We will welcome help.

13. We will not wait to communicate matters of risks. People have a right, by law, to know about risks to their health and safety. We know that failing to communicate risks generates rumors, exaggerated claims, high anxiety and an accelerated sense of urgency. Then news breaks, the story is told by others, a cover-up is suspected, public trust plummets, concern turns to resentment, anger and outrage. We know that risk must be communicated under all circumstances—when risk is immediate, under investigation, likely to be revealed, likely to be told by others, based on questionable data or fairly dependable data, is suspected but doesn't yet makes sense.

CRISIS MANAGEMENT PRINCIPLES

1. We will be prepared to manage crisis situations.

2. We will have relationships in place to deal with unexpected, known or anticipated situations.

3. We will have at the ready a Situation Team with defined responsibilities.

4. We will have tested contingency plans.

5. We will have easy access to multiple communication channels.

6. We will treat perceptions with the same importance as realities.

7. We will communicate openly with and listen to all stakeholder groups.

8. We will safeguard proprietary information, equipment and processes from public exposure.

9. We will confirm information and assess the gravity of the situation.

10. We will have an established means of refreshing our preparedness annually.

11. We will seek ways to create positive outcomes from adverse situations.

12. We will improve our preparedness from lessons learned from every crisis situation.

13. We will try to be the first source of information to employees and other stakeholder groups.

14. We will speak and listen to stakeholder groups.

CRISIS COMMUNICATION PRINCIPLES

1. We will inform the management staff of developments.

2. We will track and assess responses to our communication by media and stakeholder groups.

3. We will be thoughtful about what we say and how we say it. In our first message, we will express empathy, confirm facts and action steps, tell what we don't know and how we'll get the answers, commit

to managing the situation, and providing timely information. We are aware that every word, every eye twitch and every passing emotion resonates with heightened importance to people who are desperate for information to help them be safe and recover from a crisis.

4. We will tell it all and tell it fast.

5. We will tell what we know and don't know. What people want from leaders in a crisis is to know what the leaders know. People want and expect detailed information to allow them to come to their own conclusions. As difficult as it might be, a leader must help people reach the same conclusion the leader reached by sharing with them what was learned to reach that conclusion.

6. We will tell the good and bad news. We know that bad news does not get better over time. It is known from the experience of many others that the faster you give up bad news the better, because holding back implies guilt and arrogance. People can cope with bad news and the anticipation of bad things to come. For very good reasons, some information must be withheld. When that is the case, we can tell people we are withholding information and give the reasons why.

7. We will ensure that all credible sources share the same facts. When faced with a new threat, people want a consistent and simple recommendation. They want to hear absolute agreement about what they should do from multiple experts through multiple sources.

8. We will treat perceptions with the same importance we give to realities.

9. We will think about what the public expects. We need to live up to the public's expectations of our leadership.

10. We will stay on course. We will focus attention on the most important aspects of the problem and move the entire process forward to resolution, even in a contentious environment.

11. We will care for all stakeholder groups. It is important to address the needs of all groups of persons affected– victims and their families, indirect victims, all employees and their families, community residents and others.

12. We will keep employees informed. We should make every effort to ensure that employees get news of a situation from the company first.

13. We will assess queries for news value. We will grant interviews to state, clarify or simplify our position. We will not respond to or grant interviews about rumors, speculation, reactions from unidentified sources.

14. We will be accurate with the facts. In the first message in a crisis, people will be listening for factual information, and some will be expecting to hear a recommendation for action. We will repeat the facts consistently and avoid sketchy details from the start.

CRISIS SPOKESPERSON PRINCIPLES

1. We will be prepared to deliver key messages. Our messages will be 10 to 12 second sound bites and will be repeated frequently. Messages, for example, might emphasize dedication to do what's right, or to care for victims, or praise emergency service personnel.

2. We will issue statements. They will provide this information: what happened; where; when; number of persons injured; where victims were taken for treatment; what equipment or property was damaged; positives to be acknowledged. They will not provide: dollar estimates of damage; time estimates for resuming operation; possible causes of the accident or incident; original cost estimates of equipment involved; names of injured or their condition; estimates of insurance coverage or other settlements. The statement will be properly cleared by internal authorities, will reassure that appropriate authorities are taking control, that the company is stepping up to its responsibilities, that top management is apprised and providing support; that praise is due to police, fire and rescue for prompt service.

3. We will treat everyone with respect. We know that when we treat people as intelligent adults they will act like intelligent adults. If treated any other way, they will either turn on you or behave in ways that seem illogical to you. When we engage people in the process it is reasonable to expect that they will follow.

4. We will acknowledge the fear. The worst thing we can do is tell a frightened person they have no reason to be frightened. We will not utter the words, "There's no reason to be afraid." We will make no statement about wanting it to go away. We will tell what we know that makes people less afraid. Example: "I understand that anything related to radiation can seem frightening. Let me tell you what I know …"

5. We will be compassionate. When we show compassion, even people who are frightened will feel less like victims and will be inclined to become helpers.

6. We will give people what they expect of a spokesperson in a crisis. We will be on the scene fast, in touch, providing details, taking charge, explaining action steps with positive endorsements by objective, third-party authorities.

7. We will address the public in the manner of a statesman—maintaining a sense of integrity and an impartial concern for the public good.

8. We will tell people what we know. People want and expect detailed information to allow them to come to their own conclusions.

9. We will be accurate with facts and precise in our use of words. A spokesperson can have a real, measurable affect on the well being of people through words used, speed of delivery, and tone in which they are spoken. We know that every word, every eye twitch and every passing

emotion resonates with heightened importance to people who are desperate for information to help them be safe and recover from the crisis. In making a statement before television cameras, our spokesperson will look into the lens of the camera, see friends and neighbors, and talk to them.

10. We will try to answer every question. It's important to show concern for every question asked.

11. We will prepare for interviews. When the broadcast media calls, we will be politely persistent in finding out what the interview will be about. The caller may be in a hurry, but this is the one time to get valuable information so we can decide whether or not to have the interview and, if so, prepare and rehearse. We will think about possible questions, including ones we don't want to be asked.

12. We will use key messages to help stay in control of interviews.

13. We will have interviews monitored. We have another representative of the company monitor an interview, or record it, or video record it to help ensure that the context is always clear, understood and accurate.

14. We will be alert to being "on record." We know that as soon as we are in the presence or within microphone distance of reporters before, during and after an interview, news briefing or conference, that equipment is running and we are "on record" with everything seen and heard. We

never go "off the record," without exception.

15. We will tell the truth, never lie.

16. We will talk to be understood. We will always be honest and forthright, answer questions in short, simple sentences, avoid the use of jargon and volunteering long-winded explanations.

17. We will remain skilled in the use of communication techniques. For example, if we don't like the way a question was asked, we will rephrase it before giving an answer. A reporter might ask: "How many other near-death mishaps have you had at this plant?" This can be restated in a positive way: "Are you asking what our safety record has been? If we do not want a reporter to dwell on a certain subject, we can bridge to something else. A reporter might ask: "What if the price goes down even lower?" A reply could be: "That is only speculation—let's focus on current inventories." We will refute anything with which we disagree. A reporter might say: "You have to admit that negligence could have been a factor in her death." A strong reply would be: "No. A full investigation should reveal the truth of what happened." If a reporter tries to draw us into a challenging situation, we can anchor our position. A reporter might say: "The Department of Ecology said your plant poses numerous health hazards." A response could be: "I have not heard those comments, and we don't respond to rumors."

Know What Reporters Want

- A front seat to all action and information–now!
- An exclusive
- Equal access to information
- Honest answers to their questions
- Timely release of information
- Backgrounders, fact sheets, bios, visuals
- Rumors quashed quickly
- Schedule for updates
- Interviews with subject matter experts
- Calls to be returned

18. We will always comment. If we cannot comment, we will avoid saying, "No comment." For example, a reporter could ask: "What are the current terms being negotiated?" Possible response: We will announce the terms when the agreement is ratified. Other ways to avoid the phrase "no comment" are: We're following an investigative process and will provide details at the appropriate time. There is proprietary information involved that we cannot divulge. There are legal issues involved. We've just learned of the situation and are getting information now. I'm not an authority on the subject; I will put you in touch with a source. We're preparing a statement and will have a copy for you. We don't respond to comments from "unidentified sources" We don't respond to rumors.

CRISIS MEDIA RELATIONS PRINCIPLES

1. We will log media calls. Reporters will be assured that their calls will be returned promptly and that there will be frequent updates as information becomes available.

2. We will return calls promptly. We will let reporters know that their calls will be returned promptly, and when, where and how information will be made available.

3. We will be clear with the media. We will issue a media alert to call a press conference or press briefing. We will be accurate with the media in all respects. If we have breaking news or a major announcement we will call a press conference. If we have updates and progress reports, we will call news briefings. It is not wise to set up expectations for a major announcement when we have only a progress report.

4. We will post information on our Web site.

5. We will treat reporters as partners.

6. We will accommodate reporters. We will provide a news briefing room or area of adequate size, wireless Internet connection, phone, fax and multiple power outlets.

7. We will greet reporters upon their arrival. If they arrive on the scene before the PR manager, they will be told that a spokesperson will soon provide the facts. We will host their visit and do what we can to assist them with their work.

8. We will keep reporters informed. We will provide frequent, even regularly scheduled updates, and be present at scheduled briefing times even if only to repeat information. We will convey new information to reporters as soon as it becomes available and is properly cleared.

9. We will provide reporters will relevant background (paper or electronic). We will have prepared in advanced backgrounders, fact sheets, bios, and we will also issue statements on the current incident or situation.

10. We will educate reporters. When the initial work is done and reporters have even a little extra time, we will use the opportunity to go beyond event-specific information–educate with background information, provide content sources on relevant subjects, teach them what we would like them to know for future reports and articles.

11. We will keep media restricted to the briefing area. We will provide company escorts for them when they leave the area.

12. We will convey new information as soon as it becomes available.

13. We will allow pictures only in the media briefing area.

14. We will decide at the time about media tours. We will decide on a case-by-case basis whether or not to let reporters, photographers and TV crews tour an incident or accident area.

15. When and if properly approved we will tour the incident or accident site. Reporters, photographers and authorized others will be escorted by company personnel and will be asked to respect the privacy of employees and not attempt interviews at the site.

16. We will monitor media reports and immediately correct erroneous information.

17. We will monitor new and social media. We will spike rumors and correct inaccurate information on the Internet.

18. We will answer all questions. Further, we will show concern for every question asked.

We Will Know the Needs of All Stakeholders in a Crisis

Stakeholders are people or organizations with a special connection to us and our involvement in an emergency. We will anticipate and assess an incident from the stakeholders' perspective. They will be most interested in how the incident will affect them. Stakeholders are expecting something from us. It could be as simple as information released through a Web site and e-mail message or as complex as in-person meetings with key organization officials. An emergency or crisis may be an opportunity to strengthen our partner and stakeholder relationships as they see us in action. A positive response will enhance our organization's credibility. We will not forget to consider existing stakeholder controversies or concerns and how the ongoing relationship will color attitudes during an incident.

CRISIS CODE OF CONDUCT

PREPAREDNESS

Preparedness is a responsibility of every employee of (organization). It is an integral part of our organization's culture. It has the priority of our principal operating strategies and is embodied in this Crisis Code of Conduct.

INTEGRITY

We assess difficult situations with integrity and align our thinking with that of all of our stakeholder groups

CORE VALUES

We rely on our core values to guide our actions in a crisis situation. When we align ourselves with our core values it gives us energy and a sense of dedication to do what's right in resolving a situation. We know that critical decisions backed by core values are respected by all stakeholders as a display of an organization's true strength.

Our core values are that we will be

1. transparent in our actions;
2. accountable; and
3. empathetic.

RULE OF ADVANCED ENGAGEMENT

Our preparedness strategy requires that we have a situation team. The team's job is to assess difficult situations and recommend courses of action to the chief executive. It also requires members of the team to follow the Rule of Advanced Engagement—know whom they must work with in a crisis situation and agree in advance to work together according to the principles contained in our Crisis Code of Conduct.

CRISIS LEADERSHIP PRINCIPLES

Our leader will

1. be visible and in charge immediately;
2. own up to responsibilities; and
3. lay out action steps.

CRISIS CODE OF CONDUCT

PREPAREDNESS

Preparedness is a responsibility of every employee of (organization). It is an integral part of our organization's culture. It has the priority of our principal operating strategies and is embodied in this Crisis Code of Conduct.

INTEGRITY

We assess difficult situations with integrity and align our thinking with that of all of our stakeholder groups

CORE VALUES

We rely on our core values to guide our actions in a crisis situation. When we align ourselves with our core values it gives us energy and a sense of dedication to do what's right in resolving a situation. We know that critical decisions backed by core values are respected by all stakeholders as a display of an organization's true strength.

Our core values are that we will be

1. transparent in our actions;
2. accountable; and
3. empathetic.

RULE OF ADVANCED ENGAGEMENT

Our preparedness strategy requires that we have a situation team. The team's job is to assess difficult situations and recommend courses of action to the chief executive. It also requires members of the team to follow the Rule of Advanced Engagement—know whom they must work with in a crisis situation and agree in advance to work together according to the principles contained in our Crisis Code of Conduct.

CRISIS LEADERSHIP PRINCIPLES

Our leader will

1. be visible and in charge immediately;
2. own up to responsibilities; and
3. lay out action steps.

CRISIS CODE OF CONDUCT

PREPAREDNESS

Preparedness is a responsibility of every employee of (organization). It is an integral part of our organization's culture. It has the priority of our principal operating strategies and is embodied in this Crisis Code of Conduct.

INTEGRITY

We assess difficult situations with integrity and align our thinking with that of all of our stakeholder groups

CORE VALUES

We rely on our core values to guide our actions in a crisis situation. When we align ourselves with our core values it gives us energy and a sense of dedication to do what's right in resolving a situation. We know that critical decisions backed by core values are respected by all stakeholders as a display of an organization's true strength.

Our core values are that we will be

1. transparent in our actions;
2. accountable; and
3. empathetic.

RULE OF ADVANCED ENGAGEMENT

Our preparedness strategy requires that we have a situation team. The team's job is to assess difficult situations and recommend courses of action to the chief executive. It also requires members of the team to follow the Rule of Advanced Engagement—know whom they must work with in a crisis situation and agree in advance to work together according to the principles contained in our Crisis Code of Conduct.

CRISIS LEADERSHIP PRINCIPLES

Our leader will

1. be visible and in charge immediately;
2. own up to responsibilities; and
3. lay out action steps.

CRISIS CODE OF CONDUCT

PREPAREDNESS

Preparedness is a responsibility of every employee of (organization). It is an integral part of our organization's culture. It has the priority of our principal operating strategies and is embodied in this Crisis Code of Conduct.

INTEGRITY

We assess difficult situations with integrity and align our thinking with that of all of our stakeholder groups

CORE VALUES

We rely on our core values to guide our actions in a crisis situation. When we align ourselves with our core values it gives us energy and a sense of dedication to do what's right in resolving a situation. We know that critical decisions backed by core values are respected by all stakeholders as a display of an organization's true strength.

Our core values are that we will be

1. transparent in our actions;
2. accountable; and
3. empathetic.

RULE OF ADVANCED ENGAGEMENT

Our preparedness strategy requires that we have a situation team. The team's job is to assess difficult situations and recommend courses of action to the chief executive. It also requires members of the team to follow the Rule of Advanced Engagement—know whom they must work with in a crisis situation and agree in advance to work together according to the principles contained in our Crisis Code of Conduct.

CRISIS LEADERSHIP PRINCIPLES

Our leader will

1. be visible and in charge immediately;
2. own up to responsibilities; and
3. lay out action steps.

CRISIS MANAGEMENT PRINCIPLES

Our Situation Team will

1. recommend actions based on the organization's core values and lessons learned by others in similar situations;
2. respect the public's right to know, especially in matters of risk to health and safety;
3. care for the information needs of all stakeholder groups, continuously promoting two-way communication.

CRISIS COMMUNICATION PRINCIPLES

1. We will tell it all and tell it fast.
2. We will tell the whole truth upfront.
3. We will be accurate with the facts.

CRISIS MEDIA RELATIONS PRINCIPLES

1. We will treat reporters as partners.
2. We will keep reporters informed.
3. We will correct inaccurate reports.

CRISIS SPOKESPERSON PRINCIPLES

1. We will treat everyone with respect.
2. We will be thoughtful and precise in our use of words.
3. We will listen as carefully as we speak and answer all questions to the best of our ability.

A STRATEGY TO REFRESH & SUSTAIN

We will keep our preparedness strategy alive and energized. We will conduct an Annual Preparedness Forum during September, National Preparedness Month, as a recurring event to cycle the strategy and keep it current and top of mind. The forum will show that preparedness has the same high priority as the organization's overarching operational strategies. Every functional area of our organization–finance, planning, sales, marketing, human resources, production–will determine how its respective unit will contribute to reducing risk and support the organization in carrying out its preparedness strategy.

CRISIS MANAGEMENT PRINCIPLES

Our Situation Team will

1. recommend actions based on the organization's core values and lessons learned by others in similar situations;
2. respect the public's right to know, especially in matters of risk to health and safety;
3. care for the information needs of all stakeholder groups, continuously promoting two-way communication.

CRISIS COMMUNICATION PRINCIPLES

1. We will tell it all and tell it fast.
2. We will tell the whole truth upfront.
3. We will be accurate with the facts.

CRISIS MEDIA RELATIONS PRINCIPLES

1. We will treat reporters as partners.
2. We will keep reporters informed.
3. We will correct inaccurate reports.

CRISIS SPOKESPERSON PRINCIPLES

1. We will treat everyone with respect.
2. We will be thoughtful and precise in our use of words.
3. We will listen as carefully as we speak and answer all questions to the best of our ability.

A STRATEGY TO REFRESH & SUSTAIN

We will keep our preparedness strategy alive and energized. We will conduct an Annual Preparedness Forum during September, National Preparedness Month, as a recurring event to cycle the strategy and keep it current and top of mind. The forum will show that preparedness has the same high priority as the organization's overarching operational strategies. Every functional area of our organization–finance, planning, sales, marketing, human resources, production–will determine how its respective unit will contribute to reducing risk and support the organization in carrying out its preparedness strategy.

CRISIS MANAGEMENT PRINCIPLES

Our Situation Team will

1. recommend actions based on the organization's core values and lessons learned by others in similar situations;
2. respect the public's right to know, especially in matters of risk to health and safety;
3. care for the information needs of all stakeholder groups, continuously promoting two-way communication.

CRISIS COMMUNICATION PRINCIPLES

1. We will tell it all and tell it fast.
2. We will tell the whole truth upfront.
3. We will be accurate with the facts.

CRISIS MEDIA RELATIONS PRINCIPLES

1. We will treat reporters as partners.
2. We will keep reporters informed.
3. We will correct inaccurate reports.

CRISIS SPOKESPERSON PRINCIPLES

1. We will treat everyone with respect.
2. We will be thoughtful and precise in our use of words.
3. We will listen as carefully as we speak and answer all questions to the best of our ability.

A STRATEGY TO REFRESH & SUSTAIN

We will keep our preparedness strategy alive and energized. We will conduct an Annual Preparedness Forum during September, National Preparedness Month, as a recurring event to cycle the strategy and keep it current and top of mind. The forum will show that preparedness has the same high priority as the organization's overarching operational strategies. Every functional area of our organization–finance, planning, sales, marketing, human resources, production–will determine how its respective unit will contribute to reducing risk and support the organization in carrying out its preparedness strategy.

CRISIS MANAGEMENT PRINCIPLES

Our Situation Team will

1. recommend actions based on the organization's core values and lessons learned by others in similar situations;
2. respect the public's right to know, especially in matters of risk to health and safety;
3. care for the information needs of all stakeholder groups, continuously promoting two-way communication.

CRISIS COMMUNICATION PRINCIPLES

1. We will tell it all and tell it fast.
2. We will tell the whole truth upfront.
3. We will be accurate with the facts.

CRISIS MEDIA RELATIONS PRINCIPLES

1. We will treat reporters as partners.
2. We will keep reporters informed.
3. We will correct inaccurate reports.

CRISIS SPOKESPERSON PRINCIPLES

1. We will treat everyone with respect.
2. We will be thoughtful and precise in our use of words.
3. We will listen as carefully as we speak and answer all questions to the best of our ability.

A STRATEGY TO REFRESH & SUSTAIN

We will keep our preparedness strategy alive and energized. We will conduct an Annual Preparedness Forum during September, National Preparedness Month, as a recurring event to cycle the strategy and keep it current and top of mind. The forum will show that preparedness has the same high priority as the organization's overarching operational strategies. Every functional area of our organization–finance, planning, sales, marketing, human resources, production–will determine how its respective unit will contribute to reducing risk and support the organization in carrying out its preparedness strategy.

Case
Fourteen
Government
Relations

GIVE AND TAKE AWAY

Citizens elected to positions in state government—from state representative to governor—have a responsibility for the state's economic health. States compete among each other to attract investments, such as the building of a plant or headquarters relocation that will strengthen a state's economy by providing revenues in terms of wages, taxes and local purchases. State competition includes providing incentives, such as tax credits, infrastructure improvements and additions, land packages, expedited permit processing, worker training programs, etc. Companies base their site selections, in part, on these state government incentives.

In this case, some members of a state's legislature are proposing to rescind an incentive once given to companies that selected the state for their operations. The chief executive officer (CEO) of the company you serve is not about to stand idly by and give up the incentive that was promised to his company.

Team and individual assignments are on the next page followed by background details of the case. As you will see, the CEO of ChannelGate Electronics needs to be seen as a strong leader so you will want to read about how professional writers can help executives create a commanding presence in the article on page 318 titled, "Does every CEO have a ghostwriter?" It would be useful also to search the Internet for information on how a bill becomes a law in state government.

Team Assignment

Your team comprises the public relations department of ChannelGate Electronics, Inc. located in Overton, Anystate. Norman Gate, ChannelGate CEO, has instructed your department to see that the state legislature does not approve H.B. 3540, a proposed measure that would rescind tax credits that were granted to electronics companies as an incentive for locating their operations in the state. Gate wants to see a public relations plan that develops for his company enough political clout to eliminate H.B. 3540 from further consideration by legislators. He wants his company to be operating with the benefit of tax credits indefinitely. Your plan must be developed right away and must include provisions for orchestrating support–individuals and organization heads who will testify in favor of maintaining the tax credits during a public hearing on H.B. 3540 scheduled one work week from today at 3 p.m. in the state capital.

Individual Team Member Assignments

Each team member is to complete a different one of the following items that might or might not be included in the design of your plan.

1. Write a one-page letter from your CEO to the head of the Association of Anystate Businesses presenting your case and urging the organization to take a position against H.B. 3540.

2. Write an e-mail message from your CEO to be sent individually to every member of the Anystate House of Representatives urging them to oppose H.B. 3540.

3. Write a one-page memo (legislative alert) from your CEO to ChannelGate employees presenting your case and urging them to write to their elected representatives in the House and asking them not to consider H.B. 3540.

4. Write a one-page information sheet to be used electronically as a .pdf file in assembling a coalition to defeat the proposed measure. It should give information about H.B.3540, identify its sponsors, provide reasons for opposing H.B. 3540 and instructions for contacting members of the House. This should be a persuasive document in the form of an issue bulletin.

5. Write text for a pocket point card with facts about H.B. 3540, reasons why it should not be considered by the legislature, instructions for contacting members of the house, plus your organization's contact information.

6. Write a one-page letter from your CEO personally addressed to individuals and organizations that supported incentives, originally, such as a tax credit, to recruit your company to locate in the state. The letter should express appreciation

for their support in recruiting your firm, describe the current situation with the proposed H.B. 3540, and ask them to contact the CEO to confirm that they will testify in support of retaining tax credits at a public hearing scheduled for (make up the date) at the state capital.

7. Write 90 seconds of opening testimony against H.B. 3540 to be given by Norman Gate before members of the House Revenue Committee chaired by Representative Oscar Harrison.

Background

Six elected representatives of the state legislature are sponsoring a measure that would amend legislation passed in 1995 that gave ChannelGate in Overton, Anystate, and six major electronics firms in Circuitville, tax credits for an understood indefinite period as an incentive for locating their operations in the state. The incentive amounts to a 50 percent credit on each firm's state business and occupation tax. The six state representatives are working aggressively to eliminate the tax credit granted to the electronics firms in 1995 because of the state's dire financial position.

The managements of ChannelGate and the other six affected electronics firms were surprised and upset about the initiative to eliminate what once was promised as an incentive for the firms to locate in Anystate. The annual contribution of the seven electronics firms to the state's economy in terms of wages, taxes and local purchases, totaling $552 million far exceeds

the tax credit totaling $24 million. The firms question how reneging on the incentive would look to other firms considering Anystate as a place to locate a business. The CEO of ChannelGate, Norman Gate, insists that his PR department block any measure to take away the firm's tax credit. Your team is ChannelGate's PR department and has responsibility for government relations. Your department head is a registered lobbyist in Anystate.

You begin to assess the situation. First you consider home base. Your area of the state is represented by three elected officials—two members of the House of Representatives (Alfred Peabody and Charlie Bismark) and one member of the Senate (Holly Green). When your firm was considering Overton for its operation, Mayor Helen Fish and the entire city council welcomed ChannelGate with opened arms. Included in the grand welcome was the Overton Chamber of Commerce headed by George Harman, the Overton Economic Development Council headed by Sandra Dollars, as well as the town's many service clubs, particularly the Rotary Club of Overton led by 86-year-old Charlie Dobetter. As you assess the situation you are thinking about developing as much political clout as possible by bringing these key contacts and possible coalitions together on the issue to rally to your cause.

Looking beyond home base you consider that ChannelGate is a member of the Association of Anystate Businesses, a statewide organization of businesses headed by Randy King. And your CEO, Norman Gate, is a member of the influential Anystate Business Roundtable in Appleton led by Executive Director Butch Bartolli. Your state representative, Alfred Peabody is a member of the Revenue Committee of the House of Representatives. The governor of Anystate is Elsie Greenbach.

The elected officials sponsoring the measure to eliminate the B&O tax credit are Bruce Fisher and Allen Giverback of Plum Valley; Molly Wantsmore and Jim Glover of Artichoke Hill; and Byron Bick and Karen Greedy of Crabapple. Your CEO is so upset about the situation he wants you to send individualized e-mails to every member of the House.

The measure to eliminate tax credits, H.B. 3540, is expected to be sent to the floor for a vote of the House of Representatives sometime within the next three weeks. A public hearing on the proposed measure is scheduled one work week from today at 3 p.m. in the state capital.

As a seasoned lobbyist and head of your public relations department you know that it is best always to take the high road–to work as a statesman, to argue positions on the basis of their merits. You know to attack the issue and never its supporters because opponents today might be needed as allies to tomorrow. It is not unusual for a lobbyist to argue an issue intensely with an opponent in a public hearing and relax afterwards with the same opponent over wine and dinner. You proudly regard maintaining respectful relationships as a mark of good statesmanship.

ARTICLE: DOES EVERY CHIEF EXECUTIVE OFFICER HAVE A GHOSTWRITER?

We probably will never have a definitive answer to the question: Does every chief executive officer have a ghostwriter? CEOs who have good writers are not inclined to talk about it. However, many CEOs do have talented, highly-skilled ghostwriters. And for reasons that will become obvious, having such writers is an invaluable capability.

A highly-skilled ghostwriter can give a CEO a commanding presence in any situation.

In any situation? A commanding presence? How do ghostwriters do that? How do they know what to write? How do CEOs find talented ghostwriters?

I can help you discover answers to these questions because I was a ghostwriter for corporate executives of Fortune 500 companies for more than 30 years.

In what kinds of situations do ghostwriters give CEOs a commanding presence?

Highly-skilled ghostwriters give CEOs a commanding presence before members of the board, industry analysts, shareholders, customers, employees, journalists, government officials, potential investors and many other important audiences.

How are ghostwriters able to give CEOs a commanding presence in such diverse situations?

Highly-skilled ghostwriters are able in what they write to give CEOs a commanding presence in virtually any situation because they:

- have experience in working with CEOs and have learned to think like CEOs;
- are able to assimilate the mind-set of CEOs and can write in ways that reflect their character, values, beliefs and goals;
- are adept researchers, able to gather even the most complex and technical information, organize it and translate it into plain English;
- keep abreast of management trends and jargon and incorporate current management thinking into their writing to help keep CEOs on the cutting edge;
- provide CEOs with ideas and concepts that help shape policy, crystallize visions, solidify goals and articulate positions;
- stay connected with and analyze the attitudes and beliefs of important CEO audiences and in their writing enable CEOs to effectively influence the attitudes and beliefs of these audiences.

How do ghostwriters know what to write?
Ghostwriters usually get their direction directly from the CEOs.

Talented ghostwriters require surprisingly little direction from CEOs, provided that the CEOs give their writers ample opportunity to get to know and understand who they are, what they stand for and where they are heading.

Once a working relationship is established with a ghostwriter, a CEO is able to make assignments in terse form and expect, with little or no further discussion, first class results in an appropriate form, which might be a keynote speech, formal letter, informal remarks, testimony, presentation narrative or script, position paper, by-lined article or just a list of talking points.

With a good ghostwriter, all that a CEO needs to say is, I would like …

- to make these three points before this audience in a 20-minute presentation;
- a by-lined article on this subject for this magazine;
- a position paper on this issue to submit to this Congressional committee;
- talking points in preparation for my interview with this reporter;
- a draft of my letter to shareholders for the annual report;

- a technical paper and scripted presentation with visuals to give before this trade conference;
- a response to this shareholder's letter;
- a proposal on this for the board;
- informal remarks for the upcoming employee awards dinner;
- a persuasive argument in opposition to this issue for my meeting with the head of this government agency.

How do CEOs find talented ghostwriters?

Shopping for a ghostwriter is not something done easily by an executive recruiter or by a human resources director. Ghostwriters can come from various disciplines, such as public relations, marketing, law, human resources, finance.

However, first and foremost, ghostwriters are highly skilled editors, writers and researchers. They are good listeners and interviewers. They have strong intuitive qualities. They have a sense of what leadership is all about. They respect and appreciate the value of corporate reviews and clearance procedures. And, above all else, they have good chemistry and unshakable trust with CEOs.

Many CEOs do have ghostwriters. Many CEOs have more than one. For busy executives, good ghostwriters are an invaluable resource, an indispensable capability.

Highly-skilled, experienced ghostwriters can give CEOs a commanding presence in any situation.

Case Fifteen
Crisis
Recovery

METHA-DON'T

It would be nice to be called before something becomes a major problem; too often, it doesn't happen that way, as in the case of Metha-DON'T. The complete slogan, "Metha-DON'T put a methadone clinic in this community" was borrowed by protestors from another town that tried unsuccessfully to block the placement of a clinic in its community. Your public relations agency has been hired by Pivotal Directions, Inc., an expanding methadone clinic operator, to do what should have been done in the beginning to win acceptance for establishing a methadone treatment clinic in a community. The mishandling of this situation takes this organization back to square one—requiring that it follow federal guidelines and conduct a community relations and education effort before moving in and opening its doors. Conducting such a program would be a challenge, but recovering from public outrage, misinformation, crippling rumors, and conducting a successful outreach program will be a monumental challenge for your agency and your new client, PDI.

Your agency team is scheduled to meet with the executive management of PDI for an in-depth discussion of PDI's expectations of your services, especially about how progress will be tracked and results will be evaluated. The meeting will be held at PDI tomorrow afternoon, so your team will be working late to prepare for the discussion. Prepare? Oh, yes. If you want this business for your firm, you need to show the client that you have a knowledgeable interest in its goal.

Team Assignment

The goal is for Pivotal Directions to be operating a methadone treatment clinic in Lighthouse Bay with community acceptance. Your PR agency's job is to develop with PDI a plan to recover from public rejection, educate residents on the importance of providing methadone treatment and, ultimately, winning acceptance for establishing a treatment facility in Lighthouse Bay to serve this area of the state. For case details, read the memo from the new clinic director, Harold Clifton, to his boss, Ted Blake, who asked for a status report on the situation in Lighthouse Bay. Also conduct the role play of a public information meeting during which outraged residents refused to listen to Clifton.

Individual Writing Assignments

Each member of your team is to select and complete a different one of the following writing assignments:

1. Prepare notes for your first client meeting with PDI. Research the Internet for brief answers to the following questions. What is a methadone clinic? What services does one

provide? Methadone is an addictive drug; is it safe? What is methadone maintenance treatment? What's the difference between methadone and meth? Who are the clinic's clients– addicts? Are they dangerous people? Why or why not? Do methadone clinics' clients attract drug dealers?

2. Read PDI's situation report in the memo from Harold Clifton to Ted Blake and write an assessment of how you see the situation as a public relations professional. Express yourself in no more than one page of type singled-spaced.

3. Search the Internet for recent blogs about methadone and methadone clinics. Make note of negative or critical comments and explain briefly how such comments might have a bearing on work for your new client, PDI (a fictitious name).

4. Read the resource information about risk communication on pages 323–326, review in the role play what Harold Clifton said to an angry crowd at the public information meeting, then write comments (about 150 words) he could have made, initially, to ease emotions and settle things down.

5. Assume that your team decided to create a Web site for the Pivotal Directions clinic to be established in Lighthouse Bay. Make a list of critical information needs revealed in the case and what you would show on the home page to instantly direct visitors to what they want and need to know.

6. In this case, the writer of an editorial in the local newspaper referred to the Pivotal Directions clinic as a "meth" clinic. Compose an e-mail to the writer showing how you would correct the error in a manner than would be accepted by the writer as constructive, not critical.

7. As a member of your PR team, you have volunteered to write part of your proposed PR plan that explains how you would search the social media to identify community leaders in the Lighthouse Bay area. Write a paragraph, as an "activity" entry for your plan, that identifies electronic devices you would use, what you would be searching for with each device, and keywords you would be using.

MEMO

January 18, 20xx

TO: Ted Blake
FROM: Harold Clifton
RE: **Lighthouse Bay Situation Report**

Ted, you asked for a report on the situation here at Lighthouse Bay to use for possibly orienting a PR firm on our unsuccessful attempts to win public acceptance for siting one of our methadone treatment clinics in this community. I have tried in this report to provide an objective view of what has transpired over the past months. There's no question but that we need professional help.

People learned about the clinic from a article in the Lighthouse Community Beacon that said that the county had approved its location on Sea Drive near the high school. Citizen concerns about the clinic caused one of the county commissioners to ask state officials to hold a community forum about the facility before it opens its doors. The state Division of Alcohol and Substance Abuse announced that it would hold a public information meeting on the clinic, Feb. 1, and a public hearing, Feb. 22.

I was completely surprised at the information meeting. People acted outraged and demanded that we put the clinic in some other town. Every time I tried to talk about methadone and methadone treatment, the audience interrupted and shouted all sorts of accusations. They were angry about putting the clinic near the local high school. As you know, we met with a resident while we were looking for a site for the clinic. We said, at the time, that we would be willing to meet with residents. By not doing enough to ask for their input during the planning stage for the clinic, we apparently have made them feel as though we do not value their opinions. They seem madder about being excluded than about having the clinic, which they know nothing about. The only thing that some know is that methadone is a drug for treating heroin addiction.

Believe me, I tried to explain. They don't know what goes on inside a clinic and they are afraid that drug dealers are going to hang around trying to sell to people trying to fight an addiction. You know, I tried to tell them nicely that the decision to put the clinic in Lighthouse Bay was already made and that they can't do anything about it. Here's a link to an audio file of the meeting. [Assume that the role play on page 327 is the audio file.]

An editorial in the Beacon argued that the fears of residents were unfounded and that helping addicts recover can bring benefits to the community. Unfortunately, the writer referred to the methadone clinic as a "meth" clinic. As you know, Ted, a lot of people believe that methadone is related to methamphetamine, so the editorial just reenforced the belief.

Several community leaders took their concerns to county government and said the community was committed to keep the clinic from opening on Feb. 15. Feeling the pressure, the county asked state government officials not to move ahead with the clinic until PDI provided a community outreach plan. They got attention. State officials put the clinic on hold. I thought that would calm things down, but I found out that residents were planning to demonstrate on the day of the clinic's open house.

You saw the letter we got from the county commissioners recommending that we "start over in our search for a viable location for the clinic."

In preparation for the public hearing scheduled by the state for Feb. 22, residents began posting fliers with the slogan Metha-DON'T, as well as writing e-mails to the local media. They also established an elaborate Web site. We haven't had anything about this on the PDI Web site.

The public hearing on Feb. 22 didn't go well. Instead of digging in our heals, I think we should have apologized for not doing more to keep the community informed and that we would like to involve the community in future decisions. Instead of arguing, we should have done more informing, educating people. I don't think anyone realizes that there are more than 1500 heroin addicts in this county.

The commissioners got another letter from residents, this time insisting that they delay any decisions regarding the certification of the clinic until PDI has demonstrated that it can effectively meet state and local standards for community relations. They said they would take their votes elsewhere if the commissioners failed to act on their behalf. The county then issued a cease and desist order to prevent PDI from moving into the clinic and offering treatment. This showed just how serious the county is about making sure that the community's fears are adequately addressed. The order stated that no PDI employee was allowed inside the clinic. Unfortunately, Ted, someone saw me inside preparing for the open house. That's when we canceled the open house to show the commissioners that we were willing to comply with the county's order. It was crystal clear that we were not going to open the clinic without first presenting a community relations plan that was acceptable to residents.

PDI then got a letter from School Superintendent John Pupil. He said that he wasn't concerned about the clinic's proposed proximity to the high school, but rather about traffic if the clinic had several hundred people coming for treatment everyday, before and after work. We hadn't met with the superintendent and decided to make a visit. It was clear that he was siding with the community. He asked about security. He wanted to know about PDI's experience at other sites. He said the school already has its hands full with families where one person works and the other is in prison or some type of rehabilitation program. He wanted to know how many patients will be drawn in from outside the town.

Shortly after our meeting with Superintendent Pupil, we caught wind of a rumor among local bloggers that the daughter of one of our newly hired employees, who is an active drug addict, was involved in a local drug-related crime spree. We're not sure how it started.

So here we are, weeks behind schedule, on the wrong side of the community, and under government pressure to produce a community outreach plan. We need desperately to get into the good graces of the community and to show county commissioners how we intend to comply with federal guidelines on community relations and education.

I looked up the federal guidelines. Here's what is required:

XVIII. Community Relations and Education

Discussion: Before a new program moves in and opens its doors, there is a strong need to educate all entities impacted by the program, including the medical community, neighbors, and those who will be asked to provide support services.

For existing and/or new programs, to help minimize negative impact on the community, promote peaceful coexistence, and plan for change and program growth, programs develop and implement a general set of practices, policies, and procedures that

1. consider community need and impact in siting programs.
2. elicit input from the community on the program's impact in the neighborhood.
3. ensure that the facility's physical appearance is clean and orderly and that the physical setting does not impede pedestrian or traffic flow.

4. identify community leaders for the purpose of fostering good community relations, and establish interpersonal contact, and proactive associations with those identified people. For example:
    a. publicly elected representatives;
    b. local health, substance abuse, social, human service agency directors;
    c. business organization leaders;
    d. community and health planning agency directors;
    e. grass roots community organization leaders;
    f. local police and law enforcement officials;
    g. religious and spiritual leaders.
5. develop and support a community relations plan specific to the configuration and needs of the program within its community that includes the following steps:
    a. establishing a liaison with community representatives to share information about the program and community and mutual issues;
    b. identifying program personnel who will function as community relations coordinators and define the goals and procedures of the community relations plan;
    c. serving as a community resources on substance abuse and related health and social issues, as well as promoting the benefit of methadone/LAAM therapy in preserving the public health;
    d. soliciting community input about methadone/LAAM therapy and the program's presence in the community;
    e. developing program policies and procedures to effectively address or resolve community problems (including patient loitering and medication diversion), and ensuring that program operations do not adversely affect community life.
6. document community relations efforts and community contacts, evaluate these efforts and contacts over time, and address outstanding problems or deficiencies.
7. devise communication mechanisms so that interested parties and potential patients may obtain general information about the program outside4 regular operating hours.
8. develop a plan in place for contingencies, emergencies, closure, transportation of staff during poor weather, etc.

ROLE PLAY

Presume this role play to be the audio file referred to in Harold Clifton's status report.

Cast

Narrator
Ron Alder, state Department of Alcohol and Substance Abuse (DASA)
Lauren Butterworth, Homes on the Bluff Association
Harold Clifton, PDI clinic manager
Deputy Sheriff
Helen Coats, DASA clinic certification manager
Irate Resident #1
Irate Resident #2
Irate Resident #3
Irate Resident #4
Irate Resident #5
Irate Resident #6
Irate Resident #7
Irate Resident #8
Un-named Resident
Un-named methadone client

From Parking Lot into Community Center

Harold Clifton, manager of the new Pivotal Directions, Inc. clinic, walks toward the community center and tries to be friendly with a town resident. He smiles and says hello; the resident frowns and turns away. In the center people look and sound agitated. They are talking in loud voices, picking up or ignoring PDI handouts from a table near the entrance. Ron Alder, state Division of Alcohol and Substance Abuse, calls the meeting to order.

Ron Alder, DASA

(taps microphone)
May I have … (pause) … May I … Please… Ladies and gentlemen…

All Irate Actors

(irate residents purposely ignore speaker, jabber loudly among themselves)

Ron Alder, DASA

(serious, assertive)
Hello. It's time … Ladies and gentlemen …

All Irate Actors

(boo the speaker)
Boo! Boo! Go back to where you came from!! (chant) Go back! Go back! Go back!

Ron Alder, DASA

(persists)
Please! (pause) Let's … Let's be respectful and get things under way.

(Crowd settles down)

Ron Alder, DASA

This meeting was called by the state Division of Alcohol and Substance Abuse. The purpose is to provide information about placing a methadone clinic in Lighthouse Bay.

Irate Resident #1

(Irate resident interrupts, shouting)
Who decided we needed a clinic?

Irate Resident #2

(shouting)
We don't-a-want no meth lab here!!

Irate Resident #3

(shouting)
Yea! (pause) I mean no! We don't!!!

Irate Resident #4

(Irate resident stands up and sternly instructs the speaker)
Just tell us what we have to do to keep the clinic out of here!

Ron Alder, DASA

Could we please just give our speakers a chance to talk? (long pause) … Thank you. … Thank you. The first person on the agenda is Harold Clifton. He's the new manager of the clinic.

(Harold steps up to the microphone)

Harold Clifton, PDI Clinic Manager

I have some prepared remarks that I would like to read. But first I'd like to ask you to think kindly about the people who really need this clinic … people who are fighting different addictions … people who …

Irate Resident #5

(shouting) Take your druggies and treat'em someplace else!! Go back home and take PDI with you!

Irate Resident #6

Where did this idea come from, anyway? Who decided we needed drug treatment?

Ron Alder, DASA

(steps back up to the microphone)
The Division of Alcohol and Substance Abuse held a hearing here a year ago. We took comments about the need for a methadone clinic.

Lauren Butterworth

I'm Lauren Butterworth. I'm here for the Homes On The Bluff Association. I never knew about a hearing held last year.

Ron Alder, DASA

Well, we didn't exactly have a hearing on a specific site in the Bay.

Lauren Butterworth

Well, you should have.

Irate Resident #7

(shouts out)
Darn right! Go Lauren!!!

Lauren Butterworth

The county, the state … you people did not do due diligence when you selected this location.

Irate Resident #8

(shouts)
Tell 'em Lauren!!

Ron Alder, DASA

At last year's meeting, that's when it was decided a clinic was needed.

Irate Resident #1

That's when who decided? … the secret Sneak-It-In-Here Club???

Ron Alder, DASA

There were 28 people at the hearing …

Irate Resident #2

(with great sarcasm)
Wow! Nearly the whole county!

Lauren Butterworth

Well the state, the county and PDI must have had a cozy little get together. No one around here knows about any such decision. You left the citizens out of the loop. And it looks like you did it deliberately!

All Irate Actors

(start chanting)
Metha-DON'T! Metha-DON'T! Metha-DON'T! Metha-DON'T!

Ron Alder, DASA

Please! Please! Let's try to be orderly. Please, we have a speaker with important information.

(Harold Clifton steps back to the microphone)

Harold Clifton, PDI Clinic Manager

The purpose of the clinic is …

Irate Resident #3

(interrupts)
We know your purpose Clifton. It's to make money off the druggies. Look for addicts somewhere else.

Harold Clifton, PDI Clinic Manager

(losing his patience; using a reprimanding voice)
Listen friends, the decision has been made. (pause) Like it or not, we're going to hold an open house and start treating people.

(The crowd jeers. Irate resident #4 stands, raising up a book as if winding up to throw it at the speaker. She faces off with a deputy sheriff.)

Deputy Sheriff

Hey, it's my job to throw the book at people.

Irate Resident #4

You think I'm a problem? Just wait 'til the felons start lining up. How big is your jail? (pause) You better start fluffin' pillows, big guy.

(Irate resident retreats to her seat)

Harold Clifton, PDI Clinic Manager

About 8 to 12 percent of our clients will be from this area.

Irate Resident #5

8 to 12!!! So 90 percent of these addicts are coming from outside our area! From where? Oystershells!!

Irate Resident #6

Put the clinic in Oystershells!!!

Irate Resident #7

Yea! Put it across the bay!!

Irate Resident #8

I'm really upset about this. I can't believe you want to put this clinic next to the high school! Drug dealers are going to be all over the place trying to sell to your addicts.

Irate Resident #1

This is terrible. What have they been smoking at DASA?

Helen Coats, state certification manager for medical clinics, steps up to the microphone. Harold Clifton is relieved to be out of the spotlight and walks over to a chair and sits down with an exhausted and somewhat exasperated expression.

Helen Coats, DASA

I hear your anger and your frustration and I'm not discounting that in the least. I have some prepared remarks and I'm going to set them aside. There are several requirements that aren't completed. Part of what we are concerned about is mitigating concerns that you have.

Irate Resident #2

With all due respect, we don't want to hear what they're going to do to make us like them. We just want to know what we have to do to make them leave.

Irate Resident #3

(Looks over at County Commissioner Jack Hokesman)
We can vote certain people out of office. Find another site for the meth lab, Jack!

Ron Alder, DASA

We're not talking about a meth lab. Methadone is a legal replacement for heroin.

Lauren Butterworth, Homes On The Bluff Association

So you're replacing an illegal drug with a legal drug. Is that some kind of cure, or do the legal druggies just have a new master?

Ron Alder, DASA

Methadone is legal when a licensed clinic controls it. When it's taken daily in a maintenance dose, it allows people addicted to heroin or prescription pain pills to manage their addiction and lead normal lives.

Harold Clifton, PDI Clinic Manager

(stands and comments)
We have 12 other methadone clinics. The one here will only serve insured patients and those who pay privately.

Irate Resident #4

That's nice. We would feel much better having only white collar felons.

Ron Alder, DASA

I have licensed every methadone clinic in the state. In the 20 years that I've been doing that we never received a single complaint from a citizen or a neighborhood.

Irate Resident #5

Ah. That explains why you don't bother to tell people where you're going to put them.

Irate Resident #6

If you've been doing this for 20 years, you shouldn't have any trouble putting this one someplace else!!

A methadone client in the back of the room tries to explain that people using methadone under a doctor's supervision can live normal lives.

Unnamed Methadone Client

Excuse me. I take methadone and I drive a cab. A lot of public transportation employees take methadone. We aren't unstable people. We can drive. We feel perfectly normal. And you're perfectly safe in my cab.

All Irate Actors

(begin chanting)
No addicts. No addicts. No addicts. No addicts. No addicts. No addicts.

Harold Clifton, PDI Clinic Manager

(stands, once again)
Some of our clinics are treating Iraq war veterans. They got addicted to pain pills when they were getting treated for war injuries.

Unnamed Resident

Please don't talk about veterans like they're drug addicts.

Irate Resident #7

Listen everybody. I've heard about all I need to hear. If you think this is outrage, you haven't seen anything.

Ron Alder, DASA

I want to thank …

(Crowd starts gathering belongings, talks in aggressive tones about stopping the clinic. Harold Clifton turns to Ron Alder. He's dumbstruck over how hostile people can be. Ron Alder, DASA, says quietly, "We should have had some formal public involvement. That's what they're angry about.")

Case Sixteen
Crisis
Communication

COMMUNITY ALARMED

Crisis is a time of great danger, a time of serious trouble. It's a decisive time, a crucial time. Most important, a crisis is a turning point because its outcome will determine its consequences. Answers to how an organization should handle a crisis can be found in a plethora of books. However, it is the court of public opinion with its own set of expectations as to how a crisis should be handled that is the ultimate judge of crisis management. It doesn't matter if the crisis is real or perceived, the situation must be managed as a crisis. In this case a reputable company is about to be thrust into the public spotlight for its use of hazardous chemicals. Case details are presented following the team and individual assignments in a series of news reports. The heads of organizations must be visible leaders, especially in times of crisis and you will want to understand this imperative by reading the article on page 339 titled "CEOs must be visible leaders."

Team Assignment

Your team has been hired as a public relations agency by Wafermaker, Inc., one of many silicon wafer manufacturers, to develop a public relations plan to address mounting concerns among community residents about health and safety risks associated with the company's use, storage and transportation of hazardous chemicals. Tensions are so high among residents that the company expects its association with hazardous chemicals to surface in the news media at any time in a way that could put the company on the defensive and possibly tarnish an otherwise sterling reputation as a corporate citizen. Begin by reading the case background.

Individual Team Member Assignments

Each team member is to complete a different one of the following items that might or might not be included in the design of the team plan.

1.   Your agency is asked by Wafermaker to draft a letter from Parks Elementary School Principal Henry File to parents inviting them to an informational meeting to be held at the school (you select a date). School officials and officials of Wafermaker, Inc. will be at the meeting to provide information and answer questions. You are to draft the letter for the principal's signature.

2.   In deliberations with your agency team, Wafermaker officials consider calling a news conference or briefing. In considering such an

event, Wafermaker officials discuss what they might say in opening remarks at a conference or briefing to set the tone and tenor for their response to what is sure to be an intense community demand for information. You are to write 90 seconds of opening remarks for George Sanders, Wafermaker vice president for manufacturing, for a news conference or briefing. (You decide if it is to be a news briefing or news conference and what Sanders should say to put the company in the best light before the media and the community.) In your remarks you will want to welcome reporters and thank them for coming, tell them why you called the meeting (briefly recap the fire incident, the mention of chemicals in news reports and resulting concern in the community, especially among parents of children attending nearby Parks Elementary School. The remarks are to lead up to a briefing by company representatives about its use, storage and transportation of chemicals. Set the tone of the conference by making known the company's desire to provide complete and accurate information, about the company's standing in the community and how it wants to uphold its reputation by being completely open and forthright in its communication with the public. Be careful not to try to persuade the media of anything; let the information presented in the meeting stand on its own merits to provide a convincing argument that living near Wafermaker is an acceptable risk. Your remarks should close with the line, "And now I would like to present the staff members who will provide you with a briefing.

3. In deliberations with your public relations agency team, Wafermaker officials discuss possible communication with customers. Assume that it is decided to contact customers. Draft a letter from George Sanders, Wafermaker vice president for manufacturing, to customers. Assume that Sanders told you to acknowledge the incident and assure customers that it would not have any bearing on the scheduled shipments of their orders or on the quality of the silicon wafers. The same letter is to be sent to every customer but will be addressed to individuals. In the letter you will want to acknowledge the fire so that customers learn about it firsthand from Wafermaker, but you will not want to provide details that will unnecessarily cause concern among customers.

4. In deliberations with your public relations agency team, Wafermaker officials agree that you should develop a fact sheet listing the chemicals it uses with two or three practical, common, worthwhile applications for each chemical. For this assignment you will have to research the uses for the following: acetic acid, hydrochloric acid, hydrofluoric acid, nitric acid, sulfuric acid, ammonium hydroxide, potassium hydroxide, sodium hydroxide, sodium sulfide, methanol, trichlorethane, trichlorosilane, argon, nitrogen, hydrogen, hydrogen chloride, oxygen, diborane, phosphine, hydrogen peroxide, chromium trioxide, potassium dichromate, isopropyl alcohol and silane.

5. In deliberations with your public relations agency team, Wafermaker officials request that you develop a list of all questions (including rude ones) that might be asked at a news conference or briefing. The list is to form the basis of a Q & A sheet.

6. Wafermaker officials ask your agency to develop a one-page backgrounder describing silicon wafer production in terms that can be used easily by journalists. (Search the Internet for information.)

7. Explain how you would develop a digital dashboard to monitor social media for dialogue about the plant situation.

8. Draft a list of messages that would be important for Wafermaker to make to each of its stakeholder audiences.

In developing communication to parents, the media and customers, it is best not to make assumptions about what people know or how they feel. Also it is best not to try to persuade anyone of anything. To influence behavior it is most effective to provide information and firsthand experience that will enable people to persuade themselves. It is best to provide complete, objective and factual information. For example, you might begin your communication as follows: "On Friday, January 11, Wafermaker had a fire that was believed to be caused by a faulty heater. No one was injured; damage was estimated" and so forth. Resist the temptation to promise more than you can deliver (e.g. "students are perfectly safe"), to make assumptions, especially negative ones (e.g. "no reason that the plant might have to be moved); or to presume what people know or don't know (e.g. "many of you think …"); or guess how people feel (e.g. "many of you are afraid …); or to speak on behalf of something over which you have no control (e.g. Not acceptable for the school principal to write: "You can rest assured that Wafermaker operates safely.")

Background

A series of unexpected events creates a crisis situation for Wafermaker in Oakleaf, U.S.A. As you read the news reports that follow imagine how quickly emotions must begin to intensify among community residents. Consider how easily a company's hard-earned reputation can be seriously damaged. Try to empathize with Wafermaker management as they contemplate a situation with which they have no experience. Share management's feeling that at any minute issues can come into the public eye, and Wafermaker with its sterling reputation as a model corporate citizen can be put on the defensive by the same people who earlier welcomed it to the area with open arms.

The region had aggressively recruited electronics plants, considering them to be safe, clean and

non-polluting, a preferred alternative to traditional basic industries. There were no known reasons why such plants could not be integrated into the community in business parks and on property sharing borders with stores, schools and residences. However, an incident in India focused world attention on industrial hazards and an incident in Oakleaf brought the matter of concern even closer to home.

Day 1
Gas Kills 300 in India

Gas from a pesticide plant escaped into a city in central India this morning and killed at least 300 people and injured thousands more.

Day 5
Top Executive Arrested, Then Freed

The chairman of an American company whose plant was associated with a gas leak that killed more than 1,600 people was taken into custody by India police today. He was released later.

Day 7
Death Toll in India Hits 1,900 from Gas Leak

The official death toll from a poison gas leak at a pesticide plant rose to about 1,900 yesterday.

U.S. Company's Reputation Severely Damaged

Reputation of the U.S. company with a majority ownership in the pesticide plant in India where leaking of a deadly chemical cost most than 2,000 lives has suffered substantially in the eyes of the American public.

Day 9

Fire Damages Wafermaker Plant

A fire today damaged the Wafermaker plant in Oakleaf. Firefighters entering the plant were sprayed by what at first was feared to be chemicals but instead was water from the plant's sprinkler system. Damage was estimated to be about $1 million.

Day 10

Mention of chemicals in the news reports was the first time that the community became aware of the use of chemicals in electronics plants, such as Wafermaker's. Parents of the 500 children enrolled at Parks Elementary School located near the Wafermaker plant were particularly interested in the reference to chemicals. When parents talked about the plant at home, their children told how they looked through the school windows at people in baggy suits moving big barrels behind the plant. They told about how trucks bring barrels and take barrels away.

Day 12

Phone calls began pouring into the principal's office at Parks school. Parents wanted to know more about the school and its safety procedures should there ever be a chemical accident at the Wafermaker plant. Phone calls of community residents to the silicon wafer manufacture also increased and became more emotionally intense as callers pressed for information about chemical use.

Day 14

Wafermaker management requests professional public relations advice.

Additional Background

- Wafermaker employs 700 people at its Oakleaf plant
- Wafermaker makes silicon wafers for the computer industry
- The fire caused about $1 million damage, according to company officials
- Cleanup work is under way
- The company does not expect any of its employees to be off the job because of the fire
- About 30 people will be used in the cleanup operation. Another 50 to 75 workers will move their operation to a nearby warehouse while duct work is replaced at the plant and soot and dust are cleaned up
- The fire was started by a malfunctioning electrical switch.
- Most of the damage was from smoke. About 20,000 square feet of the plant's 200,000 square feet were affected by the fire. Damage to walls and equipment was minimal.
- The cleanup process will affect the silicon wafer polishing area, final inspection area and the packaging operation
- Some machinery has already been moved to temporary quarters

- The plant manufactures silicon wafers used in making computer chips. Numerous chemicals are used at the facility, but none of the chemicals was burned or released during the fire.
- The fire was nearly out by the time firefighters arrived, but it produced extensive smoke
- Wafermaker operates in an ultra-clean environment. Manufacturing the wafers and maintaining the clean environment involves the use of chemicals. Because of possible chemical contamination of workers, the facility has safety showers. A worker who is accidentally contaminated can enter a shower that releases a large volume of water to promptly wash off any chemicals
- Wafermaker said the majority of chemicals used there are hazardous, but if handled properly are safe
- Employees handling chemicals are required to wear protective suits to prevent any possible harm to themselves.
- Wafermaker said a worst-case scenario would involve liquefied hydrochloric acid. If it escaped all safety systems, a gaseous cloud would form and depending on the weather could hang over the area. People would know to move away because of the odor. Prolonged exposure could be harmful to people, according to the company.
- Wafermaker said it takes every possible precaution and safeguard to protect its employees, the environment and neighbors.
- the company spent more than $5 million on environmental control systems for the plant.
- Fearful of the chemical hazard, some parents wanted to keep their children from going to the Parks Elementary School near the plant
- Leaders of the Parent Teacher Organization began contacting local, county and state government agencies to learn more about the plant's use of chemicals
- Most chemicals are stored in tanks in an area that has concrete walls and floors painted with an acid-proof resin. Pipes carry the chemicals to work areas through a concrete tunnel also painted with the acid-proof resin. Wastes are piped through the tunnel to a treatment facility in a similarly secure area, according to Wafermaker.
- Acid and bases are neutralized and piped into the city sewer system. Nothing is disposed of on plant property except purified water used in the manufacturing process.
- A chemical spill is highly unlikely, according to the company
- The company emphasized that the plant was planned to operate in close proximity with a community and so was designed with the best available safety systems. Plant managers and workers live in the community and have children who attend area schools.
- Wafermaker was aware that its use, storage and transportation of chemicals was under intense scrutiny by the community, that rumors were rampant, and that the company could expect media attention any day–any minute.

ARTICLE: CEOS MUST BE VISIBLE LEADERS

The watchword for every organization in today's environment is preparedness. We are looking to our leaders for information, direction, safety and moral support. Our leaders include the chief executive officers of American business.

Chief executives have a responsibility to visibly lead their organizations back to a state of business as usual. By stepping up to this responsibility, CEOs have an unprecedented opportunity to earn an extraordinary measure of employee respect, admiration and commitment.

Why must CEOs be visible leaders?

For employees to take up work as usual under the looming threat of terrorism requires strong assurances from the highest authority that all precautions are being taken to safeguard employee health and safety in the workplace.

Health and safety in this uncertain environment cannot be relegated by CEOs to personnel and security departments. Securing the workplace under the shadow of terrorism requires executive oversight on a daily basis to enable CEOs to make crucial decisions in time to protect employees from potential harm.

In addition, employees need reassurances that their organizations have leaders at the helm who are in control of the communication and resources necessary to take the organization through a crisis situation if necessary. In an uncertain, challenging environment over-communication is impossible.

Employees reach out for evidence that the situation is being addressed with care and competence. People feel comforted and more in control when they are connected to others through communication. The frequency of communication is just as important as its substance. Waiting to communicate until there is something to say is anything but comforting.

What should CEOs do to be visible leaders to employees?

Chief executives must provide more face time with members of their organizations. They can do it personally to some extent, electronically to a greater extent, and they can do it throughout the organization by encouraging management face time with employees at all levels of supervision.

Practices, such as Hewlett-Packard's MBWA, are particularly important. At H-P, the practice is Management By Walking About. This practice is exemplified in the public sector by the highly commendable leadership of New York Mayor Rudy Giuliani.

Communicating the presence of leadership and responsible, caring management, as Mr. Giuliani has done so diligently, is a message that people under duress need to receive over and over in every way possible.

Chief executives should encourage managers to communicate in meaningful gestures—greeting employees in the morning, visiting employees in their lunch setting, offering a friendly comment at the coffee machine, sending an unexpected e-mail message, such as, "Let's all have a good day and enjoy working together." These various forms of communication enable employees to stay connected with those who have the authority and resources to help ensure their health and safety.

Why can't CEOs delegate the leadership responsibility to others and just carry on the way they have in the past?

Any one of America's CEOs could be thrust unexpectedly into managing a crisis situation. Real or perceived, their organization will be in danger. The chief executive will have 45 minutes to 12 hours, at most, to set the direction for the way in which the situation will be managed. A crisis is a turning point. Its outcome will determine the consequences to an organization. There could be potential for employee injury or loss of life, as well as long-term damage to an organization's image, reputation, profitability and stock value.

If the crisis is managed properly, there is potential for employee well being and public admiration. The CEO's organization can garner great respect for disclosure, candor, prudent action, total regard, commitment and contrition as appropriate.

Contrary to public belief, many organizations do not have crisis communication plans ready to implement at a moment's notice. Many chief executives take the risk of hoping a crisis will not occur. Chief executives unprepared for managing a crisis fall into a reactive, defensive mode that gets communicated instantly by the news media sometimes throughout the world.

What is expected of a CEO in a crisis?

The role of a CEO in a crisis situation is not defined by the CEO, the board or industry peers. The role is defined and evaluated by the general public. In a crisis situation, the public expects an organization's top leader to:

- step forward immediately, publicly and take charge;
- provide information completely and truthfully as soon as it becomes available;
- own up to responsibilities; lay out immediate action steps;
- show concern for everyone's needs;
- cooperate with the news media; give lots of "face time," communicating regularly and frequently.

Business leaders have an extraordinary opportunity to bond with employees in taking organizations back to business as usual.

By stepping up to these leadership responsibilities, chief executive officers can earn an extraordinary measure of employee respect, admiration and commitment.

Case
Seventeen
Fundraising

WHAT IN THE WORLD WOULD YOU LIKE TO SHARE?

A development officer at a major university thought about the importance of staying in touch with donors especially during economic downturns. She appealed to faculty members to think of gift ideas in the range of $1,000 to $3,000 that friends, alumni donors and prospective donors would find of interest to support. She encouraged one-time funding opportunities that would be of special value and even lead to long-term investment and giving. Her examples included: send a student to Ghana, endow a scholarship to support study abroad, support a weekend workshop or endow a workshop series. The opportunities would be relatively small donations with immediate impact and long-term potential.

Her appeal sparked an idea from a faculty member who suggested a program called "What in the world would you like to share?" The proposed program captured the interest of areas throughout the university and created a challenge in how to launch it. For this case, assume you are one of a small group of students in the school of journalism and communication that has decided to assist the development office in announcing the program.

Team Assignment

Your task is to develop a public relations plan to announce the program, "What in the world would you like to share?" to three audiences: students, faculty, and potential donors.

Background

"What in the world would you like to share?" is a personalized way to learn something firsthand and share the knowledge gained with many others.

In this program, students have an opportunity to propose experiencing something in the world that they would like to share with others. Examples are attending a session of the United Nations, observing the news operation of CNN in Atlanta, interviewing a world leader or a celebrity, visiting with a family in Ghana, discussing fundraising challenges with the director of a raptor center in Sitka, Alaska, interviewing a foreign ambassador to the U.S., meeting to discuss an issue with an official of the Environmental Protection Agency in Washington, D.C., meeting with the head of an advocacy organization, such as the National Resource Defense Council, and many other diverse educational experiences students are encouraged to propose.

An important part of the application process is for students to describe the experience they would like to have and specifically how they will share their experience with others based on a detailed paper they are required to submit upon their return. Their participation in the program requires the oversight of a faculty advisor.

Through this program students engage in both a learning and teaching experience. As Bill Moyers has said, "Sharing is the essence of teaching." Students also learn what is required to be effective ambassadors to their school.

Donors supporting this program are contributing not only to the university, but also to an even higher cause of promoting personalized sharing of knowledge through human interactions around the world. A unique aspect of the program is using social media to keep in close touch with potential donors. Donors who agree to participate in the program receive, electronically, opportunities to fund student proposals. Students are required in their proposals to package their experience as an irresistible funding opportunity clearly stating the benefits to a donor, the student and the school. Using electronic means, the development office surprises donors with messages to their i-phones, Twitter or Facebook accounts about recently approved and available, amazing student proposals, which donors can select to support, instantly. Donors also receive flash reports of student experiences in progress and later completed.

Participants in the program join the ranks of what Bill Moyers calls, "public thinkers."

Individual Writing Assignments

Each team member is to complete a different one of the following items that might or might not be included in the design of the team's plan.

What in the world would I like to share?

1. Write an e-mail message announcing the new program to students in a way that attracts interest and motivates them to get more information on a specified Web site.

2. Write a blog of no less than 150 words about the program that attracts student attention and stimulates Internet buzz about what students might propose.

3. Decide on an experience that you would like to share with others through the program and summarize it in no less than 150 words as an irresistible funding opportunity for potential donors that could be conveyed by electronic means. Describe how the proposed experience would be of benefit to you, a donor and the university.

4. Explain how Twitter could be used to get students to express things they would like to share with others as a way of promoting the program.

5. Write a script of no less than 200 words for announcing the program at luncheon meetings of business, trade and civic organizations whose members could be potential donors.

6. Write a social media news release announcing the program that would be posted on the development office Web site.

7. Explain in a memo to the development officer how the program's irresistible funding opportunities could be conveyed electronically to potential donors and how donors could simply decide on the spot to fund a student proposal and notify the development office instantly to reserve the selection.

8. Write a backgrounder on the program and use your imagination to embellish the description with creative examples and ways that would make the program effective.

Case Eighteen
Corporate
Communication

DOWNSIZE

This is a case of closing a major production facility. It is representative of a phenomenon commonly referred to as downsizing that ran rampant in the 1980s and '90s and continues to appear, especially in the manufacturing sector.

What is downsizing? It's the act of reducing the size and complexity of an organization. How is it done? It's usually done by any one or combination of the following: decreasing the number of employees, closing facilities, exiting selected markets, dropping product lines, shedding activities unrelated to a firm's core business. In business, this activity is given various names, such as restructuring, re-engineering, reorganizing, redesigning and reinventing.

Why do organization's downsize? Reasons frequently offered: escalating domestic and or global competition, increasing costs, declining markets, weak economy, increased use of technology. Reasons never offered: overstaffing, over-estimating, over-spending.

What are the benefits of downsizing? We have yet to see a definitive answer to this and other questions. If jobs are eliminated to improve a company's competitive position, will employee morale and/or productivity also improve? If a company reduces its workforce and sheds activities outside its core business will its stock price increase? If a company simplifies its operations will there be an actual cost savings? Will reducing a workforce temporarily and rebuilding it when market conditions improve automatically restore an organization to its original strength? Are the benefits of downsizing shared by everyone in an organization? Benefits have to be assessed on a case by case basis. In general, benefits are arguable. Nevertheless, the practice continues. What is known is that the process imposes multiple pressures that produce stress that is real and can be harmful and expensive. These effects can be mitigated to a significant extent through thoughtfully planned and professionally implemented communication and by heeding the lessons learned by others who have experienced the process.

Team Assignment

Your team assignment is to develop a public relations plan for closing Houston Operations, one of eight production plants owned and managed by Supercore International, Inc., a leader in the design and production of structural products for commercial buildings. Background information for this case begins on the next page with a role play of the chief executive officer's assignment to the public relations director and another of discourse among executives of a core group in a private communication planning meeting. Information for individual team member assignments will be found in correspondence among core group members.

Individual Team Member Assignments

Each team member is to complete a different one of the following items that might or might not be included in the design of the team's plan. It is up to you to decide what the content should be for each element.

1. Develop a news release announcing closure of Supercore's Houston Operations. See Maple's notes on page 351.
2. Write a script for a video message from Houston Operations Manager Bill Cabot to employees announcing the company's decision to close the plant indefinitely. See Cabot's memo on page 296.
3. Draft in no more than 300 words the business rationale for closing Houston Operations. See page 360.
4. Draft a Q & A sheet addressing employment matters to be placed on the plant's Web site. See page 363.
5. Draft an e-mail message announcing the plant closure to be sent to Supercore's distribution centers.
6. Draft a Q & A addressing the plant closure for use by supervisory and management staff throughout Supercore International.
7. Develop a script for a video news release for use on TV business news about Supercore's downsizing and how it will benefit the company.

ROLE PLAY #1
Cast

Chief Executive Officer George Waters
Public Relations Director David Maple

Monday Meeting, July 8, 19XX

CEO George Waters' Office

CEO George Waters:

I want to talk to you about a move we are about to make. This is highly confidential. You are among a select few to know about this decision.

PR Director David Maple:

I understand.

CEO George Waters:

We're going to close the Houston plant. This will affect about 200 employees. I want to do this in keeping with the reputation we have for upholding quality and acting responsibly. I want this announcement made, and to be operating with minimal negative impacts from the closure on the overall business.

PR Director David Maple:

I'd like to know more specifically about the rationale for closing this particular plant.

CEO George Waters:

Tom Oaks will give you those details. I want the announcement to be made in three weeks.

PR Director David Maple:

Who will I be working with?

CEO George Waters:

There will be a core group of five, including you.

PR Director David Maple:

Will that include the plant manager?

CEO George Waters:

Yes. I've known Bill Cabot for more than 15 years. I trust him completely. He'll do what's right for the company. You can work with Bill, Tom, Gayle and Harvy. I want to have a communication plan from this core group by noon Friday.

Meeting Adjourns

ROLE PLAY #2
Cast

VP Operations Tom Oaks
VP Marketing/Sales Gayle Hopkins
VP Human Resources Harvy Collins
PR Director David Maple
(Manager Houston Operations Bill Cabot not included in this meeting)

Tuesday Meeting of Core Group, July 9, 19XX
A Conference Room

VP Operations Tom Oaks:

David, communication planning is your area; how should we prepare for this announcement?

PR Director David Maple:

We don't have a track record in closing plants. Not this company. In fact, this will be our first experience. But other companies have closed more than one facility and have good advice to offer. I called the resource center of Public Relations Society of America in New York. Had them send articles about Fortune 500 companies that have learned about announcing plant closings. Ten lessons. These points go beyond communication, but they're all important considerations.

VP Operations Tom Oaks:

A lot of people are going to take an interest in this announcement, not just employees.

PR Director David Maple:

That's a good place to begin, Tom. Let's talk about audiences. Within the organization we have Houston Operations employees, including sales, customer service and estimating personnel. Externally, we have Houston's customers and certain suppliers. In the community we have community leaders, government representatives on the local, county, state and federal level. And we have the media—local, business, financial and trade press. We're privately owned so we don't need to worry about investors. This points to the first lesson learned by others: We need to be first to communicate fully to everyone concerned.

VP Human Resources Harvy Collins:

It's going to take some time to reach all of those groups.

PR Director David Maple:

It has to be done all at once. I'll show you how we can reach everyone in a single morning. That's the function of a good plan.

VP Marketing & Sales Gayle Hopkins:

So how do we decide what to tell these different groups?

PR Director David Maple:

Key question, Gayle. We have to have a crystal clear business rationale for the decision to close Houston. That rationale will be the basis of every communication. Our credibility with all of these audiences depends on the soundness of our rationale for closing the plant. Tom, if you will provide me with the basic information, I'll draft the rationale. If we can't explain the business reasons for a closure to ourselves, we can't expect anyone else to understand why the facility must be shut down. The rationale will be at the heart of every communication we develop. In our next work session, tomorrow, we need to decide on message points for each audience—Houston employees, customers and corporate-wide employees, field sales reps, distribution center managers, the media and the community.

VP Marketing & Sales Gayle Hopkins:

What about Bill? Isn't he supposed to be working with us?

PR Director David Maple:

That happens to be third on my list of lessons learned. It's essential to have full support of the plant manager. George said we can trust Bill Cabot completely and that he will do what's best for the company, even though he will be retired in the process. Bill will get an audio file of this meeting. We would have to alter our strategy if we had a manager who might take issue with the decision or resist talking about the decision. Most people would rather avoid confrontation and controversy. A plant manager who has been operating for years in the comfort zone of a routine operation could have a tough time with this. He suddenly gets thrust into having to confront people within and outside the plant on a difficult subject. It's much easier, even with someone as loyal as Bill, to follow a comprehensive, agreed upon plan.

VP Human Relations Harvy Collins:

One of your points must focus on the 200 employees who will lose their jobs.

PR Director David Maple:

Yes. Every Fortune 500 company I read about emphasized the importance of putting a high priority on human needs. You will need a Q & A on HR stuff, Harv. We're talking about job information …

VP Human Relations Harvy Collins:

I know, … relocation opportunities, if any, early retirements, jobs training. We're going to want to provide financial, family, emotional, career counseling, psychological counseling for managers. We will need to provide letters of recommendation, help with resume writing and whatever placement services are needed. You know this announcement can also cause people to jump ship. We need to make sure we identify and contact people we want to keep elsewhere in the organization.

PR Director David Maple:

Another lesson learned is to protect against demoralization elsewhere in the organization. Employees easily identify with one

another. How the Houston employees are treated will be of interest to every employee in the company. They will draw conclusions about how they might be treated. That reinforces the importance of having a sound business rationale for the decision to shut down. Another thing we have to protect is the safety and security of everyone at Houston. It's another lesson point. What's the physical layout at that plant?

VP Operations Tom Oaks:

If it's what you're thinking, the operation is wide open. Someone could walk in …

VP Human Relations Harvy Collins:

Like an emotionally distraught employee?

VP Operations Tom Oaks:

Yes. Someone like that could walk right in the front door and have dozens of production people in his or her sights. We'll take a look at security. We also have to think about the unlikely possibility of vandalism, looting, sabotage and any other form of reprisal. David, according to my notes, that's six points.

PR Director David Maple:

I have four more. One is keeping the planning confidential with a core group, which we have. Another is having a comprehensive plan. We're working on that. Once we have a plan we have to commit to following it. The plan will have to have contingency provisions for dealing with problems like leaks and rumors. A third one is in your area, Harvy–meeting all local, state and federal laws for closing a facility. The fourth is leaving the community in a way that the community would welcome our return in the future. This closure will impact the local economy in terms of revenue from wages, taxes and local purchases. The community needs to understand our decision and not feel that it could or should have done something to secure the plant's future. We might even consider gifting the community some property, park equipment or public improvement.

Let me wrap up this part of our meeting with a summary of lessons learned:

1. Have a crystal clear rationale.
2. Work confidentially with a core staff.
3. Follow a comprehensive plan.
4. Place a high priority on human needs.
5. Have full support of the person in charge of the facility to be closed.
6. Meet all local, state and federal requirements.
7. Protect against demoralization elsewhere.
8. Ensure safety and tight security.
9. Leave the community in a way that the community would welcome our return.
10. Be first to communicate fully to everyone concerned.

VP Operations Tom Oaks:

We have to regroup tomorrow … here, 9 o'clock.

Tuesday night in the office of PR Director David Maple

Maple is reviewing his research on plant closings from PRSA headquarters in New York. The experience in plant closings by more than a dozen Fortune 500 companies reveals 10 important communication points. Maple decides to present them at Wednesday's planning meeting in a PowerPoint presentation. He finishes the last slide and checks his e-mail before leaving the office. There's a message from VP Operations Tom Oaks and a file attachment. Message: The information you wanted for drafting the rationale is in the attached file. Maple opens the file, which is in a memo format—

SUPERCORE INTERNATIONAL, INC.
Inter-Office Correspondence

CONFIDENTIAL

JULY 9, 19XX

TO: DAVID MAPLE
FROM: TOM OAKS
COPIES: George Waters, Harvy Collins, Gayle Hopkins, Bill Cabot
RE: **BUSINESS RATIONALE FOR HOUSTON CLOSING**

Following is the information you will need for developing a statement of our business rationale for closing Houston Operations. Supercore International, Inc. has provided the standard of quality in structural products for commercial buildings in countries around the world for more than half a century. We are a leading international supplier of custom designed products and systems. We have 51 facilities. They employ 5, 221 people in North and South America, Europe and Asia.

We have been the market leader in North America and have been steadily increasing market shares in Europe and Asia. However, business conditions in our major market, specifically the United States, are causing us to adjust our production capacity. The U.S. commercial building market is experiencing a major recession. Volume of construction business has dropped dramatically over the past five years. Many parts of the country are overbuilt in commercial construction. Contractors are constrained financially. Financing for construction projects is hard to get. Supercore and its competitors have seen their market drop 37 percent in five years. Industry analysts expect that it will be another 18 months with a further decline next year, before this market begins to turn around. Competition for the reduced volume of business has put enormous downward pressure on pricing. That, plus the cost of maintaining excess production capacity caused us to assess what could be done to reduce operating costs and still maintain the same high level of sales and service to our customers.

We decided our production capacity had to be brought in line with market conditions. By the end of this year Supercore will consolidate its manufacturing operations in the United States, reducing the number of production plants from eight to seven. Houston Operations was the likely candidate for an indefinite closure. The Southwest has had the weakest construction environment in the country for the past five years, and this has led to a substantial decline in the plant's sales volume from levels 10 years ago. The depressed regional economy, resulting from a major decline in oil prices, a rash of major bankruptcies, together with an oversupply of commercial buildings, has severely reduced market demand for our products. Houston has been operating significantly under capacity for several years. Work there can be handled easily by our other facilities.

Actually, the Southwestern market is relatively small and isn't expected to improve much in the foreseeable future, which is another reason we focused our decision on Houston. But the main reason we selected Houston over other plants was the its closing would be least disruptive in terms of the company's ability to serve its national dealer network. We will serve the Southwest as effectively and aggressively as ever using the same sales organization. The Houston area sales districts and their distribution centers will become part of our Southeastern Area operations.

We are confident that reducing our production plants from eight to seven will leave us ample capacity to supply customer needs for the coming years. Even with the closing of Houston Operations, Supercore will continue to be one of the largest international producers of structural products for commercial buildings. We are generally considered to be the industry's quality leader with service that outperforms our competition.

Our outlook is positive, despite current market conditions. Commercial building represents a big market in the United States and around the world. Our brand has enjoyed a major market position and we have always been a full participant in economic recoveries. We see excellent market potential in Europe and in developing parts of the world. We have built our organization not on business but on relationships with employees, suppliers, customers, dealers, the media, social and environmental activists and with the communities and countries in which we operate.

* * *

David, that should give you something to work with in developing our business rationale statement.

T.O.

Meeting Transcript
Wednesday Morning Meeting of Core Group, July 10, 19XX

A Conference Room

Participants

VP Operations Tom Oaks
VP Marketing/Sales Gayle Hopkins
VP Human Resources Harvy Collins
PR Director David Maple
(Manager Houston Operations Bill Cabot not included in this meeting)

PR Director David Maple:

Tom, I read your memo. Thanks for the information for the rationale. Last night I gleaned more helpful information from my research on lessons learned by other companies. This information focuses directly on communication. In the interest of time, I'll quickly cover 10 points that I have summarized in a PowerPoint presentation.

1. Announce the closing according to a plan. The logistics of getting key

messages to a diverse number of audiences all at one particular time requires meticulous planning and scheduling. We must have a plan and follow it through to the last detail.

2. Use prepared Q & A's When it comes to work like this, I know from experience that only birds can wing it. We will need a Q & A on each major subject area and we will have to supply them to everyone who has a responsibility for communicating the information.

3. Spike rumors. We need to offer every company communicator guidance on how to spike rumors and deal with news leaks.

4. Stay in touch with the media. A plant closure is a major news item. We can expect calls from the local, business, financial and trade press. We can minimize calls and conversations by developing a news announcement that anticipates and responds to what journalists will want to know about the closure. This will help ensure the accuracy of what is reported. No matter what we do there will always be more questions, so it's essential that we stay in touch with the media until all information needs are satisfied.

5. Assess audience reactions. The point here is that effective communication is a two-way process. We communicate. We listen. We respond to feedback. And the process continues until we're satisfied that the communication is complete and accurate.

6. Respond to problems. When an announcement is planned properly, people involved in the announcement activities develop a sense of ownership and commit to identifying and dealing with problems to help ensure a successful outcome. We want everyone involved in this announcement to have confidence in the plan and all the information they need so they will feel compelled to help head off potential problems.

7. Communicate frequently with employees. When an organization gets into a stressful situation, especially one that pertains to health, safety or job security, people need face time with their leaders. They need to be in touch to have a sense that someone is in charge and providing direction. So it's important for managers and supervisors to be in touch on a personal face-to-face basis even when there is nothing new to communicate.

8. Show concern and commitment. The way in which we make the announcement in Houston needs to show everyone affected by it that the company is taking an action that is absolutely necessary and that we are doing it with compassion, understanding and a commitment to make good on every promise.

9. Generate positive follow-up publicity. We have opportunities to follow the announcement with positive news by publicizing successful personnel placements and any goodwill gestures to the community

like a donation of property or park equipment.

10. Leave the community in a way that would invite our return. We need to make sure community leaders and government representatives are not blind sided by the announcement, that they are well informed and prepared to respond to questions from their constituents. We need to make known that we will continue to serve the Southwest market with products and services from our other facilities. We need to reposition, not sever, our relationship with the community.

These are the 10 communication points derived from the lessons learned by others.

VP Marketing/Sales Gayle Hopkins

Well, we're going to look to you for how we apply this. What do you need from us so we can get down to the specifics of developing the announcement plan?

PR Director David Maple

Gayle, I need you to provide key message points we want to make to distribution center managers, to field sales personnel and to customers. We'll have to talk to Bill about the message points for Houston plant employees and key suppliers. Tom, I will need from you and Harvy message points for employees company-wide. I think I have what I need to draft the news announcement and the message points for community leaders and government representatives.

If you all agree, I think we should take some time now to rough out a time line

that will become our communication schedule. Then, let's meet again tomorrow morning [Thursday, July 11]. I will have a draft announcement plan and time line for us to review. We should have a final draft by the end of the day. Tom, do you want to schedule a meeting with George for Friday [July 12]?

VP Operations Tom Oaks

I'll do that. Let's get to this schedule.

PR Director David Maple

We need to bring Bill into the planning group. Why don't we have him join us on Monday, July 15?

VP Human Relations Harvy Collins

We have a lot of stuff to review, probably revise and get approved. It might be good to schedule a three-day work session.

PR Director David Maple

What about doing that next week, Wednesday thru Friday [July17–19]?

VP Operations Tom Oaks

That should include review and approval of an operations shutdown plan and timetable.

PR Director David Maple

It's also the time we should decide if this core group needs to be expanded and who that should include.

Vp Human Relations Harvy Collins

I will have the retention plan ready. We can do a final review of government requirements for a closure. We can review the employment information Q & A. I will also have a description of employment assistance services we will be providing. And we can review security arrangements.

PR Director David Maple

We can finalize the communication plan and time line. It will contain contingency provisions for handling news leaks and rumors. The business rationale and news announcement need to be reviewed and approved, as well as the communication to all of the various stakeholders. For the announcement, I would see notifying the general managers of each of our operations by phone on July 26 and sending them information kits via courier to arrive the same day. We'll get Bill's opinion on how soon to notify key staff in Houston. We should courier information kits to sales reps and distribution center managers. I think we should schedule the announcement for Tuesday, July 30. On announcement day we need to cover the following something like this:

- Bill Cabot personally notifies supervisors
- Houston supervisors notify employees and distribute letter from Cabot
- Facility managers company-wide distribute CEO letter to employees with business rationale attached
- Bill meets with Houston customer service representatives and estimators
- Headquarters faxes sales reps company-wide with instructions to notify Southwest customers by phone
- News release to headquarters personnel (electronically) and to Houston media and via news distribution service to state wires, national business, financial and trade media

- Bill and selected staff members call community leaders and local government representatives
- Houston faxes government representatives at state and federal offices
- Houston mails news release and letter to Houston customers and suppliers
- In the days following the announcement, Houston will be operating counseling services, employment assistance and we should be looking for opportunities to generate some positive publicity. [end]

David Maple's notes for writing the news announcement

- Dateline should be from headquarters, THYME, Ill., July 30, 19xx
- Indefinite closure structural building products plant to bring production capacity in line with market conditions consolidating our manufacturing resources in the United States by reducing the number of production plants from eight to seven.
- This adjustment will enable us to reduce operating costs and still provide the same high level of sales and service to our customers
- With the U.S. commercial construction market in the midst of a major recession, the market for the company's products has dropped by approximately 39 percent, nationwide, over the past six years
- Will be another 18 months, with a further decline in the coming year, before this market begins to turn around
- Supercore International will retain the same Southwest sales organization

and distribution centers in Houston, Denver and Wichita. These centers will be supplied by production facilities in Tennessee, Illinois, Alabama

- Closure expected to be completed by year-end
- Will affect approximately 200 employees
- Some employees will have an opportunity to relocate to other Supercore International facilities
- The company will provide employees with a severance pay package and job placement services
- Houston has always had highly-skilled, productive employees; closure is regretful; we will work hard to help them find other employment
- The plant started operating in 1980
- Business grew rapidly
- Ran at near capacity during the building boom of the early 80s.
- Houston was well situated to serve the Southwest, and in particular, the Texas markets, which had major levels of construction back in that period
- This period was followed by a virtual collapse of building activity in the region
- Supercore gave Houston Operations some of the company's international work and jobs from other parts of the country; it still operated below capacity levels
- Depressed conditions hit other regions and Houston's operating level was reduced further
- Market conditions caused us to assess our situation in the U.S.
- Supercore made a thorough analysis and concluded that of the eight

production facilities, closure of Houston Operations would have the least effect on the company's ability to serve our customers nationally

- Conditions are what they are and we have to adjust our production capacity
- Houston plant was built in 1979
- Supercore International, Inc., is a leading international producer of structural building products and systems for the non-residential market
- Headquartered in Thyme, Illinois
- Supercore International has 50 facilities employing approximately 5,000 people in North America, Europe and Asia.

David Maple's notes for writing Q&A

We'll be asked why. We're closing one of eight U.S. plants to bring production in line with market conditions.

Some may think we're over-reacting; they'll try to point to indicators that we're coming out of the recession. But commercial construction business in the U.S. is in the midst of a major recession. Construction work has dropped significantly over the past six years. Supercore and other manufacturers have seen their market drop by approximately 39 percent in the past six years. It will be another 18 months before this market begins to turn around.

Not everyone understands why construction is in worse shape than the general economy. There's been substantial overbuilding in many parts of the country. Building activity is down substantially. Developers are constrained financially. They are unable to attract capital for projects.

We'll get plenty of questions on why Houston? Fact is, the Southwest has been the weakest section of the country for construction for the past six years. Why? Breakdown of the energy belt economy with the big drop in oil prices, consequences of the savings and loan crisis and lots of bankruptcies. It's likely to be a weak market for the foreseeable future. But the major reason behind selecting Houston was that it would have a minimal effect on our overall operation.

We have been in Houston so long that it will probably seem to some that we are pulling out of this market. So we need to be direct in letting people know that we're going to serve this market as well as ever before. We will continue to operate our distribution center in Houston. That center and those in Denver and Wichita will be supplied by production facilities in Tennessee, Illinois and Alabama. These plants can handle additional volume.

About 200 employees will be affected by the closure. Some will be given opportunities to relocate to other facilities.

Severance. We'll get some questions about the package. It has two elements. Employees will be offered incentive pay to work until their individual assignments have been completed. All employees will get a severance amount whether or not they work until their jobs end.

We might be asked about a possible employee buy-out. That's not possible. We're not interested in selling these assets. We may have use for them elsewhere in the future.

The end date? Closing date? We haven't set an exact date. We have to allow enough time for transferring work to other plants.

Should be able to have everything done before the end of December.

As for other plants … People will be wondering if other plants will be closed. The answer is no. According to our market outlook, we think this adjustment of reducing our U.S. capacity from eight to seven plants will give us the right size capacity to supply customers for the near future.

We know this is going to have an impact on the local economy. We'll get questions about that. The Houston plant has contributed about $20 million a year in wages, taxes and local purchases.

There will probably be people who expect us to somehow make up this deficit, this loss of income to the community. What can we say? We've been a solid contributor to the local economy for many years. We've provided good paying jobs. But business conditions no longer support this plant. We're in a position that many others are in. We can't justify our cost of operating here and there's no way to continue contributing to the economy.

We'll probably get asked about the possibility of re-opening the plant in the future. The closure is indefinite. The Southwest building market is severely depressed. We expect it to be that way for quite some time.

Someone will probably persist and ask if it will ever be opened again. But who could possibly know what conditions will be into the long term? We can make any projections, let alone commitments.

We have had such a good relationship with local and state government representatives that some of them are going to be wondering if there is anything they can do to change our decision. But there isn't anything they can do. The decision is based on business conditions in the Southwest and around the country.

I suppose someone could wonder if putting this plant here was a mistake in the first place. That certainly isn't true. It really took off into the mid '80s and was well situated to serve the Southwest. Texas had lots going on then. Major construction projects were under way. But that period didn't last. Things pretty much collapsed. Who could have predicted the S & L debacle?

Employees at Houston had nothing to do with the decision. They are good, smart, hardworking individuals. They were always making suggestions on how to improve things, quality and production. Other employers should take a hard look at the talent that will be available from this plant.

Employees at our other plants might wonder if any of them might get bumped by a relocated Houston employee. First of all, there will be a limited number of relocations. We place a high value on our human resources and will be very thoughtful in any placements.

That brings up the matter of employees who are not relocated. We will provide employment services, like preparing resumes and training for making a job search and how to interview. We'll be talking to local employers to describe the kinds of work people have been doing for us and how their skills might relate to other business operations. We'll give employees time off for job interviews. We will make a concerted effort to help everyone as much as we can.

The announcement may seem abrupt and someone might ask if we couldn't have given more notice. But we made the announcement as soon as we finished our analysis of the market situation. With the closure targeted for year-end employees will have an opportunity to work and be looking for other jobs for many weeks.

Let's see, we made the decision to close the plant in June, after our study was completed and assessed. The final decision came in mid-July. So there weren't any unusual delays in going through the process and making it known publicly.

The Houston plant … We'll secure it, probably move the equipment and eventually sell the property.

The Houston plant was built in 1979. It started up in 1980

It produces structural building products and pre-engineering building systems for the non-residential market.

It's not a union plant.

As for the outlook … We'll see an even greater decline in the market in the coming year and it will be at least 18 months before things begin to turn around. We will be stepping up our sales and marketing efforts. When things pick up we'll be in position to participate in the recovery as we have in the past.

SUPERCORE INTERNATIONAL, INC.
Inter-Office Correspondence

CONFIDENTIAL

JULY 10, 19XX

TO: DAVID MAPLE
FROM: HARVY COLLINS
COPIES: George Waters, Tom Oaks, Gayle Hopkins, Bill Cabot
RE: **INFORMATION FOR Q & A ON PEOPLE RELATED ISSUES**

Following is information you can use in writing a Q & A on people related issues:

There will be severance pay for salaried and hourly employees. At the time of termination, each employee will receive a base severance payment. It will amount to the person's weekly pay times the individual's years of service up to 25. Partial years will be prorated.

There will also be an incentive severance payment for individuals who work up to a time we specify or the particular job ends. Employees who qualify will be given $1000 if they have less than two years of service and $2500 if they have two or more years of service. The incentive will be paid when their jobs terminate.

The severance base pay and incentive pay will be payable to employees who are offered relocations to other plants, even if the individual does not accept the relocation offer.

Anyone who resigns before their jobs end must give us two weeks' notice in order to get their base severance pay. There's some flexibility on this requirement depending on circumstances.

Acts of misconduct related to the company, customers or other employees will disqualify a person from receiving severance payments.

We will get questions about benefits. Benefits end with job terminations. Hourly and salary employees may continue their medical insurance at their own expense according to "COBRA" provisions. We'll have more on COBRA later.

As for retirement benefits … Individuals who qualify for retirement or early retirement under either hourly or salary retirement plans can do so and receive retirement benefits. We'll have more details on this later.

We will be pressed hard on how many Houston employees will be transferred to jobs in other facilities. Actually, we don't know at this point. We have to see what's needed at other plants and we'll have to see who is willing to relocate of those who could be offered the opportunity. As soon as the announcement is made other plants will be assessing their personnel needs. We will have a more accurate idea when we have reports from the other seven plants. It won't be a large number.

Likely transferees will be employees in managerial, supervisory or technical jobs.

We'll probably be asked where the relocations could be. Most likely places would be Cilantro, Tennessee, Sage, Illinois, and Rosemary, Alabama.

As for when transfers might be made, I would say beginning in September and going through the end of the year.

Unfortunately, most employees will not have an opportunity to transfer. There's no cut-off date for employment. It will be different for each individual. It depends on how their work relates to the transition and if they accept the incentive to work as long as we need them. We will try to be more specific about this in the coming weeks.

If an employee wants to be transferred, and that refers to salaried employees in managerial and technical jobs, they will be given an opportunity to complete a form that will be sent to appropriate personnel for consideration.

It's different for hourly employees. A transfer might be possible for jobs with specialized skills. However, the individual would be responsible for moving expenses.

H.C.

SUPERCORE INTERNATIONAL, INC.
Inter-Office Correspondence

CONFIDENTIAL

JULY 10, 19XX

TO: DAVID MAPLE
FROM: BILL CABOT
COPIES: George Waters, Tom Oaks, Gayle Hopkins, Harvy Collins
RE: **INFORMATION FOR MY MEMO TO HOUSTON EMPLOYEES**

David, I'd appreciate a little help with writing my memo to the Houston employees. I've known many of these folks for more than a dozen years. If you would rough out something I will personalize it.

Some of the points I'd like to include are:

- Very difficult; we have operated like a family
- Proud of the teamwork we've shown
- Struggled through some lean times together, but always recovered
- I personally believe the decision to close was justified from a business assessment
- Need to support each other as we prepare for looking in new directions
- Can't help but wonder, why us? But there's nothing we could have done to alter the outcome. That's clear when we face the facts:

a. Supercore has too much under utilized production capacity and will have for some time to come
b. The market our plant serves is the by far the softest in the country
c. Prices have eroded, profits are down, no way to cover the cost of operating this facility
d. Unfortunately for us, our customers can be easily served by other plants
e. The Southwest distribution center will serve to anchor Supercore's business in this market
f. I'll be talking with everyone in smaller groups as we move forward … we'll go over personnel concerns
g. I know we all have mixed emotions over this … we will have to make a special effort to rely on our professionalism to maintain the teamwork needed to work through the shut down process
h. We have always given our customers a level of quality that always meets and often exceeds company standards … they deserve our continuing commitment and a smooth hand-off to our other plants … you know the rapport we have enjoyed … nothing has changed in that regard … we will continue working together in an open, straight-forward, totally honest relationship

In all honesty, I have to admit this is the most difficult memo I have ever had to write See what you can do with that. Thanks, David.

B.C.

SUPERCORE INTERNATIONAL, INC.
Inter-Office Correspondence

CONFIDENTIAL

JULY 10, 19XX

TO: DAVID MAPLE
FROM: GAYLE HOPKINS
COPIES: George Waters, Tom Oaks, Harvy Collins, Bill Cabot
RE: **INFORMATION FOR MY MEMO TO DISTRIBUTION CENTERS**

I appreciate your help with this communication, David. I am providing the main points that I think should be written in my memo to be sent to Supercore's distribution center managers.

- ... you were notified this morning about the company's decision to close Houston Operations
- ... I talked by speaker phone to the staff at the Houston distribution center. As you know, that facility will remain in operation. Southwest Area Sales will also remain as usual.
- ... we're all going to have our own thoughts about the shut-down and we're certainly entitled to that ...
- ... we have a responsibility to fully understand and be able to discuss the business reasons for the decision ...
- ... urge you to read and study the business rationale in your information kits ...
- ... as members of the sales organization, our biggest responsibility is to maintain our current business and make every effort to keep from losing any business as other plants begin to supply Houston customers ...
- ... to protect our position will require a stronger than ever commitment to the company and its strategic direction ...
- ... I know we are up to the challenge ...
- ... no matter how we plan, there will be some rough situations ... some not easy or even possible to see
- ... will place great demands on our ability to work together ...
- ... can't emphasize enough the importance of reading and studying all of the materials in your information kits ... you must know this material well enough to show complete confidence in Supercore's decision about Houston ...
- ... we need time to go over the transition plan in detail ... plan to attend a meeting of all distribution center managers at headquarters on Friday, August 2, at 11 a.m. in the main conference room ... your attendance is mandatory ... we have a big job ahead of us and I know we can handle it when we tackle it as a team ...

That's about what needs to be said, David. I'll look forward to your draft. Thanks.

G.H.

SUPERCORE INTERNATIONAL, INC.
Inter-Office Correspondence

CONFIDENTIAL

JULY 10, 19XX
TO: DAVID MAPLE
FROM: TOM OAKS
COPIES: George Waters, Gayle Hopkins, Harvy Collins, Bill Cobot
RE: **INFORMATION FOR MEMO FROM CEO TO ALL EMPLOYEES**

David, we'll need a memo written from George Waters to all employees. I would see it containing these points:

- For a company that holds its employees in highest regard, putting business realities ahead of our personal relationships is extremely difficult
- I have a responsibility to our organization to keep us in a strong competitive position
- Market conditions, as we all know, are heavily taxing our ability to generate the sales necessary to earn some return on investment. … In the U.S. we have experienced swings from no orders to 'round-the-clock production …
- The bottom line is that we have to face the reality of bringing our capacity in line with market conditions that are expected to remain depressed for the foreseeable future …
- Because the situation is serious, I asked for a thorough market study and comprehensive study of our production capacity and operating options. … It became evident that the way to restructure with minimal effects on our overall business is to shut down the Houston plant …
- It is with deep regret that we have to pursue a decision that will affect nearly 200 hard-working employees, some of whom have been with us for more than a dozen years … We will provide severance and employment services, including working with Houston employers to make local placements wherever possible
- So that everyone is able to know the details behind our decision to close Houston I have included with this letter to all employees a copy of our business rationale for this action
- You will see clearly from the rational that Houston has always been a top performer and closure is entirely due to market conditions

David, let me have a draft by tomorrow. George asked for a draft ASAP. Thanks.

T.O.

ARTICLE: DOWNSIZING: FOCUS ON PEOPLE

You don't have to go far to find examples of companies in the process of down-sizing—DaimlerChrysler, Hewlett-Packard Co., Amazon.com, OfficeMax, Xerox, Freightliner and many more. You do have to look harder to identify companies that treat downsizing with the respect that it deserves.

One way to judge how well a company manages downsizing is by the way in which it announces its restructuring plans. By focusing on people rather than on the downsizing process, companies are in a better position to promptly resume business operations.

This commentary is based on lessons learned by ARCO Chemical Co., UJB Financial Corp., Campbell Soup Company, NatWest Bank and my experience with other companies to answer three questions: 1) Why is it important to focus on people rather than on the downsizing process? 2) How do you focus on people rather than on process? 3) How does focusing on people enable a company to promptly resume business operations?

1. Why is it important to focus on people rather than on the downsizing process?

Studies have shown that downsizing has one guaranteed result: it reduces personnel. Research also concludes that downsizing does not ensure increased operating profits, employee motivation or morale for the short or long term.

Restructuring is a people-threatening process that can leave an entire staff and work force feeling like lucky survivors rather than valued employees. The dominant part of such a feeling is employee ambivalence toward one's work, employer, and continuing association.

That is why it is important to treat everyone involved in downsizing with respect and to take especially good care of employees who will comprise a company's "new" organization

2. How do you focus on people rather than process?

The answer to this question, based on lessons learned by many companies, is found in the quality of corporate downsizing announcement plans.

Generally, announcement activity should consider:

*   educating everyone about the reasons for downsizing;
*   showing consideration and respect for employees whose jobs will be eliminated;

- reassuring employees who will be retained that their value is recognized and appreciated;
- announcing the news to all affected and interested parties on a scheduled date;
- having contingency plans to deal with rumors and news leaks in order to adhere to the scheduled announcement date.

Announcement activity should consider all parties:

- all employees (all locations);
- news media
- customers
- major suppliers
- government representatives—all levels;
- appropriate government agencies;
- community opinion leaders;
- financial community—investors, bankers, securities analysts.

The downsizing message should consider:

- revealing the full extent of the reduction in force;
- establishing an 800 information number;
- providing a detailed business rationale for the downsizing and benefits to be derived;
- being totally open about how departing employees will be compensated;
- enabling retained employees to feel like important partners rather than fortunate survivors.

The announcement follow-up activity should consider:

- facilitating and assessing feedback from all interested parties and adjusting to developments;
- having an appropriate event for all retained employees that marks the end of restructuring and commemorates a new beginning.

3. How does focusing on people enable a company to promptly resume business operations?

Focusing on people throughout the downsizing announcement process as described above cultivates mutual respect within an organization. It reduces uncertainty and speculation and enhances an organization's credibility with all of its important audiences from which support is needed. It enables employees to return their undivided attention to the work at hand.

By focusing on people rather than on the downsizing process, companies are in a better position to promptly resume their business operations.

Case Nineteen
Celebrity Image Building

SUPERSTAR ENTREPRENEUR

This is a case of image building and centers on a superstar entrepreneur. Much research has been done in attempts to characterize entrepreneurs. Many are driven by the desire to make a lot more money than they could with some other application of their skills and energy. What every entrepreneur must decide is whether the rewards of their respective enterprise will justify the cost, sacrifice and risk involved in achieving some degree of success.

George Bernard Shaw said, "The reasonable man adapts himself to the world; the unreasonable man attempts to adapt the world to himself. Therefore all progress depends upon the unreasonable man." The character of the superstar in this case lies somewhere between reasonable and unreasonable. As you develop this case using the public relations file notes that follow the team and individual team member assignments, you will want to think about what makes this superstar tick and how the personality traits of this entrepreneur can be put to good use in building a business.

The article, "Work with journalists and make CEO profiles soar," should stimulate further thought in the development of your public relations plan.

Team Assignment

For this case assume that your team has been hired by superstar entrepreneur Jan Overbrook. Your superstar has a tenacious spirit that has enabled her to turn some ideas into profitable ventures. Your team has collected information about Overbook and has a file of interview notes that reveals secrets behind your client's successes and failures. Overbrook has hired your team to develop a public relations plan spanning 12 months that will promote her image as a superstar entrepreneur in ways that will propel the expansion of her latest business venture, Wellness Advocates, Inc. Overbrook wants to use her entire promotional budget on leveraging the credibility of public relations to expand WAI services, initially, throughout New York—in Albany, the Bronx, Vahalla, Brooklyn, Buffalo, Stoneybrook and Old Westbury.

Individual Team Member Assignments

Each team member is to complete a different one of the following items that might or might not be part of the design of your team's plan:

1. Draft a personality profile of the superstar.
2. Write a phone pitch script to an assistant program director to get TV coverage of the superstar.
3. Write an e-mail to the superstar client proposing an unusual attention-getting book-signing event/tour.
4. Write a pitch to bloggers to generate interest in the entrepreneur.
5. Draft a concise description of Wellness Advocates, Inc. and the superstar for use on a Web site.
6. Write a prompting sheet for the superstar to use for a TV talk show. Describe Wellness Advocates and its purpose. Use short conversational phrases. Illustrate how WAI helps a person take responsibility for his or her health using acid reflux disease as an example—describe what it is and list questions that a patient should ask the doctor about the condition, its treatment, as well as how to avoid the problem. Arrange the information in the order it might be asked for by the talk show host.
7. Draft an op-ed article about the need for people to take more responsibility for their own health.

Client File on Jan Overbrook
Facts and interview notes 12/05/20XX

Observations: Overbrook seems to be a "pro" at getting things done. She obviously likes to run the show and make things happen. Her energy is boundless. We [the agency] had better be as precise about organization and detail as she is. When she goes for the goal it's done cost-effectively and on schedule. If there's one thing we learned at the last meeting, it was be prepared; she makes decisions! She's analytical and objective. She's also quick. And what we present had better be logical. Forget theory and any abstract ideas. Overbrook wants practical applications; she cares about what's here and now. She's outgoing and sociable; she's also matter-of-fact and direct.

Random quotes from the interview with Overbrook: I know I'm analytical and that can seem impersonal and uncaring to some people. So I have to remind myself to think about how others think and feel. I've been successful and I tend to get caught up in the success of things. I've surrounded myself with talented people and I have to remember to credit them and make sure they know they're appreciated. If this relationship lasts [with the agency], you'll see that I make rapid-fire decisions. I know I should spend time listening more, so if I get too far out in front I want you to tell me. Don't let me jump to conclusions when you have stuff that I should know. When the work is good, we'll be fine. When it's not, brace yourself because I don't pull punches when it comes to criticizing.

Client's story of what inspired the new business: My latest venture is Wellness Advocates, Inc. I started it a year ago, on January 1. The idea for it was inspired a year before that. A dear friend of mine, Jason Adams, drove himself to City Hospital as he was having a heart attack. He had been video taping a friend's wedding and left the camera running to as not to disappoint his friend. He was transferred to General Hospital where they put a double stent in one of his arteries. Another artery was 80 percent blocked, but they decided to treat that with drugs. Bad decision.

Seven months later, on August 8, Jason had shortness of breath and chest pains. He was rushed to General. The double stent had failed but vessels near it had regenerated. A chemical-release-type stent was placed in the other clogged artery. No one volunteered to tell him the condition of other arteries and he finally had to press hard for answers before leaving the hospital.

On August 15, Jason awoke with tremendous pains in his chest. Off to General once again. Jason waved to friendly faces as he was wheeled on a gurney to critical care. The welcome got serious when they started the heart catheterization treatment. He said it was like some medieval torture chamber. Narrow bed. Doctors and nurses outfitted like Martians to fend off the radioactivity. A sharp jab in the groin with a long metal stick. Big cameras pointing down as he strained to hold the pose for 30 minutes. A shot of morphine eased the pain, but Jason begged for more and more. Meanwhile, down in accounting, the figure in the ledger was reaching into a sixth column.

He awoke to the voices of heart surgeons who said his heart was "fine." Jason said, "Great, so why all the pain? They told him it must be his lungs or stomach. He said it was obvious their area of expertise and interest was the heart; stomachs and lungs were someone else's area.

Jason was released and sent to cardiac rehab at County Hospital. For half an hour he walked a treadmill, rode a stationery bike, lifted weights, then passed out. His blood pressure fell to 64 over 50. He was rushed to ER. Another battery of blood tests. By now his arm was numb from all the blood taking.

"Jason, your heart is fine," the doctor said. "The problem might be your liver." Liver? Lungs? Stomach? Heart? Totally exasperated, Jason's wife said, "Enough is enough! She called the family doctor, told him the situation, and without seeing Jason at General, he told her to take Jason back to City Hospital and have them insert a scope to look at his stomach.

Jason had nothing to wear because he had thrown up on his clothes on the way to ER. So he had to wear his General Hospital gown to City. A security guard at General saw Jason in his gown and hassled him because he thought Jason was trying to leave the hospital without permission. Finally he was admitted to City. They insisted on another full examination routine, telling him his heart was fine but that they could not perform the scope procedure right away because he needed to fast for 24 hours.

By this time Jason just wanted to go home. Enough doctors, hospitals, IVs and blood tests. His weight dropped from 269 at the time of his first attack to under 200 and was continuing to decline.

Finally, the family doctor told Jason that his most recent attack was from acute acid reflux. Jason had never heard of it. Some of the symptoms are the same as those of a heart attack—chest pains, heavy breathing, nausea, even passing out. He was told more pills. More exercise. Better diet control. Better diet was a joke to Jason. He hadn't eaten anything of substance for the past three weeks.

The doctor scheduled the scope procedure at still another hospital, Parkview, for September 23. But Jason decided he needed a new family doctor. He wanted a coordinated approach to his problems. He wanted someone to take a holistic look at his physical condition, to review the list of drugs (and potential interactions) that had been prescribed by a battery of different physicians. He wanted to see details of the many examinations. He wanted to know if he was in a life-threatening situation. He wanted better advice about diet and exercise and dreaded the thought of passing out again on some piece of equipment. He wanted to know more about acute acid reflux.

It was the experience of this very dear friend that inspired me to establish Wellness Advocates, Inc.

Client's comments on the mission and operation of Wellness Advocates, Inc.: The mission of WAI is to show clients how to take responsibility for their health and wellness. At WAI we have a staff of facilitators. They are not medical advisors. Their job is to show clients how to overcome any feelings of trepidation for white smocks and stethoscopes and become medically conversant about their health and wellness. That means suggesting sources of information and teaching them how to ask questions and insist on satisfactory answers. It means showing them how to stay current on the latest developments in medical discoveries, new procedures, medicine and research. It means showing clients how important it is to take a personal interest in everything they put into their bodies—from food to pharmacy products. It means showing clients how to take a holistic approach to their health and wellness and finding qualified medical professionals who subscribe to such an enlightened view.

At WAI we show clients how to create and maintain a personal medical file, what health indicators to track and record, what records to include and how to obtain them.

We also provide support so that when a client feels like he or she is being led down a blind alley we can help them avoid an experience like Jason's by showing them how get complete and honest information to enlighten and ensure themselves that they are on the right course.

WAI has a staff of six facilitators who collectively are educated in a full range of medical subjects from diet to drugs. We have offices in New York City, Syracuse and Rochester . We have over 700 clients. The fee for our service is $48 per month. We have a Web site. We have the private financial backing necessary to begin expanding the business nationally. We have an information kit that explains everything for potential clients. We have a stellar reputation. We are not widely known yet, but those who meet us and become acquainted with our mission in nearly every case become clients. Our service becomes so valuable that when we get together with a client the meeting always begins with a big hug.

Observations and random client comments on managing a business: When we first started I tried to do everything, because I feel better when I have complete control. Then we started to expand and I hired people who could carry out my ideas and my ways of working with clients. I've had other ventures, like a chain of gift shops in New York hospitals, a wellness newsletter published nationally, and a florist in Old Westbury that specialized in patient bouquets that were delivered by volunteer care givers who spent five to 10 minutes talking with each hospital recipient. But WAI has, by far, been the most successful and most rewarding venture. What I love is meeting people, getting acquainted and getting hired.

Trying to control everything is a real challenge, especially when I don't like the nitty-gritty accounting work and meeting all of the regulatory and other administrative requirements. Dividing my attention between serving clients and managing the business gets real stressful. But I'm determined to do this no matter what it takes.

I have an exercise routine and I try to spend time outdoors. But I hate the thought of taking time for a vacation. I love to work. I was married once and had two children. They were my primary interest. My husband died and the children are grown. I couldn't have ventured into my own business while they were growing up. I remarried. My husband, Banks, manages a venture capital firm. Convenient arrangement! Not really. The businesses are kept separate. He's a workaholic too. But we both plan to expand operations, hire staff and quit killing ourselves. I feel good about the business. I have done well and I've been rewarded for a tireless effort.

Client's views on secrets of her success: I'm results-oriented in a tenacious way. When I set a goal nothing discourages me from reaching it. When I make a commitment it is rock solid; you can count on it. You'd be surprised at how tough I can get. And I make good decisions. You have to be a risk taker. I have a good sense about things and know just how far to go. One way to uncover business opportunities is to look for dissatisfaction among consumers. Finding effective ways to eliminate dissatisfaction can lead to a viable business venture, just as Wellness Advocates responds to Jason's frustration with the medical community. I think you also have to know how your talents, interests, background, and values combine with your particular personality to enable you to do what you are most suited to do. Did I tell you I have a book about to be published called simply, "Wellness Advocates, Inc."?

ARTICLE: WORK WITH JOURNALISTS AND MAKE CEO PROFILES SOAR

Many chief executive officers would like high profiles in the media. The reasons for wanting or needing public visibility are diverse and far ranging. The need, for example, might be to show leadership in an industry. Or the desire might be to become better known in the local business community.

A CEO's success in getting media attention depends largely on the chief executive's attitude toward journalists. At one extreme, some CEOs regard journalists as a necessary nuisance. At the other extreme, CEOs see journalists as gateways to important audiences.

Having worked with the news media for more than 30 years, I can tell you that having an effective relationship with the media requires consistent cooperation with journalists. Responding to reporters through others with, "Tell him I'll call him back," or "Tell her I will have to make some calls to get the information," and not responding is not an expression of cooperation.

Journalists, like securities analysts and others in the information gathering business, have a job to do. Helping them accomplish their work by being an accessible, responsive, useful source of information, consistently, goes a long way in developing mutually beneficial relationships.

One way to ensure consistent cooperation with the media is for CEOs to treat journalists as they would treat customers. By treating journalists the way major customers are treated CEOs can watch their public profiles soar.

So, what must a CEO do to treat journalists the way major customers are treated?

When a journalist calls, a CEO must respond promptly, not when it's convenient. Yes, that means walking out of an important meeting to take a press call, just as the CEO would respond promptly to a major customer who needed information. A missed call is a missed opportunity for publicity and for developing a working relationship with a reporter.

When a journalist schedules a meeting, a CEO must be there on time. Would a chief executive leave a major customer waiting in the lobby for 10 or even five minutes? A CEO must show the same respect for a reporter or news crew as would be shown for a major customer.

When in an interview, a CEO must participate with undivided attention. Would a chief executive interrupt a meeting with a major customer by responding to intercom messages, phone calls or executive assistants passing written notes? The task at hand is to convey information thoughtfully and accurately and that demands uninterrupted concentration.

When a journalist asks for information, a CEO must provide details, including background that might help the journalist complete the assignment. Would a CEO expect a major customer to make purchasing decisions with incomplete information and unanswered questions? Reporters are expected to develop articles regardless of their depth of knowledge of a particular event or business development. Effective reporters have the acumen to ask the right questions to get the background and information they need to write a story. A CEO who takes the time to assist a reporter with an assignment takes a giant step forward in becoming a valuable news source.

When a photojournalist—a news photographer— wants to take pictures, a CEO must relax and allow ample time to enjoy the session as one would enjoy being photographed with a major customer. Claiming to be under tremendous pressure with no time to spare will result in a news photo of a stressed executive whose clock has run out.

When journalists call, a CEO must make a concerted effort to recognize frequent callers by name and affiliation just as a major customer would be acknowledged. It's an important part of the relationship building process.

Like major customers, journalists need timely contact, useful information, undivided attention and respectful recognition.

This advice applies to the heads of public, private and not-for-profit organizations. Many such organizations have public relations personnel responsible for media relations who handle much of the day-to-day work. However, to achieve a high public profile, a chief executive must work in partnership with public relations personnel and actively share the media relations responsibilities.

By treating journalists the way major customers are treated, CEOs can watch their public profiles soar.

Case Twenty
Marketing Communication

CAMPUS CAFÉS

Some coffee houses, are highly successful. This is a case of a coffee house company in trouble. Happy Roasters Cafés, Inc., a fictitious name, was incorporated more than a decade ago with the aim of giving people a way to step out of their busy lives into an environment wafting with good smells, good tastes, good music and good spirits. Like many successful businesses, Happy Roasters lost its focus and like a plane with a stalled engine started a free fall with but a chance to regain control. Its stock plummeted. Market leadership fell to competing with fast-food franchisers. The business pursuit appeared to be revenue growth rather than profitability, automation over custom brewing, crowded stores with high-priced merchandise, the aroma of freshly ground coffee accessible only through push-button vents on packaged beans. The company is in a tail spin with industry analysts crying out advice: "Train your people." "Improve the food." "Improve the coffee." "Brighten up the stores." "Stop opening stores." "Forget about growth; fix your problems."

It is in this downward spiral that Happy Roasters is hiring public relations firms to drive sales by market segment. Your PR firm has a contract to promote retail sales

for which the company will pay $10,000. The proposal time line must allow for conducting research.

Team Assignment

To be clear, your PR firm is to develop a marketing communication plan to promote retail sales at Happy Roaster Cafés located near colleges and universities. Strategies in the plan must be backed by recommendations for research specifically designed to validate strategies proposed in the plan that is to show results in 12 months and preferably sooner. See the article on page 378, "Keep it Simple."

at Happy Roaster Cafés located near college and university campuses. Your proposed plan must be backed by recommended research (including aim and methodology) specifically designed to validate your strategies. Your proposal must creatively capture the interests and meet the needs of college students. Your proposal must refocus the company on its original aim to give people a way to step out of their busy lives into an environment wafting with good smells, good tastes, good music and good spirits. Your PR firm's role, in this case, has been expanded from communication to "marketing communication," which means that you are expected to consider the total sales environment, including physical layout, customer service, collateral merchandise, pricing considerations, and promotional programs. Your firm is to develop a proposal

Individual Writing Assignments

If you are working this case as a team, each team member is to select a different one of the following individual writing assignments that may pertain to the same coffee house:

1.   Select a coffee house near a college campus. Visit the company's Web site and read its business purpose or mission statement. Visit the coffee house and through personal observation determine how well

its operation lives up to the company's mission statement. Write your findings and conclusions in a one-page, 1.5 spaced report titled Coffee House Research—Personal Observation.

2. Select a coffee house near a college campus. Search the archives of the local newspaper. Study the content of stories mentioning the coffee house and determine the image (positive and negative) of the coffee house or company projected by the article(s). Write your findings and conclusions in a one-page, 1.5 spaced report titled Coffee House Research—Media Content Analysis. Include a list, by date and headline, of articles covered in your analysis.

3. Select a coffee house near a college campus. Search the Internet for and find at least six blogs by different bloggers in which the company is mentioned. Study the content of the blogs and determine why the company is mentioned and in what context. Write your findings and conclusions in a one-page, 1.5 spaced report titled Coffee House Research: Content Analysis of Blogs.

4. Select a coffee house near a college campus. Search Twitter for mentions of the company and determine why the company is mentioned and in what context. Write your findings and conclusions in a one-page, 1.5 spaced report titled Coffee House Research: Content Analysis of Tweets.

5. Select a coffee house near a college campus. Conduct personal

interviews of 10 students, and get their views on what would make the coffee house more attractive to students. Write your findings and conclusions in a one-page, 1.5-spaced report titled Coffee House Research—Personal Interviews.

6. Conduct an on-the-street survey of 20 students to determine where they usually go to buy a cup of coffee, what type of drink they buy and why they patronize that particular vendor. Write your findings and conclusions in a one-page, 1.5 spaced report titled Coffee House Research: On-The-Street Survey.

7. Select a coffee house near a college campus. Research the company's policy on sponsoring events, activities and organizations. Write your findings and conclusions in a one-page, 1.5 spaced report title Coffee House Research: Sponsorships.

ARTICLE: KEEP IT SIMPLE
Marketing Communication

How should I write a marketing communication plan? The over arching principle should be keep it simple–no noisy, showy and exciting activity and display designed to attract and impress plan reviewers. Write to be clear; research to be convincing. Use the structure that you have been using to write winning plans and proposals and stick to the rules for writing a plan's 10 components.

The situation analysis sets the course for the journey into marketing communication. The analysis must be logical, based on reliable information, and honest. I say honest because all claims of product benefits must be substantiated for legal reasons. For this case, the analysis should focus on questions, such as:

1. What is the mission of the business?
2. Does the business live up to its mission? If not, explain why. Your plan should tell what must be done to reconcile the difference.
3. Is the mission of the business reflected accurately by the traditional and social media? If not, explain why. Your plan should tell what must be done to reconcile the difference.
4. What does the business offer its market?
5. What does the market think the business offers? If there is a perceived difference between what the business offers and what the market thinks it offers, explain the difference. Your plan should tell how the difference should be reconciled.
6. What would the market like the business to offer?
7. Where does the market get what it prefers to have from this type of business? Give reasons why people prefer to patronize the competition. Your plan should explain how to redirect these potential customers to the client's business.
8. What does the business profess to stand for in the community?
9. What does the market think the business stands for in the community? If there is a difference between what the business professes to stand for in the community and what the market thinks it stands for explain. Your plan should tell how to reconcile the difference.
10. In summary, what is an honest appraisal of the strengths and weaknesses of the business and what factors must be reconciled in order to have the marketable assets needed to be a successful business?

Do a good job on the situation analysis. Write your plan in terms that enable measurement. Write the goal, objectives and strategies by the rules. Keep it simple and you will have a marketing communication plan worthy of serious consideration.

Index

CPSIA information can be obtained at www.ICGtesting.com
Printed in the USA
LVIW01n1930230617
539188LV00001B/1

9 781934 269961